# LEAN AND LUSCIOUS

Revised and Updated Edition

BOBBIE HINMAN & MILLIE SNYDER

Illustrator: Vonnie Winslow Crist

PRIMA PUBLISHING

PRIMA PUBLISHING, its colophon, and LEAN AND LUSCIOUS are trademarks of Prima Communications, Inc.

Cover design: The Dunlavey Studio
Cover photograph: ©1995 Kent Lacin

**Library of Congress Cataloging-in-Publication Data**

Hinman, Bobbie.
　　Lean and Luscious / Bobbie Hinman and Millie Snyder.
　　　　p.　　　cm.
　　Includes index.
　　ISBN 0-7615-0015-4
　　1. Vegetarian cookery.　2. Reducing diets—Cookery.　I. Snyder, Millie.　II. Title
　　RM236.H56　1995
　　641.5'635—dc20　　　　　　　　　　　　　　　　　　95-3362
　　　　　　　　　　　　　　　　　　　　　　　　　　　　　　CIP

95 96 97 98 99　AA　10　9　8　7　6　5　4　3　2　1

Printed in the United States of America

**How to Order:**
Single copies may be ordered from Prima Publishing, P.O. Box 1260BK, Rocklin, CA 95677; telephone (916) 632-4400. Quantity discounts are also available. On your letterhead, include information concerning the intended use of the books and the number of books you wish to purchase.

*This book is dedicated to all of the wonderful people who are striving for a healthier lifestyle. Thanks for making our books a part of your life.*

*Enjoy and be healthy!*

# *Contents*

# Special Thanks

A very special thanks to our trustworthy recipe tester, Barbara Tabibian, along with her taste-testers, Mark, Jessica, and Ashley, for working so hard and helping so much!

# *Important*

This book is not intended as a promotion or recommendation for any specific diet, nor as a substitute for your physician's advice. Its purpose is to show you how you can follow a balanced diet that is low in fat and high in fiber, and still enjoy tasty meals.

# Introduction:
## About Our Book

*Lean and Luscious* was originally created in 1985 as a collection of recipes designed to allow you to enjoy your favorite foods without adding unnecessary calories or fat. As so often happens, times and ideas change and knowledge is gained. Huge strides have been made in the fields of health and nutrition. In order to keep up with the many scientific breakthroughs, we have adapted our cooking styles, making use of the latest information on health and diet.

We are very excited about this newly revised book. We have eliminated some of the dishes that we felt were too high in fat to ever be transformed. We have changed most of the remaining recipes, substituting high-fat ingredients with their new lowfat counterparts. We have lowered the fat content of these recipes and have converted them in a way that now makes them available to the health-conscious people of the world. And we have added many, many new recipes, created just for you. It is our wish that using these recipes will help you to create a new, healthful way of cooking and eating. Our quick, easy-to-prepare dishes will transform ordinary meals into culinary delights, while teaching you and your family new and healthier eating habits.

For each recipe, we have included calorie counts as well as a complete nutritional breakdown. We hope that you will use this information to prepare satisfying and well-balanced meals.

In transforming and creating our recipes, we have always tried to keep in mind the fact that foods have their own built-in flavors. We have used spices to enhance, not hide, these flavors. We have attempted to bring out the best in food by eliminating the use of excess sugar, salt, and fats and replacing them with unique, flavorful combinations of extracts and spices. Our goal is to make foods taste so good that this enlightened way of eating can easily become a way of life.

## What Is a Balanced Diet?

Throughout this book we refer to a "balanced diet." This term has changed over the years and now has come to mean a diet low in fat and high in fiber. Health professionals feel that our diet should be rich in carbohydrates, such as whole grain breads, grains, dried peas and beans, fruits, vegetables, and pasta. These should be the focus of the meal, with lean meat, poultry, fish, and lowfat or nonfat dairy products playing smaller roles.

Many health professionals recommend that we get *less than* 30% of our total daily calories from fat. Of the total number, most of this should come from unsaturated fat. To figure your own daily fat allowance, multiply your daily calorie intake by .30 (to find 30% of calories). Then divide your answer by 9 for the number of fat grams that you would be allowed each day.

Example: 1,500 calories × .30 = 450 ÷ 9 = 50 grams of fat daily

Remember that it is figured *by the day,* not the individual food, so if you eat a little more fat in one meal, you can compensate by eating less fat in the other meals. Ideally, the formula should be used to evaluate your daily or weekly diet rather than single foods.

In addition to lowering our fat intake, studies have shown that eating a high-fiber diet may be our first line of defense against heart disease and several forms of cancer. Many health professionals recommend that we eat 20 to 25 grams of fiber daily. Fiber is abundant in many plant foods, including whole grains, fruits, vegetables, and dried peas and beans. (Meats contain no fiber.) These high-fiber foods are also relatively low in calories, so if you plan your diet around fresh fruits and vegetables, along with whole grains and beans, and use smaller portions of meats and dairy products, it becomes easy to eat fewer calories. Isn't it nice that most of the foods that are low in fat are high in fiber and also low in calories?

Sugar is high in calories and low in nutrients and should, therefore, be used sparingly. In all of our recipes, we have kept the use of sugar to a minimum. We found that we can greatly reduce the amount of sugar in a recipe and, by increasing the vanilla extract, still achieve delicious, sweet results. (There is controversy surrounding the safety of artificial sweeteners, and, wanting our recipes to be as wholesome as possible, we have chosen not to use any artificial sweeteners in these recipes.)

Although sodium is a mineral that occurs naturally in many foods, most of the sodium in the American diet comes from table salt and from sodium that is added to processed foods and beverages. Although some sodium is essential to our health, the recommendation from many health professionals is that we limit our daily sodium intake to 2,400 to 3,000 milligrams, or about 1 to 1 1/2 teaspoons of salt. In our recipes, we have used herbs and spices in place of most of the salt, and we always recommend tasting the finished product and then adding salt only if necessary. We also choose low-sodium or salt-free canned foods whenever available and recommend rinsing canned beans to remove excess salt.

## Can Food *Really* Be Both Lean *and* Luscious?

Growing up in typical American homes, we always thought that meats had to be smothered with sauce or gravy in order to taste good. We thought that desserts had to be laden with butter and sugar if they were to have any flavor at all. And, like so many people, we thought that "lowfat" meant "low flavor." Faced with the awesome responsibility of changing our own and our family's eating habits, we were determined to keep the flavor while eliminating fat and calories. The good news is that it works. Over the years, we have found 3 basic ways to accomplish this goal:

1. Choose healthful cooking methods: Eliminate deep-frying and sautéing in lots of butter and oil. Healthier cooking methods include steaming, broiling, grilling, poaching, and stir-frying.
2. Rely on herbs, spices, and extracts for flavor. Experiment with the vast selection of flavors that will enhance your food without adding fat.
3. Substitute high-fat ingredients with their lowfat counterparts.

Following are some basic substitutions to guide you.

### BASIC SUBSTITUTIONS

| Instead of: | Use: |
| --- | --- |
| Whole eggs | Two egg whites in place of each egg, or use egg substitutes |
| Whole milk | Skim milk |
| Cream | Evaporated skim milk or plain nonfat yogurt |
| Sour cream | Fat-free sour cream or plain nonfat yogurt |
| Ice cream | Reduced-fat or nonfat ice cream or frozen yogurt |
| Whipped cream (as a dessert topping) | Vanilla nonfat yogurt |

*Basic Substitutions, continued*

| Instead of: | Use: |
| --- | --- |
| Cream cheese | Fat-free cream cheese |
| Cheese | Reduced-fat or fat-free cheese |
| Mayonnaise | Reduced-calorie mayonnaise |
| Butter | Margarine that lists a liquid oil as the first ingredient, or vegetable oil (however, all are high in fat and should be used sparingly) |
| Vegetable oil | An oil with a high amount of monounsaturated fat, such as olive oil or canola oil |
| | Nonstick cooking spray for greasing pans |
| Salad dressings with lots of oil | Replace *half* the oil with water or fruit juice |
| High-fat marinades | Nonfat salad dressings |
| Sugar | Use *half* the amount called for (this works in most recipes except cookies) |
| White rice | Brown rice or other whole grains |
| All-purpose flour | Replace *half* with whole wheat flour |
| French fries | Baked potatoes (with a lowfat topping such as nonfat yogurt and chopped chives) |
| Meat in casseroles | Replace *half* with beans |

## Food Families

In order to help you develop healthy eating habits, we have divided foods into basic food groups, or food families. These groupings are similar to the exchanges used by the American Dietetic Association and several major weight reduction groups, making them easy to use in conjunction with these plans. We hope that these food groupings will help you to plan variable menus and to greatly simplify your portion control. If you wish to lose weight, you should consult your physician or other weight control expert regarding the number of servings from each food family that would be the best for your particular daily needs.

The foods found in each family are foods of comparable nutritional and calorie values. At the end of each recipe, in addition to the nutritional analysis, you will find the number of servings from each food family (example: 2 Protein Servings, 1 Fruit Serving, etc.). If you vary your menu but choose foods from each family daily, you will have all the nutrients needed for a balanced diet.

## Family #1: Protein

The Protein family is made up of meats, poultry, seafood, eggs, cheese, legumes (beans), and tofu. While all of these foods are valuable sources of protein, it is important to choose wisely in this group. Select cuts of meat carefully, choosing those that are lowest in fat. Whenever possible, remove skin from poultry before cooking and choose white meat over dark. Choose lowfat or nonfat cheeses, and replace whole eggs with egg whites or liquid egg substitutes. Legumes and tofu are not of animal origin, and so while high in protein, they contain no cholesterol and low amounts of saturated fat.

One serving from the Protein family contains approximately 60 to 70 calories.

## Family #2: Breads

The Bread family is made up of breads, crackers, cereals, grains, and starchy vegetables. Whenever possible, choose whole grains, such as brown rice and whole wheat flour, and products made from whole grains. We have included starchy vegetables (such as corn, peas, potatoes, and sweet potatoes) in this family, because their carbohydrate levels are about the same as an equivalent serving of bread. The Bread family is a good source of fiber in the diet.

One serving from the Bread family contains approximately 75 to 85 calories.

## Family #3: Vegetables

The Vegetable family consists of fresh, canned, or frozen vegetables other than the starchy vegetables. This family provides valuable sources of vitamins, minerals, and fiber. Vegetables retain more nutrients when cooked only until tender-crisp. Also, you will retain more nutrients if you leave the skin on vegetables whenever possible.

One serving from the Vegetable family contains approximately 25 to 30 calories.

## Family #4: Fats

The Fat family is made up of margarine, mayonnaise, vegetable oils, and salad dressings. Many health professionals recommend using oils that are high in monounsaturated fats, such as canola or olive oil, and margarine in place of butter, since butter is high in saturated fat. When choosing margarine, select one that contains a liquid vegetable oil as the first oil listed. Whichever fats you choose, remember that they should be used in very small amounts.

One serving from the Fat family contains approximately 40 to 45 calories.

## Family #5: Fruit

The Fruit family consists of fruits and fruit juices. This family provides valuable sources of vitamins, minerals, and fiber. Fruits may be fresh, canned, dried, or frozen. Be sure when choosing canned or frozen fruit that the fruit has been packed in water or unsweetened fruit juice. Whenever possible, leave the skin on fruits.

One serving from the Fruit family contains approximately 50 calories.

## Family #6: Milk

The Milk family is made up of milk and milk products. This family is an excellent source of vitamins, minerals, protein, and calcium. In order to cut down on calories and fats, choose skim milk and other nonfat or lowfat dairy products.

One serving from the Milk family contains approximately 80 to 90 calories.

## Family #7: Free Foods

The Free Food family consists of foods that appear in our recipes but provide no nutritional value. They are used to enhance the taste of each dish. Included in this family are spices, extracts, vinegar, lemon juice, mustard, and soy sauce. While we call them "free," some of these foods are very high in sodium, and it is best to choose their low- or reduced-sodium counterpart when available and also to use them in moderation.

Each serving from the Free Food family contains a negligible amount of calories.

## Family #8: Additional Calories

The Additional Calories family consists of foods that appear in our recipes in small amounts and, while they do not appreciably alter the nutritional value of each dish, they do add calories. Among these foods are sugar, honey, ketchup, jams and jellies, nuts, cocoa, broth mix, cornstarch, egg whites,* and coconut.

In each recipe we have figured the Additional Calories for you. They appear at the end of each list of food family servings where applicable.

## How to Use the Nutritional Information Found in This Book

After each recipe, you will find a box that contains the nutritional information for that particular recipe.

Here's an example:

| | | | |
|---|---|---|---|
| Each serving provides: | | | |
| | **200 Calories** | | |
| 2 | Protein Servings | 7 g | Protein |
| 1 | Vegetable Serving | 4 g | Fat (18% of calories) |
| 4 | Additional Calories | 24 g | Carbohydrate |
| | | 46 mg | Sodium |
| | | 3 mg | Cholesterol |
| | | 1 g | Fiber |

If you are following a weight reduction organization diet, you can tell at a glance how many servings from each food family are contained in one portion. In this example, each serving contains 2 servings from the Protein family, 1 serving from the Vegetable family, and 4 calories from the Additional Calories family.

The information in the box also tells you that each serving contains 200 calories, 7 grams of protein, 4 grams of fat, 24 grams of carbohydrate, 46 milligrams of sodium, 3 milligrams of cholesterol, and 1

*For our purposes, 3 egg whites will count as 1 Protein Serving. If we use less than 3 egg whites, we count them under Additional Calories.

gram of fiber. In this particular recipe, 18% of the calories come from fat.

When there is a choice of two ingredients, such as "salt-free (or regular) tomato sauce," the analysis is based on the first one mentioned. It is important to note that the nutritional analysis may vary slightly depending on the brands of food that are used. If a recipe contains less than 1/2 gram of protein, fat, or carbohydrate, or less than 1/2 milligram of sodium or cholesterol, the number will either be listed as zero or as "trace."

We hope that you will use this information to help you to select recipes and to balance your diet in a delicious and healthful way.

# SUGGESTED MENUS

## Breakfast

South Sea Salad (page 38)
Toasted Bagel with Jam
Orange Juice

Cold Cereal with Sliced Banana
Skim Milk
Cinnamon Yogurt Muffin
(page 308)

Half Melon
15-Minute Muesli (page 237)
Whole Wheat Toast

Broiled Grapefruit Delight
(page 336)
Scrambled Eggs Florentine
(page 69)
Maple Bran Muffin (page 310)

Orange Upside-Down French Toast (page 91)
Fresh Fruit Cup

## Lunch

"Pretend" Salmon Salad (page 107)
on Whole Wheat Pita
with Lettuce and Tomato
Apricot-Almond Cranberry Sauce
(page 330)

Tossed Salad
with Fat-Free Dressing
Bean and Cheese Quesadillas
(page 168)
Fresh Fruit Salad

French Onion Soup (page 21)
Tuna Mousse (page 4)
Crackers
Baked Pears (page 327)

Barbecue Turkey Loaf (page 155)
on Whole Wheat Bread
with Lettuce and Tomato
Fresh Fruit

Tossed Salad with
Cheesy Herb Dressing (page 61)
Spinach Frittata (page 72)
Whole Wheat Bread
Half Melon

## Dinner

Tossed Salad with
Dijon Vinaigrette (page 60)
Snapper Creole (page 102)
Brown Rice
Golden Carrot Loaf (page 247)
Apple Crisp (page 430)

Sherried Mushroom Soup
(page 29)
Chinese Pepper Steak (page 196)
Oriental Fried Rice (page 228)
Steamed Green Beans
Baked Pineapple Tapioca (page 332)

Tossed Salad
with Fat-Free Dressing
Bean Stroganoff (page 173)
Yolk-Free Noodles
Steamed Green Beans
Company Fruit Compote
(page 320)

Cucumbers Dijon (page 49)
on Bed of Lettuce
Golden Crowned Chicken (page 133)
Steamed Broccoli
Favorite Rice Casserole (page 229)
Mixed Fruit Sherbet (page 374)

Tossed Salad with
Creamy Italian Dressing (page 62)
Pacific Pasta Sauce with Salmon (page 218)
over Pasta
French Bread
Orange Fruit Cups (page 337)

# Appetizers, Dips,
# and Spreads

Used as party foods, meal-starters, or delicious snacks, the selections in this chapter are meant to whet your appetite or simply offer some easy "munchies."

We've kept the fat content as low as possible by using only lowfat and nonfat dairy products. However, it's important to remember that dairy products contain no fiber. For that reason, we recommend using fresh fruits and vegetables as "dippers" and whole grain, lowfat crackers, or breads for our spreads. It's important to note that most packaged chips, often used for dipping, are usually fried and are very high in fat.

Also, remember that many salads and fruits make ideal appetizers, so be sure to check the other chapters.

# Clams Casino

*Entertaining is so elegant with this delectable appetizer. If you can get some real clam shells and scrub them well, you can serve this special dish right in the shells. There are also a variety of ceramic shells available in specialty shops.*

*Makes 8 servings*

3 10-ounce cans minced clams, drained (This will yield about 16 ounces of clams.) (Reserve 1/2 cup of the clam juice.)
3/4 cup dry bread crumbs
2 tablespoons minced onion flakes
2 teaspoons dried parsley flakes
1/2 teaspoon dried oregano
1/4 teaspoon garlic powder
1/4 teaspoon salt
1 tablespoon plus 1 teaspoon grated Parmesan cheese
Lemon wedges

Preheat oven to 375°.

Spray 8 clam shells (either real or ceramic) with nonstick cooking spray.

In a medium bowl, combine all ingredients (including clam juice), *except* Parmesan cheese and lemon wedges. Mix well.

Divide mixture evenly and spoon into prepared shells. Sprinkle with Parmesan cheese.

Place shells on a baking sheet.

Bake 25 minutes, until hot and bubbly.

Serve with lemon wedges.

---

Each serving provides:

**134 Calories**

| | | | |
|---|---|---|---|
| 1 | Protein Serving | 16 g | Protein |
| 1/2 | Bread Serving | 2 g | Fat (16% of calories) |
| 6 | Additional Calories | 11 g | Carbohydrate |
| | | 266 mg | Sodium |
| | | 39 mg | Cholesterol |
| | | 0 g | Fiber |

# Tuna Mousse

*This elegant-looking mousse can also be made with salmon. It makes a beautiful and very tasty appetizer that is an ideal party centerpiece. We've also served it with crusty bread as a light lunch dish.*

*Makes 12 servings*
*(2 1/2 tablespoons each serving)*

| | |
|---|---|
| 1 | envelope unflavored gelatin |
| 1/2 | cup water |
| 1 | 8-ounce can salt-free (or regular) tomato sauce |
| 1 | 6 1/2-ounce can tuna (packed in water), drained |
| 2/3 | cup lowfat (1%) cottage cheese |
| 2 | tablespoons reduced-calorie mayonnaise |
| 1 | tablespoon sugar |
| 1/4 | teaspoon pepper |
| 1/8 | teaspoon salt |
| 1/2 | cup finely chopped celery |
| 2 | tablespoons finely chopped onion |

Sprinkle gelatin over water in a small bowl and let soften a few minutes.

In a small saucepan, over medium heat, heat tomato sauce to boiling. Reduce heat to low and stir in gelatin mixture. Heat, stirring, for 1 minute.

In a blender container, combine tuna, cottage cheese, mayonnaise, sugar, pepper, and salt. Add tomato sauce mixture. Blend until smooth.

Stir in celery and onion.

Pour mixture into a 3-cup mold.

Chill until firm.

Unmold to serve.

---

Each serving provides:

**48 Calories**

| | | | |
|---|---|---|---|
| 1/3 | Protein Serving | 6 g | Protein |
| 1/2 | Vegetable Serving | 1 g | Fat ( 18% of calories) |
| 1/4 | Fat Serving | 3 g | Carbohydrate |
| 4 | Additional Calories | 146 mg | Sodium |
| | | 7 mg | Cholesterol |
| | | 0 g | Fiber |

# Chesapeake Bay Crab Puffs

*Our unusual version of this normally deep-fried delicacy is actually a crab-filled muffin. It can be served alongside a tossed salad as an appetizer or a delicious light lunch.*

*Makes 4 muffins*

| | |
|---|---|
| 1/2 | cup liquid egg substitute |
| 1 | slice whole wheat bread (1-ounce slice), crumbled |
| 1/3 | cup nonfat dry milk |
| 1/3 | cup water |
| 1 | tablespoon plus 1 teaspoon all-purpose flour |
| 1 | tablespoon vegetable oil |
| 1 1/2 | teaspoons Worcestershire sauce |
| 1 | teaspoon lemon juice |
| 1 | teaspoon baking powder |
| 1/2 | teaspoon baking soda |
| 1/2 | teaspoon seafood seasoning (such as Old Bay) |
| 1/2 | cup crab meat (4 ounces) |

Preheat oven to 350°.

Spray 4 muffin cups with nonstick cooking spray.

In a blender container, combine all ingredients, *except* crab meat. Blend until smooth. Combine *half* of this mixture with the crab meat in a small bowl. Mix well.

Divide crab mixture evenly into prepared muffin cups. Pour remaining batter evenly over crab mixture.

Spray the tops of the muffins with nonstick cooking spray.

Bake 12 to 15 minutes, or until firm and lightly browned.

Cool in pan 5 minutes, then serve.

---

Each muffin provides:

**115 Calories**

| | | | |
|---|---|---|---|
| 1 | Protein Serving | 10 g | Protein |
| 1/4 | Bread Serving | 5 g | Fat (37% of calories) |
| 3/4 | Fat Serving | 8 g | Carbohydrate |
| 1/4 | Milk Serving | 564 mg | Sodium |
| 10 | Additional Calories | 29 mg | Cholesterol |
| | | 1 g | Fiber |

# Spinach Cheese Balls

*Great for parties, these cheesy cornmeal balls can be made a day ahead and refrigerated until it's time to bake them.*

*Makes 12 servings*
*(3 cheese balls each serving)*

| | |
|---|---|
| 2 | teaspoons vegetable oil |
| 1/2 | cup chopped onion |
| 1 | 10-ounce package frozen chopped spinach, thawed and drained well |
| 1/2 | cup liquid egg substitute |
| 1 1/2 | ounces shredded reduced-fat Cheddar cheese (1/3 cup) |
| 1/4 | cup grated Parmesan cheese |
| 1/4 | cup bottled fat-free Italian dressing |
| 1/4 | teaspoon garlic powder |
| 2 | teaspoons baking powder |
| 3/4 | cup yellow cornmeal (4 1/2 ounces) |

Heat oil in a large nonstick skillet oven medium-high heat. Add onion and cook until golden, stirring frequently. Remove from heat. Stir in spinach.

In a small bowl, combine egg substitute, both cheeses, Italian dressing, and garlic powder. Mix well. Stir into spinach.

Stir baking powder into cornmeal and add to spinach mixture, mixing thoroughly.

Place mixture in a bowl and chill several hours or overnight.

Shape chilled mixture into balls, about 1 1/2 inches in diameter.

Preheat oven to 375°.

Place cheese balls on a nonstick baking sheet.

Bake 10 to 12 minutes, until bottoms are lightly browned.

Serve hot.

---

Each serving provides:

**79 Calories**

| | | | |
|---|---|---|---|
| 1/3 | Protein Serving | 4 g | Protein |
| 1/2 | Bread Serving | 2 g | Fat (24% of calories) |
| 1/2 | Vegetable Serving | 11 g | Carbohydrate |
| 18 | Additional Calories | 223 mg | Sodium |
| | | 4 mg | Cholesterol |
| | | 1 g | Fiber |

# Onion Dip

*A take-off on the ever-popular party dip, this version has all of the flavor with only a trace of the fat. We've replaced the sour cream with nonfat yogurt, making a dip that's still as creamy and delicious as ever.*

*Makes 8 servings*
*(3 tablespoons each serving)*

1 1/2 cups plain nonfat yogurt
2 tablespoons minced onion flakes
2 packets low-sodium instant beef-flavored broth mix

In a small bowl, combine all ingredients, mixing well.
Chill several hours to blend flavors.
Serve with vegetable dippers.

---

Each serving provides:

**29 Calories**

| | | | |
|---|---|---|---|
| 1/4 | Milk Serving | 3 g | Protein |
| 3 | Additional Calories | trace | Fat (3% of calories) |
| | | 4 g | Carbohydrate |
| | | 35 mg | Sodium |
| | | 1 mg | Cholesterol |
| | | 0 g | Fiber |

# Party Clam Dip

*A favorite party dish goes lowfat and no one will ever guess! Garnished with chopped chives, either fresh or dried, and served with vegetables or melba toast rounds, this makes a wonderful party dish.*

*Makes 12 servings*
*(2 1/2 tablespoons each serving)*

| | |
|---|---|
| 1 1/2 | cups plain nonfat yogurt* |
| 1 | 10 1/2-ounce can minced clams, drained (This will yield about 6 ounces of clams.) |
| 1 1/2 | tablespoons minced onion flakes |
| 1 1/2 | teaspoons Worcestershire sauce |
| 1/4 | teaspoon salt |
| 1/4 | teaspoon pepper |
| 1/8 | teaspoon garlic powder |

In a small bowl, combine all ingredients. Mix well.
Chill several hours to blend flavors.
Serve with vegetable dippers.

*If desired, you can substitute nonfat sour cream for the yogurt.

---

Each serving provides:

**39 Calories**

| | | | |
|---|---|---|---|
| 1/4 | Protein Serving | 5 g | Protein |
| 1/4 | Milk Serving | trace | Fat (8% of calories) |
| 4 | Additional Calories | 3 g | Carbohydrate |
| | | 89 mg | Sodium |
| | | 10 mg | Cholesterol |
| | | 0 g | Fiber |

# Yogurt Cheese

*This creamy, cream cheese-like spread can also be made with flavored yogurt, such as vanilla or lemon. It also works with yogurt containing fruit. Just stir the fruit into the yogurt first. You can use the cheese as is or in place of cream cheese in your favorite recipe. (This process will not work with yogurt that contains gelatin.)*

*Makes 8 servings*
*(2 tablespoons each serving)*

2      cups nonfat yogurt

Line a colander with several layers of cheesecloth (or you can use a coffee filter placed in a strainer). Fill with yogurt.
Place colander in a pan to catch the drippings.
Refrigerate 24 hours.
Remove cheese and place in a small bowl.
Refrigerate until needed.

---

Each serving provides:

**25 Calories**

| 1/4 Milk Serving | | |
|---|---|---|
| | 3 g | Protein |
| | 1 g | Fat (29 % of calories) |
| | 1 g | Carbohydrate |
| | 18 mg | Sodium |
| | 1 mg | Cholesterol |
| | 0 g | Fiber |

# Crab and Cheese Ball

*You can either use the yogurt cheese on page 9 or fat-free cream cheese in this wonderful spread that has a lively taste with a bit of a kick. It looks lovely garnished with fresh chives or parsley.*

*Makes 8 servings*
*(3 tablespoons each serving)*

| | |
|---|---|
| 1 | cup yogurt cheese (see page 9)* |
| 1/2 | cup crab meat (4 ounces) |
| 1 | tablespoon lemon juice |
| 1 | tablespoon prepared horseradish |
| 2 | teaspoons minced onion flakes |
| 1/2 | teaspoon dried chives |
| 1/8 | teaspoon salt |
| | Dash Worcestershire sauce |

Combine all ingredients in a bowl. Blend well with a fork. Chill at least 1 hour, until firm.

Shape mixture into a ball or log.

Chill.

To serve, spread on crackers or vegetable dippers.

* If desired, you can substitute fat-free cream cheese for the yogurt cheese.

---

Each serving provides:

**41 Calories**

| | | | |
|---|---|---|---|
| 1/4 | Protein Serving | 6 g | Protein |
| 1/4 | Milk Serving | 1 g | Fat (23% of calories) |
| | | 2 g | Carbohydrate |
| | | 95 mg | Sodium |
| | | 16 mg | Cholesterol |
| | | 0 g | Fiber |

# Three-Cheese Spread

*A tantalizing blend of flavors awaits the cheese lover in this delicious spread.*

*Makes 8 servings*
*(3 tablespoons each serving)*

1       cup yogurt cheese (see page 9)*
1/2    cup reduced-fat Cheddar cheese (2 ounces)
1/3    cup blue cheese, crumbled (2 ounces)
1/8    teaspoon garlic powder
       Few drops bottled pepper hot sauce

Combine all ingredients in a bowl. Mix with a fork until well blended.

Line a small bowl with plastic wrap. Spoon cheese into bowl and press down firmly.

Chill.

To serve, invert cheese onto a serving plate and remove plastic wrap. Spread cheese on crackers or celery stalks.

*If desired, you can substitute fat-free cream cheese for the yogurt cheese.

---

Each serving provides:

### 70 Calories

| | | | |
|---|---|---|---|
| 1/2 | Protein Serving | 7 g | Protein |
| 1/4 | Milk Serving | 4 g | Fat (53% of calories) |
| 10 | Additional Calories | 1 g | Carbohydrate |
| | | 173 mg | Sodium |
| | | 12 mg | Cholesterol |
| | | 0 g | Fiber |

# Chili-Cheddar Cheese Spread

*Spread on crackers or sliced veggies, this is a great Sunday afternoon football snack.*

*Makes 12 servings*
*(2 1/2 tablespoons each serving)*

| | |
|---|---|
| 1 | cup yogurt cheese (see page 9)* |
| 4 | ounces shredded reduced-fat Cheddar cheese (1 cup) |
| 2 | tablespoons very finely minced onion |
| 2 | tablespoons bottled chili sauce |
| 1 | teaspoon dry mustard |
| 1/4 | teaspoon garlic powder |

In a large bowl, combine all ingredients. Mix with a fork until well blended.

Chill several hours to blend flavors.

*If desired, you can substitute fat-free cream cheese for the yogurt cheese.

---

Each serving provides:

**48 Calories**

| | | | |
|---|---|---|---|
| 1/3 | Protein Serving | 5 g | Protein |
| 25 | Additional Calories | 2 g | Fat (43% of calories) |
| | | 2 g | Carbohydrate |
| | | 123 mg | Sodium |
| | | 8 mg | Cholesterol |
| | | 0 g | Fiber |

# Mexican Pinto Spread

*This spicy spread is not only delicious on crackers, but it also makes a wonderful sandwich. Either way, its flavor is enhanced by the addition of fresh, sliced tomatoes.*

*Makes 8 servings*
*(3 tablespoons each serving)*

| | |
|---|---|
| 1/4 | cup chopped onion |
| 2 | cloves garlic, coarsely chopped |
| 1 | 1-pound can pinto beans, rinsed and drained (This will yield approximately 9 ounces of cooked beans.) |
| 1 | teaspoon vinegar |
| 1 | teaspoon chili powder |
| 1/2 | teaspoon ground cumin |
| 1/2 | teaspoon dried oregano |

Place onion and garlic in a food processor. Process with a steel blade until finely chopped. Add beans, vinegar, and spices. Process until smooth. (A blender can be used, but you will need to blend the mixture in small batches and be careful not to let the mixture get soupy.)

Spoon mixture into a bowl and chill thoroughly.

Each serving provides:

**36 Calories**

| 1/2 | Protein Serving | 2 g | Protein |
|---|---|---|---|
| 4 | Additional Calories | trace | Fat (8% of calories) |
| | | 6 g | Carbohydrate |
| | | 95 mg | Sodium |
| | | 0 mg | Cholesterol |
| | | 2 g | Fiber |

# Caraway Cheese Spread

*An adaptation of an Eastern European recipe, this unusual dish can be spread on thin slices of dark party rye or on crackers, and it also makes a tasty stuffing for celery sticks.*

*Makes 8 servings*
*(3 tablespoons each serving)*

| | |
|---|---|
| 1¹/₂ | cups nonfat ricotta cheese |
| 1 | tablespoon Dijon mustard |
| 3 | tablespoons very finely minced onion |
| 2 | teaspoons caraway seeds |
| 2 | teaspoons paprika |

In a small bowl, combine all ingredients, mixing well. Chill several hours, or overnight, to blend flavors.

---

Each serving provides:

**44 Calories**

| | | | |
|---|---|---|---|
| ¹/₂ | Protein Serving | 6 g | Protein |
| 8 | Additional Calories | trace | Fat (4% of calories) |
| | | 2 g | Carbohydrate |
| | | 98 mg | Sodium |
| | | 0 mg | Cholesterol |
| | | 0 g | Fiber |

# Salmon Paté

*This elegant spread is delicious on crackers or on cucumber slices. For a pretty presentation, chill the paté in a bowl that is lined with plastic wrap, then invert it onto a serving plate and peel off the plastic.*

*Makes 8 servings*
*(2 tablespoons each serving)*

| | |
|---|---|
| 8 | ounces drained canned salmon |
| 2 | teaspoons lemon juice |
| 1 | teaspoon dill weed |
| $^1/_2$ | teaspoon dried tarragon |
| $^1/_2$ | teaspoon onion powder |
| $^1/_4$ | teaspoon garlic powder |
| $^1/_8$ | teaspoon pepper |

Combine all ingredients in a food processor. With a steel blade, process until smooth. Spoon into a bowl.

Chill several hours or overnight.

Each serving provides:

**42 Calories**

| | | | |
|---|---|---|---|
| 1 | Protein Serving | 6 g | Protein |
| | | 2 g | Fat (35% of calories) |
| | | 0 g | Carbohydrate |
| | | 139 mg | Sodium |
| | | 11 mg | Cholesterol |
| | | 0 g | Fiber |

# Stuffed Figs with Orange-Cheese Filling

*These pretty confections make such an attractive dish. They can be served as an appetizer, dessert, snack, or even breakfast fare.*

*Makes 12 servings*
*(2 figs each serving)*

| | |
|---|---|
| 24 | large dried figs (³/₄-ounce each) |
| 1/2 | cup fat-free cream cheese |
| 1 | tablespoon sugar |
| 1/4 | teaspoon orange extract |
| 24 | walnut pieces (about 1 ounce) |
| | Ground cinnamon |

Place figs in a large saucepan. Add water to cover and bring to a boil over medium heat. Cook, uncovered, 5 minutes, or until figs are just tender. Drain and cool. Then chill several hours.

Combine cream cheese, sugar, and orange extract in a bowl. Mix until smooth. Chill several hours.

To assemble, slice the top (stem end) off of each fig and open each one up, using your finger or the back of a spoon. Spoon 1 teaspoon of cheese mixture into each fig, mounding it slightly. Top each one with a piece of walnut. Sprinkle very lightly with cinnamon. Serve right away or chill several hours, or overnight, until serving time.

---

Each serving provides:

**137 Calories**

| | | | |
|---|---|---|---|
| 2 | Fruit Servings | 3 g | Protein |
| 26 | Additional Calories | 2 g | Fat (12% of calories) |
| | | 30 g | Carbohydrate |
| | | 50 mg | Sodium |
| | | 1 mg | Cholesterol |
| | | 4 g | Fiber |

# Chocolate Ricotta Spread

*This unusual, sweet spread makes a great appetizer when served with thin apple or pear slices. It can also be served as a light, refreshing dessert.*

*Makes 4 servings*
*(2 tablespoons each serving)*

| | |
|---|---|
| 1/2 | cup part-skim ricotta cheese |
| 1 | tablespoon sugar |
| 2 | teaspoons cocoa (unsweetened) |
| 1/2 | teaspoon vanilla extract |
| 1/4 | teaspoon rum or almond extract |

Combine all ingredients in a small bowl. Mix well.
Serve right away or chill for later serving.

---

Each serving provides:

**60 Calories**

| | | | |
|---|---|---|---|
| 1/2 | Protein Serving | 4 g | Protein |
| 15 | Additional Calories | 3 g | Fat (38% of calories) |
| | | 5 g | Carbohydrate |
| | | 39 mg | Sodium |
| | | 10 mg | Cholesterol |
| | | 0 g | Fiber |

# Tofu, Peanut Butter, and Banana Spread

*Kids love this sweet spread. It's delicious on toast or crackers and also tastes great on apple slices. You'll have to try this one to believe it!*

*Makes 4 servings*
*(2 1/4 tablespoons each serving)*

| | |
|---|---|
| 3 | ounces silken (or soft) tofu (1/3 cup) |
| 1/2 | medium ripe banana, mashed |
| 1 | tablespoon peanut butter (Choose one without added sugar or fat.) |
| 2 | teaspoons sugar |
| 1 | teaspoon lemon juice |
| 1 | teaspoon honey |
| 1 | teaspoon vanilla extract |
| | Ground cinnamon |

In a small bowl, combine tofu and banana. Mash with a fork or potato masher. Add remaining ingredients, *except* cinnamon. Mix well, then beat vigorously with a fork or wire whisk until blended. (If a creamier spread is desired, place mixture in a blender container and blend just until smooth, but do not let mixture get soupy.)

Chill.

Before serving, mix well, then sprinkle with cinnamon.

---

Each serving provides:

**69 Calories**

| | | | |
|---|---|---|---|
| 1/2 | Protein Serving | 3 g | Protein |
| 1/4 | Fat Serving | 3 g | Fat (33% of calories) |
| 1/4 | Fruit Serving | 9 g | Carbohydrate |
| 13 | Additional Calories | 30 mg | Sodium |
| | | 0 mg | Cholesterol |
| | | 0 g | Fiber |

# Soups

There's nothing like a bowl of hot soup to warm your bones and cheer your feelings.

Most soups are made from stock or broth, with several choices available to you. If you prefer to make a homemade stock, by simmering chicken and/or vegetables in water along with herbs, it's important to chill the stock before using it in a soup so that the fat can be easily skimmed off the top. If you prefer to use a canned broth, choose a low-sodium variety. Remember, you can always add salt if needed. Packets of low-sodium instant broth mix can also be used, and added to the soup with the specified amount of water.

As a meal starter or as the entrée itself, these soups will prove to be delicious and satisfying—without a lot of calories, fat, or fuss.

# French Onion Soup

*Instead of being covered with "gobs" of cheese, this version proves to be tasty with only a sprinkling of Parmesan. It's light, simple, and very elegant. Vive la France!*

*Makes 4 servings*
*(1 cup each serving)*

| | |
|---|---|
| 2 | teaspoons vegetable oil |
| 2 | cups thinly sliced onion |
| 4 | cups low-sodium beef broth (or 4 cups of water and 4 packets low-sodium instant beef-flavored broth mix) |
| 1/4 | cup dry red wine |
| 1 | bay leaf |
| | Salt and pepper to taste |
| 2 | tablespoons grated Parmesan cheese |

Heat oil in a medium saucepan over medium heat. Add onions and cook until golden, stirring frequently, and separating slices into rings. Add small amounts of water if necessary (a few teaspoons at a time), to prevent sticking. (A nonstick saucepan is ideal for making this soup.)

Add broth, wine, and bay leaf. Bring soup to a boil. Reduce heat to medium-low, cover, and simmer 20 minutes, stirring occasionally. Add salt and pepper to taste.

Remove and discard bay leaf.

Spoon soup into serving bowls and sprinkle each serving with Parmesan cheese, using 1 1/2 teaspoons for each serving.

---

Each serving provides:

**90 Calories**

| | | | |
|---|---|---|---|
| 1 | Vegetable Serving | 5 g | Protein |
| 1/2 | Fat Serving | 3 g | Fat (34% of calories) |
| 48 | Additional Calories | 9 g | Carbohydrate |
| | | 678 mg | Sodium |
| | | 2 mg | Cholesterol |
| | | 1 g | Fiber |

# Manhattan Clam Chowder

*With its exquisite blend of flavors, you'll see why this thick, chunky chowder is so popular.*

*Makes 6 servings*
*(1 1/3 cups each serving)*

| | |
|---|---|
| 2 | teaspoons vegetable oil |
| 1 | cup sliced onion |
| 1 | cup diced carrots |
| 1 | cup diced celery |
| 1 | 1-pound can salt-free (or regular) tomatoes, chopped and drained (Reserve liquid.) |
| 1 | large cooked potato (12 ounces), diced (You can either bake, boil, or microwave the potato.) |
| 4 | whole black peppercorns |
| 1 | bay leaf |
| 1 | tablespoon dried parsley flakes |
| 1 1/2 | teaspoons dried thyme |
| 1/4 | teaspoon dried basil |
| 1 | 10 1/2 ounce can clams, drained (Reserve liquid.) This will yield approximately 6 ounces of clams. |
| | Salt to taste |

Heat oil in a medium saucepan over medium heat. Add onion, carrots, and celery. Cook 5 minutes, stirring frequently. Add small amounts of water as necessary (about a tablespoon at a time), to prevent sticking.

Add tomatoes, potato, and spices.

In a 1-quart bowl or jar, combine reserved tomato liquid and clam liquid. Add water to make 1 quart. Pour liquid over vegetables and bring to a boil. Cover, reduce heat to medium-low, and simmer 45 minutes.

Add clams. Simmer, covered, 15 minutes more.
Remove and discard bay leaf before serving.
Add salt to taste.

Each serving provides:

**139 Calories**

| | | | |
|---|---|---|---|
| 1/2 | Protein Serving | 9 g | Protein |
| 1/2 | Bread Serving | 2 g | Fat (15% of calories) |
| 1 3/4 | Vegetable Servings | 21 g | Carbohydrate |
| 1/4 | Fat Serving | 67 mg | Sodium |
| 3 | Additional Calories | 17 mg | Cholesterol |
| | | 3 g | Fiber |

# Old World Cabbage Soup

*This delectable soup tastes just like Mom's, but it takes half the time to pre-
pare. It tastes best when reheated, so we always plan to make it a day ahead.*

*Makes 8 servings*
*( 1 1/4 cups each serving)*

2       1-pound cans salt-free (or regular) tomatoes, chopped and
        undrained
4       cups thinly shredded cabbage
1/2     cup finely chopped onion
1/3     cup lemon juice
1       cup low-sodium instant chicken- or vegetable-flavored broth
        (or 1 cup of water and 1 packet low-sodium instant chicken
        or vegetable broth mix)
2       teaspoons sugar
        Salt and pepper to taste

Combine all ingredients in a large saucepan. Bring to a boil over
medium heat. Reduce heat to medium-low, cover, and simmer 40
minutes, or until cabbage is tender.

Add additional lemon juice or sugar to taste.

---

Each serving provides:

**44 Calories**

| 2 | Vegetable Servings | 2 g | Protein |
|---|---|---|---|
| 7 | Additional Calories | trace | Fat (7% of calories) |
| | | 9 g | Carbohydrate |
| | | 93 mg | Sodium |
| | | 0 mg | Cholesterol |
| | | 2 g | Fiber |

# Creamy Chicken Chowder

*Cottage cheese and skim milk replace the cream in this rich-tasting chowder that's so thick and creamy, you won't believe it's so low in fat. And what a great use for leftover chicken.*

*Makes 4 servings*
*(1 1/4 cups each serving)*

| | |
|---|---|
| 1 | cup sliced mushrooms |
| 1 | cup lowfat (1%) cottage cheese |
| 1 | cup skim milk |
| 3 | cups low-sodium chicken or vegetable broth (or 3 cups of water and 3 packets low-sodium instant chicken- or vegetable-flavored broth mix) |
| 2 | tablespoons dried chives |
| 1 | teaspoon paprika |
| 1/8 | teaspoon pepper |
| 1/8 | teaspoon ground nutmeg |
| 6 | ounces cooked chicken, cut into small cubes, skin discarded (1 1/2 cups) |

Place mushrooms in a medium saucepan over medium heat. Cook, stirring frequently, until tender, 3 to 5 minutes. Add small amounts of water if necessary (about a tablespoon at a time), to prevent sticking.

In a blender container, combine cottage cheese and milk. Blend until smooth. Add to saucepan. Add remaining ingredients, except chicken. Heat over low heat, stirring constantly, until mixture just starts to boil.

Add chicken. Cook, stirring, until heated through.

---

Each serving provides:

**165 Calories**

| | | | |
|---|---|---|---|
| 2 1/4 | Protein Servings | 23 g | Protein |
| 1/2 | Vegetable Serving | 4 g | Fat (24% of calories) |
| 1/4 | Milk Serving | 6 g | Carbohydrate |
| 15 | Additional Calories | 719 mg | Sodium |
| | | 41 mg | Cholesterol |
| | | 0 g | Fiber |

# Chicken Rice Soup

*The dill adds a nice touch to this delicious soup that's not only warm and homey, but also easy to prepare. You can have comfort food in no time. If you store leftover cooked rice in the freezer, it's always ready for times like this.*

*Makes 4 servings*
*(1 1/4 cups each serving)*

| | |
|---|---|
| 2 | teaspoons vegetable oil |
| 1/4 | cup diced onion |
| 1/2 | cup diced celery |
| 1/4 | cup diced carrots |
| 4 | cups low-sodium chicken broth (or 4 cups of water and 4 packets low-sodium instant chicken-flavored broth mix) |
| 1/2 | teaspoon poultry seasoning |
| 1/4 | teaspoon dill weed |
| 4 | ounces cooked chicken, cubed, skin discarded (1 cup) |
| 1 | cup cooked rice |
| | Salt and pepper to taste |

Heat oil in a medium saucepan over medium heat. Add onion, celery, and carrots. Cook, stirring frequently, until tender, about 5 minutes. Add small amounts of water as necessary (a few teaspoons at a time), to prevent sticking.

Add broth, poultry seasoning, and dill weed. Bring mixture to a boil, then reduce heat to medium-low, cover, and simmer 20 minutes.

Add chicken and rice. Heat through.

Add salt and pepper to taste.

---

Each serving provides:

**170 Calories**

| | | | |
|---|---|---|---|
| 1 | Protein Serving | 12 g | Protein |
| 1/2 | Bread Serving | 5 g | Fat (27% of calories) |
| 1/2 | Vegetable Serving | 17 g | Carbohydrate |
| 1/2 | Fat Serving | 601 mg | Sodium |
| 20 | Additional Calories | 25 mg | Cholesterol |
| | | 1 g | Fiber |

# Creole Seafood Chowder

*This colorful, tasty dish provides a delectable way to use leftover seafood, and it's hearty enough to be a meal in itself. It's party-perfect when garnished with fresh parsley and oyster crackers.*

*Makes 4 servings*
*(1 1/4 cups each serving)*

| | |
|---|---|
| 2 | teaspoons vegetable oil |
| 1/4 | cup *each* chopped onion, celery, and green bell pepper |
| 2/3 | cup lowfat (1%) cottage cheese |
| 1 | 1-pound can salt-free (or regular) tomatoes, undrained |
| 1/2 | cup water |
| 1 | packet low-sodium instant chicken- or vegetable-flavored broth mix |
| 1/2 | teaspoon dried oregano |
| 1/2 | teaspoon dried parsley flakes |
| 1/4 | teaspoon dried basil |
| 1/8 | teaspoon dried thyme |
| 4 | ounces cooked and diced fish, crab, or shrimp (or any combination of cooked seafood) (1 1/2 cups) |
| | Salt and pepper to taste |
| | Dash seafood seasoning (such as Old Bay) |

Heat oil in a medium saucepan over medium heat. Add onion, celery, and green pepper. Cook, stirring frequently, until vegetables are tender, about 8 minutes. Add small amounts of water as necessary (about a tablespoon at a time), to prevent sticking.

In a blender container, combine remaining ingredients, *except* seafood, salt, pepper, and seafood seasoning. Blend until smooth. Add to saucepan. Reduce heat to low and bring mixture to a simmer, stirring frequently. Add seafood and heat through, stirring.

Add salt and pepper to taste and a dash of seafood seasoning.

---

Each serving provides:

**115 Calories**

| | | | |
|---|---|---|---|
| 1 | Protein Serving | 13 g | Protein |
| 1 1/2 | Vegetable Servings | 3 g | Fat (27% of calories) |
| 1/2 | Fat Serving | 8 g | Carbohydrate |
| 3 | Additional Calories | 218 mg | Sodium |
| | | 21 mg | Cholesterol |
| | | 1 g | Fiber |

# Cream of Carrot Soup

*This version of a French favorite is quick and easy and much, much lower in fat than the original. Evaporated skim milk replaces the cream, and the result is still silky and rich.*

*Makes 6 servings*
*(1 cup each serving)*

| | |
|---|---|
| 2 | teaspoons vegetable oil |
| 3 | cups chopped carrots |
| 1/2 | cup chopped onion |
| 3 1/2 | cups low-sodium chicken or vegetable broth (or 3 1/2 cups of water and 3 packets low-sodium instant chicken- or vegetable-flavored broth mix) |
| 1 | bay leaf |
| 1 1/2 | cups evaporated skim milk |
| | Salt and pepper to taste |

Heat oil in a medium saucepan over medium heat. Add carrots and onion. Cook 5 minutes, stirring frequently. Add small amounts of water (about a tablespoon at a time), to prevent sticking.

Add broth and bay leaf. Bring mixture to a boil, then cover, reduce heat to medium-low, and simmer 30 minutes, or until carrots are tender. Remove and discard bay leaf.

Place soup in a blender container, reserving about 1/4 cup of the carrot and onion. Blend until smooth. Return to saucepan and add reserved vegetables.

Stir in milk. Heat through, but do not boil.

Add salt and pepper to taste.

---

Each serving provides:
### 104 Calories

| | | | |
|---|---|---|---|
| 1 1/4 | Vegetable Servings | 7 g | Protein |
| 1/4 | Fat Serving | 2 g | Fat (16% of calories) |
| 1/4 | Milk Serving | 14 g | Carbohydrate |
| 23 | Additional Calories | 420 mg | Sodium |
| | | 3 mg | Cholesterol |
| | | 2 g | Fiber |

# Sherried Mushroom Soup

*If your supermarket has different varieties of fresh mushrooms, you can really make an exotic-tasting soup. The splash of sherry at the end adds a wonderful, delicate flavor that really enhances this woodland vegetable.*

*Makes 6 servings*
*(1 cup each serving)*

| | |
|---|---|
| 2 | teaspoons vegetable oil |
| 1 | pound fresh mushrooms, sliced |
| 2 | cups thinly sliced carrots |
| 1/2 | cup chopped onion |
| 5 | cups low-sodium chicken or vegetable broth (or 5 cups of water and 5 packets low-sodium instant chicken- or vegetable-flavored broth mix) |
| 1/2 | teaspoon dried thyme |
| 1/8 | teaspoon pepper |
| 2 | tablespoons dry sherry |
| | Salt to taste |

Heat oil in a large saucepan over medium heat. Add mushrooms, carrots, and onion. Cook, stirring frequently, 5 minutes. Add small amounts of water if necessary (about a tablespoon at a time), to prevent sticking.

Add broth, thyme, and pepper. When mixture boils, reduce heat to medium-low, cover, and simmer 45 minutes, or until vegetables are tender.

Remove from heat and stir in sherry and salt to taste.

---

Each serving provides:

**77 Calories**

| | | | |
|---|---|---|---|
| 1 1/2 | Vegetable Servings | 4 g | Protein |
| 1/4 | Fat Serving | 2 g | Fat (26% of calories) |
| 21 | Additional Calories | 9 g | Carbohydrate |
| | | 483 mg | Sodium |
| | | 0 mg | Cholesterol |
| | | 2 g | Fiber |

# Garlic and White Bean Soup

*Sounds exotic, doesn't it? No one will believe it only takes a few minutes to make this delectable soup. Keep canned beans on hand in the pantry and you'll be able to throw this together with only a moment's notice.*

*Makes 6 servings*
*(1 cup each serving)*

| | |
|---|---|
| 2 | 1-pound cans white kidney beans (cannellini), rinsed and drained (This will yield 2 cups, or 1 1/4 pounds, of cooked beans.) |
| 3 | cups low-sodium chicken or vegetable broth (or 3 cups of water and 3 packets low-sodium instant chicken- or vegetable-flavored broth mix) |
| 2 | cloves garlic, coarsely chopped |
| 2 | tablespoons dried parsley flakes |
| 2 | teaspoons dried basil |
| 2 | tablespoons grated Parmesan cheese |
| | Salt and pepper to taste |

In a blender container, combine all ingredients, *except* salt and pepper. Blend until smooth.

Pour mixture into a medium saucepan. Heat through and add salt and pepper to taste.

---

Each serving provides:

**127 Calories**

| | | | |
|---|---|---|---|
| 1 1/2 | Protein Servings | 10 g | Protein |
| 30 | Additional Calories | 1 g | Fat (10% of calories) |
| | | 18 g | Carbohydrate |
| | | 500 mg | Sodium |
| | | 1 mg | Cholesterol |
| | | 6 g | Fiber |

# Creamy Potato Soup

*A delight served hot on a chilly day or served cold on a hot day, this versatile soup is a real taste treat. It has a thick, creamy texture that tastes a lot like real cream.*

*Makes 4 servings*
*(1 cup each serving)*

| | |
|---|---|
| 2 | cups evaporated skim milk |
| 1 | pound cooked potatoes, peeled and diced (You can either bake, boil, or microwave the potatoes.) |
| 2 | tablespoons minced onion flakes |
| 2 | packets low-sodium instant chicken- or vegetable-flavored broth mix |
| 1/4 | teaspoon celery salt |
| 2 | teaspoons margarine |
| | Freshly ground black pepper to taste |
| 1 | teaspoon dried chives |

In a medium saucepan, combine milk, potatoes, onion flakes, broth mix, and celery salt. Cook on low heat, stirring frequently, until mixture is hot. Do not boil.

Remove soup from heat and stir in margarine.

Spoon into serving bowls and sprinkle with pepper and dried chives.

---

Each serving provides:

**220 Calories**

| | | | |
|---|---|---|---|
| 1 | Bread Serving | 12 g | Protein |
| 1/2 | Fat Serving | 2 g | Fat (9% of calories) |
| 1 | Milk Serving | 39 g | Carbohydrate |
| 5 | Additional Calories | 216 mg | Sodium |
| | | 5 mg | Cholesterol |
| | | 2 g | Fiber |

# Tomato Butternut Soup

*An exciting combination of flavors awaits you in this delicately spiced soup.*
*The recipe calls for butternut squash, but any winter squash will do.*

*Makes 6 servings*
*(1 cup each serving)*

2       teaspoons vegetable oil
1/2     cup chopped onion
2       cloves garlic, finely chopped
2       cups butternut squash, peeled and cut into 1/2 - to 1-inch cubes
            (about 9 ounces)
1       1-pound can salt-free (or regular) tomatoes, chopped and
            undrained
21/2    cups low-sodium chicken or vegetable broth (or 21/2 cups of
            water and 21/2 packets low-sodium instant chicken- or
            vegetable-flavored broth mix)
2       tablespoons dried parsley flakes
1       teaspoon dried basil
1/8     teaspoon dried thyme
1       bay leaf
2       tablespoons dry sherry

Heat oil in a medium saucepan over medium heat. Add onion and
garlic. Cook, stirring frequently, until onion is tender, 3 to 5 minutes.
Add small amounts of water if necessary (a few teaspoons at a time),
to prevent sticking.

Add remaining ingredients, *except* sherry. Bring mixture to a boil.
Reduce heat, cover, and simmer 30 minutes, or until squash is tender.
Remove from heat and stir in sherry.

Remove and discard bay leaf before serving.

(Optional: You can puree the soup if you want a creamier texture.)

---

Each serving provides:

**72 Calories**

| | | | |
|---|---|---|---|
| 1/4 | Bread Serving | 2 g | Protein |
| 3/4 | Vegetable Serving | 2 g | Fat (24% of calories) |
| 1/4 | Fat Serving | 11 g | Carbohydrate |
| 23 | Additional Calories | 246 mg | Sodium |
| | | 0 mg | Cholesterol |
| | | 2 g | Fiber |

# Salads and
# Salad Dressings

Salads are so versatile. A salad can be an appetizer, a side dish, a snack, a main course, or even a dessert. Made with fruits and vegetables, salads are valuable sources of vitamins, minerals, and fiber.

To reduce the amount of fat in salads, we recommend using nonfat yogurt in place of sour cream and replacing part of the oil with fruit juice or water. The oils that we use in our recipes are monounsaturated oils, such as canola oil or olive oil. When mayonnaise is used, we specify reduced-calorie mayonnaise, which has been whipped with water to reduce the fat and calories.

It's important to note that even though some of the salads and dressings contain more than the recommended 30% of calories from fat, each serving contains only a few grams of fat. It's important to practice portion control and not smother your salads with dressing. Also, remember that the percentage of calories should be figured *by the day,* not the individual food, so if you eat a little more fat in one meal or one dish, you can compensate by eating less fat in the other meals or dishes. Ideally, you should evaluate your daily or weekly diet rather than single foods.

Enjoy our taste-tempting delights.

# Our Waldorf Salad

*It's easy to lower the fat content of mayonnaise-based salads by doing what we've done here. We've replaced the mayonnaise with a combination of non-fat yogurt and reduced-calorie mayonnaise. It's still one of our favorite crunchy salads. (For a new taste, try tossing in a sliced banana.)*

*Makes 4 servings*

| | |
|---|---|
| 1/2 | cup plain nonfat yogurt |
| 2 | tablespoons reduced-calorie mayonnaise |
| 1 | teaspoon lemon juice |
| 1 | tablespoon sugar |
| 4 | small, sweet apples, unpeeled, chopped |
| 1 | cup chopped celery |
| 2 | tablespoons chopped walnuts (1/2 ounce) |

In a medium bowl, combine yogurt, mayonnaise, lemon juice, and sugar. Mix well.

Add remaining ingredients, mixing thoroughly.

Chill several hours to blend flavors.

---

Each serving provides:

**139 Calories**

| | | | |
|---|---|---|---|
| 1/2 | Vegetable Serving | 3 g | Protein |
| 1 | Fat Serving | 5 g | Fat (30% of calories) |
| 1 | Fruit Serving | 24 g | Carbohydrate |
| 35 | Additional Calories | 89 mg | Sodium |
| | | 3 mg | Cholesterol |
| | | 3 g | Fiber |

# Tropical Ambrosia Salad

*We've replaced the usual sour cream with nonfat yogurt and taken out most of the high-fat coconut. Yet, this cool, delicious salad retains the wonderful, refreshing flavors of the Caribbean.*

*Makes 4 servings*

| | |
|---|---|
| 1 | 8-ounce can pineapple chunks or tidbits (packed in juice), drained |
| 1 | 8-ounce can mandarin orange slices (packed in juice), drained |
| 1 | cup vanilla nonfat yogurt |
| 2 | teaspoons shredded coconut (unsweetened) |
| 1 | teaspoon vanilla extract |
| 1/4 | teaspoon coconut extract |

Place pineapple and oranges in a medium bowl.

In a small bowl, combine remaining ingredients, mixing well. Add to fruit, stirring until well blended.

Chill.

---

Each serving provides:

**114 Calories**

| | | | |
|---|---|---|---|
| 1 | Fruit Serving | 4 g | Protein |
| 1/4 | Milk Serving | trace | Fat (4% of calories) |
| 15 | Additional Calories | 24 g | Carbohydrate |
| | | 44 mg | Sodium |
| | | 2 mg | Cholesterol |
| | | 0 g | Fiber |

# Carrot and Raisin Salad

*You've probably met the high-fat cousin of this popular salad. It's offered at many salad bars and usually contains a lot more than the 3 grams of fat in each of our servings. Served alone or on a bed of greens, this is truly a tempting salad.*

*Makes 4 servings*

| | |
|---|---|
| 2 | cups finely shredded carrots |
| 1 | 8-ounce can crushed pineapple (packed in juice), drained |
| 1/4 | cup raisins |
| 2 | tablespoons plus 2 teaspoons reduced-calorie mayonnaise |
| 1 | tablespoon lemon juice |
| 2 | teaspoons sugar |
| 1/4 | teaspoon coconut extract |

Place carrots, pineapple, and raisins in a medium bowl. Toss to combine.

In a small bowl or custard cup, stir together remaining ingredients. Add to carrot mixture, mixing well.

Chill.

---

Each serving provides:

**121 Calories**

| | | | |
|---|---|---|---|
| 1 | Vegetable Serving | 1 g | Protein |
| 1 | Fat Serving | 3 g | Fat (20% of calories) |
| 1 | Fruit Serving | 25 g | Carbohydrate |
| 8 | Additional Calories | 76 mg | Sodium |
| | | 3 mg | Cholesterol |
| | | 3 g | Fiber |

# South Sea Salad

*This refreshing salad makes an ideal brunch dish. We like to serve it on a bed of greens, accompanied by a toasted bagel with jam. It's lovely to look at and oh-so delicious.*

*Makes 2 servings*

| | |
|---|---|
| 1 | cup lowfat (1%) cottage cheese |
| 1/2 | teaspoon vanilla extract |
| 1/2 | cup strawberries, sliced |
| 1/4 | cup canned crushed pineapple (packed in juice), drained |
| 1 | teaspoon shredded coconut (unsweetened) |

Combine all ingredients and mix well.
Chill several hours to blend flavors.

---

Each serving provides:

**120 Calories**

| | | | |
|---|---|---|---|
| 1 1/2 | Protein Servings | 14 g | Protein |
| 1/2 | Fruit Serving | 2 g | Fat (13% of calories) |
| 3 | Additional Calories | 11 g | Carbohydrate |
| | | 460 mg | Sodium |
| | | 5 mg | Cholesterol |
| | | 1 g | Fiber |

# Cranberry Salad Mold

*Not just for Thanksgiving, this colorful mold with its interesting texture provides a cool accompaniment to any dinner. Using unflavored gelatin greatly reduces the number of calories normally found in gelatin molds.*

*Makes 4 servings*

| | |
|---|---|
| 2 | cups cranberries |
| 1 | small, sweet apple, unpeeled, chopped |
| 1/2 | cup canned crushed pineapple (packed in juice), drained (Reserve 2 tablespoons of the juice.) |
| 1/3 | cup sugar |
| 1 | cup water |
| 2 | envelopes unflavored gelatin |
| 1 | cup small ice cubes |
| 1/2 | cup finely chopped celery |
| 1 | teaspoon lemon extract |
| 1 | teaspoon orange extract |

In a blender container or food processor, combine cranberries, apple, pineapple, reserved pineapple juice, and sugar. Turn blender on and off a few times to finely chop the fruits.

Place water in a small saucepan. Sprinkle gelatin over water and let stand a few minutes to soften. Heat, stirring frequently, over low heat, until gelatin is completely dissolved. Remove from heat.

Stir ice cubes into gelatin mixture. Stir until gelatin just begins to thicken. Remove and discard any remaining ice.

Stir chopped fruit into gelatin. Add celery and extracts, mixing well. Pour mixture into a 3-cup mold.

Chill until firm.

Unmold to serve. (If you prefer, you can chill the mixture in a bowl and serve it right from the bowl.)

---

Each serving provides:

**151 Calories**

| | | | |
|---|---|---|---|
| 1/4 | Vegetable Serving | 3 g | Protein |
| 1 | Fruit Serving | trace | Fat (1% of calories) |
| 64 | Additional Calories | 33 g | Carbohydrate |
| | | 21 mg | Sodium |
| | | 0 mg | Cholesterol |
| | | 3 g | Fiber |

# Tangy Aspic Mold

*A great lunch consists of a serving of this delicious mold alongside a scoop of lowfat cottage cheese, accompanied by a chunk of crusty French bread.*

*Makes 4 servings*

| | |
|---|---|
| 2 | tablespoons cold water |
| 1 | tablespoon lemon juice |
| 1 | envelope unflavored gelatin |
| 2 | cups tomato juice |
| 2 | tablespoons minced onion flakes |
| 1 | tablespoon firmly packed brown sugar |
| 1 | bay leaf |
| 2 | whole cloves |
| 3 | whole peppercorns |
| 2 | whole allspice |
| 1/2 | teaspoon celery seed |
| 1/4 | teaspoon dried basil |
| 1/4 | teaspoon salt |
| | Bottled hot sauce to taste |

In a small bowl, combine water and lemon juice. Sprinkle gelatin over this mixture and set aside for a few minutes to soften.

In a medium saucepan, combine remaining ingredients, *except* hot sauce. Bring to a boil over medium heat. Reduce heat to medium-low and simmer 15 minutes. Remove from heat, strain, and discard spices. Add hot sauce to taste.

Add gelatin mixture to tomato juice. Stir until gelatin is completely dissolved. Pour mixture into a small mold.

Chill until firm.

Unmold to serve.

---

Each serving provides:

**48 Calories**

| | | | |
|---|---|---|---|
| 1 | Vegetable Serving | 3 g | Protein |
| 12 | Additional Calories | trace | Fat (3% of calories) |
| | | 11 g | Carbohydrate |
| | | 584 mg | Sodium |
| | | 0 mg | Cholesterol |
| | | 0 g | Fiber |

# Marinated Artichoke Hearts

*This tangy salad is a perfect addition to an antipasto. Just arrange a medley of fresh and pickled vegetables, along with an assortment of reduced-fat cheeses, on a bed of lettuce, pile these artichoke hearts in the middle, and serve it proudly at any gathering.*

*Makes 4 servings*

| | |
|---|---|
| 1 | 1-pound can artichoke hearts, drained |
| 2 | tablespoons red wine vinegar |
| 1 | tablespoon water |
| 1 | tablespoon vegetable oil |
| 1 | teaspoon sugar |
| $1/2$ | teaspoon dried oregano |
| $1/4$ | teaspoon dry mustard |
| $1/4$ | teaspoon garlic powder |
| $1/4$ | teaspoon salt |
| $1/8$ | teaspoon pepper |

Place artichoke hearts in a medium bowl.

In a small bowl, combine remaining ingredients, mixing well. Pour over artichoke hearts and toss until evenly coated.

Chill overnight to blend flavors. Stir occasionally while chilling.

---

Each serving provides:

**63 Calories**

| | | | |
|---|---|---|---|
| 1 | Vegetable Serving | 2 g | Protein |
| $3/4$ | Fat Serving | 3 g | Fat (47% of calories) |
| 4 | Additional Calories | 7 g | Carbohydrate |
| | | 135 mg | Sodium |
| | | 0 mg | Cholesterol |
| | | 1 g | Fiber |

# Easy Italian Green Bean Salad

*Either fresh or frozen green beans will work in this easy salad, and the fat-free dressing allows you to add all of the flavor without adding fat. If the dressing you choose has a lot of herbs and spices, you may not even need to add the ones in the recipe.*

*Makes 4 servings*

| | |
|---|---|
| 1 | 10-ounce package frozen cut green beans |
| 1 | cup sliced mushrooms |
| $1/2$ | cup salt-free (or regular) tomato sauce |
| 2 | tablespoons bottled fat-free Italian dressing |
| $1/4$ | teaspoon dried oregano |
| $1/4$ | teaspoon dried basil |
| $1/8$ | teaspoon garlic powder |

Cook green beans according to package directions, adding mushrooms and cooking them along with the beans. Drain and place in a medium bowl.

Combine remaining ingredients in a small bowl and mix well. Pour over green beans.

Chill several hours or overnight.

---

Each serving provides:

**41 Calories**

| | | | |
|---|---|---|---|
| 2 | Vegetable Servings | 2 g | Protein |
| 3 | Additional Calories | trace | Fat (6% of calories) |
| | | 9 g | Carbohydrate |
| | | 82 mg | Sodium |
| | | 0 mg | Cholesterol |
| | | 2 g | Fiber |

# Gourmet Zucchini Salad

*This salad is so simple, yet it tastes so elegant. It's at home with a family dinner or at a fancy dinner party.*

*Makes 4 servings*

| | |
|---|---|
| 1 1/2 | cups zucchini, unpeeled and sliced crosswise into 1/8-inch slices |
| 1/2 | cup thinly sliced celery |
| 1/4 | cup thinly sliced onion |
| 1/4 | cup thinly sliced green pepper |
| 1/4 | cup red wine vinegar |
| 2 | tablespoons sugar |
| 1 | tablespoon plus 1 1/2 teaspoons vegetable oil |
| 2 | tablespoons water |
| 1/2 | teaspoon dried basil |
| 1/4 | teaspoon salt |
| 1/8 | teaspoon pepper |

Combine vegetables in a shallow bowl.

Combine remaining ingredients in a small bowl, mixing well. Pour over vegetables.

Chill overnight to blend flavors. Stir several times while chilling.

---

Each serving provides:

**87 Calories**

| | | | |
|---|---|---|---|
| 1 1/4 | Vegetable Servings | 1 g | Protein |
| 1 | Fat Serving | 5 g | Fat (52% of calories) |
| 29 | Additional Calories | 10 g | Carbohydrate |
| | | 150 mg | Sodium |
| | | 0 mg | Cholesterol |
| | | 1 g | Fiber |

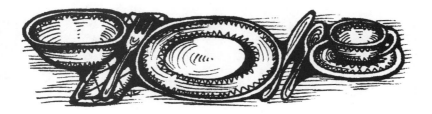

# Herbed Potato Salad

*Nonfat yogurt replaces the mayonnaise, and red onions add a splash of color in this sweet and tangy version of an all-American favorite.*

*Makes 6 servings*

| | |
|---|---|
| 2 | large potatoes (20 ounces total) |
| 1/2 | cup finely chopped red onion |
| 1/2 | cup finely chopped cucumber, peeled and seeded |
| 1/2 | cup plain nonfat yogurt |
| 1 | tablespoon vinegar |
| 2 | teaspoons vegetable oil |
| 2 | teaspoons dried parsley flakes |
| 1 | teaspoon sugar |
| 1/2 | teaspoon dill weed |
| 1/4 | teaspoon dried oregano |
| 1/4 | teaspoon salt |
| 1/8 | teaspoon pepper |

Place potatoes in 2 inches of boiling water in a medium saucepan. Cover and cook over medium heat 15 to 20 minutes, or until potatoes are tender. Do not let them get mushy. (Length of cooking time will depend on the variety of potatoes used.)

Drain potatoes and let them sit until cool enough to handle. Remove skin and cut potatoes into 1-inch chunks. Place in a large bowl. Add onion and cucumber and mix well.

In a small bowl, combine remaining ingredients. Mix well and add to potatoes. Toss until potatoes are evenly coated.

Chill several hours to blend flavors.

---

Each serving provides:

**100 Calories**

| | | | |
|---|---|---|---|
| 1/2 | Bread Serving | 3 g | Protein |
| 1/3 | Vegetable Serving | 2 g | Fat (14% of calories) |
| 1/4 | Fat Serving | 19 g | Carbohydrate |
| 37 | Additional Calories | 111 mg | Sodium |
| | | 0 mg | Cholesterol |
| | | 1 g | Fiber |

# Best Cole Slaw

*An old family standby for years, no backyard cookout is ever complete without it.*

*Makes 8 servings*

| | |
|---|---|
| 1 | small cabbage, thinly shredded (4 cups) |
| 1 | medium carrot, grated |
| 3 | tablespoons sugar |
| 1 | teaspoon celery seed |
| 1 | teaspoon salt |
| 1/2 | cup reduced-calorie mayonnaise |
| 3 | tablespoons plain nonfat yogurt |
| 2 | tablespoons vinegar |
| | Freshly ground black pepper |

Place cabbage and carrot in a large bowl. Sprinkle sugar, celery seed, and salt on top. Let stand for 5 minutes.

In a small bowl, combine mayonnaise, yogurt, and vinegar, mixing well. Spoon over cabbage. Toss to blend.

Add pepper to taste.

Chill several hours or overnight. Mix occasionally while chilling.

---

Each serving provides:

**78 Calories**

| | | | |
|---|---|---|---|
| 1 1/4 | Vegetable Servings | 1 g | Protein |
| 1 1/2 | Fat Servings | 4 g | Fat (47% of calories) |
| 21 | Additional Calories | 10 g | Carbohydrates |
| | | 372 mg | Sodium |
| | | 5 mg | Cholesterol |
| | | 1 g | Fiber |

# Cucumber and Onion Salad

*This salad makes an excellent side dish for light summer meals and cookouts. It's also a great addition to a tossed salad and even tastes great on sandwiches.*

*Makes 4 servings*

1¹/₂   cups cucumber, peeled and sliced paper-thin
¹/₂    cup onion, sliced paper-thin
¹/₃    cup vinegar
¹/₃    cup water
¹/₃    cup sugar
¹/₄    teaspoon salt
      Dash pepper

Layer cucumber and onion in a jar or bowl. Combine remaining ingredients and pour over vegetables.

Chill overnight, stirring several times.

---

Each serving provides:

**81 Calories**

| | | |
|---|---|---|
| 1 | Vegetable Serving | 1 g | Protein |
| 64 | Additional Calories | trace | Fat (1% of calories) |
| | | 21 g | Carbohydrate |
| | | 139 mg | Sodium |
| | | 0 mg | Cholesterol |
| | | 1 g | Fiber |

# Brown Rice and Vegetable Salad

*Loaded with fiber and flavor, this hearty salad makes a tasty dinner accompaniment or a filling lunch. We like to serve it on a bed of fresh spinach, garnished with sliced tomato and cucumber.*

*Makes 4 servings*

| | |
|---|---|
| 2 | cups cooked brown rice |
| 1/2 | cup shredded carrots |
| 1/2 | cup shredded zucchini, unpeeled |
| 2 | tablespoons finely chopped onion |
| 1/4 | cup lemon juice |
| 1 | tablespoon plus 1 teaspoon vegetable oil |
| 1 | tablespoon dried parsley flakes |
| 1/2 | teaspoon dried thyme |
| 1/2 | teaspoon garlic powder |
| 1/2 | teaspoon salt |
| | Pepper to taste |

In a medium bowl, combine rice, carrots, zucchini, and onion. Toss to combine.

In a small bowl, combine remaining ingredients. Pour over rice mixture.

Chill several hours.

Mix before serving.

---

Each serving provides:

**163 Calories**

| | | | |
|---|---|---|---|
| 1 | Bread Serving | 3 g | Protein |
| 1/2 | Vegetable Serving | 5 g | Fat (30% of calories) |
| 1 | Fat Serving | 26 g | Carbohydrate |
| | | 287 mg | Sodium |
| | | 0 mg | Cholesterol |
| | | 2 g | Fiber |

# Caesar Salad

*This is a slimmed-down, easy version of an ever-popular salad. It makes a perfect beginning to almost any meal.*

*Makes 4 servings*

| | |
|---|---|
| 2 | slices (1 ounce each) whole wheat bread, cubed |
| 2 | tablespoons grated Parmesan cheese |
| 1 | small head romaine lettuce, chilled, torn into bite-size pieces (about 4 cups) |
| 1/4 | cup red wine vinegar |
| 2 | tablespoons vegetable oil |
| 2 | tablespoons lemon juice |
| 1/2 | teaspoon Worcestershire sauce |
| 1/2 | teaspoon salt |
| 1/4 | teaspoon dry mustard |
| 1/4 | teaspoon garlic powder |
| | Freshly ground black pepper to taste |

To make croutons, spread bread cubes in a single layer on an ungreased baking sheet. Toast in a 300° oven until dry and light brown. Spray bread cubes lightly with nonstick cooking spray and sprinkle them with *half* of the Parmesan cheese.

Place lettuce in a large bowl.

In a small bowl, combine remaining ingredients *except* remaining Parmesan cheese and pepper. Mix well and pour over lettuce. Toss to coat lettuce evenly.

Divide evenly onto 4 salad plates. Top each serving with remaining Parmesan cheese, freshly ground pepper, and croutons.

---

Each serving provides:

**124 Calories**

| | | | |
|---|---|---|---|
| 1/2 | Bread Serving | 3 g | Protein |
| 2 | Vegetable Servings | 9 g | Fat (61% of calories) |
| 1 1/2 | Fat Servings | 9 g | Carbohydrate |
| 15 | Additional Calories | 408 mg | Sodium |
| | | 2 mg | Cholesterol |
| | | 2 g | Fiber |

# Cucumbers Dijon

*This super-quick salad has a nice "kick" and makes a great addition to any tossed salad. It's also delicious packed into pita bread with sliced turkey and tomato.*

*Makes 4 servings*

| | |
|---|---|
| 1/4 | cup plain nonfat yogurt |
| 1 | tablespoon plus 1 1/2 teaspoons Dijon mustard |
| 2 | cups cucumber, peeled, sliced very thin |
| 2 | teaspoons dried chives |

In a medium bowl, combine yogurt and mustard. Stir in cucumber and chives.

Chill several hours.

(This salad tastes best when served the same day.)

---

Each serving provides:

**23 Calories**

| 1 | Vegetable Serving | 1 g | Protein |
|---|---|---|---|
| 8 | Additional Calories | trace | Fat (4% of calories) |
| | | 3 g | Carbohydrate |
| | | 150 mg | Sodium |
| | | 0 mg | Cholesterol |
| | | 0 g | Fiber |

# Italian Mushroom Salad

*As an appetizer, salad, or side dish, this easy dish dresses any meal, and it's so easy to prepare.*

*Makes 4 servings*

3    tablespoons bottled fat-free Italian dressing
1    tablespoon grated Parmesan cheese
2    cups mushrooms, thinly sliced

In a medium bowl, combine dressing and Parmesan cheese, mixing well. Stir in mushrooms.
Chill several hours.

---

Each serving provides:
### 18 Calories

| | | | |
|---|---|---|---|
| 1 | Vegetable Serving | 1 g | Protein |
| 11 | Additional Calories | 1 g | Fat (24% of calories) |
| | | 2 g | Carbohydrate |
| | | 133 mg | Sodium |
| | | 1 mg | Cholesterol |
| | | 0 g | Fiber |

# Marinated Vegetable Salad

*A colorful and tasty addition to any meal, this has become a family favorite in our house. If you like, you can eliminate one cup of the cauliflower and add one cup of broccoli in its place.*

*Makes 6 servings*

| | |
|---|---|
| 2 | cups cauliflower, cut into small flowerets |
| 1 | cup carrots, cut crosswise into 1/2-inch slices |
| 1 | cup celery, cut into 1-inch slices |
| 1 | medium, green bell pepper, cut into 1/2-inch strips |
| 1 | cup small mushrooms (or larger mushrooms cut into quarters) |
| 1/2 | cup chopped red onion |
| 10 | small stuffed green olives, cut in half crosswise |
| 1/2 | cup water |
| 1/4 | cup vinegar |
| 2 | tablespoons vegetable oil |
| 2 | tablespoons plus 2 teaspoons sugar |
| 1 1/2 | teaspoons dried oregano |
| 3/4 | teaspoon salt |
| 1/2 | teaspoon pepper |
| 1/4 | teaspoon garlic powder |

Combine all ingredients in a large nonstick skillet. Bring to a boil over medium heat, stirring occasionally.

Reduce heat to medium-low, cover, and simmer 5 minutes, or until vegetables are barely tender-crisp.

Place salad in a bowl and chill overnight.

---

Each serving provides:

**102 Calories**

| | | | |
|---|---|---|---|
| 2 1/4 | Vegetable Servings | 2 g | Protein |
| 1 | Fat Serving | 5 g | Fat (44% of calories) |
| 28 | Additional Calories | 14 g | Carbohydrate |
| | | 419 mg | Sodium |
| | | 0 mg | Cholesterol |
| | | 2 g | Fiber |

# Hot German Potato Salad

*Who said salads have to be cold? This tangy, hot salad is high in flavor and surprisingly low in fat.*

*Makes 4 servings*

| | |
|---|---|
| 15 | ounces red-skinned potatoes |
| 2 | tablespoons very finely minced onion |
| 1 | tablespoon dried chives |
| 2 | teaspoons imitation bacon bits |
| 1 | teaspoon dry mustard |
| 1/4 | teaspoon salt |
| | Pepper to taste |
| | Dash celery seed |
| 1/4 | cup vinegar |
| 2 | tablespoons water |
| 1 | teaspoon sugar |

Place potatoes in 2 inches of boiling water in a medium saucepan. Cover and cook over medium heat 10 to 15 minutes, or until potatoes are tender. Do not let them get mushy. (Length of cooking time will depend on the variety of potatoes used.)

Drain potatoes and let them sit until cool enough to handle. Cut potatoes into 1-inch chunks. Place in a large bowl. Toss with onion, chives, and bacon bits.

Sprinkle mustard, salt, pepper, and celery seed over potatoes. Mix well.

In a small saucepan, heat vinegar, water, and sugar until hot, stirring to dissolve sugar. Pour over potatoes.

Toss and serve.

---

Each serving provides:

**92 Calories**

| | | | |
|---|---|---|---|
| 3/4 | Bread Serving | 3 g | Protein |
| 9 | Additional Calories | 1 g | Fat (5% of calories) |
| | | 20 g | Carbohydrate |
| | | 173 mg | Sodium |
| | | 0 mg | Cholesterol |
| | | 2 g | Fiber |

# Carrot Slaw

*This colorful, festive salad really comes to life when presented on a bed of greens and garnished with ripe, red tomato wedges.*

*Makes 4 servings*

| | |
|---|---|
| 2 | cups coarsely shredded carrots |
| 1/2 | cup finely chopped green bell pepper |
| 1/4 | cup plus 2 tablespoons raisins |
| 1/4 | cup finely chopped onion |
| 1 | small, sweet apple, unpeeled, coarsely shredded |
| 2 | tablespoons plus 1 1/2 teaspoons vinegar |
| 1 | tablespoon plus 1 teaspoon vegetable oil |
| 1 | tablespoon water |
| 1 | tablespoon plus 1 teaspoon sugar |
| 1/4 | teaspoon salt |
| 1/4 | teaspoon celery seed |
| 1/4 | teaspoon dry mustard |

In a large bowl, combine carrots, green pepper, raisins, onion, and apple. Toss to combine.

Add remaining ingredients and mix well.

Chill overnight.

---

Each serving provides:

**145 Calories**

| | | | |
|---|---|---|---|
| 1 1/2 | Vegetable Servings | 1 g | Protein |
| 1 | Fat Serving | 5 g | Fat (28% of calories) |
| 1 | Fruit Serving | 27 g | Carbohydrate |
| 16 | Additional Calories | 157 mg | Sodium |
| | | 0 mg | Cholesterol |
| | | 3 g | Fiber |

# Middle East Eggplant Salad

*This delicious salad also makes a great sandwich when piled into a crusty roll and topped with a slice of reduced-fat cheese.*

*Makes 6 servings*

| | |
|---|---|
| 1 | tablespoon olive oil |
| 3 | cups eggplant, peeled and cut into small cubes |
| 1/2 | cup chopped onion |
| 1/2 | cup chopped green bell pepper |
| 2 | cloves garlic, crushed |
| 1/2 | cup chopped tomato |
| 2 | tablespoons red wine vinegar |
| 1 | tablespoon dried parsley flakes |
| | Salt and pepper to taste |

Heat oil in a large nonstick skillet over medium-high heat. Add eggplant, onion, green pepper, and garlic. Cook, stirring frequently, until eggplant is tender and begins to brown.

Spoon eggplant mixture into a large bowl. Add remaining ingredients and mix well.

Chill several hours or overnight.

---

Each serving provides:

**43 Calories**

| 1 1/2 | Vegetable Servings | 1 g | Protein |
|---|---|---|---|
| 1/2 | Fat Serving | 2 g | Fat (46% of calories) |
| | | 5 g | Carbohydrate |
| | | 4 mg | Sodium |
| | | 0 mg | Cholesterol |
| | | 1 g | Fiber |

# Italian Cauliflower Salad

*Simple and delicious, this salad is a perfect way to start any Italian meal.*

*Makes 6 servings*

| | |
|---|---|
| 3 | cups cauliflower, cut into small flowerets |
| 2 | tablespoons finely chopped green bell pepper |
| 2 | tablespoons finely chopped onion |
| 1/4 | cup water |
| 3 | tablespoons bottled fat-free Italian dressing |
| 1/4 | teaspoon salt |
| 1/8 | teaspoon dried oregano |
| 1/8 | teaspoon dried basil |
| 1/8 | teaspoon garlic powder |

Combine all ingredients in a medium saucepan. Cover and cook over medium heat, stirring occasionally, until cauliflower is tender-crisp, about 10 minutes.

Chill thoroughly.

---

Each serving provides:

**17 Calories**

| | | | |
|---|---|---|---|
| 1 | Vegetable Serving | 1 g | Protein |
| 3 | Additional Calories | trace | Fat (4% of calories) |
| | | 3 g | Carbohydrate |
| | | 170 mg | Sodium |
| | | 0 mg | Cholesterol |
| | | 1 g | Fiber |

# Asparagus Vinaigrette

*For years, this has been one of our favorite dinner party dishes. Someone always asks for the recipe. It has just a few simple ingredients, yet the blend of flavors is exquisite.*

*Makes 4 servings*

| | |
|---|---|
| 1 | 10-ounce package frozen asparagus spears |
| 3 | tablespoons red wine vinegar |
| 1 | teaspoon Dijon mustard |
| 2 | tablespoons plus 1 1/2 teaspoons water |
| 1 | tablespoon plus 1 teaspoon vegetable oil |
| 2 | teaspoons dried chives |
| 1/2 | teaspoon dried parsley flakes |
| | Salt and pepper to taste |

Cook asparagus according to package directions. Drain and place in a shallow bowl.

Stir vinegar into mustard in a small bowl until blended. Add water, oil, chives, parsley, salt, and pepper. Mix well. Spoon over asparagus.

Chill several hours, turning asparagus occasionally.

Spoon a little of the marinade over each serving.

---

Each serving provides:

**60 Calories**

| | | | |
|---|---|---|---|
| 1 | Vegetable Serving | 2 g | Protein |
| 1 | Fat Serving | 5 g | Fat (65% of calories) |
| | | 3 g | Carbohydrate |
| | | 36 mg | Sodium |
| | | 0 mg | Cholesterol |
| | | 2 g | Fiber |

# Dilly Beans

*This is a great dish to make in the summer when tender, fresh green beans are plentiful. The tangy beans can be served anyplace you would ordinarily serve pickles.*

*Makes 6 servings*

| | |
|---|---|
| 1 | pound green beans, ends trimmed and strings removed |
| 1/2 | cup thinly sliced onion |
| 1/2 | cup vinegar |
| 2 | tablespoons vegetable oil |
| 2 | cloves garlic, cut into paper-thin slivers |
| 1 | teaspoon sugar |
| 1 | teaspoon dill weed |
| 1/2 | teaspoon dry mustard |
| 1/4 | teaspoon salt |
| 1/8 | teaspoon pepper |

Cook beans, covered, in 1 inch of boiling water until just tender-crisp, about 15 minutes. Drain, reserving cooking liquid. Place beans in a shallow bowl.

Add water to reserved liquid to make 1 cup. Combine liquid with remaining ingredients in a small bowl. Pour over beans.

Cover and chill 1 to 2 days.

---

Each serving provides:

**74 Calories**

| | | | |
|---|---|---|---|
| 1 | Vegetable Serving | 1 g | Protein |
| 1 | Fat Serving | 5 g | Fat (52% of calories) |
| 3 | Additional Calories | 8 g | Carbohydrate |
| | | 95 mg | Sodium |
| | | 0 mg | Cholesterol |
| | | 1 g | Fiber |

# Pineapple Slaw

*A refreshing change-of-pace salad, this easy slaw has the sweetness of pineapple and is laced with the exotic flavor of curry powder.*

*Makes 4 servings*

2      cups finely shredded cabbage
1/2    cup canned crushed pineapple (packed in juice), drained
1/4    cup finely chopped green bell pepper
2      tablespoons finely chopped onion
2      tablespoons reduced-calorie mayonnaise
1      teaspoon sugar
1/2    teaspoon curry powder
1/4    teaspoon celery seed
1/4    teaspoon salt
      Pepper to taste

Combine cabbage, pineapple, green pepper, and onion in a large bowl. Toss to combine.

Place mayonnaise in a small bowl. Stir in spices. Spoon over cabbage mixture. Mix well.

Chill several hours or overnight.

Mix well before serving.

---

Each serving provides:

**56 Calories**

| | | | |
|---|---|---|---|
| 1 1/4 | Vegetable Servings | 1 g | Protein |
| 3/4 | Fat Serving | 2 g | Fat (33% of calories) |
| 1/4 | Fruit Serving | 9 g | Carbohydrate |
| 4 | Additional Calories | 183 mg | Sodium |
| | | 2 mg | Cholesterol |
| | | 1 g | Fiber |

# Herbed Yogurt Dressing

*Nonfat yogurt makes a delicious, creamy base for salad dressings. Be creative and vary the herbs and spices, and you can create lots of different flavor combinations.*

*Makes 8 servings*
*(2 1/2 tablespoons each serving)*

| | |
|---|---|
| 2 | teaspoons vegetable oil |
| 1 | cup plain nonfat yogurt |
| 2 | tablespoons red wine vinegar |
| 1 | tablespoon minced onion flakes |
| 1/2 | teaspoon dried oregano |
| 1/2 | teaspoon dill weed |
| 1/8 | teaspoon garlic powder |
| | Salt and pepper to taste |

Stir oil into yogurt. Add remaining ingredients, mixing well.
Chill several hours to blend flavors.
Stir before serving.

Each serving provides:

**28 Calories**

| | | | |
|---|---|---|---|
| 1/4 | Fat Serving | 2 g | Protein |
| 15 | Additional Calories | 1 g | Fat (37% of calories) |
| | | 3 g | Carbohydrate |
| | | 22 mg | Sodium |
| | | 1 mg | Cholesterol |
| | | 0 g | Fiber |

# Dijon Vinaigrette

*Try this tangy dressing on steamed broccoli or asparagus as well as on a
tossed salad.*

*Makes 4 servings*
*(2 tablespoons each serving)*

| | |
|---|---|
| 3 | tablespoons red wine vinegar |
| 2 | tablespoons water |
| 1 | tablespoon plus 1 teaspoon vegetable oil |
| 1 | tablespoon plus 1 teaspoon Dijon mustard |
| 1/4 | teaspoon garlic powder |

Combine all ingredients in a small bowl. Beat with a fork or wire
whisk until blended.

Chill several hours to blend flavors.

Each serving provides:

**47 Calories**

| | | | |
|---|---|---|---|
| 1 | Fat Serving | 0 g | Protein |
| | | 5 g | Fat (95% of calories) |
| | | 0 g | Carbohydrate |
| | | 120 mg | Sodium |
| | | 0 mg | Cholesterol |
| | | 0 g | Fiber |

# Cheesy Herb Dressing

*This thick, cheese-flavored dressing also doubles as a delicious sandwich spread.*

*Makes 6 servings*
*(2 tablespoons each serving)*

| | |
|---|---|
| 1/2 | cup plain nonfat yogurt |
| 1 | tablespoon vegetable oil |
| 1 | tablespoon grated Parmesan cheese |
| 1 | tablespoon dried parsley flakes |
| 1 1/2 | teaspoons lemon juice |
| 1/4 | teaspoon garlic powder |
| 1/4 | teaspoon dried basil |

Combine all ingredients and mix well.
Chill several hours to blend flavors.

---

Each serving provides:

**35 Calories**

| 1/2 | Fat Serving | 1 g | Protein |
|---|---|---|---|
| 15 | Additional Calories | 3 g | Fat (65% of calories) |
| | | 2 g | Carbohydrate |
| | | 30 mg | Sodium |
| | | 1 mg | Cholesterol |
| | | 0 g | Fiber |

# Creamy Italian Dressing

*Turn an ordinary tossed salad into a gourmet delight with this creamy, herbed dressing.*

*Makes 8 servings*
*(2 tablespoons each serving)*

| | |
|---|---|
| 3/4 | cup plain nonfat yogurt |
| 1/4 | cup reduced-calorie mayonnaise |
| 2 | tablespoons skim milk |
| 1 | tablespoon red wine vinegar |
| 1/2 | teaspoon dried oregano |
| 1/2 | teaspoon dried basil |
| 1/2 | teaspoon sugar |
| 1/8 | teaspoon garlic powder |
| | Salt and pepper to taste |

In a large bowl, combine all ingredients, mixing well.
Chill several hours to blend flavors.

---

Each serving provides:

**35 Calories**

| 3/4 | Fat Serving | 1 g | Protein |
|---|---|---|---|
| 13 | Additional Calories | 2 g | Fat (52% of calories) |
| | | 3 g | Carbohydrate |
| | | 59 mg | Sodium |
| | | 3 mg | Cholesterol |
| | | 0 g | Fiber |

# French Tomato Dressing

*This tart and tangy dressing makes greens come alive. It's also a delicious dressing to spoon over a platter of sliced tomatoes and onions.*

*Makes 6 servings*
*(2 tablespoons each serving)*

| | |
|---|---|
| 1/2 | cup tomato juice |
| 2 | tablespoons vegetable oil |
| 2 | tablespoons red wine vinegar |
| 1 | teaspoon Dijon mustard |
| 1 | teaspoon sugar |
| 1/2 | teaspoon Worcestershire sauce |
| 1/2 | teaspoon dried oregano |
| 1/4 | teaspoon salt |
| 1/4 | teaspoon dried basil |
| 1/4 | teaspoon pepper |

Combine all ingredients in a small jar and shake well.
Chill to blend flavors.

---

Each serving provides:

**49 Calories**

| | | | |
|---|---|---|---|
| 1/4 | Vegetable Serving | 0 g | Protein |
| 1 | Fat Serving | 5 g | Fat (83% of calories) |
| 3 | Additional Calories | 2 g | Carbohydrate |
| | | 188 mg | Sodium |
| | | 0 mg | Cholesterol |
| | | 0 g | Fiber |

# Cheesy Thousand Island Dressing

*Lowfat cottage cheese replaces the mayonnaise in this creamy version of an all-time favorite dressing. It also makes a delicious spread for a sliced turkey and tomato sandwich.*

*Makes 12 servings*
*(2 tablespoons each serving)*

| | |
|---|---|
| 1 | cup lowfat (1%) cottage cheese |
| 1/4 | cup ketchup |
| 1 | tablespoon vegetable oil |
| 1 | teaspoon paprika |
| 1/4 | teaspoon salt |
| 1/8 | teaspoon pepper |
| 2 | tablespoons finely minced celery |
| 2 | tablespoons finely minced green pepper |
| 2 | tablespoons finely minced onion |
| 1 | tablespoon sweet pickle relish |

In a blender container, combine cottage cheese, ketchup, oil, paprika, salt, and pepper. Blend until smooth.

Stir in remaining ingredients.

Chill several hours to blend flavors.

---

Each serving provides:

**33 Calories**

| | | | |
|---|---|---|---|
| 1/4 | Protein Serving | 2 g | Protein |
| 1/4 | Fat Serving | 1 g | Fat (37% of calories) |
| 6 | Additional Calories | 3 g | Carbohydrate |
| | | 192 mg | Sodium |
| | | 1 mg | Cholesterol |
| | | 0 g | Fiber |

# Blue Cheese Dressing

*The distinctive flavor of blue cheese plays to its full advantage in this creamy dressing, and "diluting" the cheese with lowfat cottage cheese really helps lower the total fat.*

*Makes 8 servings*
*(2 tablespoons each serving)*

| | |
|---|---|
| 2/3 | cup lowfat (1%) cottage cheese |
| 1 1/2 | ounces blue cheese, crumbled (1/4 cup) |
| 2 | teaspoons vegetable oil |
| 2 | teaspoons red wine vinegar |
| 1 | teaspoon dry mustard |
| 1 | teaspoon minced onion flakes |
| | Salt and pepper to taste |

Combine all ingredients in a blender container. Blend until smooth. Chill several hours to blend flavors.

---

Each serving provides:

**44 Calories**

| 1/2 | Protein Serving | 4 g | Protein |
|---|---|---|---|
| 1/4 | Fat Serving | 3 g | Fat (60% of calories) |
| 5 | Additional Calories | 1 g | Carbohydrate |
| | | 151 mg | Sodium |
| | | 5 mg | Cholesterol |
| | | 0 g | Fiber |

# Creamy Orange Dressing

*Spoon this delectable dressing over fresh fruit and create an appetizer or a
light dessert with a delicious difference.*

*Makes 8 servings*
*(2 1/2 tablespoons each serving)*

1      cup plain nonfat yogurt
1/4    cup frozen orange juice concentrate, thawed

In a small bowl, combine yogurt and juice concentrate. Mix well.
Chill several hours.

---

Each serving provides:

**30 Calories**

| | | | |
|---|---|---|---|
| 1/4 | Fruit Serving | 2 g | Protein |
| 15 | Additional Calories | trace | Fat (2% of calories) |
| | | 6 g | Carbohydrate |
| | | 22 mg | Sodium |
| | | 1 mg | Cholesterol |
| | | 0 g | Fiber |

# Eggs and Cheese

There are an endless number of recipes available for eggs and cheese. Both are versatile, tasty, and inexpensive. There's only one problem: Both eggs and cheese are high in fat and cholesterol. Fortunately, there are a few easy solutions to the problem.

The cholesterol in eggs is found entirely in the yolk. The easiest way around this dilemma is to use either 2 egg whites to replace each whole egg or a liquid egg substitute. Either will work in baked goods and most recipes that call for eggs. In omelets, many people prefer the flavor and the ease of the egg substitutes.

Cheese is a perfect match for so many foods. There are reduced-fat and fat-free versions of most cheeses. Some of the fat-free cheeses seem to lack flavor and "meltability," so our choice is usually the reduced-fat versions. Some cheeses, such as feta and Parmesan, have a rich, distinctive taste that goes a long way, so by simply cutting back on the amount used, you can still enjoy their wonderful flavors.

We've made the adjustments for you and combined eggs and cheese with many other delicious ingredients, bringing you many scrumptious taste delights.

# Scrambled Eggs Florentine

*Spinach makes a colorful and nutritious addition to this favorite American breakfast. You can also turn this into a great sandwich by placing the cooked eggs between 2 slices of whole wheat toast, with a little ketchup or tomato sauce.*

*Makes 4 servings*

| | |
|---|---|
| 2 | cups liquid egg substitute |
| 1 | 10-ounce package frozen chopped spinach, thawed and drained well |
| 2 | tablespoons minced onion flakes |
| 2 | tablespoons grated Parmesan cheese |
| 1 | tablespoon imitation bacon bits |
| $1/2$ | teaspoon garlic powder |
| $1/16$ | teaspoon ground nutmeg |
| | Freshly ground black pepper to taste |

In a large bowl, combine all ingredients. Mix well.

Spray a large nonstick skillet or griddle with nonstick cooking spray. Heat over medium heat.

Pour egg mixture into skillet. Cook, stirring frequently, until eggs are done to taste.

---

Each serving provides:

**103 Calories**

| | | | |
|---|---|---|---|
| 2 | Protein Servings | 16 g | Protein |
| 1 | Vegetable Serving | 1 g | Fat (12% of calories) |
| 23 | Additional Calories | 7 g | Carbohydrate |
| | | 344 mg | Sodium |
| | | 2 mg | Cholesterol |
| | | 2 g | Fiber |

# Spanish Omelet

*Easy and delicious, this omelet makes a perfect brunch dish or weekend treat.*

*Makes 4 servings*

## Omelet

| | |
|---|---|
| 2 | teaspoons vegetable oil |
| 1 | cup chopped onion |
| 1 | cup chopped green bell pepper |
| 2 | cups liquid egg substitute |
| 1/4 | teaspoon garlic powder |
| 1/8 | teaspoon pepper |
| | Salt to taste |

## Sauce

| | |
|---|---|
| 1 | 8-ounce can salt-free (or regular) tomato sauce |
| 1/4 | teaspoon *each* dried basil and oregano |
| 1/8 | teaspoon garlic powder |

Heat oil in a large nonstick skillet over medium heat. Add onion and green pepper. Cook, stirring frequently, until lightly browned, about 10 minutes.

While onion and pepper are browning, combine all sauce ingredients in a small saucepan. Heat until hot and bubbly.

Place egg substitute in a large bowl and add garlic powder and pepper, mixing well. Add to skillet. Cook, stirring frequently, until eggs are done to taste.

To serve, divide egg mixture onto 4 serving plates. Top with sauce.

---

Each serving provides:

**124 Calories**

| | | | |
|---|---|---|---|
| 2 | Protein Servings | 13 g | Protein |
| 2 | Vegetable Servings | 3 g | Fat (19% of calories) |
| 1/2 | Fat Serving | 12 g | Carbohydrate |
| | | 214 mg | Sodium |
| | | 0 mg | Cholesterol |
| | | 2 g | Fiber |

# Mexican Tomato Omelet

*Tomato slices add color and flavor to this upside-down omelet. Garnish it with fresh basil, serve it with salsa, and it really reflects the Mexican cuisine's use of color.*

*Makes 2 servings*

| | |
|---|---|
| 2 | teaspoons vegetable oil |
| 1 | cup liquid egg substitute |
| 1 | teaspoon dried basil |
| 1 | teaspoon ground cumin |
| 1/4 | teaspoon garlic powder |
| | Salt and pepper to taste |
| 1 | tablespoon grated Parmesan cheese |
| 1 | tablespoon skim milk |
| 1 | medium ripe tomato, sliced |

Heat oil in an 8-inch nonstick skillet over medium heat.

In a medium bowl, combine egg substitute with remaining ingredients, *except* tomato slices. Beat with a fork or wire whisk until blended. Pour into hot skillet.

Reduce heat to medium-low, cover skillet, and cook 5 minutes. Arrange tomato slices over eggs and continue to cook, covered, 5 minutes more, or until eggs are set enough to invert without breaking.

Slide omelet out of pan onto a plate. Then, invert into pan so that tomatoes are now on the bottom. Cook, uncovered, 1 minute, or until eggs are set.

Invert onto serving plate tomato-side up.

---

Each serving provides:

**137 Calories**

| | | | |
|---|---|---|---|
| 2 | Protein Servings | 14 g | Protein |
| 1 | Vegetable Serving | 6 g | Fat (38% of calories) |
| 1 | Fat Serving | 7 g | Carbohydrate |
| 18 | Additional Calories | 259 mg | Sodium |
| | | 2 mg | Cholesterol |
| | | 1 g | Fiber |

# Spinach Frittata

*This hearty dish is fit for any meal, from a Sunday brunch to a quick and inexpensive dinner. For variations, feel free to add any leftover cooked vegetables.*

*Makes 8 servings*

| | |
|---|---|
| 2 | teaspoons olive oil |
| 1 | cup chopped onion |
| 3 | cups liquid egg substitute |
| 2 | 10-ounce packages frozen chopped spinach, thawed and drained well |
| 1/2 | teaspoon garlic powder |
| 1/4 | teaspoon ground nutmeg |
| | Salt and pepper to taste |
| 3 | tablespoons grated Parmesan cheese |

Preheat oven to 375°.

Heat oil in a 10-inch heavy, ovenproof skillet over medium heat. Add onion. Cook, stirring frequently, until tender, about 5 minutes.

Combine egg substitute, spinach, garlic powder, nutmeg, salt, pepper, and half of the Parmesan cheese. Mix well and pour into skillet. Sprinkle with remaining cheese. Cook for 2 minutes without stirring, then place skillet in oven.

Bake, uncovered, until eggs are set and lightly browned.

Cut into pie-shaped wedges to serve.

---

Each serving provides:

**89 Calories**

| | | | |
|---|---|---|---|
| 1 1/2 | Protein Servings | 12 g | Protein |
| 1 1/4 | Vegetable Servings | 2 g | Fat (19% of calories) |
| 1/4 | Fat Serving | 6 g | Carbohydrate |
| 11 | Additional Calories | 238 mg | Sodium |
| | | 1 mg | Cholesterol |
| | | 2 g | Fiber |

# Company Egg Cups

*Similar to miniature quiches, these egg cups are fun to serve, but you don't really have to wait for company to try them.*

*Makes 4 servings*

| | |
|---|---|
| 1/4 | cup *each* finely chopped mushrooms, onion, and green bell pepper |
| 2 | cloves garlic, finely chopped |
| 1/2 | teaspoon dried oregano |
| | Salt and pepper to taste |
| 2 | teaspoons reduced-calorie margarine |
| 4 | slices thin-sliced whole wheat bread (1/2-ounce slices) |
| 1 | cup liquid egg substitute |
| 4 | teaspoons grated Parmesan cheese |

Preheat oven to 375°.

Heat a small nonstick skillet over medium heat. Add mushrooms, onion, green pepper, and garlic. Sprinkle with oregano, salt, and pepper. Cook, stirring frequently, until vegetables are tender, about 5 minutes. Add small amounts of water if necessary to prevent sticking.

Spread 1/2 teaspoon of margarine on each slice of bread. Press each slice, margarine-side down, into the cup of a muffin pan, forming a cup.

Divide vegetable mixture evenly into the crusts. Fill with egg substitute. Sprinkle 1 teaspoon of Parmesan cheese over the top of each cup.

Bake, uncovered, 15 minutes, or until eggs are set.

---

Each serving provides:

**90 Calories**

| | | | |
|---|---|---|---|
| 1 | Protein Serving | 8 g | Protein |
| 1/2 | Bread Serving | 2 g | Fat (20% of calories) |
| 1/2 | Vegetable Serving | 10 g | Carbohydrate |
| 1/4 | Fat Serving | 229 mg | Sodium |
| 10 | Additional Calories | 1 mg | Cholesterol |
| | | 1 g | Fiber |

# Fruittata

*We've combined eggs with vegetables. Now, why not combine eggs with fruit? This unique omelet, topped with a creamy, rum-flavored sauce, makes a truly elegant brunch dish.*

*Makes 4 servings*

### Fruittata
| | |
|---|---|
| 1 | cup liquid egg substitute |
| 1 | tablespoon sugar |
| 1 | teaspoon vanilla extract |
| 1/4 | teaspoon rum extract |
| 1/4 | teaspoon orange or lemon extract |
| 1/4 | teaspoon ground cinnamon |
| 1/3 | cup nonfat dry milk |
| 1/3 | cup water |
| 2 | teaspoons margarine |
| 1/2 | cup blueberries, fresh or frozen |
| 1/3 | cup canned crushed pineapple (packed in juice), drained |
| 1/3 | cup canned peaches (packed in juice), drained and cut into small chunks |
| | Ground cinnamon |

### Vanilla-Rum Topping
| | |
|---|---|
| 3/4 | cup vanilla nonfat yogurt |
| 1/2 | teaspoon rum extract |

Preheat oven to 375°.

In a medium bowl, combine egg substitute, sugar, extracts, cinnamon, dry milk, and water. Beat with a fork or wire whisk until blended.

Melt margarine in a 7- or 8-inch ovenproof skillet or baking dish over medium heat. Add fruit, stirring to distribute evenly in pan. Pour egg mixture over fruit. Sprinkle lightly with additional cinnamon. Cook for 2 minutes without stirring, then place pan in oven.

Bake, uncovered, 20 to 25 minutes, or until eggs are set.

Combine yogurt and rum extract. Serve as a topping on hot fruittata.

---

Each serving provides:

**154 Calories**

| | | | |
|---|---|---|---|
| 1 | Protein Serving | 11 g | Protein |
| 1/2 | Fat Serving | 2 g | Fat (12% of calories) |
| 1/2 | Fruit Serving | 22 g | Carbohydrate |
| 1/4 | Milk Serving | 185 mg | Sodium |
| 48 | Additional Calories | 2 mg | Cholesterol |
| | | 1 g | Fiber |

# Banana Puff

*If you were to cross an omelet with a soufflé, the result would be this delicious breakfast treat. Adding the maple syrup at the end really makes this dish taste wonderful.*

*Makes 4 servings*

| | |
|---|---|
| 1/4 | cup liquid egg substitute |
| 3/4 | cup vanilla nonfat yogurt |
| 2 | tablespoons sugar |
| 1 | teaspoon vanilla extract |
| 1/4 | teaspoon rum extract |
| 3/4 | cup all-purpose flour |
| 2 | teaspoons baking powder |
| 1 | teaspoon baking soda |
| 1/4 | teaspoon ground cinnamon |
| 3 | egg whites (Do not use egg substitute.) |
| 1 | medium ripe banana, diced |
| 4 | teaspoons maple syrup |

Preheat oven to 400°.

Spray a 9-inch cake pan with nonstick cooking spray.

Combine egg substitute, yogurt, sugar, and extracts in a large bowl. Beat on low speed of an electric mixer until blended. Continue to beat 1 minute more.

In a small bowl, combine flour, baking powder, baking soda, and cinnamon, mixing well. Add to first mixture, beating on low speed until all ingredients are moistened.

In a separate bowl, with clean, dry beaters, beat egg whites on high speed until stiff. Fold into batter, gently but thoroughly. Fold in banana.

Spread batter in prepared cake pan. Sprinkle lightly with additional cinnamon.

Bake 20 minutes, or until puffy and lightly browned.

Drizzle each serving with 1 teaspoon of the maple syrup.

Each serving provides:

**218 Calories**

| | | | |
|---|---|---|---|
| 1/2 | Protein Serving | 9 g | Protein |
| 1 | Bread Serving | 1 g | Fat (3% of calories) |
| 1/2 | Fruit Serving | 44 g | Carbohydrate |
| 87 | Additional Calories | 657 mg | Sodium |
| | | 1 mg | Cholesterol |
| | | 1 g | Fiber |

# Lemon Soufflé

*As an elegant brunch dish or an inspired dessert, this popular dish is sure to please. It's usually made with whole eggs, which are separated and then beaten. We've replaced the yolks with egg substitute, and the taste is still divine. It will definitely impress!*

*Makes 4 servings*

| | |
|---|---|
| 1/2 | cup liquid egg substitute |
| 3 | tablespoons sugar |
| 1 | teaspoon lemon extract |
| 1/2 | teaspoon vanilla extract |
| 1/2 | teaspoon grated fresh lemon peel |
| 4 | egg whites (Do not use egg substitute.) |
| 1/4 | teaspoon cream of tartar |

Preheat oven to 350°.

Spray a 1 1/2-quart soufflé dish or deep baking dish with nonstick cooking spray.

In a large bowl, beat egg substitute on medium speed of an electric mixer for 1 minute. Add 2 tablespoons of the sugar, the extracts, and lemon peel. Beat on high speed for 2 minutes.

In another bowl, using clean, dry beaters, beat egg whites and cream of tartar on high speed until soft peaks form. Add remaining sugar and beat until egg whites are stiff.

Fold egg whites into first mixture, a third at a time, folding gently, until the two mixtures are just blended. Pour mixture into prepared dish. Place in a shallow baking pan and pour hot water into larger pan to a depth of 1 inch.

Bake 30 minutes, or until soufflé has puffed and top is lightly browned. Serve right away.

---

Each serving provides:

**78 Calories**

| | | | |
|---|---|---|---|
| 3/4 | Protein Serving | 7 g | Protein |
| 41 | Additional Calories | trace | Fat (3% of calories) |
| | | 11 g | Carbohydrate |
| | | 105 mg | Sodium |
| | | 0 mg | Cholesterol |
| | | 0 g | Fiber |

# Almond Bread Puff

*This sensational version of French toast is light and lots of fun to eat. The taste is great, and you can vary the flavors by replacing the almond extract with any other favorite extract.*

*Makes 2 servings*

| | |
|---|---|
| 1/4 | cup liquid egg substitute |
| 2 | tablespoons skim milk |
| 1 | tablespoon sugar |
| 2 | teaspoons vanilla extract |
| 1/2 | teaspoon almond extract |
| 2 | slices whole wheat bread (1-ounce slices) |
| 2 | egg whites (Do not use egg substitute.) |

Preheat oven to 350°.

Spray a 4 × 8-inch loaf pan with nonstick cooking spray.

In a small bowl, combine egg substitute, milk, *half* of the sugar, *half* of the vanilla extract, and *half* of the almond extract. Mix well and pour into prepared pan. Place bread in mixture, turning carefully until all of the liquid has been absorbed.

Bake 15 minutes. Remove from oven.

In a medium bowl, beat egg whites until stiff, using high speed of an electric mixer. Beat in remaining sugar and extracts. Spread over bread. Return to oven and continue to bake for 10 more minutes, or until nicely browned.

---

Each serving provides:

**156 Calories**

| | | | |
|---|---|---|---|
| 1/2 | Protein Serving | 10 g | Protein |
| 1 | Bread Serving | 2 g | Fat (13% of calories) |
| 50 | Additional Calories | 22 g | Carbohydrate |
| | | 262 mg | Sodium |
| | | 0 mg | Cholesterol |
| | | 2 g | Fiber |

# Dutch Apple Pancake

*This unique cross between an omelet and a pancake is delicious topped with
either maple syrup, confectioners' sugar, or a mix of sugar and cinnamon.
It's also good topped with the Vanilla-Rum Topping that's served with the
Fruittata on page 74.*

*Makes 2 servings*

| | |
|---|---|
| 2 | teaspoons margarine |
| 2 | small, sweet apples, peeled and cut into 1/2-inch cubes |
| 1/2 | cup liquid egg substitute |
| 1/3 | cup nonfat dry milk |
| 1/4 | cup water |
| 3 | tablespoons all-purpose flour |
| 2 | tablespoons sugar |
| 1/2 | teaspoon ground cinnamon |
| 1/4 | teaspoon ground nutmeg |
| 1/4 | teaspoon baking powder |
| 1 | teaspoon vanilla extract |
| 1/4 | teaspoon almond extract |

Melt margarine in a 10-inch heavy, ovenproof skillet over medium-
high heat. Add apples. Cook, stirring frequently, until apples are tender, about 5 minutes. Remove from heat.

Preheat oven to 500°.

Combine remaining ingredients in a blender container. Blend until
smooth. Pour over apples. Bake, uncovered, 10 minutes, or until eggs
are set and lightly browned.

---

Each serving provides:

**263 Calories**

| | | | |
|---|---|---|---|
| 1 | Protein Serving | 11 g | Protein |
| 1/2 | Bread Serving | 4 g | Fat (15% of calories) |
| 1 | Fat Serving | 44 g | Carbohydrate |
| 1 | Fruit Serving | 267 mg | Sodium |
| 1/2 | Milk Serving | 2 mg | Cholesterol |
| 48 | Additional Calories | 2 g | Fiber |

# Broccoli and Cheese Pancakes

*A light meal of tuna salad, a tossed salad, and these cheesy pancakes is often a welcome change of pace from a heavy meat and potato dinner.*

*Makes 4 servings*
*(4 pancakes each serving)*

| | |
|---|---|
| 1 | 10-ounce package frozen chopped broccoli, thawed and drained |
| 1/2 | cup liquid egg substitute |
| 2/3 | cup lowfat (1%) cottage cheese |
| 1/4 | cup thinly sliced green onion (green part only) |
| 3 | tablespoons all-purpose flour |
| 1 | tablespoon grated Parmesan cheese |
| 1/4 | teaspoon garlic powder |
| | Salt and pepper to taste |
| | Dash ground nutmeg |

Place broccoli in a large bowl.

In a blender container, combine egg substitute and cottage cheese. Blend until smooth. Stir in remaining ingredients and add to broccoli, mixing well.

Spray a large nonstick griddle or skillet with nonstick cooking spray. Preheat over medium heat.

Drop cheese mixture onto griddle, using 2 tablespoons for each pancake. Cook, turning once, until pancakes are lightly browned on both sides.

---

Each serving provides:

**94 Calories**

| | | | |
|---|---|---|---|
| 1 | Protein Serving | 11 g | Protein |
| 1/4 | Bread Serving | 2 g | Fat (14% of calories) |
| 1 | Vegetable Serving | 10 g | Carbohydrate |
| 8 | Additional Calories | 245 mg | Sodium |
| | | 2 mg | Cholesterol |
| | | 2 g | Fiber |

# Asparagus Cheese Tart

*This elegant no-crust, quiche-like pie serves 8 as a side dish or 6 as a light en-trée. It's so easy to make with no pie crust to roll.*

*Makes 8 servings*

| | |
|---|---|
| 1 | 10-ounce package frozen asparagus spears |
| 1 1/3 | cups lowfat (1%) cottage cheese |
| 2/3 | cup nonfat dry milk |
| 1/2 | cup water |
| 1/4 | cup plus 2 tablespoons all-purpose flour |
| 2 | teaspoons baking powder |
| 2 | tablespoons plus 2 teaspoons reduced-calorie margarine |
| 3/4 | cup liquid egg substitute |
| 2 | teaspoons minced onion flakes |
| 1 | packet low-sodium instant chicken- or vegetable-flavored broth mix |
| 3 | tablespoons grated Parmesan cheese (1 ounce) |

Cook asparagus according to package directions. Drain.

Preheat oven to 350°.

Spray a 9-inch pie pan with nonstick cooking spray.

Cut each asparagus spear into 3 pieces. Arrange pieces in prepared pan.

In a blender container, combine remaining ingredients, using only *half* of the Parmesan cheese. Blend until smooth. Pour over asparagus. Sprinkle with remaining Parmesan cheese.

Bake 30 minutes, or until set and lightly browned.

Cool 5 minutes before serving.

---

Each serving provides:

**125 Calories**

| | | | |
|---|---|---|---|
| 3/4 | Protein Serving | 12 g | Protein |
| 1/4 | Bread Serving | 4 g | Fat (25% of calories) |
| 1/2 | Vegetable Serving | 11 g | Carbohydrate |
| 1/2 | Fat Serving | 458 mg | Sodium |
| 1/4 | Milk Serving | 5 mg | Cholesterol |
| 23 | Additional Calories | 1 g | Fiber |

# Easy Cheesy

*Yes, it's easy and it's cheesy. This quick casserole is suitable for any meal, from breakfast to dinner. You can add lots of different touches if you wish, such as sliced green onions, sliced olives, imitation bacon bits, chopped jalapeño peppers . . .*

*Makes 6 servings*

| | |
|---|---|
| 1⅓ | cups lowfat (1%) cottage cheese |
| 4 | ounces shredded reduced-fat Cheddar cheese (1 cup) |
| 1 | cup liquid egg substitute |
| 1½ | teaspoons vegetable oil |
| 1 | tablespoon all-purpose flour |
| 1 | tablespoon minced onion flakes |
| 1 | packet low-sodium instant chicken-flavored broth mix |
| ⅛ | teaspoon garlic powder |

Preheat oven to 350°.

Spray an 8-inch square baking pan with nonstick cooking spray.

In a blender container, combine all ingredients. Blend until smooth. Pour into prepared pan.

Bake, uncovered, 30 minutes, or until puffy and lightly browned.

Cut into squares and serve hot.

---

Each serving provides:

**129 Calories**

| | | | |
|---|---|---|---|
| 2 | Protein Servings | 17 g | Protein |
| ¼ | Fat Serving | 5 g | Fat (36% of calories) |
| 20 | Additional Calories | 4 g | Carbohydrate |
| | | 418 mg | Sodium |
| | | 15 mg | Cholesterol |
| | | 0 g | Fiber |

# Broccoli Cheese Puff

*Simple, yet elegant, this dish can be prepared up to a day ahead and baked when you are ready. It serves 6 as a side dish or 4 as a delicious, light entrée.*

*Makes 6 servings*

| | |
|---|---|
| 4 | slices whole wheat bread (1-ounce slices) |
| 4 | ounces shredded reduced-fat Cheddar cheese (1 cup) |
| 1 | 10-ounce package frozen chopped broccoli, thawed and drained |
| 1 | cup liquid egg substitute |
| 2 | cups skim milk |
| 2 | teaspoons minced onion flakes |
| 1/2 | teaspoon dry mustard |
| 1/4 | teaspoon salt |
| 1/8 | teaspoon pepper |
| 1/8 | teaspoon garlic powder |

Spray a 4 × 8-inch loaf pan with nonstick cooking spray.

Place 2 slices of the bread in the prepared pan. Sprinkle with *half* of the cheese. Spread broccoli over the cheese and top with remaining cheese, followed by remaining bread slices.

In a blender container, combine egg substitute and remaining ingredients. Blend until smooth. Pour evenly over bread.

Refrigerate at least 1 hour, up to 24 hours. Remove from refrigerator 30 minutes before baking.

Preheat oven to 350°.

Bake, uncovered, 40 minutes, or until golden brown.

---

Each serving provides:

**165 Calories**

| | | | |
|---|---|---|---|
| 1 1/2 | Protein Servings | 16 g | Protein |
| 1/2 | Bread Serving | 5 g | Fat (25% of calories) |
| 3/4 | Vegetable Serving | 16 g | Carbohydrate |
| 1/4 | Milk Serving | 457 mg | Sodium |
| 24 | Additional Calories | 15 mg | Cholesterol |
| | | 2 g | Fiber |

# Potato-Cheese Casserole

*You can either bake or boil the potatoes for this rich, cheesy casserole. If you are making baked potatoes for dinner one night, why not pop a few extra ones into the oven so you can make this great casserole the next night?*

*Makes 6 servings*

| | |
|---|---|
| 12 | ounces cooked potatoes, peeled and thinly sliced (2 small baking potatoes) |
| 3 | ounces shredded reduced-fat Cheddar cheese (3/4 cup) |
| 1/2 | cup liquid egg substitute |
| 2/3 | cup lowfat (1%) cottage cheese |
| 1 | teaspoon dried parsley flakes |
| 1/8 | teaspoon garlic powder |
| | Salt and pepper to taste |
| 1/2 | cup thinly sliced green onions (green part only) |

Preheat oven to 350°.

Spray a 1 1/2-quart baking dish with nonstick cooking spray.

Arrange *half* of the potatoes in prepared pan. Top with *half* of the Cheddar cheese, then the remaining potatoes, followed by the remaining Cheddar.

In a blender container, combine remaining ingredients, *except* green onions. Blend until smooth. Stir in green onions. Pour over potatoes.

Bake, uncovered, 30 minutes, or until hot and lightly browned.

---

Each serving provides:

**121 Calories**

| | | | |
|---|---|---|---|
| 1 1/4 | Protein Servings | 11 g | Protein |
| 1/2 | Bread Serving | 3 g | Fat (22% of calories) |
| 1/4 | Vegetable Serving | 13 g | Carbohydrate |
| 5 | Additional Calories | 250 mg | Sodium |
| | | 11 mg | Cholesterol |
| | | 1 g | Fiber |

# Baked Cauliflower and Cheese

*The combination of the ricotta and Parmesan cheeses gives this dish a very rich taste. It makes a lovely buffet dish.*

*Makes 4 servings*

| | |
|---|---|
| 4 | cups cauliflower, cut into flowerets (or two 10-ounce packages frozen caluiflower) |
| 1/2 | cup part-skim ricotta cheese |
| 1/2 | cup liquid egg substitute |
| 1 | tablespoon grated Parmesan cheese |
| 2 | teaspoons minced onion flakes |
| | Salt and pepper to taste |

Place cauliflower in a steamer rack over boiling water in a medium saucepan. Cook, covered, 5 minutes. (If using frozen cauliflower, cook according to package directions, choosing the shorter amount of cooking time given.)

Preheat oven to 350°.

Spray a 1-quart baking dish with nonstick cooking spray.

Place cauliflower in prepared pan.

Combine remaining ingredients in a small bowl. Beat with a fork or wire whisk until blended. Spoon over cauliflower.

Bake, uncovered, 25 minutes, or until lightly browned.

---

Each serving provides:

**91 Calories**

| | | | |
|---|---|---|---|
| 1 | Protein Serving | 9 g | Protein |
| 2 | Vegetable Servings | 3 g | Fat (30% of calories) |
| 8 | Additional Calories | 8 g | Carbohydrate |
| | | 127 mg | Sodium |
| | | 11 mg | Cholesterol |
| | | 2 g | Fiber |

# Spaghetti Squash Kugel

*Spaghetti squash takes the place of noodles in this rich, cheesy dish. It can be served warm or cold, and it is a good side dish to serve with the "Pretend" Salmon Salad on page 107.*

*Makes 8 servings*

| | |
|---|---|
| 1 | cup liquid egg substitute |
| 1¹/₃ | cups lowfat (1%) cottage cheese |
| ¹/₄ | cup sugar |
| 2 | teaspoons vanilla extract |
| ¹/₂ | teaspoon ground cinnamon |
| 3 | cups cooked, drained spaghetti squash* |

Preheat oven to 350°.

Spray an 8-inch square baking pan with nonstick cooking spray.

In a large bowl, combine egg substitute, cottage cheese, sugar, vanilla, and cinnamon. Beat with a fork or wire whisk until blended.

Add spaghetti squash to egg mixture. Mix well. Spoon into prepared pan. Sprinkle lightly with additional cinnamon.

Bake 40 minutes, or until set and lightly browned.


*To cook spaghetti squash, cut squash in half lengthwise. Remove seeds. Bake, cut-side down in a baking pan containing 1 inch of water, at 350°, for 45 minutes, or until tender. Drain halves cut-side down. Pull strands free with a fork.

---

Each serving provides:

**88 Calories**

| 1 | Protein Serving | 8 g | Protein |
|---|---|---|---|
| ³/₄ | Vegetable Serving | 1 g | Fat (7% of calories) |
| 24 | Additional Calories | 12 g | Carbohydrate |
| | | 213 mg | Sodium |
| | | 2 mg | Cholesterol |
| | | 0 g | Fiber |

# Italian Eggplant and Cheese Casserole

*Serve this easy favorite with rice or noodles and a green vegetable, and dinner is complete. As an entrée for 6 or a filling side dish for 8, this one will be requested again and again.*

*Makes 6 servings*

| | |
|---|---|
| 1 | large eggplant (1 1/4 pounds), peeled and cut crosswise into 1/2-inch slices |
| 2 | cups reduced-fat, meatless spaghetti sauce, or marinara sauce |
| 2 | cups part-skim ricotta cheese |
| 2 | ounces part-skim Mozzarella cheese (1/2 cup) |
| 1 | tablespoon grated Parmesan cheese |

Preheat broiler.

Arrange eggplant slices in a single layer on a nonstick baking sheet. Broil until lightly browned on both sides, turning slices once.

Reduce oven temperature to 375°.

Spray a 9 × 13-inch baking pan with nonstick cooking spray.

Spread a thin layer of the sauce in the bottom of the prepared pan. Arrange half of the eggplant slices over the sauce. Drop ricotta cheese by spoonfuls onto eggplant. Top with 2/3 cup of sauce.

Top with remaining eggplant slices, pressing them down gently. Top with remaining sauce, then sprinkle with Mozzarella and Parmesan cheeses.

Bake, uncovered, 35 minutes.

Let stand 3 to 5 minutes before serving.

---

Each serving provides:

**195 Calories**

| | | | |
|---|---|---|---|
| 1 1/2 | Protein Servings | 14 g | Protein |
| 2 1/4 | Vegetable Servings | 9 g | Fat (40% of calories) |
| 1 | Fat Serving | 16 g | Carbohydrate |
| 22 | Additional Calories | 425 mg | Sodium |
| | | 32 mg | Cholesterol |
| | | 2 g | Fiber |

# Quiche for One

*You can enjoy the glorious flavor of quiche without all the muss and fuss. Go ahead—treat yourself!*

*Makes 1 serving*

| | |
|---|---|
| 1/4 | cup liquid egg substitute |
| 1/2 | cup skim milk |
| 1/8 | teaspoon salt |
| 1/8 | teaspoon pepper |
| | Dash ground nutmeg |
| 1/2 | cup chopped mushrooms, fresh or canned |
| 1 | ounce shredded reduced-sodium Swiss cheese (1/4 cup) |
| 2 | tablespoons thinly slice green onion (green part only) |
| 1 | teaspoon imitation bacon bits |

Preheat oven to 350°.

Spray a small individual casserole with nonstick cooking spray.

In a small bowl, combine egg substitute, milk, salt, pepper, and nutmeg. Beat with a fork or wire whisk until blended. Stir in remaining ingredients. Pour into prepared pan.

Bake 30 minutes, or until set.

Let stand 5 minutes before serving.

---

Each serving provides:

**192 Calories**

| | | | |
|---|---|---|---|
| 2 | Protein Servings | 22 g | Protein |
| 1 1/4 | Vegetable Servings | 7 g | Fat (31% of calories) |
| 1/2 | Milk Serving | 11 g | Carbohydrate |
| 30 | Additional Calories | 549 mg | Sodium |
| | | 22 mg | Cholesterol |
| | | 1 g | Fiber |

# Italian Cheese-Stuffed Pita

*For cheese lovers, this is an easy sandwich that can be varied by choosing different cheese combinations. For instance, Swiss or Provolone add their own distinctive flavors.*

*Makes 2 servings*

| | |
|---|---|
| 1/4 | cup part-skim ricotta cheese |
| 2 | ounces shredded reduced-fat Cheddar cheese |
| 1 | teaspoon grated Parmesan cheese |
| 1/2 | teaspoon dried basil |
| 1/4 | teaspoon onion powder |
| | Dash garlic powder |
| | Pepper to taste |
| 2 | 1-ounce whole wheat pita breads |
| 2 | slices tomato |

Preheat oven to 350°.

In a small bowl, combine cheeses with basil, onion powder, garlic powder, and pepper. Mix well.

Split open one end of each pita, forming a pocket. Place tomato slices inside pita, then divide cheese mixture and spoon into the pita.

Wrap sandwiches in foil and bake 20 minutes.

---

Each serving provides:

**206 Calories**

| 1 1/2 | Protein Servings | 16 g | Protein |
|---|---|---|---|
| 1 | Bread Serving | 8 g | Fat (36% of calories) |
| 1/4 | Vegetable Serving | 18 g | Carbohydrate |
| 25 | Additional Calories | 426 mg | Sodium |
| | | 30 mg | Cholesterol |
| | | 2 g | Fiber |

# Orange Upside-Down French Toast

*A wonderful orange flavor makes this version of an all-time favorite quite unique. And baking the toast rather than frying makes it puffier and fluffier. For a special company touch, you can dust the toast lightly with confectioners' sugar just before serving.*

*Makes 4 servings*

| | |
|---|---|
| 2 | teaspoons margarine |
| 2 | tablespoons sugar |
| 1/2 | teaspoon ground cinnamon |
| 1 | cup liquid egg substitute |
| 1/2 | teaspoon orange extract |
| 1/2 | teaspoon vanilla extract |
| 1/2 | teaspoon maple extract |
| 1/4 | cup frozen orange juice concentrate, thawed |
| 1/4 | cup water |
| 4 | slices whole wheat bread (1-ounce slices) |

Preheat oven to 400°.

Place margarine in an 8-inch square baking pan and place in oven until margarine is melted. Remove pan from oven and spread margarine evenly over bottom of pan.

Combine sugar and cinnamon. Sprinkle evenly over margarine.

In a shallow bowl, combine egg substitute, extracts, orange juice concentrate, and water. Dip each slice of bread in egg mixture, soaking well. Arrange bread in pan. Spoon any remaining egg mixture on bread.

Bake 25 minutes, until eggs are set.

Let stand 1 minute, then turn cinnamon-side up to serve.

---

Each serving provides:

**175 Calories**

| | | | |
|---|---|---|---|
| 1 | Protein Serving | 9 g | Protein |
| 1 | Bread Serving | 3 g | Fat (16% of calories) |
| 1/2 | Fat Serving | 28 g | Carbohydrate |
| 1/2 | Fruit Serving | 272 mg | Sodium |
| 24 | Additional Calories | 0 mg | Cholesterol |
| | | 2 g | Fiber |

# Cream Cheese and Jelly French Toast

*A real favorite among our kids, this is a popular sandwich transformed into a breakfast treat.*

*Makes 2 servings*

| | |
|---|---|
| 4 | slices thin-sliced whole wheat bread ($^1/_2$-ounce slices) |
| 4 | teaspoons fat-free cream cheese |
| 4 | teaspoons fruit-only spread, any flavor |
| $^1/_4$ | cup liquid egg substitute |
| $^1/_4$ | cup skim milk |
| $^1/_2$ | teaspoon vanilla extract |

Make 2 sandwiches by dividing the cream cheese and fruit spread, spreading it on 2 slices of the bread, and topping with remaining bread.

In a shallow bowl, combine egg substitute, milk, and vanilla extract. Beat with a fork until blended. Dip the sandwiches in the egg mixture, turning carefully, until all of the mixture is absorbed.

Spray a large nonstick skillet with nonstick cooking spray. Preheat over medium heat.

Place sandwiches in skillet. Cook, turning sandwiches several times, until browned on both sides.

---

Each serving provides:

**139 Calories**

| | | | |
|---|---|---|---|
| $^1/_2$ | Protein Serving | 8 g | Protein |
| 1 | Bread Serving | 2 g | Fat (11% of calories) |
| $^1/_2$ | Fruit Serving | 23 g | Carbohydrate |
| 31 | Additional Calories | 260 mg | Sodium |
| | | 2 mg | Cholesterol |
| | | 2 g | Fiber |

# Cottage Cheese Cinnamon Toast

*For breakfast or a light, hot lunch, this easy, toasted sandwich can't be beat.*
*For a delicious variation, it can also be made with raisin bread.*

*Makes 2 servings*

2/3     cup lowfat (1%) cottage cheese
1     teaspoon sugar
1     teaspoon vanilla extract
1/2     teaspoon ground cinnamon
2     slices whole wheat bread (1-ounce slices), lightly toasted

Preheat broiler.

Have an ungreased shallow baking pan or baking sheet ready.

In a small bowl, combine cottage cheese, sugar, vanilla, and cinnamon. Mix well.

Spread on toast. Sprinkle lightly with additional cinnamon.

Place toast in pan. Broil 2 to 3 minutes, or until cheese is hot and bubbly.

Serve hot.

---

Each serving provides:

**141 Calories**

| | | | |
|---|---|---|---|
| 1 | Protein Serving | 12 g | Protein |
| 1 | Bread Serving | 2 g | Fat (13% of calories) |
| 8 | Additional Calories | 18 g | Carbohydrate |
| | | 457 mg | Sodium |
| | | 3 mg | Cholesterol |
| | | 2 g | Fiber |

# Pineapple-Orange Danish Toast

*This variation of the preceding recipe is also sweet and delicious, and you can make it in no time!*

*Makes 2 servings*

| | |
|---|---|
| ²/₃ | cup lowfat (1%) cottage cheese |
| ¹/₄ | cup canned crushed pineapple (packed in juice), drained |
| 2 | tablespoons fruit-only orange marmalade |
| ¹/₄ | teaspoon ground cinnamon |
| 2 | slices whole wheat bread (1-ounce slices), lightly toasted |

Preheat broiler.

Have an ungreased shallow baking pan or baking sheet ready.

In a small bowl, combine cottage cheese, pineapple, marmalade, and cinnamon. Spread on toast.

Place toast in pan. Broil 2 to 3 minutes, or until cheese is hot and bubbly.

Serve hot.

---

Each serving provides:

**186 Calories**

| | | | |
|---|---|---|---|
| 1 | Protein Serving | 12 g | Protein |
| 1 | Bread Serving | 2 g | Fat (9% of calories) |
| 1¹/₄ | Fruit Servings | 31 g | Carbohydrate |
| | | 457 mg | Sodium |
| | | 3 mg | Cholesterol |
| | | 2 g | Fiber |

# Fish and Seafood

Many varieties of fish and seafood are low in fat and fit nicely into a balanced diet. Often, if dishes are high in fat, it is not the seafood that is the culprit, but the way in which it is prepared. So, for our sauces we are careful to choose ingredients such as lemon juice, broth, and vegetables, along with a delectable array of spices. Now you can have all of the flavor without the fat.

Seafood contains no fiber. Therefore, we recommend adding a whole grain, such as brown rice or barley, to every meal. In addition, if you serve a salad and a steamed vegetable, you have a beautifully balanced, and filling, meal.

Our selection of seafood dishes will definitely please your taste buds and delight your family and friends.

# Sole and Peppers

*In this colorful dish, a delicious blend of herbs are combined with the green peppers and tomato sauce to create a dish fit for a king.*

*Makes 4 servings*

| | |
|---|---|
| 2 | teaspoons vegetable oil |
| 2 | medium, green bell peppers, cut into 1/4-inch strips |
| 1/2 | cup chopped onion |
| 1 | packet low-sodium instant beef- or chicken-flavored broth mix |
| 2 | 8-ounce cans salt-free (or regular) tomato sauce |
| 1/2 | teaspoon dried oregano |
| 1/4 | teaspoon dried thyme |
| 1/8 | teaspoon garlic powder |
| 1 | bay leaf |
| 1 1/4 | pounds sole or flounder fillets |

Heat oil in a large nonstick skillet over medium heat. Add green peppers, onion, and broth mix. Cook, stirring frequently, until vegetables are tender. Add small amounts of water if necessary (about a tablespoon at a time) to prevent sticking.

Add tomato sauce and spices. Reduce heat slightly and simmer, uncovered, 10 minutes. Remove and discard bay leaf.

Preheat oven to 375°.

Spray a 7 × 11-inch baking pan with nonstick cooking spray.

Arrange fish in pan. Pour sauce evenly over fish.

Bake, uncovered, 20 minutes, or until fish flakes easily when tested with a fork.

---

Each serving provides:

**222 Calories**

| | | | |
|---|---|---|---|
| 2 | Protein Servings | 29 g | Protein |
| 3 1/4 | Vegetable Servings | 5 g | Fat (20% of calories) |
| 1/2 | Fat Serving | 16 g | Carbohydrate |
| 3 | Additional Calories | 144 mg | Sodium |
| | | 68 mg | Cholesterol |
| | | 3 g | Fiber |

# Flounder Parmigiana

*The fish is rolled in seasoned bread crumbs and topped with a delicately herbed sauce, then sprinkled lightly with Parmesan cheese. It's a very impressive dinner.*

*Makes 4 servings*

| | |
|---|---|
| 3/4 | cup dry bread crumbs |
| 2 | teaspoons dried oregano |
| 1/8 | teaspoon garlic powder |
| 1 1/4 | pounds flounder fillets |
| 1 | 8-ounce can salt-free (or regular) tomato sauce |
| 2 | tablespoons minced onion flakes |
| 1/4 | teaspoon dried basil |
| 1/4 | teaspoon dried oregano |
| 1/8 | teaspoon garlic powder |
| 3 | tablespoons grated Parmesan cheese |

Preheat oven to 350°.

Spray a 7 × 11-inch baking pan with nonstick cooking spray.

In a shallow bowl, combine bread crumbs, oregano, and garlic powder. Dip fish fillets first into a bowl of water and then in crumbs. Place fish in prepared pan. Sprinkle any remaining crumbs over fish. Spray fish evenly with nonstick spray.

Bake, uncovered, 10 minutes.

Combine tomato sauce and spices in a small bowl and pour evenly over fish. Sprinkle with Parmesan cheese.

Bake 20 minutes longer, or until fish flakes easily when tested with a fork.

---

Each serving provides:

**260 Calories**

| | | | |
|---|---|---|---|
| 2 | Protein Servings | 32 g | Protein |
| 1 | Bread Serving | 5 g | Fat (17% of calories) |
| 1 | Vegetable Serving | 21 g | Carbohydrate |
| 23 | Additional Calories | 372 mg | Sodium |
| | | 71 mg | Cholesterol |
| | | 2 g | Fiber |

# Breaded Fillet of Sole

*Fast, with no fuss, this delicious fish needs only a squeeze of fresh lemon to enhance its delicate flavor.*

*Makes 4 servings*

1/4     cup plus 2 tablespoons Italian seasoned bread crumbs
1/3     cup nonfat dry milk
2       tablespoons minced onion flakes
1/8     teaspoon garlic powder
1 1/4   pounds sole or flounder fillets

Preheat oven to 400°.

Spray a 7 × 11-inch baking pan with nonstick cooking spray.

In a shallow bowl, combine bread crumbs, dry milk, onion flakes, and garlic powder. Mix well.

Dip each fish fillet first in a bowl of water and then in crumb mixture. Place fillets in prepared pan. Sprinkle any remaining crumb mixture evenly over fish. Spray fish evenly with cooking spray.

Bake, uncovered, 10 minutes, or until fish flakes easily when tested with a fork.

| Each serving provides: | | | |
|---|---|---|---|
| | | **190 Calories** | |
| 2 | Protein Servings | 29 g | Protein |
| 1/4 | Bread Serving | 3 g | Fat (15% of calories) |
| 1/4 | Milk Serving | 10 g | Carbohydrate |
| | | 424 mg | Sodium |
| | | 69 mg | Cholesterol |
| | | 0 g | Fiber |

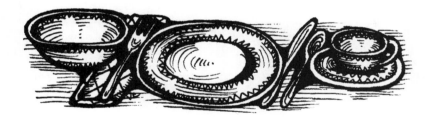

# Caribbean Fish

*The unique blend of flavors is reminiscent of the exotic tastes of the Caribbean. It's delicate and complex at the same time.*

*Makes 4 servings*

| | |
|---|---|
| 1 1/4 | pounds flounder, sole, or orange roughy fillets |
| 1 | 6-ounce can tomato paste |
| 1/2 | cup water |
| 1 1/2 | tablespoons lime juice |
| 1 1/2 | teaspoons coconut extract |
| 1/2 | teaspoon dried oregano |
| 1/2 | teaspoon onion powder |
| 1/4 | teaspoon garlic powder |
| 1/4 | teaspoon salt |
| 1/4 | teaspoon pepper |
| 1 | bay leaf, crumbled |

Preheat oven to 375°.

Spray a 7 × 11-inch baking pan with nonstick cooking spray.

Place fish fillets in prepared pan.

In a small bowl, combine remaining ingredients, mixing well. Spoon evenly over fish.

Bake, uncovered, 20 minutes, or until fish flakes easily when tested with a fork.

---

Each serving provides:

**175 Calories**

| | | | |
|---|---|---|---|
| 2 | Protein Servings | 28 g | Protein |
| 1 1/2 | Vegetable Servings | 3 g | Fat (13% of calories) |
| | | 10 g | Carbohydrate |
| | | 587 mg | Sodium |
| | | 68 mg | Cholesterol |
| | | 2 g | Fiber |

# French Fish

*The savory sauce is so easy to make and it really dresses up this fish. When buying French dressing, choose one that has a deep, dark color—those usually have a richer flavor.*

*Makes 4 servings*

1¹/₄    pounds flounder, sole, or orange roughy fillets
¹/₄      cup bottled fat-free French dressing
2        tablespoons grated Parmesan cheese
2        tablespoons minced onion flakes
1        tablespoon lemon juice
1        tablespoon water

Arrange fish in a single layer in a shallow baking pan.

Combine remaining ingredients in a small bowl, mixing well. Spread evenly over fish. Marinate in the refrigerator 4 to 5 hours, or overnight, turning fish several times.

Preheat oven to 375°.

Bake fish, uncovered, 20 minutes, or until fish flakes easily when tested with a fork.

For a crisper fish, place it under the broiler for a few minutes before serving.

---

Each serving provides:

**167 Calories**

|     |                      |        |                       |
|-----|----------------------|--------|-----------------------|
| 2   | Protein Servings     | 28 g   | Protein               |
| 35  | Additional Calories  | 2 g    | Fat (14% of calories) |
|     |                      | 6 g    | Carbohydrate          |
|     |                      | 283 mg | Sodium                |
|     |                      | 70 mg  | Cholesterol           |
|     |                      | 0 g    | Fiber                 |

# Snapper Creole

*You can also use haddock or grouper for this classic Southern dish. The fish is baked first, then heated in a rich, savory sauce. It's perfect over brown rice or noodles.*

*Makes 4 servings*

| | |
|---|---|
| 1¹/₄ | pounds snapper fillets |
| 2 | teaspoons vegetable oil |
| ¹/₂ | cup chopped onion |
| ¹/₂ | cup celery, thinly sliced |
| ¹/₂ | medium, green bell pepper, thinly sliced |
| 2 | cloves garlic, finely chopped |
| 2 | 8-ounce cans salt-free (or regular) tomato sauce |
| ¹/₂ | cup water |
| 1 | tablespoon vinegar |
| 1 | teaspoon Worcestershire sauce |
| 1 | teaspoon sugar |
| 2 | bay leaves |
| 1 | teaspoon dried oregano |
| ¹/₂ | teaspoon dried thyme |
| ¹/₂ | teaspoon chili powder |
| | Bottled hot pepper sauce |

Bake fish in a 400° oven for 10 minutes, or until fish flakes easily when tested with a fork.

Heat oil in a large saucepan over medium heat. Add onion, celery, green pepper, and garlic. Cook, stirring frequently, until vegetables are tender, about 8 minutes. Add small amounts of water if necessary (about a tablespoon at a time) to prevent sticking.

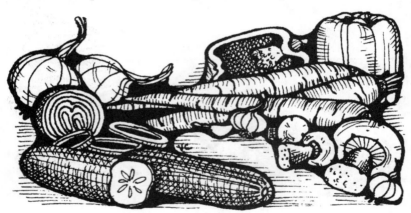

Add remaining ingredients, *except* hot pepper sauce, to saucepan. When mixture boils, reduce heat to medium-low, cover, and simmer 15 minutes. Add fish. Continue to cook, covered, 10 minutes more. Add hot pepper sauce to taste.

Remove and discard bay leaves.

Each serving provides:

**229 Calories**

| | | | |
|---|---|---|---|
| 2 | Protein Servings | 31 g | Protein |
| 2³/₄ | Vegetable Servings | 5 g | Fat (19% of calories) |
| ¹/₂ | Fat Serving | 15 g | Carbohydrate |
| 4 | Additional Calories | 147 mg | Sodium |
| | | 52 mg | Cholesterol |
| | | 3 g | Fiber |

# Italian Baked Fish

*You can mix the marinade up quickly and put the fish in the refrigerator in the morning; then just pop it in the oven when ready. It's also great on a grill and makes a quick and easy summertime entrée.*

*Makes 4 servings*

| | |
|---|---|
| 1¹/₄ | pounds flounder, sole, or orange roughy fillets |
| ¹/₄ | cup bottled fat-free Italian dressing |
| 2 | tablespoons lemon juice |
| 1 | tablespoon Worcestershire sauce |
| ¹/₈ | teaspoon garlic powder |

Arrange fish in a single layer in a shallow baking pan.

Combine remaining ingredients in a small bowl, mixing well. Spoon over fish. Marinate in the refrigerator 4 to 5 hours, or overnight, turning fish occasionally.

Preheat oven to 375°.

Bake fish, uncovered, 20 minutes, or until fish flakes easily when tested with a fork.

For a crisper fish, place it under the broiler for a few minutes before serving.

---

Each serving provides:

**140 Calories**

| | | | |
|---|---|---|---|
| 2 | Protein Servings | 27 g | Protein |
| 5 | Additional Calories | 2 g | Fat (12% of calories) |
| | | 2 g | Carbohydrate |
| | | 303 mg | Sodium |
| | | 68 mg | Cholesterol |
| | | 0 g | Fiber |

# Springtime Broiled Fish

*This easy, herbed fish is also great on a grill and makes a delicious dish for summertime entertaining.*

*Makes 4 servings*

| | |
|---|---|
| 1 1/4 | pounds flounder, sole, or orange roughy fillets |
| 2 | tablespoons reduced-calorie margarine |
| 1 | tablespoon lemon juice |
| 1 | teaspoon dill weed |
| 1/2 | teaspoon onion powder |
| 1/2 | teaspoon grated fresh lemon peel |
| 1/4 | teaspoon dried oregano |
| 1/8 | teaspoon salt |
| 1/8 | teaspoon pepper |
| | Dash paprika |

Place fish in a shallow broiler pan.

Place margarine in a small saucepan and heat over low heat until almost melted. Remove from heat and stir in remaining ingredients. Spread half of the mixture evenly over fish.

Place fish, margarine-side up, under a preheated broiler. Cook 3 to 5 minutes, then turn fish, spread with remaining margarine mixture, and broil 3 to 5 minutes more, or until fish flakes easily when tested with a fork.

---

Each serving provides:

**157 Calories**

| | | | |
|---|---|---|---|
| 2 | Protein Servings | 27 g | Protein |
| 3/4 | Fat Serving | 4 g | Fat (27% of calories) |
| | | 1 g | Carbohydrate |
| | | 254 mg | Sodium |
| | | 68 mg | Cholesterol |
| | | 0 g | Fiber |

# Spicy Fish Cakes

*A wonderful stand-in for crab cakes, these delectable patties can be made from any non-oily, mild fish, such as flounder, sole, or orange roughy. You can make them "on purpose," or whenever you have leftover fish.*

*Makes 4 servings*
*(2 fish cakes each serving)*

12    ounces cooked fish, flaked
2     slices whole wheat bread (1-ounce slices), crumbled
2     egg whites
1     tablespoon plus 1 teaspoon reduced-calorie mayonnaise
1     teaspoon Worcestershire sauce
1     teaspoon baking powder
1     teaspoon seafood seasoning (such as Old Bay)
      Salt and pepper to taste

In a large bowl, combine fish and bread crumbs. Combine remaining ingredients in a small bowl and mix well. Add to fish and mix with a fork until well blended.

Divide mixture evenly and shape into 8 patties, 1/2- to 3/4-inch thick.

Spray a large nonstick skillet or griddle with nonstick cooking spray and preheat over medium heat.

Place fish cakes in skillet and cook, turning several times, until nicely browned on both sides.

---

Each serving provides:

**162 Calories**

| | | | |
|---|---|---|---|
| 1 1/2 | Protein Servings | 24 g | Protein |
| 1/2 | Bread Serving | 4 g | Fat (20% of calories) |
| 1/2 | Fat Serving | 8 g | Carbohydrate |
| 10 | Additional Calories | 530 mg | Sodium |
| | | 60 mg | Cholesterol |
| | | 0 g | Fiber |

# "Pretend" Salmon Salad

*Less expensive than salmon, haddock fillets make a wonderful cold salad that will please even the most discriminating gourmet. Make this dish up to a day ahead and chill it thoroughly to blend the wonderful flavors.*

*Makes 4 servings*

| | |
|---|---|
| 1 1/4 | pounds haddock fillets |
| 2 | tablespoons lemon juice |
| 1/2 | cup plain nonfat yogurt |
| 1/4 | cup bottled chili sauce |
| 2 | tablespoons reduced-calorie mayonnaise |
| 1/2 | cup finely chopped celery |
| 2 | tablespoons finely chopped onion |
| 1 | teaspoon sugar |
| 1/4 | teaspoon celery salt |
| 1/8 | teaspoon pepper |

Preheat oven to 375°.

Place fish in a shallow pan than has been sprayed with nonstick cooking spray.

Bake 20 minutes, or until fish flakes easily when tested with a fork. Cool for 15 minutes, then flake fish into a large bowl.

Combine remaining ingredients in a small bowl and mix well. Spoon over fish and blend well with a fork.

Chill several hours or overnight to blend flavors.

---

Each serving provides:

**187 Calories**

| | | | |
|---|---|---|---|
| 2 | Protein Servings | 29 g | Protein |
| 1/4 | Vegetable Serving | 3 g | Fat (16% of calories) |
| 3/4 | Fat Serving | 9 g | Carbohydrate |
| 9 | Additional Calories | 441 mg | Sodium |
| | | 84 mg | Cholesterol |
| | | 0 g | Fiber |

# Lemony Stuffed Fish

*We used to make this luscious dish with butter and serve it at all of our din-
ner parties. Now we use reduced-calorie margarine instead, along with some
butter flavor, and, even though we've trimmed the fat, the result is still a
wonderful party dish. (Look for butter flavor with the extracts in most large
grocery stores.)*

*Makes 4 servings*

| | |
|---|---|
| ¹/₄ | cup reduced-calorie margarine |
| ¹/₂ | cup finely chopped onion |
| ¹/₂ | cup finely chopped celery |
| ¹/₂ | cup plain nonfat yogurt |
| 2 | tablespoons lemon juice |
| 1 | tablespoon grated fresh lemon peel |
| 1 | teaspoon imitation butter flavor |
| 1 | teaspoon paprika |
| 1 | teaspoon dill weed |
| ¹/₄ | teaspoon salt |
| 4 | slices whole wheat bread (1-ounce slices), cubed |
| 1¹/₄ | pounds flounder fillets |

Preheat oven to 375°.

Spray a 1-quart baking dish with nonstick cooking spray.

Melt margarine in a small nonstick skillet over medium heat. Add
onion and celery and cook, stirring frequently, until tender, about 5
minutes. Transfer to a small bowl.

Stir in yogurt, lemon juice, lemon peel, butter flavor, paprika, dill
weed, and salt. Add bread cubes, mixing well.

Place *half* of the fillets in prepared baking dish. Spoon stuffing evenly over fish. Top with remaining fillets. Press fish down firmly onto stuffing. Sprinkle with additional paprika.

Bake, uncovered, 30 minutes, or until fish flakes easily when tested with a fork.

Each serving provides:

**282 Calories**

| | | | |
|---|---|---|---|
| 2 | Protein Servings | 32 g | Protein |
| 1 | Bread Serving | 9 g | Fat (28% of calories) |
| 1/2 | Vegetable Serving | 19 g | Carbohydrate |
| 1 1/2 | Fat Servings | 573 mg | Sodium |
| 15 | Additional Calories | 69 mg | Cholesterol |
| | | 3 g | Fiber |

# Potato-Fish Patties

*Affectionately known as "coddies" when we were kids, these patties were usually topped with mustard and served between saltine crackers. They make a wonderful change-of-pace lunch.*

*Makes 4 servings*
*(2 patties each serving)*

| | |
|---|---|
| 1 | pound cod fillets |
| 1 | pound cooked potatoes, mashed (2 medium baking potatoes) |
| 1/4 | cup evaporated skim milk |
| 2 | tablespoons grated onion |
| 1 | tablespoon plus 1 teaspoon Worcestershire sauce |
| 2 | teaspoons vegetable oil |
| 1/4 | teaspoon garlic powder |
| | Salt and pepper to taste |

Preheat oven to 350°.

Bake fish for 30 minutes in a shallow pan that has been sprayed with a nonstick cooking spray, until fish flakes easily when tested with a fork. Set aside to cool.

In a large bowl, combine potatoes, milk, and onion. Mix well. Stir in remaining ingredients. Flake fish and add to bowl. Mix well. (Add a little water, a few teaspoons at a time, if mixture is too dry to hold together.)

Chill thoroughly.

Shape mixture into 8 patties about 1/2- to 3/4-inch thick.

Spray a large nonstick skillet or griddle with nonstick cooking spray and preheat over medium heat.

Place fish cakes in skillet and cook, turning several times, until nicely browned on both sides.

---

Each serving provides:

**234 Calories**

| | | | |
|---|---|---|---|
| 1 1/2 | Protein Servings | 24 g | Protein |
| 1 | Bread Serving | 4 g | Fat (14% of calories) |
| 1/2 | Fat Serving | 26 g | Carbohydrate |
| 11 | Additional Calories | 140 mg | Sodium |
| | | 50 mg | Cholesterol |
| | | 2 g | Fiber |

# Lemon-Broiled Scallops

*Incredibly easy and just as delicious, this dish can also be made on the grill.*
*Served with seasoned rice and steamed broccoli, it makes an elegant meal.*

*Makes 4 servings*

| | |
|---|---|
| 1 | pound scallops, uncooked |
| 2 | tablespoons reduced-calorie margarine, melted |
| 3 | tablespoons lemon juice |
| 1 | teaspoon grated fresh lemon peel |
| 1 | teaspoon Worcestershire sauce |
| 1/2 | teaspoon dried tarragon |
| 1/2 | teaspoon dried basil |
| 1/4 | teaspoon salt |

Preheat broiler.

Place scallops in a shallow baking pan that has been sprayed with a nonstick cooking spray.

Combine remaining ingredients in a small bowl. Baste scallops with *half* of this mixture.

Broil 3 to 5 minutes, or until edges of scallops begin to crisp. Turn scallops, baste with remaining sauce, and broil 3 to 5 minutes more, or until scallops are done.

---

Each serving provides:

**129 Calories**

| | | | |
|---|---|---|---|
| 1 1/2 | Protein Servings | 19 g | Protein |
| 3/4 | Fat Serving | 4 g | Fat (26% of calories) |
| | | 4 g | Carbohydrate |
| | | 402 mg | Sodium |
| | | 37 mg | Cholesterol |
| | | 0 g | Fiber |

# Teriyaki Scallops

*Stir-fry some veggies in a little bit of soy sauce, cook some brown rice, broil your scallops, and you have a delectable feast. This versatile marinade also works well with shrimp.*

*Makes 4 servings*

| | |
|---|---|
| 1/4 | cup reduced-sodium soy sauce |
| 2 | tablespoons dry sherry |
| 2 | teaspoons sugar |
| 1 | teaspoon ground ginger |
| 1/4 | teaspoon garlic powder |
| 1 | pound scallops, uncooked |

In a shallow bowl, combine all ingredients *except* scallops. Mix well. Add scallops. Marinate in the refrigerator for several hours. Drain, reserving marinade.

Preheat broiler.

Place scallops in a shallow broiler pan. Baste with marinade.

Broil 3 to 5 minutes, or until edges of scallops begin to crisp. Turn scallops, baste again with marinade, and broil 3 to 5 minutes more, or until scallops are done.

---

Each serving provides:

**131 Calories**

| 1 1/2 | Protein Servings | 20 g | Protein |
|---|---|---|---|
| 14 | Additional Calories | 1 g | Fat (7% of calories) |
| | | 8 g | Carbohydrate |
| | | 784 mg | Sodium |
| | | 37 mg | Cholesterol |
| | | 0 g | Fiber |

# Crab and Cheddar Casserole

*This has been one of our favorite special occasion dishes for years, with the splash of sherry adding a richness and elegance that will win you rave reviews. It can also be made with flaked fish in place of the crab.*

*Makes 4 servings*

| | |
|---|---|
| 3 | tablespoons all-purpose flour |
| 2/3 | cup nonfat dry milk |
| 1/4 | teaspoon dry mustard |
| 1/8 | teaspoon salt |
| 1/8 | teaspoon pepper |
| 1 | cup water |
| 3 | ounces shredded reduced-fat Cheddar cheese (3/4 cup) |
| 2 | tablespoons dry sherry |
| 12 | ounces crab meat (1 1/2 cups) |

Preheat oven to 350°.

Spray a 1-quart casserole with nonstick cooking spray.

In a small saucepan, combine flour, dry milk, mustard, salt, and pepper. Mix well. Gradually add water, stirring briskly to avoid lumps. Heat over medium heat, stirring constantly, until mixture thickens. Remove from heat.

Stir cheese and sherry into milk mixture, mixing until cheese is completely melted. Stir in crab meat. Place in prepared casserole.

Bake, uncovered, 20 minutes.

---

Each serving provides:

**223 Calories**

| 2 1/2 | Protein Servings | 29 g | Protein |
|---|---|---|---|
| 1/4 | Bread Serving | 6 g | Fat (24% of calories) |
| 1/2 | Milk Serving | 11 g | Carbohydrate |
| 6 | Additional Calories | 535 mg | Sodium |
| | | 102 mg | Cholesterol |
| | | 0 g | Fiber |

# French Herbed Shrimp

*Serve this deliciously herbed shrimp over rice or any other grain for an elegant and delicious dinner.*

*Makes 4 servings*

| | |
|---|---|
| 2 | teaspoons vegetable oil |
| 1/2 | cup chopped onion |
| 3 | cloves garlic, finely minced |
| 3 | tablespoons all-purpose flour |
| 2 | cups water |
| 1 | 8-ounce can salt-free (or regular) tomato sauce |
| 2 | teaspoons Worcestershire sauce |
| 1 | teaspoon lemon juice |
| 2 | bay leaves |
| 1 | teaspoon sugar |
| 1/4 | teaspoon salt |
| 1/4 | teaspoon dried thyme |
| 1/8 | teaspoon pepper |
| | Bottled hot pepper sauce to taste |
| 12 | ounces cooked, peeled shrimp |

Heat oil in a medium saucepan over medium heat. Add onion and garlic. Cook, stirring frequently, 3 to 5 minutes, until tender. Add small amounts of water if necessary, (about a tablespoon at a time) to prevent sticking.

Place flour in a small bowl. Gradually add 1/2 cup of the water, stirring briskly to avoid lumps.

Add flour mixture and remaining ingredients *except* shrimp to saucepan. Mix well. When mixture boils, reduce heat to medium-low and simmer, covered, 25 minutes, stirring occasionally.

Remove and discard bay leaves.

Add shrimp. Simmer 5 minutes more.

Each serving provides:

### 165 Calories

| | | | |
|---|---|---|---|
| 1 1/2 | Protein Servings | 20 g | Protein |
| 1/4 | Bread Serving | 4 g | Fat (20% of calories) |
| 1 1/4 | Vegetable Servings | 13 g | Carbohydrate |
| 1/2 | Fat Serving | 369 mg | Sodium |
| 4 | Additional Calories | 166 mg | Cholesterol |
| | | 1 g | Fiber |

# Shrimp Scampi

*This classic dish is always a favorite. We've removed most of the oil and substituted white wine instead, adding even more flavor to an already delicious dish.*

*Makes 4 servings*

| | |
|---|---|
| 1/3 | cup dry white wine |
| 3 | tablespoons lemon juice |
| 2 | tablespoons vegetable oil |
| 2 | tablespoons Worcestershire sauce |
| 1 | tablespoon water |
| 2 | tablespoons grated Parmesan cheese |
| 1 | tablespoon dried parsley flakes |
| 1 | teaspoon dried oregano |
| 1/4 | teaspoon garlic powder |
| 1/4 | teaspoon salt |
| 1/4 | teaspoon pepper |
| 1 1/4 | pounds cleaned raw shrimp |

Combine all ingredients *except* shrimp in a shallow bowl. Add shrimp. Marinate in the refrigerator for several hours.

Remove shrimp from marinade and place in a shallow baking pan. Broil 6 inches from heat for 8 to 10 minutes, turning occasionally, until shrimp are done.

While shrimp is broiling, bring marinade to a boil in a small saucepan. Simmer 2 minutes.

Place shrimp in a serving bowl and add marinade.

---

Each serving provides:

**247 Calories**

| | | | |
|---|---|---|---|
| 2 | Protein Servings | 30 g | Protein |
| 1 1/2 | Fat Servings | 10 g | Fat (40% of calories) |
| 32 | Additional Calories | 4 g | Carbohydrate |
| | | 477 mg | Sodium |
| | | 218 mg | Cholesterol |
| | | 0 g | Fiber |

# Tuna Noodle Casserole

*This homestyle casserole has been a family favorite for years. Although the ingredients have changed (lowfat dairy products in place of the original sour cream), this is still the best tuna casserole we have ever tasted.*

*Makes 6 servings*

| | |
|---|---|
| 6 | ounces medium yolk-free noodles, uncooked |
| 1 | cup lowfat (1%) cottage cheese |
| 3/4 | cup plain nonfat yogurt |
| 1 | tablespoon all-purpose flour |
| 2 | teaspoons Worcestershire sauce |
| 1/4 | teaspoon salt |
| 1/8 | teaspoon pepper |
| 1/8 | teaspoon garlic powder |
| 1/2 | cup frozen peas |
| 1/4 | cup finely minced onion |
| 1 | 8-ounce can mushroom pieces, drained |
| 2 | 6 1/2-ounce cans tuna (packed in water), drained and flaked (8 ounces) |
| 3 | tablespoons grated Parmesan cheese |

Preheat oven to 350°.

Spray an 8-inch square baking pan with nonstick cooking spray.

Cook noodles according to package directions. Drain.

In a large bowl, combine cottage cheese, yogurt, flour, Worcestershire sauce, salt, pepper, and garlic powder. Mix well. Stir in peas, onion, mushrooms, tuna, and noodles. Spoon into prepared baking pan.

Sprinkle Parmesan cheese evenly over casserole.

Bake, uncovered, 30 minutes, or until hot.

---

Each serving provides:

### 250 Calories

| | | | |
|---|---|---|---|
| 1 | Protein Serving | 29 g | Protein |
| 1 1/2 | Bread Servings | 2 g | Fat (9% of calories) |
| 1/2 | Vegetable Serving | 28 g | Carbohydrate |
| 45 | Additional Calories | 632 mg | Sodium |
| | | 27 mg | Cholesterol |
| | | 2 g | Fiber |

# Italian Tuna Casserole

*This delicious casserole is so tasty, you won't believe how easy it is to pre-pare. Even though it's served hot, the leftovers are also delicious cold.*

*Makes 6 servings*

| | |
|---|---|
| 2 | 6 1/2-ounce cans tuna (packed in water), drained and flaked (8 ounces) |
| 1 | 1-pound can salt-free (or regular) tomatoes, chopped and drained |
| 1 | 4-ounce can mushroom pieces, drained |
| 1/4 | cup chopped onion |
| 1/4 | cup chopped green bell pepper |
| 1 | cup liquid egg substitute |
| 1 | cup nonfat dry milk |
| 1 1/4 | cups water |
| 1 | tablespoon dry sherry |
| 1 1/2 | teaspoons dried oregano |
| 1/2 | teaspoon dried basil |
| 1/4 | teaspoon salt |
| 1/4 | teaspoon pepper |
| 2 | teaspoons grated Parmesan cheese |

Preheat oven to 350°.

Spray an 8-inch square baking pan with nonstick cooking spray.

Layer tuna, tomatoes, mushrooms, onion, and green pepper in pre-pared pan.

In a small bowl, combine remaining ingredients *except* Parmesan cheese. Beat with a fork or wire whisk until blended. Pour over tuna and vegetables. Sprinkle with Parmesan cheese.

Bake, uncovered, 40 to 45 minutes, until set.

---

Each serving provides:

**163 Calories**

| | | | |
|---|---|---|---|
| 1 1/4 | Protein Servings | 25 g | Protein |
| 1 | Vegetable Serving | 1 g | Fat (5% of calories) |
| 1/2 | Milk Serving | 12 g | Carbohydrate |
| 10 | Additional Calories | 478 mg | Sodium |
| | | 25 mg | Cholesterol |
| | | 1 g | Fiber |

# Tuna Seashell Salad

*This easy salad makes an ideal light summer dinner. Add slices of fresh toma-toes and perhaps some corn on the cob, and your dinner is complete.*

*Makes 4 servings*

| | |
|---|---|
| 2 | 6 1/2-ounce cans tuna (packed in water), drained and flaked (8 ounces) |
| 2 | cups cooked macaroni shells |
| 1 | cup thinly sliced celery |
| 1/4 | cup finely chopped onion |
| 2 | tablespoons reduced-calorie mayonnaise |
| 2 | tablespoons lemon juice |
| 1 | tablespoon vinegar |
| 1 | tablespoon dried parsley flakes |
| 1/2 | teaspoon celery seed |
| 1/2 | teaspoon dill weed |
| 1/4 | teaspoon salt |
| 1/8 | teaspoon pepper |

In a large bowl, combine flaked tuna with macaroni. Add celery and onion and toss to combine.

In a small bowl, combine remaining ingredients. Mix well. Pour over tuna mixture. Mix well.

Chill several hours to blend flavors.

---

Each serving provides:

**221 Calories**

| | | | |
|---|---|---|---|
| 1 | Protein Serving | 28 g | Protein |
| 1 | Bread Serving | 3 g | Fat (12% of calories) |
| 3/4 | Vegetable Serving | 20 g | Carbohydrate |
| 3/4 | Fat Serving | 497 mg | Sodium |
| | | 37 mg | Cholesterol |
| | | 2 g | Fiber |

# Superb Salmon Loaf

*The leftovers of this delicately flavored loaf make wonderful sandwiches. Try it between 2 slices of whole grain bread with a little ketchup and a slice of pickle for a "banquet on bread."*

*Makes 4 servings*

| | |
|---|---|
| 1 | 14 3/4-ounce can salmon, drained and flaked (12 ounces) |
| 1/2 | cup liquid egg substitute |
| 2 | slices whole wheat bread (1-ounce slices), crumbled |
| 2/3 | cup nonfat dry milk |
| 1/2 | cup finely chopped green bell pepper |
| 1/4 | cup finely chopped onion |
| 1 | teaspoon lemon juice |
| 1 | teaspoon dried basil |
| 1/2 | teaspoon grated fresh lemon peel |
| 1/2 | teaspoon dried parsley flakes |
| 1/4 | teaspoon salt |
| 1/4 | teaspoon pepper |
| 1/4 | teaspoon dry mustard |
| 1/4 | teaspoon celery seed |

Preheat oven to 350°.

Spray a 4 × 8-inch loaf pan with nonstick cooking spray.

In a large bowl, combine all ingredients, mixing well. Spoon mixture into prepared pan. Press in pan gently with the back of a spoon.

Bake, uncovered, 1 hour, or until top of loaf is golden.

Let stand 5 minutes, then remove loaf to a serving plate.

---

Each serving provides:

**200 Calories**

| | | | |
|---|---|---|---|
| 3 1/2 | Protein Servings | 25 g | Protein |
| 1/2 | Bread Serving | 6 g | Fat (27% of calories) |
| 1/2 | Vegetable Serving | 11 g | Carbohydrate |
| 1/2 | Milk Serving | 705 mg | Sodium |
| | | 35 mg | Cholesterol |
| | | 1 g | Fiber |

# Bengal Seafood Salad

*This unusual salad has an exotic flavor and a wonderful blend of textures. It's lovely served on a bed of lettuce, accompanied by sliced, fresh pineapple and tomatoes.*

*Makes 6 servings*

| | |
|---|---|
| 12 | ounces crab meat (1 1/2 cups) |
| 4 | ounces cooked, peeled shrimp, cut into 1-inch pieces |
| 1 | cup thinly sliced celery |
| 1/4 | cup finely chopped onion |
| 3 | ounces sliced water chestnuts |
| 1 | cup canned crushed pineapple (packed in juice), undrained |
| 1 1/4 | cup raisins |
| 2 | tablespoons sunflower seeds (raw or dry roasted) |
| 3/4 | cup plain nonfat yogurt |
| 3 | tablespoons reduced-calorie mayonnaise |
| 3 | tablespoons lemon juice |
| 1 | teaspoon coconut extract |
| 2 | teaspoons curry powder, or more to taste |

In a large bowl, combine crab meat, shrimp, celery, onion, water chestnuts, pineapple, raisins, and sunflower seeds. Mix well.

In a small bowl, combine remaining ingredients. Add to crab mixture and mix well.

Chill several hours to blend flavors.

---

Each serving provides:

**198 Calories**

| | | | |
|---|---|---|---|
| 1 1/4 | Protein Servings | 19 g | Protein |
| 1/2 | Vegetable Serving | 5 g | Fat (22% of calories) |
| 3/4 | Fat Serving | 20 g | Carbohydrate |
| 1/2 | Fruit Serving | 285 mg | Sodium |
| 55 | Additional Calories | 97 mg | Cholesterol |
| | | 1 g | Fiber |

# Seafood Quiche

*Most quiches are made with cream and whole eggs, making them very high in fat and cholesterol. Switching to skim milk and egg substitute lets you keep the fat content low without sacrificing flavor.*

*Makes 8 servings*

### Crust

| | |
|---|---|
| 1/2 | cup all-purpose flour |
| 1/4 | cup whole wheat flour |
| 1/4 | teaspoon baking powder |
| 1/8 | teaspoon salt |
| 2 | tablespoons plus 2 teaspoons margarine |
| 3 | tablespoons plus 2 teaspoons ice water |

### Filling

| | |
|---|---|
| 8 | ounces cooked fish, shrimp, or crab meat, cut into small chunks |
| 1 | 4-ounce can mushroom pieces, drained |
| 1/2 | cup thinly sliced green onion |
| 4 | ounces shredded reduced-fat Swiss cheese (1 cup) |
| 1 | cup liquid egg substitute |
| 1 1/4 | cups water |
| 2/3 | cup nonfat dry milk |
| 1 | tablespoon dry sherry |
| 1 | tablespoon grated Parmesan cheese |

Preheat oven to 450°.

Have a 9-inch pie pan ready.

To prepare crust:

In a medium bowl, combine both types of flour, baking powder, and salt, mixing well. Add margarine. Mix with a fork or pastry blender until mixture resembles coarse crumbs.

Add water. Mix with a fork until dry ingredients are moistened. Work dough into a ball, using your hands. (Add a little more flour if dough is sticky, or a little more water if dough is too dry.) Roll dough between 2 sheets of wax paper into an 11-inch circle. Remove top sheet of wax paper and invert crust into prepared pan. Fit crust into pan, leaving an overhang. Carefully remove remaining wax paper. Bend edges of crust under and flute dough with your fingers or a fork. Prick the bottom and sides of crust with a fork about 20 times.

Bake 8 minutes.

Reduce oven temperature to 350°.

To prepare filling:
Sprinkle seafood, mushrooms, green onion, and Swiss cheese evenly in crust. In a blender container, combine remaining ingredients. Blend until smooth. Pour over seafood.

Bake 45 minutes, or until set and lightly browned.

Let stand 5 minutes before cutting.

Each serving provides:

**198 Calories**

| | | | |
|---|---|---|---|
| 1¼ | Protein Servings | 19 g | Protein |
| ½ | Bread Serving | 7 g | Fat (33% of calories) |
| ¼ | Vegetable Serving | 14 g | Carbohydrate |
| 1 | Fat Serving | 274 mg | Sodium |
| ¼ | Milk Serving | 31 mg | Cholesterol |
| 15 | Additional Calories | 1 g | Fiber |

# Bouillabaisse

*This cross between a soup and a stew is so filling and hearty, all you need is a salad and a loaf of crusty French bread. You'll serve it time and time again.*

*Makes 6 servings*

| | |
|---|---|
| 1 | tablespoon vegetable oil |
| 1/2 | cup chopped carrots |
| 1/2 | cup chopped onion |
| 3 | cloves garlic, finely chopped |
| 2 | medium leeks, thinly sliced (white part only) |
| 1 | 1-pound can salt-free (or regular) tomatoes, chopped and drained |
| 4 | cups water |
| 1 | tablespoon dried parsley flakes |
| 1 | bay leaf |
| 1/2 | teaspoon salt |
| 1/4 | teaspoon saffron, crumbled |
| 1/4 | teaspoon dried thyme |
| | Pepper to taste |
| 1 3/4 | pounds seafood, uncooked, cut into 1-inch pieces (Use any combination of flounder, sole, haddock, scallops, shrimp, lobster, or crab meat.) |

Heat oil in a large saucepan over medium heat. Add carrots, onion, garlic, and leeks. Cook, stirring frequently, 10 minutes. Add small amounts of water if necessary (about a tablespoon at a time) to keep vegetables from sticking.

Add remaining ingredients *except* seafood. Bring to a boil, then reduce heat to medium-low, cover, and simmer 30 minutes.

Add seafood. Continue to cook, uncovered, 15 minutes, or until seafood is thoroughly cooked.

Remove and discard bay leaf before serving.

Divide seafood evenly into 6 bowls. Spoon soup over seafood.

Each serving provides:

**177 Calories**

| 1³/4 | Protein Servings | 26 g | Protein |
| 1³/4 | Vegetable Servings | 4 g | Fat (22% of calories) |
| 1/2 | Fat Serving | 8 g | Carbohydrate |
| | | 371 mg | Sodium |
| | | 90 mg | Cholesterol |
| | | 1 g | Fiber |

# Poultry

The versatility of chicken and turkey have made them universal favorites, with almost every culture having its own traditional favorites.

When buying chicken, the white meat is your best bet, because it is lower in fat than the dark meat. One very important tip in cooking chicken is to remove the skin before cooking. Because the skin itself has a very high fat content, leaving it on can add quite a bit of fat per serving. Turkey cutlets are one of our quick-cooking favorites, and ground turkey is versatile for use in meat loaves and casseroles. However, when buying ground turkey it is important to read the label carefully, as some brands may contain a high percentage of skin.

Our easy-to-prepare poultry recipes will show you that the variations are endless.

We choose our cooking methods carefully (baking and broiling rather than frying) and use lots of herbs and spices, rather than high-fat sauces, to enliven our dishes.

# Chicken and Peppers

*You can use either red or green bell peppers for this dish depending on the taste you prefer (red peppers are much sweeter than the green). Or, if you like both types of peppers, you can use half red and half green.*

*Makes 4 servings*

| | |
|---|---|
| 1 | pound boneless, skinless chicken breasts, cut into 1-inch slices |
| 3 | tablespoons reduced-sodium soy sauce |
| 1/4 | cup dry sherry |
| 2 | teaspoons ground ginger |
| 2 | teaspoons vegetable oil |
| 1 | cup chopped onion |
| 3 | cloves garlic, crushed |
| 4 | medium red or green bell peppers, sliced 1/4-inch thick |
| 1/2 | cup water |

In a medium bowl, combine chicken with soy sauce, sherry, and ginger. Marinate in the refrigerator several hours, turning chicken several times.

Heat oil in a large nonstick skillet over medium heat. Add onion and garlic. Cook, stirring frequently, 3 minutes. Add peppers and continue to cook and stir 3 more minutes.

Add chicken and marinade. Cook, stirring frequently, until chicken loses its pink color. Reduce heat to medium-low, add water, cover, and cook 15 minutes, or until chicken is done.

---

Each serving provides:

**222 Calories**

| | | | |
|---|---|---|---|
| 4 | Protein Servings | 28 g | Protein |
| 2 1/2 | Vegetable Servings | 4 g | Fat (18% of calories) |
| 1/2 | Fat Serving | 14 g | Carbohydrate |
| 4 | Additional Calories | 529 mg | Sodium |
| | | 66 mg | Cholesterol |
| | | 2 g | Fiber |

# Chicken Scampi

*You've seen it with shrimp. Now try this unique version made with chicken.*

*Makes 4 servings*

| | |
|---|---|
| 1/4 | cup dry white wine |
| 3 | tablespoons lemon juice |
| 2 | tablespoons Worcestershire sauce |
| 2 | tablespoons grated Parmesan cheese |
| 1 | tablespoon vegetable oil |
| 1 | tablespoon dried parsley flakes |
| 1 | teaspoon dried oregano |
| 1/4 | teaspoon garlic powder |
| 1/4 | teaspoon salt |
| 1/4 | teaspoon pepper |
| 1 | pound boneless, skinless chicken breasts, cut into 1-inch strips |

Combine all ingredients, *except* chicken, in a shallow bowl. Mix well. Add chicken. Turn chicken over several times to coat each piece with marinade.

Marinate in the refrigerator for several hours, turning chicken several times.

Preheat broiler.

Place chicken in a shallow pan and broil 4 to 5 inches from heat, turning chicken several times. Cook until chicken is no longer pink inside, about 6 to 8 minutes. Baste with any remaining marinade while cooking.

---

Each serving provides:

**189 Calories**

| | | | |
|---|---|---|---|
| 3 | Protein Servings | 28 g | Protein |
| 3/4 | Fat Serving | 6 g | Fat (29% of calories) |
| 28 | Additional Calories | 3 g | Carbohydrate |
| | | 341 mg | Sodium |
| | | 68 mg | Cholesterol |
| | | 0 g | Fiber |

# Oriental Chicken and Mushrooms

*This chicken is delicious served over Asian noodles. Look for the whole grain, dark-colored soba or somen noodles in health food stores and most large grocery stores.*

*Makes 4 servings*

| | |
|---|---|
| 1 | pound boneless, skinless chicken breasts |
| 1 | tablespoon minced onion flakes |
| 3 | tablespoons reduced-sodium soy sauce |
| 2 | teaspoons honey |
| 1/4 | teaspoon garlic powder |
| 1/2 | cup chopped green bell pepper |
| 2 1/2 | cups sliced mushrooms |
| 1/2 | cup low-sodium chicken broth (or 1/2 cup of water and 1/2 packet low-sodium instant chicken-flavored broth mix) |

Preheat oven to 350°.

Spray a 7 × 11-inch baking dish with nonstick cooking spray.

Place chicken in prepared pan. Sprinkle with onion flakes.

In a small bowl, combine soy sauce, honey, and garlic powder and pour evenly over chicken.

Cover and bake 30 minutes.

Spread green pepper and mushrooms evenly over chicken. Drizzle broth over chicken and continue to bake, covered, 20 minutes more.

---

Each serving provides:

**166 Calories**

| | | | |
|---|---|---|---|
| 3 | Protein Servings | 28 g | Protein |
| 9 | Additional Calories | 2 g | Fat (12% of calories) |
| | | 8 g | Carbohydrate |
| | | 596 mg | Sodium |
| | | 66 mg | Cholesterol |
| | | 1 g | Fiber |

# Chicken in Wine Sauce

*This has long been one of our favorite party dishes. It tastes best when made a day ahead and reheated, making it an easy dish for entertaining. It's delicious over couscous.*

*Makes 4 servings*

| | |
|---|---|
| 1 | cup rosé wine |
| 3 | tablespoons reduced-sodium soy sauce |
| 2 | tablespoons water |
| 3 | cloves garlic, crushed |
| 1 | tablespoon firmly packed brown sugar |
| 1 | teaspoon ground ginger |
| 1/2 | teaspoon dried oregano |
| 1 | pound boneless, skinless chicken breasts |

Combine all ingredients, *except* chicken, in a shallow casserole, mixing well. Add chicken.

Marinate in the refrigerator several hours.*

Preheat oven to 375°.

Bake, covered, 1 hour.


*If chicken is to be served the following day, marinating is not necessary. Just bake and refrigerate. Reheat before serving.

---

Each serving provides:

**192 Calories**

| 3 | Protein Servings | 27 g | Protein |
|---|---|---|---|
| 62 | Additional Calories | 1 g | Fat (9% of calories) |
| | | 6 g | Carbohydrate |
| | | 529 mg | Sodium |
| | | 66 mg | Cholesterol |
| | | 0 g | Fiber |

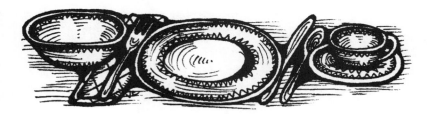

# Pineapple Mandarin Chicken

*The sweetness of orange and pineapple makes a delicious contrast to the tartness of the vinegar in this unusual dish. It really makes an attractive presentation when served on a bed of brown and wild rice.*

*Makes 4 servings*

| | |
|---|---|
| 1 | pound boneless, skinless chicken breasts |
| 1/2 | cup canned crushed pineapple (packed in juice), undrained |
| 2 | small oranges, peeled and sectioned, white membrane discarded |
| 1/4 | cup orange juice |
| 1 | tablespoon cornstarch |
| 2 | tablespoons very finely minced onion |
| 3 | tablespoons reduced-sodium soy sauce |
| 1 | tablespoon vinegar |
| 1/2 | teaspoon dry mustard |
| 1/4 | teaspoon garlic powder |

Preheat oven to 350°.

Spray a shallow baking dish with nonstick cooking spray.

Place chicken in prepared dish. Spread crushed pineapple and orange sections evenly over chicken.

In a small bowl, combine remaining ingredients, stirring until cornstarch is dissolved. Pour over chicken.

Bake, covered, 1 hour.

---

Each serving provides:

**200 Calories**

| | | | |
|---|---|---|---|
| 3 | Protein Servings | 28 g | Protein |
| 3/4 | Fruit Serving | 2 g | Fat (9% of calories) |
| 5 | Additional Calories | 18 g | Carbohydrate |
| | | 525 mg | Sodium |
| | | 66 mg | Cholesterol |
| | | 2 g | Fiber |

# Golden Crowned Chicken

*Apples and carrots make this an outstanding flavor treat as well as a colorful and attractive way to prepare chicken.*

*Makes 4 servings*

1        pound boneless, skinless chicken breasts
2        small Golden Delicious apples, peeled, cut into 1-inch chunks
1        1-pound can carrots, drained and cut into ¹/₂-inch chunks (or
            2 cups fresh carrots, steamed)
1        packet low-sodium instant chicken-flavored broth mix
1        tablespoon plus 1 teaspoon honey
¹/₄      cup plus 2 tablespoons dry bread crumbs
1        tablespoon plus 1 teaspoon reduced-calorie margarine

Preheat oven to 350°.
Spray a 1-quart shallow casserole with nonstick cooking spray.
Place chicken in prepared pan.
In a small bowl, combine apples and carrots. Stir in broth mix and honey. Spoon carrot mixture evenly over chicken. Sprinkle with bread crumbs. Dot with margarine.
Cover tightly and bake 30 minutes.
Uncover and continue to bake 30 minutes more.

Each serving provides:

**252 Calories**

| | | | | |
|---|---|---|---|---|
| 3 | Protein Servings | 28 g | Protein |
| ¹/₂ | Bread Serving | 4 g | Fat (15% of calories) |
| 1 | Vegetable Serving | 25 g | Carbohydrate |
| ¹/₂ | Fat Serving | 388 mg | Sodium |
| ¹/₂ | Fruit Serving | 66 mg | Cholesterol |
| 23 | Additional Calories | 2 g | Fiber |

# Orange Barbecue Chicken

*Orange marmalade adds a delicious, sweet flavor to this crowd-pleasing version of an all-time favorite. It's delicious and attractive served over fine, yolk-free noodles.*

*Makes 6 servings*

| | |
|---|---|
| 1 1/2 | pounds boneless, skinless chicken breasts |
| 1 | 8-ounce can salt-free (or regular) tomato sauce |
| 3 | tablespoons fruit-only orange marmalade |
| 1 | tablespoon minced onion flakes |
| 1 | teaspoon vinegar |
| 1 | teaspoon Worcestershire sauce |
| 1/4 | teaspoon garlic powder |
| | Bottled hot sauce to taste |
| | Salt and pepper to taste |

Preheat oven to 350°.

Spray a 7 × 11-inch baking pan with nonstick cooking spray.

Place chicken in prepared pan.

Combine remaining ingredients and spread *half* of the sauce over chicken. Bake, uncovered, 1 hour, basting with sauce several times. Heat remaining sauce and serve with chicken.

---

Each serving provides:

**165 Calories**

| | | | |
|---|---|---|---|
| 3 | Protein Servings | 27 g | Protein |
| 3/4 | Vegetable Serving | 2 g | Fat (11% of calories) |
| 1/2 | Fruit Serving | 9 g | Carbohydrate |
| | | 93 mg | Sodium |
| | | 66 mg | Cholesterol |
| | | 1 g | Fiber |

# Chicken in White Wine

*White wine and herbs give this easy dish a truly gourmet taste. The leftovers make a great sandwich, either hot or cold.*

*Makes 4 servings*

| | |
|---|---|
| 1 | pound boneless, skinless chicken breasts |
| 1/2 | cup dry white wine |
| 2 | tablespoons grated onion |
| 1/2 | teaspoon celery salt |
| 1/2 | teaspoon pepper |
| 1/4 | teaspoon dried thyme |
| 1/4 | teaspoon dried marjoram |
| 1/4 | teaspoon dried rosemary, crumbled |

Place chicken in a shallow baking pan. Combine remaining ingredients in a small bowl and pour over chicken. Marinate in the refrigerator several hours, turning chicken several times.

Preheat oven to 350°.

Bake chicken, uncovered, 1 hour, basting several times.

Each serving provides:

**148 Calories**

| | | | |
|---|---|---|---|
| 3 | Protein Servings | 26 g | Protein |
| 25 | Additional Calories | 1 g | Fat (10% of calories) |
| | | 1 g | Carbohydrate |
| | | 155 mg | Sodium |
| | | 66 mg | Cholesterol |
| | | 0 g | Fiber |

# Spice-Glazed Chicken

*This recipe has been a family favorite for years. When you try it, you'll see why.*

*Makes 4 servings*

| | |
|---|---|
| 1 | pound boneless, skinless chicken breasts |
| 1/3 | cup ketchup |
| 1/3 | cup water |
| 2 | tablespoons plus 2 teaspoons sugar |
| 2 | tablespoons vinegar |
| 1 | tablespoon vegetable oil |
| 1 | teaspoon Worcestershire sauce |
| 3/4 | teaspoon dry mustard |
| 1 | bay leaf |
| 1 | cup thinly sliced onion, separated into rings after measuring |

Preheat oven to 350°.

Spray a 1-quart baking pan with nonstick cooking spray.

Place chicken in prepared pan.

In a small saucepan, combine remaining ingredients. Bring to a boil over medium heat, then reduce heat to medium-low and simmer 2 minutes, stirring frequently.

Baste chicken with a little of the sauce, leaving the onions in the saucepan.

Bake chicken, uncovered, 1 hour, basting frequently with the sauce. During the last 20 minutes of baking, arrange onion rings over chicken.

Remove and discard bay leaf.

Serve any remaining sauce with the cooked chicken.

---

Each serving provides:
### 233 Calories

| | | | |
|---|---|---|---|
| 3 | Protein Servings | 27 g | Protein |
| 1/2 | Vegetable Serving | 5 g | Fat (21% of calories) |
| 3/4 | Fat Serving | 18 g | Carbohydrate |
| 52 | Additional Calories | 327 mg | Sodium |
| | | 66 mg | Cholesterol |
| | | 1 g | Fiber |

# Chicken Cacciatore

*There are many versions of this popular Italian dish, but we're particularly partial to this one. Serve it over noodles, add a green vegetable, and you have a dinner to be proud of.*

*Makes 4 servings*

| | |
|---|---|
| 2 | teaspoons olive oil |
| 1 | cup sliced onion |
| 2 | cloves garlic, finely chopped |
| 1 | 1-pound can salt-free (or regular) tomatoes, chopped and undrained |
| 1 | 8-ounce can salt-free (or regular) tomato sauce |
| 1 | teaspoon dried oregano |
| 1/2 | teaspoon celery seed |
| 1/4 | teaspoon salt |
| 1/4 | teaspoon pepper |
| 1 | bay leaf |
| 1 | pound boneless, skinless chicken breasts, cut into quarters |
| 1/4 | cup dry white wine |

Heat oil in a large saucepan over medium heat. Add onion and garlic. Cook, stirring frequently, until onion is tender, about 10 minutes. Add small amounts of water as necessary (about a tablespoon at a time) to prevent sticking.

Add tomatoes, tomato sauce, and spices, stirring to blend.

Add chicken. Cover, reduce heat to medium-low, and simmer 1 hour, stirring occasionally.

Add wine. Cook, uncovered, 15 minutes.

Remove and discard bay leaf before serving.

---

Each serving provides:

**218 Calories**

| | | | |
|---|---|---|---|
| 3 | Protein Servings | 29 g | Protein |
| 2 1/2 | Vegetable Servings | 4 g | Fat (19% of calories) |
| 1/2 | Fat Serving | 14 g | Carbohydrate |
| 13 | Additional Calories | 239 mg | Sodium |
| | | 66 mg | Cholesterol |
| | | 2 g | Fiber |

# Peachy Spiced Chicken

*Very moist and topped with peaches and spices, this is really a special dish. It's delicious with rice or any cooked grain.*

*Makes 4 servings*

| | |
|---|---|
| 1 | pound boneless, skinless chicken breasts |
| 3 | fresh peaches, peeled and sliced, or 1¹/₂ cups canned peach slices (packed in juice), drained |
| ¹/₂ | cup orange juice |
| 1 | tablespoon vinegar |
| 1 | tablespoon firmly packed brown sugar |
| ¹/₂ | teaspoon dried basil |
| ¹/₄ | teaspoon ground nutmeg |
| ¹/₄ | teaspoon garlic powder |

Several hours before baking, place chicken in an 8-inch square baking pan that has been sprayed with a nonstick cooking spray.

Combine peaches with remaining ingredients, mixing well. Pour over chicken. Marinate in the refrigerator for several hours.

Preheat oven to 350°.

Cover chicken tightly and bake 1 hour.

Each serving provides:

**196 Calories**

| | | | |
|---|---|---|---|
| 3 | Protein Servings | 27 g | Protein |
| 1 | Fruit Serving | 2 g | Fat (7% of calories) |
| 12 | Additional Calories | 18 g | Carbohydrate |
| | | 76 mg | Sodium |
| | | 66 mg | Cholesterol |
| | | 2 g | Fiber |

# Honey Crunch Chicken

*We found that "painting" the chicken with reduced-calorie mayonnaise seals in the moistness, and the cereal on the outside adds a wonderful crunch. You'll choose this one time and again.*

*Makes 4 servings*

| | |
|---|---|
| 1 | pound boneless, skinless chicken breasts |
| 2 | tablespoons plus 2 teaspoons reduced-calorie mayonnaise |
| 1¹/₂ | ounces Grape Nuts cereal, crushed (¹/₃ cup) |
| 1 | tablespoon plus 1 teaspoon honey |

Preheat oven to 375°.

Spray a 1-quart baking pan with nonstick cooking spray.

Rinse chicken and pat dry. Place in prepared pan. Using a pastry brush, spread mayonnaise over both sides of the chicken.

Sprinkle cereal evenly over top side of chicken. Drizzle evenly with honey.

Let chicken stand at room temperature for 10 minutes.

Bake, uncovered, 45 minutes.

---

Each serving provides:

**215 Calories**

| | | | |
|---|---|---|---|
| 3 | Protein Servings | 27 g | Protein |
| ¹/₂ | Bread Serving | 4 g | Fat (19% of calories) |
| 1 | Fat Serving | 15 g | Carbohydrate |
| 20 | Additional Calories | 190 mg | Sodium |
| | | 69 mg | Cholesterol |
| | | 1 g | Fiber |

# Lazy Day Chicken

*This dish got its name due to its incredible ease of preparation. When you're in a hurry or just don't feel like cooking, this dish is ideal.*

*Makes 4 servings*

| | |
|---|---|
| 1 | pound boneless, skinless chicken breasts |
| 1 | 8-ounce can salt-free (or regular) tomato sauce |
| 2 | tablespoons minced onion flakes |
| 1 | packet low-sodium instant beef-flavored broth mix |
| 1/4 | teaspoon garlic powder |
| 1/2 | cup water |

Preheat oven to 350°.

Spray a shallow casserole with nonstick cooking spray.

Place chicken in prepared pan.

In a small bowl, combine remaining ingredients, mixing well. Spoon over chicken.

Cover and bake 30 minutes.

Uncover and continue to bake 20 minutes more.

---

Each serving provides:

**156 Calories**

| | | | |
|---|---|---|---|
| 3 | Protein Servings | 27 g | Protein |
| 1 | Vegetable Serving | 2 g | Fat (11% of calories) |
| 3 | Additional Calories | 6 g | Carbohydrate |
| | | 89 mg | Sodium |
| | | 66 mg | Cholesterol |
| | | 1 g | Fiber |

# Apricot-Glazed Chicken

*Our kids' all-time favorite chicken dish, this one is so easy you won't mind making it over and over.*

*Makes 4 servings*

| | |
|---|---|
| 1 | pound boneless, skinless chicken breasts |
| 1/3 | cup bottled fat-free French dressing |
| 3 | tablespoons fruit-only apricot spread |
| 2 | tablespoons water |
| 1 | tablespoon plus 1 teaspoon vegetable oil |
| 1 | tablespoon minced onion flakes |
| 1 | packet low-sodium instant beef-flavored broth mix |

Preheat oven to 350°.

Spray a shallow casserole with nonstick cooking spray.

Place chicken in prepared pan.

In a small bowl, combine remaining ingredients, mixing well. Spread sauce evenly over chicken.

Bake, uncovered, 1 hour.

---

Each serving provides:

**230 Calories**

| | | | |
|---|---|---|---|
| 3 | Protein Servings | 27 g | Protein |
| 1 | Fat Serving | 6 g | Fat (26% of calories) |
| 3/4 | Fruit Serving | 14 g | Carbohydrate |
| 29 | Additional Calories | 235 mg | Sodium |
| | | 66 mg | Cholesterol |
| | | 0 g | Fiber |

# Chicken Dijon

*Dijon mustard and herbs make this dish spicy and delicious. It's a perfect dinner, for family or guests, served with a baked potato and a pile of steamed fresh broccoli and cauliflower.*

*Makes 4 servings*

| | |
|---|---|
| 1 | pound boneless, skinless chicken breasts |
| 2 | tablespoons Dijon mustard |
| 1 | tablespoon plus 1 teaspoon vegetable oil |
| 1 | teaspoon dried parsley flakes |
| 1/2 | teaspoon dried rosemary, crumbled |
| 1/2 | teaspoon paprika |
| 1/4 | teaspoon dried thyme |
| 1/4 | teaspoon salt |
| 1/4 | teaspoon pepper |
| 1/8 | teaspoon garlic powder |

Preheat oven to 350°.

Spray a shallow casserole with nonstick cooking spray.

Place chicken in prepared pan.

Combine remaining ingredients in a small bowl. Mix well and spread over chicken.

Cover tightly and bake 30 minutes.

Uncover, baste chicken, and bake 20 minutes more.

---

Each serving provides:

**176 Calories**

| | | | |
|---|---|---|---|
| 3 | Protein Servings | 26 g | Protein |
| 1 | Fat Serving | 6 g | Fat (34% of calories) |
| | | 0 g | Carbohydrate |
| | | 389 mg | Sodium |
| | | 66 mg | Cholesterol |
| | | 0 g | Fiber |

# Savory Roast Chicken

*This is easy to prepare, and it's ideal even for a small family because the left-overs make such great sandwiches.*

*Makes 9 servings*

| | |
|---|---|
| 1 | 4 1/2-pound roasting chicken |
| 1 | small celery stalk |
| 1/2 | small onion, peeled |
| 1 | lemon wedge (about 1/4 of a small lemon) |
| 1/4 | cup bottled fat-free Italian dressing |
| 1 | tablespoon dill weed |
| 1/4 | teaspoon pepper |

Preheat oven to 375°.

Place chicken, breast-side up, on a rack in a shallow roasting pan. Place celery, onion, and lemon wedge inside cavity.

Combine dressing, dill, and pepper. Brush chicken (including inside cavity) with the sauce. If a meat thermometer is used, insert it in the center of the thigh muscle, making sure it does not touch bone.

Roast, uncovered, 1 1/2 to 2 hours, or until the internal temperature reaches 185° on a meat thermometer. (The drumstick should feel soft and it should move up and down easily in the socket. Also, the juices should run clear when the meat is pierced with a fork.)

Remove chicken from oven, cover loosely with foil to keep warm, and let stand 10 minutes before carving.

Remove and discard skin before serving.

---

Each serving provides:

**130 Calories**

| | | | |
|---|---|---|---|
| 3 | Protein Servings | 19 g | Protein |
| 2 | Additional Calories | 5 g | Fat (36% of calories) |
| | | 1 g | Carbohydrate |
| | | 92 mg | Sodium |
| | | 57 mg | Cholesterol |
| | | 0 g | Fiber |

# Chicken and Broccoli Bake

*A perfect use for leftover chicken, this luscious casserole needs only a tossed salad and a slice of whole grain bread to make a delectable meal.*

*Makes 6 servings*

| | |
|---|---|
| 1 | 10-ounce package frozen chopped broccoli, thawed and drained |
| 1 | teaspoon vegetable oil |
| 1 | cup finely chopped onion |
| 8 | ounces cooked, cubed chicken, skin removed (2 cups) |
| 1 | cup liquid egg substitute |
| 1 | cup nonfat dry milk |
| 1¹/₄ | cups water |
| ¹/₄ | cup all-purpose flour |
| 2 | teaspoons Worcestershire sauce |
| 1 | teaspoon baking powder |
| ¹/₄ | teaspoon garlic powder |
| ¹/₄ | teaspoon salt |
| ¹/₈ | teaspoon pepper |
| 4 | ounces shredded reduced-fat Cheddar cheese (1 cup) |

Preheat oven to 350°.

Spray an 8-inch square baking pan with nonstick cooking spray. Place broccoli in prepared pan.

Heat oil in a small saucepan over medium heat. Add onion. Cook, stirring frequently, until tender, about 5 minutes. Spoon over broccoli. Spread chicken over broccoli and onion.

In a blender container, combine remaining ingredients *except* cheese. Blend until smooth. Pour over chicken. Sprinkle evenly with cheese.

Bake, uncovered, 40 minutes, until top is brown and mixture is set. Let stand 5 minutes before serving.

---

Each serving provides:

**211 Calories**

| | | | |
|---|---|---|---|
| 2³/₄ | Protein Servings | 25 g | Protein |
| 1 | Vegetable Serving | 7 g | Fat (31% of calories) |
| ¹/₂ | Milk Serving | 12 g | Carbohydrate |
| 35 | Additional Calories | 469 mg | Sodium |
| | | 48 mg | Cholesterol |
| | | 1 g | Fiber |

# Deviled Cornish Hens

*A great company dish, these hens can be marinated all day and then baked when needed. Serve them with our Favorite Rice Casserole on page 229 and some steamed fresh asparagus for a dinner they won't forget.*

*Makes 4 servings*

| | |
|---|---|
| 2 | 1 1/4-pound Cornish hens, skin removed* |
| 1/2 | cup dry red wine |
| 3 | tablespoons reduced-sodium soy sauce |
| 2 | tablespoons water |
| 2 | tablespoons dry sherry |
| 1 | tablespoon Dijon mustard |
| 2 | teaspoons vegetable oil |
| 1/2 | teaspoon bottled hot pepper sauce |
| 3 | tablespoons dry bread crumbs |

Split hens in half down the back. Place in a shallow baking pan that has been sprayed with nonstick cooking spray.

In a small bowl, combine remaining ingredients *except* bread crumbs. Mix well and pour over hens.

Marinate in the refrigerator for 4 to 5 hours, turning hens several times. Preheat oven to 350°.

Sprinkle *half* of the bread crumbs evenly over hens.

Bake, uncovered, 30 minutes.

Turn hens. Sprinkle with remaining crumbs. Bake 30 minutes more.

*To remove the skin, first cut the skin down the middle of each breast using kitchen shears. Pull the skin to each side and over each leg. Snip the skin around each wing and pull the skin over each wing. Turn hen over and use a sharp knife to remove the remaining skin on the backs. It helps to grasp the skin firmly with a paper towel when pulling it off.

---

Each serving provides:

**353 Calories**

| | | | |
|---|---|---|---|
| 4 | Protein Servings | 42 g | Protein |
| 1/4 | Bread Serving | 13 g | Fat (38% of calories) |
| 1/2 | Fat Serving | 6 g | Carbohydrate |
| 31 | Additional Calories | 724 mg | Sodium |
| | | 126 mg | Cholesterol |
| | | 0 g | Fiber |

# Cranberry-Stuffed Chicken Breasts

*Chicken breasts stuffed with a delectable cranberry stuffing make a wonderful holiday meal. But you don't have to wait for a holiday to try them. Just be sure to freeze some cranberries in the fall when they are abundant, and you can enjoy this elegant dish anytime of the year.*

*Makes 4 servings*

| | |
|---|---|
| 1 | pound boneless, skinless chicken breasts |
| 1 | cup cranberries |
| 3 | tablespoons sugar |
| 1 | teaspoon grated fresh orange peel |
| 1/4 | teaspoon salt |
| 1/4 | teaspoon ground cinnamon |
| 4 | slices whole wheat bread (1-ounce slices), cut into small cubes and toasted in a 300° oven until dry |
| 2 | tablespoons raisins |
| 2 | tablespoons water |
| | Paprika |
| | Dried parsley flakes |

Preheat oven to 350°.

Spray a 10-inch pie pan with nonstick cooking spray.

Place each chicken breast between 2 pieces of wax paper and flatten with a mallet until chicken is 1/4-inch thick.

Combine cranberries, sugar, orange peel, salt, and cinnamon in a blender or food processor. Process until cranberries are chopped.

Spoon mixture into a bowl and add bread cubes, raisins, and water, mixing well. Add a little more water if necessary to moisten stuffing.

Divide stuffing mixture evenly onto the center of each chicken breast. Pull the corners together and fold up the edges to enclose the stuffing. Turn chicken over and place, smooth-side up, in prepared pan. Sprinkle liberally with paprika and parsley flakes.

Cover pan tightly with aluminum foil and bake 40 minutes.

---

Each serving provides:

**261 Calories**

| | | | |
|---|---|---|---|
| 3 | Protein Servings | 29 g | Protein |
| 1 | Bread Serving | 3 g | Fat (10% of calories) |
| 1/2 | Fruit Serving | 30 g | Carbohydrate |
| 36 | Additional Calories | 359 mg | Sodium |
| | | 66 mg | Cholesterol |
| | | 3 g | Fiber |

# Polynesian Chicken Salad

*This delicious salad, with its exotic flair, is really a hit when served in a scooped-out pineapple shell.*

*Makes 4 servings*

| | |
|---|---|
| 1 | 1-pound can pineapple tidbits (packed in juice), drained (Reserve 1/2 cup of the juice.) |
| 1/4 | cup water |
| 2 | teaspoons cornstarch |
| 1/4 | teaspoon dry mustard |
| 2 | tablespoons vinegar |
| 2 | tablespoons ketchup |
| 2 | teaspoons Worcestershire sauce |
| 2 | teaspoons reduced-sodium soy sauce |
| 1/4 | teaspoon paprika |
| 1/4 | teaspoon garlic powder |
| 12 | ounces cooked, cubed chicken, skin removed (3 cups) |
| 1/2 | cup chopped green bell pepper |

Set pineapple aside.

In a medium saucepan, combine pineapple juice, water, cornstarch, and mustard. Cook over medium heat, stirring constantly, until thick and bubbly. Cool 10 minutes.

Stir in vinegar, ketchup, Worcestershire sauce, soy sauce, paprika, and garlic powder. Add chicken, green pepper, and pineapple. Mix well.

Chill thoroughly.

---

Each serving provides:

**254 Calories**

| | | | |
|---|---|---|---|
| 3 | Protein Servings | 26 g | Protein |
| 1/4 | Vegetable Serving | 6 g | Fat (23% of calories) |
| 1 | Fruit Serving | 23 g | Carbohydrate |
| 13 | Additional Calories | 293 mg | Sodium |
| | | 76 mg | Cholesterol |
| | | 1 g | Fiber |

# Turkey Divan

*Chicken can also be used in this slimmed-down version of a popular favorite. It's a delicious dish to serve with cooked couscous or barley.*

*Makes 6 servings*

| | |
|---|---|
| 2 | 10-ounce packages frozen broccoli |
| 12 | ounces cooked, sliced, skinless turkey breast |
| 1/4 | cup plus 2 tablespoons all-purpose flour |
| 2 | cups water |
| 2 | packets low-sodium instant chicken-flavored broth mix |
| 1/2 | cup plain nonfat yogurt |
| 1/2 | teaspoon Worcestershire sauce |
| 1 | tablespoon plus 1 teaspoon prepared yellow mustard |
| 2 | tablespoons minced onion flakes |
| 3 | tablespoons grated Parmesan cheese |
| | Pepper to taste |

Preheat oven to 400°.

Spray an 8-inch square baking pan with nonstick cooking spray.

Cook broccoli according to package directions. Drain. Place in prepared pan. Place turkey slices on top of broccoli.

Place flour in a small bowl. Gradually add water, stirring to prevent lumps. Add remaining ingredients. Mix well with a fork or wire whisk. Pour mixture over turkey.

Bake, uncovered, 30 minutes, or until hot and bubbly.

---

Each serving provides:

**166 Calories**

| | | | |
|---|---|---|---|
| 2 | Protein Servings | 23 g | Protein |
| 1/4 | Bread Serving | 2 g | Fat (10% of calories) |
| 1 1/4 | Vegetable Servings | 14 g | Carbohydrate |
| 36 | Additional Calories | 156 mg | Sodium |
| | | 49 mg | Cholesterol |
| | | 2 g | Fiber |

# Rosemary Turkey Cutlets

*Rosemary adds a wonderful, delicate flavor to the turkey in this dish that's fit for the fanciest dinner party.*

*Makes 4 servings*

| | |
|---|---|
| 1 | pound turkey breast cutlets |
| 1 | cup sliced mushrooms |
| 3/4 | cup plain nonfat yogurt* |
| 1 | tablespoon all-purpose flour |
| 1/2 | cup dry white wine |
| 2 | teaspoons Dijon mustard |
| 1 | teaspoon dried rosemary, crumbled |
| 1/4 | teaspoon garlic powder |
| | Pepper to taste |

Preheat oven to 350°.

Spray an 8-inch square baking pan with nonstick cooking spray.

Place turkey in pan. Top with mushrooms.

In a small bowl, combine remaining ingredients, mixing well. Spread evenly over turkey and mushrooms.

Bake, uncovered, 45 minutes.

*If desired, you can substitute nonfat sour cream for the yogurt.

Each serving provides:

**187 Calories**

| | | | |
|---|---|---|---|
| 3 | Protein Servings | 31 g | Protein |
| 1/2 | Vegetable Serving | 1 g | Fat (7% of calories) |
| 1/4 | Milk Serving | 6 g | Carbohydrate |
| 33 | Additional Calories | 150 mg | Sodium |
| | | 71 mg | Cholesterol |
| | | 0 g | Fiber |

# Oven-Fried Turkey Cutlets

*One of our family's favorites, these breaded cutlets can be served as is or topped with spaghetti sauce. They also make great sandwiches, hot or cold.*

*Makes 4 servings*

| | |
|---|---|
| 1 | pound turkey breast cutlets |
| 2 | tablespoons lemon juice |
| 3/4 | cup dry bread crumbs |
| 2 | tablespoons grated Parmesan cheese |
| 2 | teaspoons dried oregano |
| 1/2 | teaspoon poultry seasoning |
| 1/4 | teaspoon salt |
| 1/4 | teaspoon pepper |
| 1/4 | teaspoon garlic powder |

Preheat oven to 350°.

Spray a shallow baking pan with nonstick cooking spray.

Place turkey cutlets in a medium bowl. Cover with water. Add lemon juice.

In a shallow bowl, combine remaining ingredients. Mix well.

One at a time, take cutlets from water and dip into crumbs, turning to coat both sides of cutlets. Place in prepared pan.

Spray each cutlet lightly and evenly with cooking spray.

Bake, uncovered, 30 minutes, or until lightly browned.

---

Each serving provides:

### 231 Calories

| | | | |
|---|---|---|---|
| 3 | Protein Servings | 32 g | Protein |
| 1 | Bread Serving | 4 g | Fat (16% of calories) |
| 15 | Additional Calories | 16 g | Carbohydrate |
| | | 414 mg | Sodium |
| | | 72 mg | Cholesterol |
| | | 1 g | Fiber |

# French Turkey Cutlets

*Ready in no time, these cutlets are perfect alongside a baked potato that is topped with nonfat sour cream and chives. Add some steamed broccoli, and you have a tempting and very healthful dinner.*

*Makes 4 servings*

| | |
|---|---|
| 1 | pound turkey breast cutlets |
| 1 | teaspoon dry mustard |
| 1/2 | teaspoon salt |
| 1/2 | teaspoon pepper |
| 1/4 | teaspoon garlic powder |
| 2 | teaspoons vegetable oil |
| 2 | tablespoons lemon juice |
| 2 | teaspoons Worcestershire sauce |
| 1 | tablespoon dried chives |

Sprinkle each side of cutlets with mustard, salt, pepper, and garlic powder.

Heat oil in a large nonstick skillet over medium heat. Add turkey and cook, turning frequently, until turkey is done and is no longer pink.

Sprinkle with lemon juice, Worcestershire sauce, and chives. Cook, turning frequently, 3 minutes more.

---

Each serving provides:

**154 Calories**

| | | | |
|---|---|---|---|
| 3 | Protein Servings | 28 g | Protein |
| 1/2 | Fat Serving | 3 g | Fat (19% of calories) |
| | | 1 g | Carbohydrate |
| | | 358 mg | Sodium |
| | | 70 mg | Cholesterol |
| | | 0 g | Fiber |

# Turkey in Dilled Cream Sauce

*It sounds unusual, but the combination of sour cream (nonfat, of course) and dill seed makes an exciting, rich-tasting dish.*

*Makes 4 servings*

| | |
|---|---|
| 1 | pound turkey breast cutlets |
| 1 | cup nonfat sour cream |
| 1 | teaspoon dill seed |
| 1/4 | teaspoon salt |
| 1/8 | teaspoon pepper |
| 2 | packets low-sodium instant beef-flavored broth mix |
| 1 | tablespoon plus 1 teaspoon minced onion flakes |

Preheat oven to 350°.

Spray a shallow baking pan with nonstick cooking spray.

Place turkey in prepared pan.

In a small bowl, combine remaining ingredients, mixing well. Spread evenly over turkey.

Bake, uncovered, 1 hour.

Each serving provides:

**179 Calories**

| | | | |
|---|---|---|---|
| 3 | Protein Servings | 33 g | Protein |
| 45 | Additional Calories | 1 g | Fat (6% of calories) |
| | | 6 g | Carbohydrate |
| | | 236 mg | Sodium |
| | | 70 mg | Cholesterol |
| | | 0 g | Fiber |

# Country Turkey Loaf

*This easy loaf is loaded with vegetables, making it colorful as well as tasty and nutritious. The flavor of the soy sauce blends well with the tomato sauce, giving the taste a nice little boost.*

*Makes 4 servings*

1        pound lean ground turkey
1/2      cup chopped carrot, in 1/4-inch pieces
1/2      cup finely chopped onion
1/2      cup chopped mushrooms
1/4      cup finely chopped green pepper
1/2      cup salt-free (or regular) tomato sauce
2        tablespoons reduced-sodium soy sauce
1/4      teaspoon garlic powder
         Salt and pepper to taste

Preheat oven to 350°.

Have a shallow baking pan ready.

In a large bowl, combine turkey with remaining ingredients. Mix well. Shape into a loaf. Place loaf in prepared pan.

Bake, uncovered, 1 hour.

---

Each serving provides:

**194 Calories**

| | | | |
|---|---|---|---|
| 3 | Protein Servings | 21 g | Protein |
| 1 1/2 | Vegetable Servings | 9 g | Fat (41% of calories) |
| | | 7 g | Carbohydrate |
| | | 419 mg | Sodium |
| | | 83 mg | Cholesterol |
| | | 1 g | Fiber |

# Barbecue Turkey Loaf

*Brown sugar and vinegar added to the tomato sauce give this moist loaf a wonderful barbecue flavor. It's delicious with our Oven-Baked French "Fries" on page 286 and a pile of steamed mixed vegetables.*

*Makes 6 servings*

| | |
|---|---|
| 1 1/2 | pounds lean ground turkey |
| 1 | 8-ounce can salt-free (or regular) tomato sauce |
| 1 | cup finely chopped onion |
| | Salt to taste |
| 1/4 | teaspoon pepper |
| 1/4 | teaspoon garlic powder |
| 2 | teaspoons Worcestershire sauce |
| 2 | tablespoons firmly packed brown sugar |
| 2 | tablespoons prepared yellow mustard |
| 1 | tablespoon vinegar |

Preheat oven to 350°.

In a large bowl, combine turkey, 3/4 cup of the tomato sauce, onion, salt, pepper, garlic powder, and Worcestershire sauce. Mix well. Shape mixture into a loaf and place on a rack in a shallow baking pan.

Bake, uncovered, 20 minutes.

Combine remaining tomato sauce, brown sugar, mustard, and vinegar. Spoon over loaf.

Bake, uncovered, 40 minutes longer.

---

Each serving provides:

**208 Calories**

| | | | |
|---|---|---|---|
| 3 | Protein Servings | 21 g | Protein |
| 1 | Vegetable Serving | 9 g | Fat (39% of calories) |
| 16 | Additional Calories | 10 g | Carbohydrate |
| | | 201 mg | Sodium |
| | | 83 mg | Cholesterol |
| | | 1 g | Fiber |

# Italian Turkey Burgers

*Served on a whole grain bun or on a bed of rice or noodles, these burgers will definitely be a hit.*

*Makes 4 servings*

### Burgers
1        pound lean ground turkey
2        tablespoons grated onion
1        teaspoon dried oregano
1/2      teaspoon dried basil
1/4      teaspoon garlic powder

### Sauce
1        8-ounce can salt-free (or regular) tomato sauce
1        4-ounce can mushroom pieces, drained
1/4      teaspoon *each* dried oregano and basil
1/8      teaspoon garlic powder

In a large bowl, combine turkey with remaining burger ingredients. Mix well. Shape into 4 patties.

Spray a large nonstick griddle or skillet with nonstick cooking spray. Heat over medium heat.

Place burgers on griddle. Cook until burgers are done and are nicely browned on both sides. Turn burgers several times while cooking.

While burgers are cooking, combine sauce ingredients in a small saucepan. Heat over medium heat until hot and bubbly. Keep warm over low heat until burgers are ready.

Divide sauce evenly and spoon over burgers when serving.

---

Each serving provides:

**192 Calories**

| | | |
|---|---|---|
| 3 | Protein Servings | 21 g | Protein |
| 1 1/4 | Vegetable Servings | 9 g | Fat (43% of calories) |
| | | 6 g | Carbohydrate |
| | | 185 mg | Sodium |
| | | 83 mg | Cholesterol |
| | | 1 g | Fiber |

# Roast Turkey Breast with Peach Sauce

*The delectable peach sauce turns an ordinary turkey breast into an extraordinary dish. Serve it for dinner and slice the rest for sandwiches.*

*Makes 16 servings*

1      5-pound bone-in turkey breast
3/4    teaspoon salt
1/2    teaspoon poultry seasoning
1/4    teaspoon pepper
1/4    teaspoon dried thyme

## Sauce
1      tablespoon cornstarch
3/4    cup water
1      packet low-sodium instant chicken-flavored broth mix
1/4    cup fruit-only peach spread
1      tablespoon dry sherry

Preheat oven to 325°.

Sprinkle top and bottom of turkey breast with salt, poultry seasoning, pepper, and thyme. Place turkey, skin-side up, on a rack in a shallow roasting pan.

Roast 1 1/2 to 2 hours, or until meat is no longer pink.

Remove and discard the skin before slicing. Slice and weigh 3 pounds of turkey; reserve any remaining turkey for another use.

Just before serving, prepare sauce:

Dissolve cornstarch in water in a small saucepan. Add broth mix and peach spread and mix well. Bring sauce to a boil over medium heat, stirring constantly. Boil, stirring, 2 minutes. Remove from heat and stir in sherry.

Spoon sauce over sliced turkey.

---

Each serving provides:
### 110 Calories

| | | | |
|---|---|---|---|
| 3 | Protein Servings | 21 g | Protein |
| 15 | Additional Calories | 1 g | Fat (5% of calories) |
| | | 4 g | Carbohydrate |
| | | 89 mg | Sodium |
| | | 59 mg | Cholesterol |
| | | 0 g | Fiber |

# Mock-Sausage and Peppers

*By refrigerating the turkey with the herbs and allowing the flavors to "marry," these delicious patties taste just like the Italian specialty. Serve with pasta or on a crusty roll, topped with pasta sauce.*

*Makes 4 servings*
*(2 patties each serving)*

| | |
|---|---|
| 1 | teaspoon vegetable oil |
| 1/2 | cup finely minced green bell pepper |
| 1/2 | cup finely minced onion |
| 1 | pound lean ground turkey |
| 1/2 | teaspoon fennel seeds, crushed* |
| 1/4 | teaspoon ground sage |
| 1/4 | teaspoon dried thyme |
| 1/4 | teaspoon dried marjoram |
| 1/4 | teaspoon salt |
| 1/4 | teaspoon pepper |
| 1/8 | teaspoon ground savory |

Heat oil in a small nonstick skillet over medium heat. Add green pepper and onion. Cook, stirring frequently, until tender, about 8 minutes. Add small amounts of water as necessary (about a tablespoon at a time) to prevent sticking.

In a large bowl, combine turkey with peppers and onions. Add remaining ingredients and mix well. Refrigerate mixture for 1 to 5 hours to blend flavors.

Shape mixture into 8 thin patties.

Spray a large nonstick griddle or skillet with nonstick cooking spray. Preheat over medium heat.

Place patties on griddle. Cook until patties are done and are lightly browned on both sides. Turn patties several times while cooking.

*To crush seeds, place between 2 pieces of wax paper and crush with a rolling pin or mallet.

Each serving provides:

**186 Calories**

| 3 | Protein Servings | 20 g | Protein |
|---|---|---|---|
| 1/2 | Vegetable Serving | 10 g | Fat (49% of calories) |
| 1/4 | Fat Serving | 3 g | Carbohydrate |
| | | 243 mg | Sodium |
| | | 83 mg | Cholesterol |
| | | 1 g | Fiber |

# Marinated Turkey Roll

*A rolled turkey roast is perfect for a family dinner, and, if you have a small family, you have the added bonus of lots of leftovers for sandwiches. Just ask the butcher to bone the turkey breast and remove the skin. The rest is easy.*

*Makes 12 servings*

| | |
|---|---|
| 1 | 3-pound skinless, boneless turkey breast |
| $3/4$ | teaspoon dried thyme |
| $1/2$ | teaspoon ground ginger |
| $1/4$ | teaspoon garlic powder |
| $1/4$ | cup dry sherry |
| $1/4$ | cup reduced-sodium soy sauce |
| $1/4$ | cup orange juice |
| 2 | teaspoons honey |

Using a sharp knife, make a lengthwise slit in one side of the turkey breast, as if creating a pocket. Do not cut all the way through. Open at the pocket and lay flat.

Place turkey between 2 sheets of wax paper and flatten with a mallet to about 1 1/2-inches thick. Sprinkle *half* of the thyme, ginger, and garlic powder evenly over the turkey. Starting at one end, roll turkey like a jelly roll. Tie with a cord in 3 or 4 places.

Place turkey in a plastic bag and add remaining spices, along with sherry, soy sauce, orange juice, and honey. Close bag tightly and place in a shallow pan. Marinate in the refrigerator several hours, turning bag over several times.

To cook, place turkey and marinade in the bottom of a roasting pan. Preheat oven to 350°.

Cook, covered, 2 hours, or until meat is no longer pink.

Slice crosswise to serve.

---

Each serving provides:

**143 Calories**

| | | | |
|---|---|---|---|
| 3 | Protein Servings | 29 g | Protein |
| 10 | Additional Calories | 1 g | Fat (5% of calories) |
| | | 3 g | Carbohydrate |
| | | 257 mg | Sodium |
| | | 71 mg | Cholesterol |
| | | 0 g | Fiber |

# Barbecued Turkey Franks

*Serve this tangy dish with rice or noodles for a tasty, quick, and very inexpensive dinner. Kids will love it.*

*Makes 4 servings*

| | |
|---|---|
| 9 | ounces lowfat turkey frankfurters (up to 2 grams of fat per ounce), cut into 2-inch pieces |
| 1 | teaspoon vegetable oil |
| 1/2 | cup chopped onion |
| 1/2 | cup chopped green bell pepper |
| 2 | tablespoons chopped celery |
| 1 | 8-ounce can salt-free (or regular) tomato sauce |
| 2 | tablespoons firmly packed brown sugar |
| 1 | tablespoon prepared yellow mustard |
| 1 | tablespoon vinegar |
| 2 | teaspoons Worcestershire sauce |
| 1/8 | teaspoon garlic powder |
| | Bottled hot pepper sauce to taste |

Broil frankfurters on a rack under the broiler, until brown on all sides.

Heat oil in a large nonstick skillet over medium heat. Add onion, green pepper, and celery. Cook, stirring frequently, until tender, about 8 minutes. Add small amounts of water as necessary (about a tablespoon at a time) to prevent sticking.

Add remaining ingredients *except* frankfurters and mix well. Reduce heat to medium-low. Stir in frankfurters.

Cover and cook until hot and bubbly, about 10 minutes.

---

Each serving provides:

**143 Calories**

| | | | |
|---|---|---|---|
| 1 1/2 | Protein Servings | 8 g | Protein |
| 1 1/2 | Vegetable Servings | 3 g | Fat (20% of calories) |
| 1/4 | Fat Serving | 20 g | Carbohydrate |
| 24 | Additional Calories | 625 mg | Sodium |
| | | 30 mg | Cholesterol |
| | | 1 g | Fiber |

# Beans and Tofu

The beans in this section are actually legumes, which are the seeds from certain pod-bearing plants. Among the most popular types of legumes are kidney beans, pinto beans, chickpeas (or garbanzo beans), Great Northern beans, black beans, split peas, and lentils. Legumes are extremely versatile. They can be used to replace all or part of the meat in stews, they add fiber and texture to soups, and they even appear in some of our desserts! Beans are low in fat, high in fiber, and contain iron, B vitamins, and minerals.

Tofu is a product that is made from soybeans in much the same way that cheese is made from milk. Available in the produce section of most large grocery stores, tofu is high in protein, low in saturated fat, and contains no cholesterol. Its very mild flavor is a definite advantage, allowing the tofu to blend easily with other ingredients and take on the flavor of whatever it is combined with.

In this section, we offer delicious, creative recipes that will add variety to your meals along with a refreshing change of pace.

## Basic Cooking Directions for Legumes

Before cooking, beans need to be soaked in order to restore the water lost in drying. (Split peas and lentils, however, do not require soaking.) Soak the beans first, using either of the two following methods. Then, using 2 to 3 cups of water for each cup of beans, bring water to a boil and add beans. (There should be enough water to cover the beans by 1 inch.) Reduce heat to low, cover partially, and simmer for the amount of time specified, or until beans are tender. Cooking times may vary with the size, quality, and freshness of the legumes.

**Quick soaking method:** Place beans in a pot and add enough water to cover beans by 3 inches. Bring to a boil over medium heat. Boil 2 minutes. Remove from heat, cover, and let stand 2 hours. Drain and cook as directed.

**Overnight soaking method:** Place beans in a bowl and add enough water to cover beans by 3 inches. Soak overnight, drain, and cook as directed.

**Cooking times for legumes:** The following cooking times are for soaked beans, except for split peas and lentils, which do not require soaking:

| | |
|---|---|
| Black beans | 1 to 2 hours |
| Black-eyed peas | 30 to 45 minutes |
| Garbanzo beans (chickpeas) | 2 to 3 hours |
| Great Northern beans | 1 to 1 1/2 hours |
| Kidney beans | 1 1/2 to 2 hours |
| Lentils | 30 to 45 minutes |
| Lima beans | 1 to 1 1/2 hours |
| Navy beans | 1 1/2 to 2 hours |
| Pinto beans | 1 1/2 to 2 hours |
| Soybeans | 2 to 3 hours |
| Split peas | 30 to 45 minutes |

*Note:* Generally, 1 cup of dry legumes will yield 2 to 3 cups cooked legumes. One cup of cooked legumes will weigh approximately 6 ounces. The yield and amount of cooking time may vary with the size and quality of the legumes and the mineral content of the water used.

# Prairie Bean Tortillas

*Similar to fajitas, but made with corn tortillas rather than flour tortillas, this is a quick, easy meal to prepare.*

*Makes 4 servings*

| | |
|---|---|
| 4 | 6-inch flour tortillas |
| 1 | teaspoon vegetable oil |
| 1 | cup chopped onion |
| 2 | cloves garlic, minced |
| 1 | 1-pound can pinto beans, rinsed and drained (This will yield approximately 9 ounces of beans.) |
| 1 | 8-ounce can salt-free (or regular) tomato sauce |
| 1 | 4-ounce can chopped green chilies (hot or mild), drained |
| 1 | teaspoon ground cumin |
| 1 | teaspoon chili powder |
| 1 | teaspoon dried oregano |
| 1 | cup shredded lettuce |
| 1/2 | cup chopped tomato |
| 2 | ounces shredded reduced-fat Cheddar cheese (1/2 cup) |

Preheat oven to 350°.

Stack tortillas and wrap them tightly in foil. Heat in oven for 10 minutes.

While tortillas are heating, heat oil in a large nonstick skillet over medium heat. Add onion and garlic. Cook, stirring frequently, until onion is tender, about 5 minutes. Add beans, tomato sauce, chilies, and spices. Cook 5 minutes, stirring occasionally and mashing beans slightly with a fork.

Place each tortilla on a serving plate. Divide bean mixture evenly onto tortillas. Top with lettuce, tomato, and cheese. Roll up tortillas and serve right away.

---

Each serving provides:

**235 Calories**

| | | | |
|---|---|---|---|
| 1 3/4 | Protein Servings | 13 g | Protein |
| 1 | Bread Serving | 6 g | Fat (23% of calories) |
| 2 1/2 | Vegetable Servings | 34 g | Carbohydrate |
| 1/4 | Fat Serving | 586 mg | Sodium |
| 8 | Additional Calories | 10 mg | Cholesterol |
| | | 6 g | Fiber |

# Bean-Stuffed Eggplant

*You'll be proud to serve this elegant meal. It looks so fancy, yet it's so easy to prepare.*

*Makes 4 servings*

| | |
|---|---|
| 2 | small eggplants, about 1 1/2 pounds total |
| 2 | teaspoons vegetable oil |
| 1 | cup chopped onion |
| 2 | cloves garlic, minced |
| 1 | 1-pound can kidney beans, rinsed and drained (This will yield approximately 10 ounces of beans.) |
| 2 | cups cooked brown rice |
| 1 | teaspoon dried basil |
| 1 | teaspoon dried oregano |
| 1/4 | teaspoon dried thyme |
| 3 | ounces shredded reduced-fat Cheddar cheese (3/4 cup) |
| 1/2 | cup evaporated skim milk |
| 1 | tablespoon grated Parmesan cheese |

Preheat oven to 350°.

Spray a shallow baking pan with nonstick cooking spray.

Cut eggplants in half lengthwise. Scoop out the pulp, using a small knife or melon ball scoop, leaving 1/4-inch shells. Chop pulp.

Heat oil in a large nonstick skillet over medium heat. Add eggplant pulp, onion, and garlic. Cook, stirring frequently, 3 to 5 minutes, until onion is tender. Remove from heat and stir in remaining ingredients *except* Parmesan cheese. Stir until mixture is thoroughly combined.

Fill eggplant shells with bean mixture. Sprinkle evenly with Parmesan cheese.

Bake, uncovered, 30 minutes.

---

Each serving provides:

**365 Calories**

| | | | |
|---|---|---|---|
| 2 1/4 | Protein Servings | 21 g | Protein |
| 1 | Bread Serving | 8 g | Fat (20% of calories) |
| 2 | Vegetable Servings | 54 g | Carbohydrate |
| 1/4 | Fat Serving | 379 mg | Sodium |
| 1/4 | Milk Serving | 17 mg | Cholesterol |
| 8 | Additional Calories | 9 g | Fiber |

# Pineapple–Black Bean Salad

*As cool as the Caribbean breezes, this refreshing bean salad can be served on a bed of lettuce or piled into a pita for a delicious sandwich.*

*Makes 4 servings*

| | |
|---|---|
| 1 | 1-pound can black beans, rinsed and drained (This will yield approximately 10 ounces of beans.) |
| 1 | 8-ounce can pineapple tidbits (packed in juice), drained (Reserve 1/4 cup of the juice.) |
| 1/2 | cup finely chopped red bell pepper |
| 1/2 | cup thinly sliced green onion (green and white parts) |
| 2 | teaspoons vinegar |
| 1/2 | teaspoon ground cumin |
| 1/4 | teaspoon salt |
| | Pepper to taste |
| 1 | jalapeño pepper, finely chopped, seeds and inner membranes discarded (optional) |

Combine all ingredients in a medium bowl, including the reserved pineapple juice. Mix well.

Chill thoroughly.

Mix before serving.

---

Each serving provides:

**105 Calories**

| | | | |
|---|---|---|---|
| 1 1/4 | Protein Servings | 5 g | Protein |
| 1/2 | Vegetable Serving | 1 g | Fat (5% of calories) |
| 1/2 | Fruit Serving | 21 g | Carbohydrate |
| | | 321 mg | Sodium |
| | | 0 mg | Cholesterol |
| | | 4 g | Fiber |

# Bean and Cheese Quesadillas

*Pronounced KAY-sa-DEE-yahs, these are the Mexican answer to a quick meal. If you like, you can place some chopped tomato, green onion, or green chilies on top of the cheese before you fold the tortillas. Served with salsa, this makes a great appetizer or lunch dish.*

*Makes 4 servings*

| | |
|---|---|
| 4 | 6-inch flour tortillas |
| 1/2 | cup canned fat-free refried beans (These are available in the Mexican food section of most large grocery stores.) |
| 2 | ounces shredded reduced-fat Cheddar or Monterey Jack cheese (1/2 cup) |
| | Salsa (optional) |

Preheat a large nonstick griddle over medium heat. Spray with nonstick cooking spray.

Place tortillas on a flat surface. Place 2 tablespoons of beans on each tortilla and spread it evenly, covering just half of each tortilla. Divide cheese evenly and place on top of the beans. Add chopped green onion, etc., if desired. Fold tortillas in half and press down gently. Heat tortillas, flipping them back and forth, until cheese is melted and tortillas are hot and crispy on both sides.

Serve right away, topped with salsa if you like.

---

Each serving provides:

**134 Calories**

| | | | |
|---|---|---|---|
| 1 | Protein Serving | 8 g | Protein |
| 1 | Bread Serving | 4 g | Fat (29% of calories) |
| 28 | Additional Calories | 16 g | Carbohydrate |
| | | 306 mg | Sodium |
| | | 10 mg | Cholesterol |
| | | 2 g | Fiber |

# Cheesy Beans and Rice

*Add a tossed salad and some steamed broccoli, and you have a filling, hearty family supper. It's a good idea to keep packets of cooked rice in the freezer. That way they're always ready to use in easy casseroles like this.*

*Makes 4 servings*

| | |
|---|---|
| 2 | teaspoons vegetable oil |
| 1/2 | cup chopped onion |
| 1/2 | cup chopped carrots |
| 1/2 | cup chopped celery |
| 1 | tablespoon dried basil |
| 1/2 | teaspoon dried oregano |
| 1/4 | teaspoon garlic powder |
| 1 | 1-pound can kidney beans, rinsed and drained (This will yield approximately 10 ounces of beans.) |
| 2 | cups chopped fresh tomato |
| | Salt and pepper to taste |
| 2 | ounces shredded reduced-fat Cheddar cheese (1/2 cup) |
| 2 | cups cooked brown rice |

Heat oil in a large nonstick skillet over medium heat. Add onion, carrots, and celery. Sprinkle with basil, oregano, and garlic powder. Cook, stirring frequently, until vegetables are tender, about 10 minutes. Add small amounts of water while cooking (about a tablespoon at a time) to prevent sticking.

Stir in beans, tomato, salt, and pepper. Heat through.

Stir in cheese and rice. Heat, stirring, until mixture is hot.

Each serving provides:

**287 Calories**

| | | | |
|---|---|---|---|
| 1 3/4 | Protein Servings | 14 g | Protein |
| 1 | Bread Serving | 7 g | Fat (21% of calories) |
| 1 3/4 | Vegetable Servings | 44 g | Carbohydrate |
| 1/2 | Fat Serving | 283 mg | Sodium |
| 10 | Additional Calories | 10 mg | Cholesterol |
| | | 8 g | Fiber |

# Herbed Chickpea Patties

*Serve these deliciously herbed patties plain or topped with a little ketchup.
And use the leftovers, hot or cold, to make wonderful sandwiches.*

*Makes 4 servings
(3 patties each serving)*

| | |
|---|---|
| 1 | 1-pound can chickpeas, rinsed and drained (This will yield approximately 10 ounces of chickpeas.) |
| 1/3 | cup nonfat dry milk |
| 1/2 | cup liquid egg substitute |
| 3 | tablespoons dry bread crumbs |
| 2 | teaspoons vegetable oil |
| 1 | teaspoon reduced-sodium soy sauce |
| 1/2 | teaspoon dry mustard |
| 1/2 | teaspoon dried oregano |
| 1/2 | teaspoon dried basil |
| 1/4 | teaspoon garlic powder |
| | Salt and pepper to taste |

In a blender container, combine all ingredients. Blend until smooth.
Spray a large nonstick griddle or skillet with nonstick cooking spray. Preheat over medium heat.

Drop chickpea mixture onto griddle, making 12 patties and using about 2 tablespoons for each patty. Cook until edges of patties appear dry and bottoms are lightly browned. Turn, flatten patties with a spatula, and cook until lightly browned on both sides.

---

Each serving provides:

**157 Calories**

| | | | |
|---|---|---|---|
| 1 3/4 | Protein Servings | 10 g | Protein |
| 1 1/4 | Bread Servings | 5 g | Fat (27% of calories) |
| 1/2 | Fat Serving | 19 g | Carbohydrate |
| 1/4 | Milk Serving | 300 mg | Sodium |
| | | 1 mg | Cholesterol |
| | | 3 g | Fiber |

# Herbed Bean Soufflé

*Folding egg whites into the beans makes them light and fluffy in this unusual soufflé. You'll need to serve it right away, before it "sinks."*

*Makes 4 servings*

| | |
|---|---|
| 1 | 1-pound can cannellini (white kidney beans), rinsed and drained (This will yield approximately 10 ounces of beans.) |
| 1/2 | cup liquid egg substitute |
| 1 | tablespoon minced onion flakes |
| 2 | teaspoons dried parsley flakes |
| 1/2 | teaspoon dried marjoram |
| 1/4 | teaspoon dried thyme |
| 1/8 | teaspoon dill weed |
| | Salt and pepper to taste |
| 3 | egg whites (Egg substitute will not work here.) |

Preheat oven to 350°.

Spray a 1 1/2-quart soufflé dish or deep baking dish with nonstick cooking spray.

In a blender container, combine beans, egg substitute, onion flakes, parsley, marjoram, thyme, dill, salt, and pepper. Blend until smooth. Spoon mixture into a large bowl.

In another bowl, beat egg whites on high speed of an electric mixer until stiff. Fold into bean mixture, gently but thoroughly.

Spoon mixture into prepared baking dish.

Bake 40 to 45 minutes, until set and lightly browned.

Serve right away.

---

Each serving provides:

**113 Calories**

| | | |
|---|---|---|
| 2 | Protein Servings | |
| | 12 g | Protein |
| | 1 g | Fat (7% of calories) |
| | 14 g | Carbohydrate |
| | 233 mg | Sodium |
| | 0 mg | Cholesterol |
| | 5 g | Fiber |

# Cajun Bean Pot

*Add as little or as much hot sauce as you like to this easy dish for a crowd.
It's perfect over rice or with a chunk of crusty bread for a football Sunday.*

*Makes 8 servings*

| | |
|---|---|
| 2 | teaspoons olive oil |
| 1 | cup chopped onion |
| 1 | cup chopped green bell pepper |
| 1/2 | cup chopped celery |
| 3 | cloves garlic, finely chopped |
| 3 | 1-pound cans kidney beans, rinsed and drained, *or* you can use a mixture of 3 different kinds of beans (This will yield approximately 30 ounces of beans.) |
| 1 | 1-pound can stewed tomatoes, undrained |
| 1 | 6-ounce can tomato paste |
| 1 1/4 | cups water |
| 1 | teaspoon Worcestershire sauce |
| 1/2 | teaspoon dried oregano |
| 1/4 | teaspoon dried thyme |
| 1/8 | to 1/4 teaspoon bottled hot sauce |
| 2 | bay leaves |

Heat oil in a large saucepan over medium heat. Add onion, green pepper, celery, and garlic. Cook, stirring frequently, until tender, about 10 minutes. Add small amounts of water as necessary (about a tablespoon at a time) to prevent sticking.

Add remaining ingredients, mixing well. When mixture boils, reduce heat to medium-low, cover, and simmer 30 minutes.

Remove and discard bay leaves before serving.

---

Each serving provides:

**178 Calories**

| | | | |
|---|---|---|---|
| 1 3/4 | Protein Servings | 11 g | Protein |
| 2 | Vegetable Servings | 2 g | Fat (12% of calories) |
| 1/4 | Fat Serving | 30 g | Carbohydrate |
| 8 | Additional Calories | 541 mg | Sodium |
| | | 0 mg | Cholesterol |
| | | 10 g | Fiber |

# Bean Stroganoff

*Any variety of bean will work in this creamy dish that tastes delicious spooned over noodles.*

*Makes 4 servings*

| | |
|---|---|
| 1 | teaspoon vegetable oil |
| 1 | medium onion, sliced |
| 3 | cups sliced mushrooms |
| 3 | cloves garlic, minced |
| 3 | tablespoons all-purpose flour |
| 1 | teaspoon dill weed |
| 1 | teaspoon dry mustard |
| 1/4 | teaspoon salt |
| 1/8 | teaspoon pepper |
| | Dash ground nutmeg |
| 1 | packet low-sodium instant beef-flavored broth mix |
| 2 | tablespoons dry sherry |
| 1 | 19-ounce can kidney beans, rinsed and drained (This will yield approximately 12 ounces of beans.) |
| 1/2 | cup plain nonfat yogurt |

Heat oil in a large nonstick skillet over medium heat. Add onion, mushrooms, and garlic. Cook, stirring frequently and separating onion into rings, until tender, about 5 minutes.

Combine flour, spices, and broth mix and sprinkle over mushroom mixture. Add water, a few tablespoons at a time, stirring constantly and mixing well after each addition. Stir in sherry and beans. When mixture is hot and bubbly, stir in yogurt. Heat through but do not boil.

---

Each serving provides:
### 164 Calories

| | | | |
|---|---|---|---|
| 1 1/2 | Protein Servings | 9 g | Protein |
| 1/4 | Bread Serving | 2 g | Fat (13% of calories) |
| 1 3/4 | Vegetable Servings | 26 g | Carbohydrate |
| 1/4 | Fat Serving | 381 mg | Sodium |
| 24 | Additional Calories | 1 mg | Cholesterol |
| | | 5 g | Fiber |

# Mushroom Bean Loaf Supreme

*And supreme it is! This meatless loaf has the texture of a fine paté. Serve it hot for dinner and serve the leftovers, hot or cold, in a sandwich or on crackers as an appetizer.*

*Makes 6 servings*

| | |
|---|---|
| 1 | 1-pound can pinto beans, rinsed and drained (This will yield approximately 9 ounces of beans.) |
| 3/4 | cup liquid egg substitute |
| 2 | slices whole wheat bread (1-ounce slices), crumbled |
| 2 | teaspoons vegetable oil |
| 2 | packets low-sodium instant chicken-flavored broth mix |
| 1 | tablespoon grated onion |
| 1/4 | teaspoon garlic powder |
| | Salt and pepper to taste |
| 1 | 8-ounce can mushroom pieces, drained |

Preheat oven to 350°.

Spray a 4 × 8-inch loaf pan with nonstick cooking spray.

In a blender container, combine all ingredients *except* mushrooms. Blend until smooth. Stir in mushrooms.

Spoon mixture into prepared pan.

Bake 50 to 55 minutes, until set and lightly browned.

Let loaf stand for 5 minutes, then invert onto a serving plate.

---

Each serving provides:

**105 Calories**

| | | | |
|---|---|---|---|
| 1 1/4 | Protein Servings | 7 g | Protein |
| 1/4 | Bread Serving | 3 g | Fat (21% of calories) |
| 1/4 | Vegetable Serving | 14 g | Carbohydrate |
| 1/4 | Fat Serving | 311 mg | Sodium |
| 13 | Additional Calories | 0 mg | Cholesterol |
| | | 3 g | Fiber |

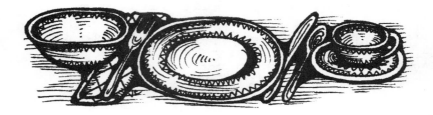

# Easy Bean Salad

*So zesty and good, this is a perfect salad for backyard picnics. It also makes a great addition to a tossed salad.*

*Makes 8 servings*

| | |
|---|---|
| 2 | 10-ounce packages frozen cut green beans |
| 1 | 1-pound can kidney beans, rinsed and drained (This will yield approximately 10 ounces of beans.) |
| 1 | 1-pound can chickpeas, rinsed and drained (This will yield approximately 10 ounces of chickpeas.) |
| 1 | tablespoon plus 1 teaspoon sweet pickle relish |
| $^1/_2$ | cup finely chopped onion |
| $^1/_4$ | cup finely chopped green bell pepper |
| 1 | tablespoon dried parsley flakes |
| $^1/_2$ | cup bottled fat-free Italian dressing |

Cook green beans according to package directions. Drain.

In a large bowl, combine all ingredients. Toss until blended.

Chill several hours to combine flavors, mixing several times while chilling.

Each serving provides:

**115 Calories**

| | | | |
|---|---|---|---|
| 1$^1/_4$ | Protein Servings | 6 g | Protein |
| 1$^1/_4$ | Vegetable Servings | 1 g | Fat (10% of calories) |
| 8 | Additional Calories | 20 g | Carbohydrate |
| | | 299 mg | Sodium |
| | | 0 mg | Cholesterol |
| | | 5 g | Fiber |

# Bean and Tuna Salad

*Pile this delectable, herbed medley into a pita, add some lettuce and a slice of tomato, and you have a delicious, filling sandwich they'll love. It's also good piled onto a bed of lettuce and served with a chunk of crusty bread.*

*Makes 6 servings*

| | |
|---|---|
| 1 | 1-pound can kidney beans, rinsed and drained (This will yield approximately 10 ounces of beans.) |
| 1 | 1-pound can chickpeas, rinsed and drained (This will yield approximately 10 ounces of chickpeas.) |
| 1 | 6¹/₂-ounce can tuna (packed in water), drained and flaked (4 ounces) |
| ¹/₄ | cup red wine vinegar |
| 2 | tablespoons vegetable oil |
| ¹/₂ | teaspoon dried marjoram |
| ¹/₂ | teaspoon dried basil |
| ¹/₂ | teaspoon dried oregano |
| ¹/₄ | teaspoon garlic powder |
| | Salt and pepper to taste |

In a large bowl, combine all ingredients. Toss until well blended.
Chill several hours, or overnight, to blend flavors.
Mix before serving.

---

Each serving provides:

**183 Calories**

| | | | |
|---|---|---|---|
| 2 | Protein Servings | 15 g | Protein |
| 1 | Fat Serving | 6 g | Fat (31% of calories) |
| | | 17 g | Carbohydrate |
| | | 275 mg | Sodium |
| | | 11 mg | Cholesterol |
| | | 5 g | Fiber |

# Pepper-Bean Casserole

*This easy casserole has an unusual and delicious flavor. It's slightly sweet, and the bacon bits add just the right amount of flavor without the fat of real bacon.*

*Makes 4 servings*

| | |
|---|---|
| 2 | 10-ounce packages frozen lima beans |
| 2 | teaspoons vegetable oil |
| 2 | medium green bell peppers, cut into 1/4-inch strips |
| 1 | 1-pound can salt-free (or regular) tomatoes, chopped, undrained |
| 1 | tablespoon imitation bacon bits |
| 1 | tablespoon molasses |
| 2 | teaspoons minced onion flakes |
| 1 | tablespoon firmly packed brown sugar |
| 1 | teaspoon dry mustard |
| 1/4 | teaspoon dried oregano |
| 1/4 | teaspoon garlic powder |

Preheat oven to 350°.

Spray a 1 1/2-quart casserole with nonstick cooking spray.

Cook beans according to package directions. Drain. Place in prepared casserole.

Heat oil in a medium nonstick skillet over medium heat. Add green peppers. Cook, stirring frequently, until tender, about 8 minutes. Add small amounts of water if necessary (about a tablespoon at a time) to prevent sticking. Add peppers to casserole.

In a small bowl, combine remaining ingredients, mixing well. Pour over beans and peppers. Toss to combine.

Cover and bake 30 minutes, or until hot and bubbly.

---

Each serving provides:

**245 Calories**

| | | | |
|---|---|---|---|
| 2 | Bread Servings | 11 g | Protein |
| 2 | Vegetable Servings | 4 g | Fat (13% of calories) |
| 1/2 | Fat Serving | 44 g | Carbohydrate |
| 31 | Additional Calories | 146 mg | Sodium |
| | | 0 mg | Cholesterol |
| | | 20 g | Fiber |

# Cranberry Beans

*Served over rice, this dish creates a deliciously different taste sensation.*

*Makes 4 servings*

| | |
|---|---|
| 1 | cup cranberries |
| 1/2 | cup canned crushed pineapple (packed in juice), drained slightly |
| 1/2 | cup orange juice |
| 1/4 | cup plus 2 tablespoons red currant jelly |
| 1 | tablespoon Dijon mustard |
| 2 | teaspoons cornstarch |
| 1 | tablespoon water |
| 1 | 1-pound can kidney beans, rinsed and drained (This will yield approximately 10 ounces of beans.) |

In a small saucepan, combine cranberries, pineapple, orange juice, jelly, and mustard. Mix well. Bring to a boil over medium heat. Reduce heat slightly and simmer 10 minutes. Spoon mixture into a blender container and blend until smooth. Return to saucepan.

Combine cornstarch and water in a small bowl or custard cup. Mix until cornstarch is dissolved. Stir into cranberry mixture.

Add beans to saucepan and mix well. Bring to a boil over medium heat. Cook, stirring constantly, 3 to 4 minutes, until sauce has thickened.

---

Each serving provides:

**212 Calories**

| | | | |
|---|---|---|---|
| 1 1/4 | Protein Servings | 6 g | Protein |
| 3/4 | Fruit Serving | 1 g | Fat (3% of calories) |
| 73 | Additional Calories | 46 g | Carbohydrate |
| | | 242 mg | Sodium |
| | | 0 mg | Cholesterol |
| | | 6 g | Fiber |

# Barbecue Black-Eyed Peas

*This quick dish can be put together fast and is delicious spooned over brown rice or noodles.*

*Makes 6 servings*

| | |
|---|---|
| 2 | 1-pound cans black-eyed peas, rinsed and drained (This will yield approximately 20 ounces of beans.) |
| 2 | 8-ounce cans salt-free (or regular) tomato sauce |
| 1/3 | cup molasses |
| 1 | tablespoon plus 1 teaspoon minced onion flakes |
| 1 | teaspoon dry mustard |
| 1/2 | teaspoon paprika |
| 1/2 | teaspoon Worcestershire sauce |
| 1/8 | teaspoon garlic powder |
| | Salt and pepper to taste |

Preheat oven to 350°.

Spray a 1 1/2-quart baking dish with nonstick cooking spray.

Combine all ingredients, mixing well. Place in prepared baking dish.

Bake, covered, 1 hour.

---

Each serving provides:

**183 Calories**

| | | | |
|---|---|---|---|
| 1 1/2 | Protein Servings | 8 g | Protein |
| 1 1/4 | Vegetable Servings | 1 g | Fat (6% of calories) |
| 50 | Additional Calories | 37 g | Carbohydrate |
| | | 256 mg | Sodium |
| | | 0 mg | Cholesterol |
| | | 7 g | Fiber |

# Baked Lentils and Tomatoes

*Lentils are relatively quick-cooking legumes and, unlike most other beans, they don't have to be soaked before cooking. This delicious casserole makes a great accompaniment to pasta or noodles.*

*Makes 4 servings*

| | |
|---|---|
| 1 | cup lentils, uncooked (7 1/2 ounces) |
| 4 | cups boiling water |
| 2 | teaspoons vegetable oil |
| 1/2 | cup chopped onion |
| 1/2 | cup chopped celery |
| 1/2 | cup chopped green bell pepper |
| 1 | 1-pound can salt-free (or regular) tomatoes, chopped and undrained |
| 1 | teaspoon dried oregano |
| 1 | teaspoon dried basil |
| 1/4 | teaspoon garlic powder |
| | Salt and pepper to taste |
| 2 | tablespoons Italian-seasoned bread crumbs |
| 2 | teaspoons grated Parmesan cheese |

Add lentils to boiling water in a medium saucepan over medium heat. Cover, reduce heat to medium-low, and simmer 40 to 45 minutes, until tender. Drain.

Heat oil in a medium nonstick skillet over medium heat. Add onion, celery, and green pepper. Cook, stirring frequently, until vegetables are tender, about 5 minutes.

Preheat oven to 350°.

Spray a 1 1/2-quart casserole with nonstick cooking spray.

In a large bowl, combine lentils, onion mixture, tomatoes, and spices. Mix well. Spoon into prepared casserole. Combine bread crumbs and Parmesan cheese and sprinkle evenly over the top.

Cover and bake 30 minutes, then uncover and continue to bake 15 minutes more.

Each serving provides:

**258 Calories**

| | | | |
|---|---|---|---|
| 2 1/2 | Protein Servings | 17 g | Protein |
| 1 3/4 | Vegetable Servings | 4 g | Fat (13% of calories) |
| 1/2 | Fat Serving | 42 g | Carbohydrate |
| 20 | Additional Calories | 149 mg | Sodium |
| | | 1 mg | Cholesterol |
| | | 8 g | Fiber |

# Tangy Baked Kidney Beans

*Apples and honey add a sweetness to this unusual and very delicious bean dish.*

*Makes 4 servings*

| | |
|---|---|
| 2 | teaspoons vegetable oil |
| 1/2 | cup chopped onion |
| 1 | packet low-sodium instant chicken-flavored broth mix |
| 1 | small apple, unpeeled, coarsely shredded |
| 1/4 | cup tomato paste |
| 2 | tablespoons vinegar |
| 2 | teaspoons honey |
| 1/2 | teaspoon dry mustard |
| 1/2 | teaspoon dried oregano |
| 1 | 19-ounce can red or white kidney beans, rinsed and drained (This will yield approximately 12 ounces of beans.) |

Preheat oven to 350°.

Spray a 1-quart casserole with nonstick cooking spray.

Heat oil in a medium nonstick skillet over medium heat. Add onion and broth mix. Cook, stirring frequently, until onion is tender, about 5 minutes. Stir in apple and continue to cook, stirring, 2 minutes more. Add remaining ingredients, mixing well. Transfer mixture to prepared casserole.

Cover and bake 40 minutes, or until hot and bubbly.

---

Each serving provides:

**170 Calories**

| | | | |
|---|---|---|---|
| 1 1/2 | Protein Servings | 8 g | Protein |
| 3/4 | Vegetable Serving | 4 g | Fat (19% of calories) |
| 1/2 | Fat Serving | 28 g | Carbohydrate |
| 1/4 | Fruit Serving | 299 mg | Sodium |
| 13 | Additional Calories | 0 mg | Cholesterol |
| | | 7 g | Fiber |

# Italian Tofu "Meatballs"

*Although these don't taste anything like real meatballs, they're fun to serve and yes, they're even delicious over pasta.*

*Makes 4 servings*

| | |
|---|---|
| 1 | pound medium or firm tofu, sliced and drained well between layers of towels |
| 2 | slices whole wheat bread (1-ounce slices), crumbled |
| 2 | tablespoons minced onion flakes |
| 2 | egg whites |
| 1 | tablespoons dried parsley flakes |
| $1/4$ | teaspoon dried oregano |
| $1/8$ | teaspoon garlic powder |
| $1/8$ | teaspoon salt |
| $1/8$ | teaspoon pepper |
| 2 | cups reduced-fat, meatless spaghetti sauce |
| 1 | tablespoon grated Parmesan cheese |

Preheat oven to 375°.

Spray a shallow baking pan with nonstick cooking spray.

In a large bowl, combine all ingredients *except* spaghetti sauce and Parmesan cheese. Mix well, mashing the ingredients with a fork, until well blended. Shape mixture into small balls, squeezing tightly.

Place tofu balls in prepared pan in a single layer. Spoon half of the sauce evenly over tofu. Sprinkle with Parmesan cheese.

Bake, uncovered, 20 minutes.

Heat remaining sauce and serve it with the "meatballs."

---

Each serving provides:

**194 Calories**

| | | | |
|---|---|---|---|
| 2 | Protein Servings | 15 g | Protein |
| $1/2$ | Bread Serving | 7 g | Fat (31% of calories) |
| $3/4$ | Vegetable Serving | 21 g | Carbohydrate |
| $3/4$ | Fat Serving | 593 mg | Sodium |
| 18 | Additional Calories | 1 mg | Cholesterol |
| | | 4 g | Fiber |

# Kidney Beans Provençal

*Simple and straightforward, this dish can be thrown together in no time. It can be served as an entrée or side dish and either alone or over noodles or rice.*

*Makes 4 servings*

| | |
|---|---|
| 2 | teaspoons olive oil |
| 2 | cloves garlic, minced |
| 1/2 | cup chopped onion |
| 1 | cup chopped mushrooms |
| 1 | 1-pound can salt-free (or regular) tomatoes, chopped, drained (Reserve liquid.) |
| 1 | tablespoon cornstarch |
| 1 | teaspoon dried basil |
| 1 | teaspoon dried oregano |
| 1 | 19-ounce can white kidney beans, rinsed and drained (This will yield approximately 12 ounces of beans.) |
| 1 | tablespoon imitation bacon bits |
| 1 | tablespoon Italian-seasoned bread crumbs |
| 1 | teaspoon grated Parmesan cheese |

Preheat oven to 350°.

Spray a 1-quart casserole with nonstick cooking spray.

Heat oil in a large nonstick skillet over medium heat. Add garlic, onion, and mushrooms. Cook, stirring frequently, until vegetables are tender, 8 to 10 minutes. Add tomatoes.

Place reserved tomato liquid in a small bowl and add cornstarch, stirring until dissolved. Add to skillet along with basil and oregano. Cook, stirring, until mixture comes to a boil. Remove skillet from heat and stir in beans and bacon bits.

Spoon mixture into prepared casserole. Combine bread crumbs and Parmesan cheese and sprinkle evenly over the top.

Bake, uncovered, 30 minutes.

Each serving provides:

**178 Calories**

| | | | |
|---|---|---|---|
| 1 1/2 | Protein Servings | 10 g | Protein |
| 1 3/4 | Vegetable Servings | 4 g | Fat (20% of calories) |
| 1/2 | Fat Serving | 27 g | Carbohydrate |
| 25 | Additional Calories | 286 mg | Sodium |
| | | 0 mg | Cholesterol |
| | | 7 g | Fiber |

# Oriental Tofu Fish Cakes

*An unusually tasty combo. Both the tofu and the fish have mellow flavors that make them wonderfully adaptable to Oriental dishes.*

*Makes 6 servings*

### Fish Cakes

| | |
|---|---|
| 12 | ounces cooked sole or flounder, flaked |
| 1 | pound medium or firm tofu, sliced and drained well between layers of towels |
| 2 | slices whole wheat bread (1-ounce slices), crumbled |
| 2 | egg whites |
| 3 | tablespoons reduced-sodium soy sauce |
| 2 | tablespoons minced onion flakes |
| 1 | tablespoon dry sherry |
| 2 | teaspoons honey |
| 1/4 | teaspoon garlic powder |
| 1/4 | teaspoon ground ginger |
| 1/4 | cup plus 2 tablespoons dry bread crumbs |

### Sauce

| | |
|---|---|
| 1/4 | cup fruit-only peach spread |
| 1 | teaspoon reduced-sodium soy sauce |
| 1 | teaspoon vinegar |
| 1 | teaspoon water |
| 1/2 | teaspoon dry mustard |

Preheat oven to 400°.

Spray a baking sheet with nonstick cooking spray.

Combine all fish cake ingredients *except* dry bread crumbs in a large bowl. Mix well, mashing the ingredients with a fork until well blended. Shape into 6 patties, pressing firmly.

Dip each patty in bread crumbs and place on prepared baking sheet.

Bake 20 minutes, or until lightly browned.

While patties are baking, combine all sauce ingredients in a small bowl or custard cup and mix well. Add a little more water if a thinner sauce is desired.

Serve sauce over patties.

---

Each serving provides:

**230 Calories**

| | | | |
|---|---|---|---|
| 2¹⁄₄ | Protein Servings | 23 g | Protein |
| ¹⁄₂ | Bread Serving | 5 g | Fat (21% of calories) |
| ¹⁄₂ | Fruit Serving | 22 g | Carbohydrate |
| 45 | Additional Calories | 549 mg | Sodium |
| | | 39 mg | Cholesterol |
| | | 2 g | Fiber |

# Tofu Cheddar Squares

*One of our quickest, easiest favorites, this dish is a perfect introduction to tofu for people who have never tried it before. It makes a filling dinner or an elegant brunch dish.*

*Makes 6 servings*

| | |
|---|---|
| 1 | tablespoon margarine, melted |
| 3 | tablespoons dry bread crumbs |
| 12 | ounces medium or firm tofu, drained slightly |
| 1 | cup liquid egg substitute |
| 4 | ounces shredded reduced-fat Cheddar cheese (1 cup) |
| 2 | tablespoons minced onion flakes |
| 1 | tablespoon all-purpose flour |
| 2 | teaspoons honey |
| 1 | teaspoon dried parsley flakes |
| 1/2 | teaspoon dry mustard |
| | Salt and pepper to taste |

Preheat oven to 350°.

Spray an 8-inch square baking pan with nonstick cooking spray.

Spread margarine in bottom of prepared pan. Sprinkle evenly with 2 tablespoons of the bread crumbs. Bake 5 minutes.

In a blender container, combine tofu with remaining ingredients *except* remaining bread crumbs. Blend until smooth. Pour mixture over the baked crumbs. Sprinkle with remaining crumbs.

Bake 25 to 30 minutes, until set and lightly browned.

Let stand 5 minutes before serving.

---

Each serving provides:

**164 Calories**

| | | | |
|---|---|---|---|
| 2 1/2 | Protein Servings | 15 g | Protein |
| 1/2 | Fat Serving | 8 g | Fat (45% of calories) |
| 28 | Additional Calories | 8 g | Carbohydrate |
| | | 269 mg | Sodium |
| | | 13 mg | Cholesterol |
| | | 1 g | Fiber |

# Cauliflower-Tofu Bake

*This tasty side dish really shows how versatile tofu can be. It adds protein while it dresses up the cauliflower. Add a salad and a baked potato, and you have a perfect light dinner or lunch.*

*Makes 4 servings*

| | |
|---|---|
| 1 | 10-ounce package frozen cauliflower |
| 6 | ounces medium or firm tofu, sliced and drained well between layers of towels |
| 2 | ounces shredded reduced-fat Cheddar cheese (1/2 cup) |
| 1/4 | cup bottled fat-free Italian dressing |

Cook cauliflower according to package directions. Drain.
Preheat oven to 375°.
Spray a 1-quart baking dish with nonstick cooking spray.
Place cauliflower in prepared baking dish.
In a small bowl, combine remaining ingredients, mixing well.
Spoon over cauliflower.
Bake, uncovered, 20 minutes.

---

Each serving provides:

**96 Calories**

| | | | |
|---|---|---|---|
| 1 1/4 | Protein Servings | 9 g | Protein |
| 1 | Vegetable Serving | 5 g | Fat (44% of calories) |
| 15 | Additional Calories | 5 g | Carbohydrate |
| | | 275 mg | Sodium |
| | | 10 mg | Cholesterol |
| | | 2 g | Fiber |

# Tofu Parmigiana

*One of our favorite ways to enjoy tofu, these crispy breaded slices can be served with pasta or rice, or used to make a wonderful submarine sandwich.*

*Makes 4 servings*

1/4     cup plus 2 tablespoons Italian-seasoned bread crumbs
2       teaspoons dried oregano
        Pepper to taste
1       pound firm tofu, sliced 1/4-inch thick
1       8-ounce can salt-free (or regular) tomato sauce
1/2     teaspoon dried basil
1/8     teaspoon garlic powder
4       ounces shredded part-skim Mozzarella cheese
1       tablespoon grated Parmesan cheese

In a small, shallow bowl, combine bread crumbs, 1 teaspoon of the oregano, and pepper, mixing well.

Place tofu slices in a bowl of water. One at a time, remove slices from water and dip in crumb mixture. Pat with a fork to press crumbs to tofu.

Spray a large nonstick skillet with nonstick cooking spray. Heat over medium heat. Cook tofu slices in skillet until browned and crisp on both sides, spraying both sides of tofu evenly with nonstick cooking spray.

Preheat oven to 400°.

Spray a shallow baking pan with nonstick cooking spray.

Combine tomato sauce, basil, garlic powder, and remaining oregano in a small bowl. Mix well. Spread a thin layer of sauce in prepared pan. Top with tofu slices, arranging them in a single layer. Spoon remaining sauce over tofu. Top with both cheeses.

Bake, uncovered, 20 minutes.

---

Each serving provides:

**310 Calories**

| | | | |
|---|---|---|---|
| 3 1/4 | Protein Servings | 28 g | Protein |
| 1/2 | Bread Serving | 16 g | Fat (44% of calories) |
| 1 | Vegetable Serving | 18 g | Carbohydrate |
| 13 | Additional Calories | 482 mg | Sodium |
| | | 17 mg | Cholesterol |
| | | 1 g | Fiber |

# Silken Banana Fritters

*Sure to become a breakfast favorite, these moist, tender little pancakes are perfect drizzled with a little maple syrup and topped with sliced bananas and strawberries.*

*Makes 6 servings*
*(5 pancakes each serving)*

| | |
|---|---|
| 1 | 10-ounce package silken (or soft) tofu |
| 1/3 | cup nonfat dry milk |
| 1/2 | cup liquid egg substitute |
| 1/4 | cup plus 2 tablespoons all-purpose flour |
| 2 | tablespoons sugar |
| 1 | teaspoon baking powder |
| 1 | teaspoon vanilla extract |
| 1/4 | teaspoon banana extract |
| 1 | medium ripe banana, sliced |

Place all ingredients in a blender container and blend until smooth.

Spray a large nonstick skillet or griddle with nonstick cooking spray.

Preheat over medium heat.

Drop mixture onto skillet, using 1 tablespoonful for each pancake. Turn pancakes when edges appear dry and bottoms are lightly browned. Cook until lightly browned on both sides.

---

Each serving provides:

**119 Calories**

| | | | |
|---|---|---|---|
| 3/4 | Protein Serving | 8 g | Protein |
| 1/4 | Bread Serving | 1 g | Fat (10% of calories) |
| 1/4 | Fruit Serving | 19 g | Carbohydrate |
| 51 | Additional Calories | 167 mg | Sodium |
| | | 1 mg | Cholesterol |
| | | 1 g | Fiber |

# Beef, Pork, and Lamb

Although there's no need to give up meat when planning a healthy diet, most health professionals do recommend that you limit the amount of meat you consume. It's also important to choose the cuts of meat carefully, choosing the leanest cuts. Extra lean ground beef, flank steak, and pork tenderloin are among the leanest choices. In addition, it is important to trim away all visible fat before cooking.

Meat contains no fiber, so it is always important to serve meat with ample portions of whole grains and vegetables. To reduce your overall fat intake, we also recommend using smaller portions of meat and larger portions of grains and vegetables.

Even though a few of our meat dishes contain more than the recommended 30% of calories from fat, remember that it should be figured *by the day*, not the individual food, so if you eat a little more fat in one meal or one dish, you can compensate by eating less fat in the other meals or dishes. Ideally, you should evaluate your daily or weekly diet rather than single foods.

In the following recipes, we've lowered the fat content and increased the flavor by emphasizing the use of herbs and spices. We know these dishes will delight the entire family.

# Steak Diane

*A lot of fine restaurants serve this elegant dish, often prepared right at the table. Now you can prepare our version at home with a lot less fat and fuss.*

*Makes 4 servings*

| | |
|---|---|
| 1 | pound boneless beef top sirloin steaks, sliced 1/2-inch thick, all visible fat removed |
| | Salt and pepper to taste |
| 1 | teaspoon dry mustard |
| 1 | tablespoon plus 1 1/2 teaspoons lemon juice |
| 1 | tablespoon plus 1 1/2 teaspoons tub-style (not diet) margarine |
| 1 | tablespoon dry sherry |
| 2 | teaspoons dried chives |
| 1 | teaspoon Worcestershire sauce |

Using a meat mallet, pound the steaks to 1/4-inch thick. Sprinkle each side with salt, pepper, and a little of the dry mustard. Rub the seasonings into the meat.

Preheat broiler.

Place meat on a rack in a broiler pan. Broil until meat is lightly browned on each side, turning meat once. Place meat on a serving dish.

While meat is browning, heat remaining ingredients to boiling in a small skillet over medium-low heat.

Pour sauce over meat and serve.

---

Each serving provides:

**214 Calories**

| | | | |
|---|---|---|---|
| 3 | Protein Servings | 26 g | Protein |
| 1/2 | Fat Serving | 11 g | Fat (47% of calories) |
| 5 | Additional Calories | 1 g | Carbohydrate |
| | | 129 mg | Sodium |
| | | 76 mg | Cholesterol |
| | | 0 g | Fiber |

# Teriyaki Flank Steak

*This is our very favorite dish for cookouts. We usually serve it with a tossed salad, the Favorite Rice Casserole on page 229 and a pile of steamed fresh green beans.*

*Makes 6 servings*

| | |
|---|---|
| 1 | 1 1/2-pound flank steak |
| 1/4 | cup reduced-sodium soy sauce |
| 1/4 | cup dry sherry |
| 1/4 | teaspoon garlic powder |
| 1/4 | teaspoon ground ginger |

Score meat diagonally on both sides, making several cuts about 1/4-inch deep. Place meat in a shallow bowl or baking dish.

Combine remaining ingredients and pour over meat. Marinate in the refrigerator 4 to 5 hours, turning meat several times.

Preheat broiler.

Place meat on a broiler rack and broil until done to taste. Turn meat several times while cooking and baste with marinade.

To slice, tilt knife blade slightly and slice meat, across the grain, into paper-thin slices.

---

Each serving provides:

**198 Calories**

| | | | |
|---|---|---|---|
| 3 | Protein Servings | 24 g | Protein |
| 8 | Additional Calories | 9 g | Fat (43% of calories) |
| | | 2 g | Carbohydrate |
| | | 471 mg | Sodium |
| | | 57 mg | Cholesterol |
| | | 0 g | Fiber |

# Chinese Pepper Steak

*A favorite in Chinese restaurants, this delectable dish is usually served over rice. The meat is best when sliced very thin, which is easier to do if it is partially frozen.*

*Makes 6 servings*

| | |
|---|---|
| 2 | teaspoons vegetable oil |
| 1 1/4 | pounds boneless beef top round steak, sliced across the grain into very thin strips |
| 1/2 | cup chopped onion |
| 3 | cloves garlic, finely chopped |
| 1 | packet low-sodium instant beef-flavored broth mix |
| 1 1/4 | cups water |
| 1 | 1-pound can salt-free (or regular) tomatoes, chopped and drained |
| 2 | large, green bell peppers, sliced vertically into 1/2-inch strips |
| 1 | tablespoon plus 1 teaspoon cornstarch dissolved in 1/4 cup water |
| 2 | tablespoons reduced-sodium soy sauce |
| 1/8 | teaspoon pepper |

Heat oil in a large nonstick skillet over medium-high heat. Add beef. Cook until browned, then remove beef from skillet and place in a covered bowl to keep warm.

Add onion and garlic to skillet. Cook, stirring frequently, about 3 minutes, until onion starts to brown. Return meat to skillet. Add broth mix, water, tomatoes, and green pepper. Reduce heat to medium, cover skillet, and simmer 5 minutes, stirring occasionally.

Combine cornstarch mixture, soy sauce, and pepper. Add to skillet. Reduce heat to medium-low and cook, stirring, until mixture has thickened slightly and is hot and bubbly, about 3 minutes.

---

Each serving provides:

**180 Calories**

| | | | |
|---|---|---|---|
| 2 1/2 | Protein Servings | 23 g | Protein |
| 1 1/2 | Vegetable Servings | 5 g | Fat (25% of calories) |
| 1/4 | Fat Serving | 10 g | Carbohydrate |
| 12 | Additional Calories | 262 mg | Sodium |
| | | 54 mg | Cholesterol |
| | | 2 g | Fiber |

# Chili Meat Loaf

*Chili powder and garlic add a wonderful zip to this easy dish. Serve it with a baked potato topped with nonfat sour cream and salsa, add a tossed salad, and dinner is complete. The leftovers make great sandwiches.*

*Makes 6 servings*

| | |
|---|---|
| 1 | pound lean ground beef (10% fat) |
| 3 | slices whole wheat bread (1-ounce slices), crumbled |
| 1 | cup salsa (hot or mild) |
| 1 | egg white |
| 2 | tablespoons grated onion |
| 1 | tablespoon prepared yellow mustard |
| 1 | teaspoon chili powder (or more to taste) |
| 1/2 | teaspoon dry mustard |
| 1/4 | teaspoon garlic powder |

Preheat oven to 350°.

In a large bowl, combine beef with remaining ingredients, mixing well. Shape mixture into a loaf. Place the loaf on a rack in a shallow baking pan.

Bake, uncovered, 1 hour.

Each serving provides:

**186 Calories**

| | | | |
|---|---|---|---|
| 2 | Protein Servings | 18 g | Protein |
| 1/2 | Bread Serving | 8 g | Fat (41% of calories) |
| 3/4 | Vegetable Serving | 10 g | Carbohydrate |
| 3 | Additional Calories | 602 mg | Sodium |
| | | 47 mg | Cholesterol |
| | | 1 g | Fiber |

# Meat Loaf Florentine

*A delightful filling of spinach and cheese awaits you as you dig into this moist meat loaf. Using bread as a "filler" lets you have bigger portions with less fat per serving.*

*Makes 6 servings*

| | |
|---|---|
| 1 | 8-ounce can salt-free (or regular) tomato sauce |
| 1 | teaspoon dried oregano |
| 1 | teaspoon dried basil |
| 1/4 | teaspoon garlic powder |
| 1 | pound lean ground beef (10% fat) |
| 3 | slices whole wheat bread (1-ounce slices), crumbled |
| 1 | egg white |
| | Salt and pepper to taste |
| 1 | 10-ounce package frozen chopped spinach, thawed and drained (Press most of the water out, but do not squeeze until too dry.) |
| 4 | ounces shredded part-skim Mozzarella cheese (1 cup) |
| 1 | tablespoon grated Parmesan cheese |

Preheat oven to 350°.

In a small bowl, combine tomato sauce, oregano, basil, and garlic powder.

In a large bowl, combine beef, bread crumbs, egg white, salt, pepper, and *half* of the tomato sauce mixture. Mix well. Spread meat on a sheet of wax paper, forming a rectangle about 8 × 10 inches.

Spread spinach over *half* of the meat. Top with Mozzarella cheese, still covering only half of the meat. Fold meat over so that spinach and cheese are inside. Pinch edges of meat to seal.

Place the meat on a rack in a shallow baking pan. Top with remaining tomato sauce. Sprinkle with Parmesan cheese.

Bake, uncovered, 1 hour.

---

Each serving provides:

**245 Calories**

| | | | |
|---|---|---|---|
| 2³/₄ | Protein Servings | 24 g | Protein |
| ¹/₂ | Bread Serving | 12 g | Fat (42% of calories) |
| 1¹/₄ | Vegetable Servings | 12 g | Carbohydrate |
| 17 | Additional Calories | 284 mg | Sodium |
| | | 59 mg | Cholesterol |
| | | 3 g | Fiber |

# Meat Sauce and Spaghetti Squash

*Spaghetti squash is a fun vegetable that is so often neglected. Its mild flavor and noodle-like texture make it a perfect accompaniment to the meat sauce in this scrumptious casserole.*

*Makes 4 servings*

| | |
|---|---|
| 1/2 | pound lean ground beef (10% fat) |
| 1 | cup chopped onion |
| 3 | cloves garlic, finely chopped |
| 2 | 8-ounce cans salt-free (or regular) tomato sauce |
| 2 | teaspoons dried oregano |
| 1 | teaspoon dried basil |
| | Dash cayenne pepper |
| 4 | cups cooked, drained spaghetti squash* |
| 1 | tablespoon grated Parmesan cheese |

Heat a large nonstick skillet over medium heat. Add beef, onion, and garlic. Cook, stirring frequently, until meat is browned. Break up the meat with a spoon while cooking. Spoon mixture onto a paper towel-lined plate to drain. Return meat to skillet.

Add tomato sauce, oregano, basil, and pepper. Cover skillet and cook 10 minutes, stirring occasionally.

Preheat oven to 375°.

Spray a 2-quart casserole with nonstick cooking spray.
Remove skillet from heat and stir in squash, tossing to blend well.
Spoon mixture into prepared casserole. Sprinkle with Parmesan cheese.
Bake, uncovered, 20 minutes.

*To cook spaghetti squash, cut squash lengthwise, remove seeds, and place cut-side down in a shallow baking pan containing 1 inch of water. Bake at 350° for 45 minutes, or until squash is tender. Remove squash from pan and drain cut-side down. Pull strands free with a fork.

Each serving provides:

**212 Calories**

| | | | | |
|---|---|---|---|---|
| 1 1/2 | Protein Servings | 15 g | Protein | |
| 4 1/2 | Vegetable Servings | 7 g | Fat (30% of calories) | |
| 8 | Additional Calories | 24 g | Carbohydrate | |
| | | 118 mg | Sodium | |
| | | 36 mg | Cholesterol | |
| | | 2 g | Fiber | |

# French Herbed Pork Roast

*This elegant dish is made with pork tenderloin, which is one of the leanest cuts of pork. This tender roast can also be made on a grill.*

*Makes 4 servings*

| | |
|---|---|
| $1/2$ | cup water |
| 1 | packet instant low-sodium chicken- or onion-flavored broth mix |
| $1/8$ | teaspoon dried rosemary, crumbled |
| $1/8$ | teaspoon dried oregano |
| $1/8$ | teaspoon dried thyme |
| $1/8$ | teaspoon garlic powder |
| $1/8$ | teaspoon salt |
| $1/8$ | teaspoon pepper |
| 1 | bay leaf |
| 1 | 1-pound boneless lean pork tenderloin, trimmed of all visible fat |

In a small bowl, combine all ingredients *except* meat. Pour into a large plastic bag. Add meat to bag and close tightly. Set bag in a shallow bowl and refrigerate overnight, turning bag over several times.

Preheat oven to 325°.

Remove meat from bag and place it on a rack in a shallow roasting pan.

Bake, uncovered, 45 minutes to 1 hour, or until meat is done.

---

Each serving provides:

**142 Calories**

| | | | |
|---|---|---|---|
| 3 | Protein Servings | 24 g | Protein |
| 3 | Additional Calories | 4 g | Fat (27% of calories) |
| | | 0 g | Carbohydrate |
| | | 81 mg | Sodium |
| | | 67 mg | Cholesterol |
| | | 0 g | Fiber |

# Pork Chops Italiano

*Makes 4 servings*

| | |
|---|---|
| 1 | pound boneless center-cut loin pork chops, trimmed of all visible fat |
| 2 | cups sliced mushrooms |
| 2 | medium, green bell peppers, cut into thin strips |
| 1/2 | cup chopped onion |
| 2 | 8-ounce cans salt-free (or regular) tomato sauce |
| 1/2 | teaspoon dried oregano |
| 1/2 | teaspoon dried basil |
| 1/4 | teaspoon garlic powder |

Lightly spray a large nonstick skillet with nonstick cooking spray. Heat over medium heat. Add chops and brown on both sides. Transfer chops to a shallow baking dish that has been sprayed with nonstick spray.

Preheat oven to 350°.

Place mushrooms, green pepper, and onion in skillet. Cook, stirring frequently, 5 minutes. Add remaining ingredients, mixing well. Continue to cook, stirring frequently, 5 more minutes. Spoon mixture evenly over chops.

Bake, uncovered, 45 minutes to1 hour, or until chops are done.

---

Each serving provides:

**299 Calories**

| | | | |
|---|---|---|---|
| 3 | Protein Servings | 26 g | Protein |
| 4 1/4 | Vegetable Servings | 15 g | Fat (46% of calories) |
| | | 15 g | Carbohydrate |
| | | 96 mg | Sodium |
| | | 76 mg | Cholesterol |
| | | 3 g | Fiber |

# Deviled Pork Chops

*Tasty and tangy, these delectable chops can also be made on the grill for a terrific summertime barbecue. Add a baked potato (also great on the grill) and a tossed salad, and enjoy.*

*Makes 4 servings*

| | |
|---|---|
| 1 | pound boneless center-cut loin pork chops, trimmed of all visible fat |
| 2 | tablespoons Dijon mustard |
| 1 | tablespoon Worcestershire sauce |
| 1 | teaspoon vegetable oil |
| 1/4 | teaspoon garlic powder |

Preheat broiler.

Place chops in a shallow pan that has been sprayed with nonstick cooking spray.

Combine remaining ingredients in a small bowl. Mix well. Spread *half* of the mixture on one side of the chops. Broil 3 inches from heat for about 5 minutes, or until chops are lightly browned and cooked through.

Turn meat and spread with remaining mixture. Broil until meat is done.

---

Each serving provides:

**197 Calories**

| | | | |
|---|---|---|---|
| 3 | Protein Servings | 26 g | Protein |
| 1/4 | Fat Serving | 8 g | Fat (42% of calories) |
| | | 1 g | Carbohydrate |
| | | 272 mg | Sodium |
| | | 70 mg | Cholesterol |
| | | 0 g | Fiber |

# Italian Grilled Pork Kabobs

*Delicious and colorful, these kabobs are perfect over rice. Feel free to add other vegetables to the skewers, such as onions and slices of corn on the cob.*

*Makes 4 servings*

1/3     cup fat-free Italian dressing
1/2     teaspoon dried oregano
1       pound boneless center cut loin pork chops, trimmed of all visible fat, cut into 1 1/2-inch cubes
2       medium zucchini, unpeeled, cut into 1- to 1 1/2-inch cubes
2       medium red or green bell peppers, cut into 1-inch squares

In a medium bowl, combine dressing and oregano. Add pork. Marinate in the refrigerator 4 to 5 hours, stirring occasionally.

Preheat broiler.

Remove meat from marinade. Alternately thread pork, zucchini, and peppers on 4 skewers. Place on a broiler rack.

Broil 3 inches from heat for about 10 minutes, or until pork is done. Turn skewers frequently and baste with any remaining marinade while broiling.

---

Each serving provides:

### 203 Calories

| | | | |
|---|---|---|---|
| 3 | Protein Servings | 27 g | Protein |
| 2 | Vegetable Servings | 7 g | Fat (32% of calories) |
| 7 | Additional Calories | 7 g | Carbohydrate |
| | | 246 mg | Sodium |
| | | 70 mg | Cholesterol |
| | | 1 g | Fiber |

# Pork Oriental

*Tender slices of pork loin, simmered in a delectable soy and pineapple sauce, make a perfect dish to serve with the Oriental Fried Rice on page 228.*

*Makes 4 servings*

| | |
|---|---|
| 2 | teaspoons vegetable oil |
| 2 | medium, green bell peppers, cut into thin strips |
| 1 | pound thinly sliced pork loin, trimmed of all visible fat |
| 2 | tablespoons reduced-sodium soy sauce |
| 2 | tablespoons sugar |
| 2 | tablespoons very finely minced onion |
| | Bottled hot pepper sauce to taste |
| 1 | cup canned pineapple chunks (packed in juice), drained (Reserve 1/4 cup of the juice.) |

Heat oil in a large nonstick skillet over medium heat. Add peppers and cook, stirring frequently, until slightly tender.

Add pork. Cook, turning pork frequently, until it is white on both sides.

Reduce heat to medium-low and add remaining ingredients to skillet, including the reserved pineapple juice. Cover and simmer until pork is cooked through, about 8 to 10 minutes.

---

Each serving provides:

**263 Calories**

|   |   |   |   |
|---|---|---|---|
| 3 | Protein Servings | 26 g | Protein |
| 1 | Vegetable Serving | 9 g | Fat (30% of calories) |
| 1/2 | Fat Serving | 20 g | Carbohydrate |
| 1/2 | Fruit Serving | 361 mg | Sodium |
| 24 | Additional Calories | 67 mg | Cholesterol |
|  |  | 1 g | Fiber |

# Grilled Ham Steak

*The smoky ham flavor is a perfect match for the sweet preserves in this easy meal. Use any flavor preserves you like, and whether made in the broiler or on the outside grill, it's sure to be a hit.*

*Makes 6 servings*

1/2     cup canned crushed pineapple (packed in juice), drained
1/4     cup fruit-only spread (choose any flavor; our favorites are
          peach, apricot, or raspberry)
1       tablespoon lemon juice
2       teaspoons dry mustard
1       teaspoon grated fresh orange peel
1/2     teaspoon cornstarch
1       1-pound slice boneless ham, cut 1 1/2 inches thick, trimmed of
          all visible fat

In a small saucepan, combine all ingredients *except* ham. Bring to a boil over medium heat, stirring constantly. Continue to cook, stirring, 2 minutes. Remove from heat.

Broil ham to desired doneness on both sides. Spread preserve mixture over top. Return to broiler until hot and bubbly.

---

Each serving provides:

**144 Calories**

| | | | |
|---|---|---|---|
| 2 | Protein Servings | 15 g | Protein |
| 3/4 | Fruit Serving | 4 g | Fat (25% of calories) |
| 6 | Additional Calories | 12 g | Carbohydrate |
| | | 1082 mg | Sodium |
| | | 36 mg | Cholesterol |
| | | 0 g | Fiber |

# Ham Barbecue on a Bun

*This is a perfect Sunday football supper. Add a bowl of soup and a salad, and enjoy the game.*

*Makes 6 sandwiches*

| | |
|---|---|
| 1 | teaspoon vegetable oil |
| 1 | cup chopped onion |
| 3 | cloves garlic, finely chopped |
| 1 | 8-ounce can salt-free (or regular) tomato sauce |
| 1/4 | cup vinegar |
| 1 | tablespoon plus 1 teaspoon lemon juice |
| 2 | tablespoons prepared yellow mustard |
| 2 | tablespoons firmly packed brown sugar |
| 1 | teaspoon Worcestershire sauce |
| | Bottled hot pepper sauce to taste |
| 1 | pound cooked boneless ham, sliced paper-thin, all visible fat removed |
| 6 | 2-ounce hamburger buns |

Heat oil in a large nonstick skillet over medium heat. Add onion and garlic. Cook, stirring frequently, until onion is tender, about 5 minutes.

Add remaining ingredients *except* ham and buns. Reduce heat to medium-low and cook, stirring frequently, 5 minutes. Add ham and heat through.

Serve on buns.

---

Each serving provides:

**328 Calories**

| 2 1/2 | Protein Servings | 22 g | Protein |
|---|---|---|---|
| 2 | Bread Servings | 8 g | Fat (23% of calories) |
| 1 | Vegetable Serving | 41 g | Carbohydrate |
| 33 | Additional Calories | 1315 mg | Sodium |
| | | 40 mg | Cholesterol |
| | | 2 g | Fiber |

# Roast Leg of Lamb

*The rosemary adds a touch of distinction to this delicious dish. It's a favorite company dish and goes well with mashed potatoes, steamed broccoli, and a tossed salad. Add a light fruit dessert, and you have a lowfat meal fit for royalty.*

*Makes 10 servings*

| | |
|---|---|
| 1 | 6-pound leg of lamb |
| 6 | large cloves garlic, peeled, cut in half lengthwise |
| 2 | teaspoons seasoned salt |
| 1 | teaspoon dried rosemary, crumbled |
| 1 | teaspoon dried thyme |
| $1/2$ | teaspoon onion powder |
| $1/4$ | teaspoon pepper |
| $1/4$ | teaspoon garlic powder |

Preheat oven to 450°.

Place lamb on a rack in a shallow roasting pan.

With a sharp knife, make twelve 1-inch-deep cuts in lamb. Place a garlic half in each cut.

Combine seasonings and rub into meat, covering entire surface.

Place pan in oven. Reduce heat to 325°.

Roast 2 to $2^1/2$ hours, or until done to taste.

Remove all visible fat before slicing. Serve 3 ounces of sliced lamb per portion, reserving remaining lamb for another time.

---

Each serving provides:

**167 Calories**

|   |   |   |   |
|---|---|---|---|
| 3 | Protein Servings | 24 g | Protein |
| | | 7 g | Fat (37% of calories) |
| | | 1 g | Carbohydrate |
| | | 99 mg | Sodium |
| | | 76 mg | Cholesterol |
| | | 0 g | Fiber |

# Pasta

Everyone's favorite, pasta is a versatile food that can change dramatically, taking on a new character with the addition of each delectable sauce. Pasta is high in carbohydrates, which is our bodies' main source of fuel. In fact, athletes are now turning to pasta for meals rather than the heavy, high-protein meals they used to consume.

We've avoided butter and cream sauces in our recipes, proving to our mothers that it isn't the pasta that adds pounds but what we put on top of it. In addition, when noodles are called for, we always choose the yolk-free variety, thereby reducing the amount of cholesterol in the dishes. We also recommend trying whole wheat pasta for a dish that's higher in carbohydrates, vitamins, minerals, and fiber than the original version.

With its variety of shapes and colors, this nutritious food can be an important part of a healthful diet.

# Greek Eggplant and Macaroni Casserole

*Similar to the Greek favorite* pastitsio, *this delectable casserole has layers of cheese, macaroni, and a thick tomato and eggplant sauce.*

*Makes 6 servings*

| | |
|---|---|
| 2 | teaspoons olive oil |
| 1 | medium eggplant, peeled and cut into 1/2-inch cubes (about 1 pound) |
| 1/2 | cup chopped onion |
| 1 | 6-ounce can tomato paste |
| 1/2 | cup dry white wine |
| 1/4 | cup water |
| 1 | teaspoon dried basil |
| 1/4 | teaspoon ground cinnamon |
| 1/4 | teaspoon salt |
| 8 | ounces elbow macaroni, uncooked |
| 1/2 | cup liquid egg substitute |
| 1 1/3 | cups lowfat (1%) cottage cheese |
| 2 | tablespoons grated Parmesan cheese |

Heat oil in a large nonstick skillet over medium heat. Add eggplant and onion. Cook 10 minutes, stirring frequently. Add small amounts of water if necessary (a few tablespoons at a time) to prevent sticking. Reduce heat to low.

Stir in tomato paste, wine, water, basil, cinnamon, and salt. Cover and simmer 15 minutes, stirring occasionally.

While eggplant is cooking, cook macaroni according to package directions. Drain.

Preheat oven to 350°.

Spray a 9-inch square baking pan with nonstick cooking spray.

In a small bowl, combine egg substitute and cheeses.

Spread 1 cup of the eggplant mixture in bottom of prepared pan. Top with macaroni, then cheese, and then remaining eggplant mixture.

Bake, uncovered, 30 minutes.

Each serving provides:

**267 Calories**

| | | | |
|---|---|---|---|
| 1 | Protein Serving | 16 g | Protein |
| 1³/₄ | Bread Servings | 4 g | Fat (13% of calories) |
| 2¹/₂ | Vegetable Servings | 41 g | Carbohydrate |
| ¹/₄ | Fat Serving | 588 mg | Sodium |
| 32 | Additional Calories | 3 mg | Cholesterol |
| | | 3 g | Fiber |

# Cheese and Noodle Casserole

*Served with a colorful tossed salad, this casserole makes a perfect dish for a luncheon or light dinner.*

*Makes 4 servings*

| | |
|---|---|
| 6 | ounces medium or thin noodles (yolk-free), uncooked |
| 1 | cup lowfat (1%) cottage cheese |
| 3 | ounces reduced-fat Cheddar cheese (3/4 cup) |
| 3/4 | cup plain nonfat yogurt |
| 2 | tablespoons grated Parmesan cheese |
| 1 | tablespoon minced onion flakes |
| 1/4 | teaspoon garlic powder |
| 1/2 | teaspoon Worcestershire sauce |
| 1 | 8-ounce can mushroom pieces, drained |

Cook noodles according to package directions. Drain.

Preheat oven to 350°.

Spray an 8-inch square baking pan with nonstick cooking spray. Place noodles in prepared pan.

In a blender container, combine cottage cheese, Cheddar cheese, yogurt, *half* of the Parmesan cheese, onion flakes, garlic powder, and Worcestershire sauce. Blend until smooth. Stir in mushrooms. Pour over noodles and mix together lightly.

Sprinkle remaining Parmesan cheese over noodles.

Bake, uncovered, 25 to 30 minutes, until hot and lightly browned.

---

Each serving provides:

**298 Calories**

| | | | |
|---|---|---|---|
| 1 3/4 | Protein Servings | 24 g | Protein |
| 2 | Bread Servings | 6 g | Fat (19% of calories) |
| 1/2 | Vegetable Serving | 37 g | Carbohydrate |
| 1/4 | Milk Serving | 621 mg | Sodium |
| 15 | Additional Calories | 20 mg | Cholesterol |
| | | 1 g | Fiber |

# Parmesan Noodles

*Turn noodles into an easy side dish by simply tossing them with a few ingredients.*

*Makes 6 servings*

6       ounces medium noodles (yolk-free), uncooked (about 1 1/2
        cups)
1       tablespoon plus 1 teaspoon tub-style (not diet) margarine
1       tablespoon plus 1 teaspoon grated Parmesan cheese
1/8     teaspoon garlic powder
        Freshly ground black pepper to taste (lots!)

Cook noodles according to package directions. Drain.
Place noodles in a serving bowl and add remaining ingredients.
Toss until blended.

---

Each serving provides:

**127 Calories**

| 1 1/4 | Bread Servings | 4 g | Protein |
| 1/2 | Fat Serving | 3 g | Fat (24% of calories) |
| 20 | Additional Calories | 20 g | Carbohydrate |
| | | 61 mg | Sodium |
| | | 1 mg | Cholesterol |
| | | 1 g | Fiber |

# Macaroni with Cheddar and Tomatoes

*An easy dinner awaits you when you alternate layers of macaroni, Cheddar cheese, and stewed tomatoes. If you like spicy food, add a finely minced jalapeño pepper to one of the tomato layers.*

*Makes 4 servings*

| | |
|---|---|
| 1 | cup elbow macaroni, uncooked (4 ounces) |
| 1 | 1-pound can salt-free (or regular) stewed tomatoes, drained |
| 4 | ounces shredded reduced-fat Cheddar cheese (1 cup) |
| 1 | tablespoon grated Parmesan cheese |
| 1/4 | teaspoon oregano |
| 1/4 | teaspoon dried basil |
| 1/8 | teaspoon pepper |
| 1 | tablespoon all-purpose flour |
| 1 | cup evaporated skim milk |
| 2 | tablespoons dry bread crumbs |

Cook macaroni according to package directions. Drain.

Preheat oven to 375°.

Spray a 1-quart casserole with nonstick cooking spray.

Place *half* of the macaroni in the prepared baking dish. Top with *half each* of the stewed tomatoes, Cheddar, Parmesan, oregano, basil, and pepper.

Repeat, using remaining tomatoes, cheeses, and spices.

Place flour in a small bowl. Gradually add milk, stirring briskly to avoid lumps. Pour milk over casserole.

Sprinkle with bread crumbs. Spray lightly and evenly with nonstick cooking spray.

Bake, uncovered, 35 minutes, or until set.

Let stand 5 minutes before serving.

---

Each serving provides:

**295 Calories**

| | | | |
|---|---|---|---|
| 1 1/4 | Protein Servings | 20 g | Protein |
| 1 1/4 | Bread Servings | 7 g | Fat (20% of calories) |
| 1 | Vegetable Serving | 40 g | Carbohydrate |
| 1/2 | Milk Serving | 368 mg | Sodium |
| 49 | Additional Calories | 24 mg | Cholesterol |
| | | 3 g | Fiber |

# Pasta à Pesto

*This delicious side dish has always been one of our family's favorite ways to enjoy pasta. Any leftovers make a delicious cold salad.*

*Makes 4 servings*

| | |
|---|---|
| 4 | ounces thin spaghetti, uncooked |
| 1 | tablespoon plus 1 teaspoon vegetable oil |
| 1 | packet low-sodium instant chicken- or vegetable-flavored broth mix |
| 1/4 | cup water |
| 2 | tablespoons grated Parmesan cheese |
| 1 | tablespoon dried parsley flakes |
| 1 | tablespoon dried basil |
| 1 | clove garlic, chopped |
| 1/8 | teaspoon ground nutmeg |

Break pasta strands in half and cook according to package directions. Drain.

While pasta is cooking, combine remaining ingredients in a blender container. Blend until smooth.

Place hot pasta in a serving bowl. Add herb mixture and toss. Serve right away.

---

Each serving provides:

**164 Calories**

| | | | |
|---|---|---|---|
| 1 1/4 | Bread Servings | 5 g | Protein |
| 1 | Fat Serving | 6 g | Fat (32% of calories) |
| 24 | Additional Calories | 23 g | Carbohydrate |
| | | 51 mg | Sodium |
| | | 2 mg | Cholesterol |
| | | 1 g | Fiber |

# Pacific Pasta Sauce with Salmon

*In the Pacific Northwest, where salmon is plentiful, this tender fish is added to lots of dishes—even pasta. This one starts with already prepared sauce. Choose your favorite lowfat brand and just add the rest.*

*Makes 6 servings*
*(3/4 cup each serving)*

| | |
|---|---|
| 1 | 28-ounce jar reduced-fat, meatless spaghetti sauce |
| 1 | tablespoon dried parsley flakes |
| 1 | teaspoon grated fresh lemon peel |
| | Pepper to taste |
| 1 | 14¹/₂-ounce can salmon, drained and flaked, skin and bones discarded (12 ounces) |

Combine spaghetti sauce, parsley, lemon peel, and pepper in a medium saucepan. Bring to a boil over medium heat. Reduce heat to medium-low, cover, and simmer 15 minutes. Add salmon.

Serve over pasta or noodles.

---

Each serving provides:

**141 Calories**

| | | | |
|---|---|---|---|
| 2 | Protein Servings | 16 g | Protein |
| 1¹/₂ | Vegetable Servings | 4 g | Fat (25% of calories) |
| ¹/₂ | Fat Serving | 11 g | Carbohydrate |
| | | 716 mg | Sodium |
| | | 24 mg | Cholesterol |
| | | 2 g | Fiber |

# Mediterranean Pasta Sauce with Artichokes

*If you love artichoke hearts, this one is for you. The sauce is thick, chunky, and just loaded with the flavors of the Mediterranean. Serve it over pasta or any cooked grain.*

*Makes 6 servings*
*(3/4 cup each serving)*

| | |
|---|---|
| 2 | teaspoons vegetable oil |
| 1 | cup chopped onion |
| 1 | cup chopped green bell pepper |
| 3 | cloves garlic, finely chopped |
| 1 | 1-pound can artichoke hearts, drained |
| 6 | large, black pitted olives, sliced |
| 1 | 26-ounce jar reduced-fat, meatless spaghetti sauce (3 cups) |
| 1 | teaspoon dill weed |

Heat oil in a medium saucepan over medium heat. Add onion, green pepper, and garlic. Cook, stirring frequently, 8 to 10 minutes, or until vegetables are tender. Add small amounts of water (about a tablespoon at a time) to prevent sticking.

Add remaining ingredients, mixing well.

When sauce boils, reduce heat to medium-low, cover, and simmer 10 minutes.

---

Each serving provides:

**102 Calories**

| | | | |
|---|---|---|---|
| 2³/4 | Vegetable Servings | 4 g | Protein |
| ¹/2 | Fat Serving | 3 g | Fat (21% of calories) |
| | | 17 g | Carbohydrate |
| | | 423 mg | Sodium |
| | | 0 mg | Cholesterol |
| | | 3 g | Fiber |

# Quick 'n' Chunky Tomato Sauce

*Canned stewed tomatoes form the base for this tangy sauce. Throw in a little wine and a few spices, cook the pasta, and dinner is ready.*

*Makes 6 servings*
*(²/₃ cup each serving)*

| | |
|---|---|
| 2 | 14¹/₂-ounce cans salt-free (or regular) stewed tomatoes |
| ¹/₃ | cup tomato paste |
| ¹/₄ | cup dry red wine |
| 1 | teaspoon sugar |
| 1 | teaspoon dried basil |
| ¹/₂ | teaspoon dried oregano |
| 2 | tablespoons grated Parmesan cheese |

In a medium saucepan, combine all ingredients except Parmesan cheese. Bring to a boil over medium heat, stirring frequently. Reduce heat to medium-low, cover, and simmer 15 minutes.

Spoon sauce over cooked pasta. Sprinkle each serving with 1 teaspoon of the Parmesan cheese.

---

Each serving provides:

**66 Calories**

| | | | |
|---|---|---|---|
| 2¹/₂ | Vegetable Servings | 3 g | Protein |
| 21 | Additional Calories | 1 g | Fat (11% of calories) |
| | | 13 g | Carbohydrate |
| | | 169 mg | Sodium |
| | | 1 mg | Cholesterol |
| | | 4 g | Fiber |

# Pasta Sauce with Rosemary and Lemon

*You feel the wonderful tang on your lips when you enjoy this tasty sauce. Spoon it over your favorite pasta, add a side dish of steamed broccoli and yellow peppers, and your dinner is colorful as well as delicious.*

*Makes 4 servings*
*(¹/2 cup each serving)*

| | |
|---|---|
| 1 | 1-pound can salt-free (or regular) tomatoes, chopped and undrained |
| 1 | 8-ounce can salt-free (or regular) tomato sauce |
| 1 | tablespoon tomato paste |
| 2 | cloves garlic, crushed |
| ¹/2 | teaspoon dried rosemary, crumbled |
| ¹/2 | teaspoon grated fresh lemon peel |
| ¹/2 | teaspoon sugar |
| ¹/4 | teaspoon dried basil |
| ¹/8 | teaspoon pepper |
| | Salt to taste |

Combine all ingredients in a medium saucepan. Bring to a boil over medium heat. Reduce heat to medium-low, cover, and simmer 30 minutes.

---

Each serving provides:

**51 Calories**

| | | | |
|---|---|---|---|
| 2 | Vegetable Servings | 2 g | Protein |
| 2 | Additional Calories | 1 g | Fat (9% of calories) |
| | | 11 g | Carbohydrate |
| | | 60 mg | Sodium |
| | | 0 mg | Cholesterol |
| | | 2 g | Fiber |

# Fruit and Noodle Kugel

*Noodle puddings have so many variations. Some are sweet, others are not so sweet. Some contain fruit, others do not. This one is sweet and it's filled with fruit. It can be served as a side dish, a brunch entrée, or even a delicious dessert.*

*Makes 8 servings*

| | |
|---|---|
| 6 | ounces fine noodles (yolk-free), uncooked (3 cups) |
| 2 | small, sweet apples, peeled and coarsely shredded |
| 1 | cup canned crushed pineapple (packed in juice), drained |
| 1/4 | cup plus 2 tablespoons raisins |
| 1 1/3 | cups lowfat (1%) cottage cheese |
| 1 | cup liquid egg substitute |
| 1/2 | cup orange juice |
| 1/4 | cup sugar |
| 2 | teaspoons vanilla extract |
| 1/2 | teaspoon ground cinnamon |

Cook noodles according to package directions. Drain.

Preheat oven to 350°.

Spray an 8-inch square baking pan with nonstick cooking spray.

In a large bowl, combine cooked noodles, apples, pineapple, and raisins. Toss to combine.

In a blender container, combine remaining ingredients. Blend until smooth. Add to noodles and mix well. Spoon into prepared pan.

Bake 45 minutes, or until set.

Serve warm or cold, cut into squares.

---

Each serving provides:

**205 Calories**

| | | | |
|---|---|---|---|
| 1 | Protein Serving | 11 g | Protein |
| 1 | Bread Serving | 1 g | Fat (5% of calories) |
| 2 | Fruit Servings | 39 g | Carbohydrate |
| 24 | Additional Calories | 209 mg | Sodium |
| | | 2 mg | Cholesterol |
| | | 2 g | Fiber |

# Little Pineapple Kugel

*Have some leftover noodles that you don't know what to do with? This easy kugel is a smaller version of our Fruit and Noodle Kugel and is perfect for a small family. If you like, you can use a coarsely chopped apple in place of the pineapple.*

*Makes 2 servings*

| | |
|---|---|
| 1/3 | cup lowfat (1%) cottage cheese |
| 2 | egg whites |
| 1/4 | cup vanilla nonfat yogurt |
| 1 | tablespoon sugar |
| 1 | teaspoon vanilla extract |
| 1/2 | teaspoon almond or rum extract |
| 1/8 | teaspoon ground cinnamon |
| 1/2 | cup canned crushed pineapple (packed in juice), undrained |
| 1/2 | cup cooked thin or medium noodles, (yolk-free) |

Preheat oven to 325°.

Spray a small baking dish with nonstick cooking spray.

In a blender container, combine cottage cheese, egg whites, yogurt, sugar, extracts, and cinnamon. Blend until smooth. Add pineapple. Blend 2 seconds. Pour mixture into a bowl and stir in noodles.

Pour mixture into prepared pan. Sprinkle with additional cinnamon.

Bake, uncovered, 40 minutes, or until set.

Serve warm or cold.

---

Each serving provides:

**182 Calories**

| | | | |
|---|---|---|---|
| 1/2 | Protein Serving | 11 g | Protein |
| 1/2 | Bread Serving | 1 g | Fat (6% of calories) |
| 1/2 | Fruit Serving | 30 g | Carbohydrate |
| 68 | Additional Calories | 229 mg | Sodium |
| | | 2 mg | Cholesterol |
| | | 1 g | Fiber |

# Grains

NEVER-FAIL RECIPE INCLUDED
100% PURE BROWN RICE

Vinnie Crist
1984

Grains are an important building block in the foundation of a healthy diet. However, many well-meaning, health-conscious eaters often eat a limited selection of grains. While there is nothing wrong with the popular choices of whole wheat bread, rice, and oatmeal, there are so many other delicious—and nutritious—possibilities.

Grains are rich in complex carbohydrates. They also provide protein, vitamin E, B vitamins, magnesium, iron, copper, and zinc. Whole grains are an excellent source of fiber and therefore may help to lower blood cholesterol and maintain bowel regularity. A cup of cooked grains provides from 3 to 11 grams of fiber, depending on the grain.

Grains are also low in fat and calories, with a cup of cooked grains providing about 200 calories. And grains are so versatile. They're not just for dinner. Cooked grains also make a filling, nutritious breakfast.

So, try them all. Some of the popular ones are barley, cornmeal, couscous, millet, oats, rice, rye, and wheat. Many health food stores also carry little-known grains such as triticale, quinoa, and teff. Be adventurous and enjoy the many delicious possibilities grains have to offer.

# BASIC COOKING DIRECTIONS FOR GRAINS

Unless the recipe specifies another method, grains are usually cooked by stirring them into boiling water or broth, covering the pot, reducing the heat, then simmering the grains until they are tender and most of the liquid has been absorbed.

The following chart is a guide; however, cooking times may vary slightly depending on the size and quality of the grains. Grains with similar cooking times may be combined and cooked together.

### COOKING CHART FOR GRAINS

| Grain | Uncooked Amount | Amount of Water | Cooking Time | Approximate Yield |
|---|---|---|---|---|
| Barley | 1 cup | 4 cups | 45 minutes | $3^1/_2$ cups |
| Bulgur | 1 cup | 2 cups | 15 minutes | 3 cups |
| Brown rice | 1 cup | $2^1/_2$ cups | 45 minutes | $3^1/_2$ cups |
| Converted rice | 1 cup | $2^1/_4$ cups | 20 minutes | $3^1/_2$ cups |
| Kasha | 1 cup | 3 cups | 15 minutes | $3^1/_2$ cups |
| Cornmeal | 1 cup | 3 cups | 25 minutes | 4 cups |
| Millet | 1 cup | 2 cups | 20 minutes | 3 cups |
| Wheat berries | 1 cup | $3^1/_2$ cups | 40 to 60 minutes | 3 cups |

# Spinach and Rice Bake

*Rosemary lends a delicate flavor to this easy casserole. It makes 8 side-dish servings and can also be used as an entrée for 6.*

*Makes 8 servings*

| | |
|---|---|
| 2 | 10-ounce packages frozen chopped spinach, thawed and drained |
| 2 | cups cooked brown rice |
| 6 | ounces shredded reduced-fat Cheddar cheese (1 1/2 cups) |
| 1/2 | cup thinly sliced green onion (green and white parts) |
| 1 | teaspoon dried rosemary, crushed |
| 1/2 | teaspoon garlic powder |
| 1/4 | teaspoon salt |
| 1/8 | teaspoon pepper |
| 2 | cups evaporated skim milk |
| 1 | cup liquid egg substitute |
| 1 | teaspoon Worcestershire sauce |

Preheat oven to 350°.

Spray an 8-inch square baking pan with nonstick cooking spray.

In a large bowl, combine spinach, rice, cheese, green onion, and rosemary. Toss to combine well. Place mixture in prepared pan.

In another bowl, combine remaining ingredients. Beat with a fork or wire whisk until blended. Pour over spinach mixture.

Bake, uncovered, 35 minutes, or until set.

---

Each serving provides:

**200 Calories**

| | | | |
|---|---|---|---|
| 2 | Protein Servings | 18 g | Protein |
| 1/2 | Bread Serving | 5 g | Fat (21% of calories) |
| 1 | Vegetable Serving | 23 g | Carbohydrate |
| 1/4 | Milk Serving | 419 mg | Sodium |
| | | 18 mg | Cholesterol |
| | | 2 g | Fiber |

# Raisin Rice Patties

*These delectable patties make a great breakfast or a special light dinner when accompanied by soup and salad. You can even make them smaller and serve them as hors d'oeuvres. They're scrumptious topped with raspberry jam.*

*Makes 4 servings*
*(three 4-inch patties each serving)*

| | |
|---|---|
| 1/2 | cup part-skim ricotta cheese |
| 1/2 | cup liquid egg substitute |
| 1 | tablespoon plus 1 teaspoon sugar |
| 1 | tablespoon all-purpose flour |
| 2 | teaspoons vanilla extract |
| 1 | teaspoon baking powder |
| 1/4 | teaspoon ground cinnamon |
| 1 | cup cooked white or brown rice |
| 1/4 | cup raisins |

In a blender container, combine all ingredients *except* rice and raisins. Blend until smooth. Pour mixture into a bowl. Stir in rice and raisins, mixing well.

Spray a large nonstick skillet or griddle with nonstick cooking spray. Preheat over medium heat.

Drop rice mixture into griddle, using 2 tablespoonfuls for each patty. Turn patties when the bottoms are lightly browned and the tops are slightly dry and bubbly. Cook until golden brown on both sides.

---

Each serving provides:

**184 Calories**

| | | | |
|---|---|---|---|
| 1 | Protein Serving | 8 g | Protein |
| 1/2 | Bread Serving | 3 g | Fat (14% of calories) |
| 1/2 | Fruit Serving | 30 g | Carbohydrate |
| 24 | Additional Calories | 213 mg | Sodium |
| | | 10 mg | Cholesterol |
| | | 1 g | Fiber |

# Oriental Fried Rice

*In fine Chinese style, this delicious dish tastes just like the rice in your favorite restaurant.*

*Makes 4 servings*

| | |
|---|---|
| 2 | tablespoons reduced-sodium soy sauce |
| 1/8 | teaspoon garlic powder |
| 1/8 | teaspoon ground ginger |
| 2 | teaspoons vegetable oil |
| 1/2 | cup liquid egg substitute |
| 4 | ounces cooked chicken (1 cup), cut into small pieces* |
| 1/2 | cup thinly sliced green onion |
| 2 | cups cooked white or brown rice |

In a small bowl or custard cup, combine soy sauce, garlic powder, and ginger. Set aside.

Preheat a large nonstick skillet over medium heat. Add 1 teaspoon of the oil. Pour in egg substitute, tilting pan to coat bottom evenly. Cook until egg is set, then remove egg from pan and cut into thin 1-inch strips. Set aside.

Add remaining oil to skillet. Add chicken, green onion, and rice. Cook, stirring, until well blended. Stir in soy sauce mixture and egg. Cook, stirring constantly, until rice is hot and sizzly.

*If desired, substitute cooked shrimp for the chicken.

---

Each serving provides:

**230 Calories**

| | | | |
|---|---|---|---|
| 1 1/2 | Protein Servings | 15 g | Protein |
| 1 | Bread Serving | 5 g | Fat (19% of calories) |
| 1/4 | Vegetable Serving | 31 g | Carbohydrate |
| 1/2 | Fat Serving | 378 mg | Sodium |
| | | 25 mg | Cholesterol |
| | | 1 g | Fiber |

# Favorite Rice Casserole

*This long-time favorite has dressed our table at many dinner parties and family gatherings. It goes with almost any entée and always adds just the right touch.*

*Makes 8 servings*

| | |
|---|---|
| 4 | teaspoons margarine |
| 1 | cup brown rice, uncooked (8 ounces) |
| 1 | 8-ounce can mushroom pieces, drained |
| 2 | packets low-sodium instant beef-flavored broth mix |
| 2 | tablespoons minced onion flakes |
| 2 3/4 | cups boiling water |

Preheat oven to 350°.

Spray a 1 1/2-quart casserole with nonstick cooking spray.

Melt margarine in a medium nonstick skillet over medium heat. Stir in rice. Cook, stirring constantly, until rice is golden, 3 to 5 minutes. Remove from heat and add remaining ingredients, mixing well. Place mixture in prepared casserole.

Bake, covered, 1 hour and 5 minutes, stirring once after 45 minutes of cooking.

---

Each serving provides:

**132 Calories**

| | | | |
|---|---|---|---|
| 1 | Bread Serving | 3 g | Protein |
| 1/4 | Vegetable Serving | 3 g | Fat (20% of calories) |
| 1/2 | Fat Serving | 24 g | Carbohydrate |
| 3 | Additional Calories | 93 mg | Sodium |
| | | 0 mg | Cholesterol |
| | | 1 g | Fiber |

# Tri-Color Rice

*The confetti-like appearance of the different peppers makes this a colorful dish to serve alongside almost any entrée.*

*Makes 4 servings*

| | |
|---|---|
| 2 | teaspoons vegetable oil |
| 1/2 | cup chopped onion |
| 1/2 | cup chopped green bell pepper |
| 1/2 | cup chopped red bell pepper |
| 1/2 | cup chopped yellow bell pepper |
| 2 | cups water |
| 1 | teaspoon dried oregano |
| 1/4 | teaspoon dried basil |
| 1/4 | teaspoon garlic powder |
| 2 | packets low-sodium instant chicken- or vegetable-flavored broth mix |
| | Salt and pepper to taste |
| 3/4 | cup converted rice, uncooked (6 ounces) |

Heat oil in a medium saucepan over medium heat. Add onion and peppers. Cook 5 minutes, stirring frequently.

Add water, oregano, basil, garlic powder, broth mix, salt and pepper. When water boils, stir in rice. Cover, reduce heat to medium-low, and simmer 20 minutes or until most of the water has been absorbed. Remove from heat and let stand 5 minutes.

Fluff rice with a fork before serving.

---

Each serving provides:

**204 Calories**

| | | | |
|---|---|---|---|
| 1 1/2 | Bread Servings | 4 g | Protein |
| 1 | Vegetable Serving | 3 g | Fat (12% of calories) |
| 1/2 | Fat Serving | 40 g | Carbohydrate |
| 5 | Additional Calories | 6 mg | Sodium |
| | | 0 mg | Cholesterol |
| | | 2 g | Fiber |

# Israeli Eggplant and Rice

*The unusual flavor and subtle sweetness of this side dish make it quite unique. It blends well with almost entrée.*

*Makes 6 servings*

| | |
|---|---|
| 2 | teaspoons vegetable oil |
| 4 | cups eggplant, peeled and cut into $1/2$-inch pieces (about $3/4$ pound) |
| 8 | large pitted dates, finely chopped |
| 2 | small, sweet apples, unpeeled, chopped into $1/2$-inch pieces |
| 1 | cup chopped mushrooms |
| $1/2$ | cup chopped onion |
| 2 | teaspoons sugar |
| $1/4$ | teaspoon salt |
| $1/8$ | teaspoon ground allspice |
| $1/2$ | teaspoon ground cinnamon |
| $1 1/2$ | cups cooked brown rice |
| 2 | tablespoons chopped walnuts or almonds ($1/2$ ounce) |

Heat oil in a large nonstick skillet over medium heat. Add eggplant, dates, apples, mushrooms, and onion, mixing well. Sprinkle with sugar, salt, allspice, and *half* of the cinnamon. Cook, stirring frequently, until vegetables are tender, about 10 to 12 minutes.

Add rice and chopped nuts and sprinkle with remaining cinnamon. Cook, stirring, until rice is heated through.

Serve hot.

---

Each serving provides:

**172 Calories**

| | | | |
|---|---|---|---|
| $1/2$ | Bread Serving | 3 g | Protein |
| $1 3/4$ | Vegetable Servings | 4 g | Fat (19% of calories) |
| $1/2$ | Fat Serving | 34 g | Carbohydrate |
| 1 | Fruit Serving | 96 mg | Sodium |
| 10 | Additional Calories | 0 mg | Cholesterol |
| | | 4 g | Fiber |

# Herbed Barley Casserole

*The wonderful, bouncy texture of barley makes it one of our favorite grains.
Baking it with herbs and spices makes an easy way to enjoy this often-neglected grain.*

*Makes 6 servings*

| | |
|---|---|
| 2 | teaspoons vegetable oil |
| $1/2$ | cup finely chopped celery |
| 1 | cup barley, uncooked ($6\,3/4$ ounces) |
| $2\,1/2$ | cups low-sodium chicken or vegetable broth, or $2\,1/2$ cups of water and 2 packets low-sodium instant chicken- or vegetable-flavored broth mix |
| $1/2$ | cup thinly sliced green onions (green and white parts) |
| 1 | teaspoon dried parsley flakes |
| $1/4$ | teaspoon garlic powder |
| | Pepper to taste |

Preheat oven to 350°.

Spray a $1\,3/4$-quart casserole with nonstick cooking spray.

Heat oil in a medium nonstick skillet over medium heat. Add celery. Cook, stirring frequently, 4 to 5 minutes, until tender.

Add barley to skillet. Cook, stirring frequently, 2 minutes. Place in prepared casserole. Stir in 1 cup of the broth, along with remaining ingredients.

Bake, covered, 25 minutes, then stir in remaining broth and continue to bake, covered, 40 minutes more, or until the liquid is absorbed and the barley is tender.

---

Each serving provides:

**140 Calories**

| | | | |
|---|---|---|---|
| $1\,1/2$ | Bread Servings | 5 g | Protein |
| $1/4$ | Vegetable Serving | 2 g | Fat (16% of calories) |
| $1/4$ | Fat Serving | 24 g | Carbohydrate |
| 12 | Additional Calories | 247 mg | Sodium |
| | | 0 mg | Cholesterol |
| | | 6 g | Fiber |

# Barley-Cheddar Sauté

*Any cooked grain will work in this delicious medley, but barley seems to add just the right texture.*

*Makes 6 servings*

| | |
|---|---|
| 2 | teaspoons olive oil |
| 1/2 | cup chopped onion |
| 1/2 | cup chopped green bell pepper |
| 2 | cloves garlic, minced |
| 1 | cup eggplant, peeled and chopped |
| 1 | cup zucchini, unpeeled, chopped |
| 2 | cups cooked barley |
| 1 | 1-pound can salt-free (or regular) tomatoes, chopped, drained slightly |
| 1 | teaspoon dried oregano |
| | Salt and pepper to taste |
| 4 | ounces shredded reduced-fat Cheddar cheese (1 cup) |

Heat oil in a large nonstick skillet over medium heat. Add onion, green pepper, and garlic. Cook, stirring frequently, 5 minutes.

Add eggplant and zucchini to skillet. Cook, stirring frequently, 5 minutes.

Add barley, tomatoes, oregano, salt, and pepper. Cook, stirring frequently, until mixture is hot and bubbly and eggplant and zucchini are tender, about 10 minutes.

Sprinkle cheese evenly over vegetables. Remove from heat, cover skillet, and let stand 5 minutes to melt cheese.

Each serving provides:

**162 Calories**

| | | | |
|---|---|---|---|
| 3/4 | Protein Serving | 9 g | Protein |
| 1/2 | Bread Serving | 5 g | Fat (28% of calories) |
| 1 3/4 | Vegetable Servings | 22 g | Carbohydrate |
| 1/4 | Fat Serving | 160 mg | Sodium |
| 25 | Additional Calories | 13 mg | Cholesterol |
| | | 4 g | Fiber |

# Buckwheat-Cheese Bake

*Hearty and satisfying, this is almost a meal in itself. All you really need to add is a salad and a steamed vegetable, and you have a filling and delicious meatless meal.*

*Makes 6 servings*

| | |
|---|---|
| 1¹/₃ | cups lowfat (1%) cottage cheese |
| 1 | cup liquid egg substitute |
| 1 | tablespoon all-purpose flour |
| 2 | teaspoons minced onion flakes |
| 1 | teaspoon dried parsley flakes |
| 1 | teaspoon dried basil |
| ¹/₂ | teaspoon dried thyme |
| 1 | packet low-sodium instant chicken-flavored broth mix |
| | Salt and pepper to taste |
| 2 | cups cooked buckwheat groats (kasha). Cook kasha according to package directions, eliminating the margarine completely and using an egg white in place of the whole egg that is usually recommended. |

Preheat oven to 375°.

Spray an 8-inch square baking pan with nonstick cooking spray.

In a blender container, combine all ingredients *except* buckwheat. Blend until smooth. Pour into a large bowl and stir in buckwheat. Mix well.

Pour mixture into prepared pan.

Bake, uncovered, 30 minutes, or until set and lightly browned.

---

Each serving provides:

**132 Calories**

| | | | |
|---|---|---|---|
| 1¹/₄ | Protein Servings | 13 g | Protein |
| ¹/₂ | Bread Serving | 1 g | Fat (8% of calories) |
| 25 | Additional Calories | 18 g | Carbohydrate |
| | | 282 mg | Sodium |
| | | 2 mg | Cholesterol |
| | | 2 g | Fiber |

# Baked Bulgur Wheat

*Look for bulgur wheat with either the cereals or grains in most large grocery stores. It has a wonderful texture and makes a nice change of pace from rice.*

*Makes 4 servings*

| | |
|---|---|
| 2 | teaspoons vegetable oil |
| 1/2 | cup chopped onion |
| 1 | large clove garlic, finely chopped |
| 2/3 | cup bulgur wheat (4 ounces), uncooked |
| 1/2 | teaspoon dried marjoram |
| 1 1/3 | cups boiling water |
| 2 | packets low-sodium instant beef-flavored broth mix |
| 1 | 4-ounce can mushroom pieces, drained |

Preheat oven to 350°.

Spray a 1-quart baking dish with nonstick cooking spray.

Heat oil in a small nonstick skillet over medium heat. Add onion and garlic. Cook, stirring frequently, until onion is lightly browned. Remove from heat and stir in remaining ingredients. Mix well and spoon into prepared baking dish.

Bake, covered, 20 to 25 minutes, or until liquid has been absorbed. Fluff with a fork before serving.

---

Each serving provides:

**138 Calories**

| | | | |
|---|---|---|---|
| 1 | Bread Serving | 5 g | Protein |
| 1/2 | Vegetable Serving | 3 g | Fat (18% of calories) |
| 1/2 | Fat Serving | 25 g | Carbohydrate |
| 5 | Additional Calories | 124 mg | Sodium |
| | | 0 mg | Cholesterol |
| | | 6 g | Fiber |

# Bombay Millet

*Millet offers another nice change of pace from rice. Its small size allows it to cook more quickly than brown rice, while still offering the high quality and fiber of a whole grain. Look for millet in health food stores and many large grocery stores.*

*Makes 4 servings*

| | |
|---|---|
| 1 1/2 | cups low-sodium chicken broth, or 1 1/2 cups of water and 1 packet low-sodium instant chicken-flavored broth mix |
| 1/2 | cup millet, uncooked (3 ounces) |
| 1 | teaspoon curry powder |
| 1/4 | teaspoon ground cumin |
| 1/4 | teaspoon ground ginger |
| 1/8 | teaspoon ground allspice |
| 1/8 | teaspoon *each* salt and pepper |

Bring broth to a boil in a small saucepan over medium heat. Stir in remaining ingredients. When water returns to a boil, reduce heat to medium-low, cover, and simmer 25 minutes, or until the broth has been absorbed.

Fluff with a fork before serving.

---

Each serving provides:

**91 Calories**

| | | | |
|---|---|---|---|
| 1 | Bread Serving | 3 g | Protein |
| 8 | Additional Calories | 1 g | Fat (10% of calories) |
| | | 16 g | Carbohydrate |
| | | 281 mg | Sodium |
| | | 0 mg | Cholesterol |
| | | 2 g | Fiber |

# 15-Minute Muesli

*This traditional Swiss breakfast is just the right way to start the day. It needs to soak for at least 15 minutes, so you can put it together and let it sit while you get dressed. There's no cooking involved, and it's ready when you are.*

*Makes 2 servings*

| | |
|---|---|
| 1/2 | cup rolled oats, uncooked (1 1/2 ounces) |
| 1 | cup orange juice |
| 1/3 | cup nonfat dry milk |
| 1 | small apple, unpeeled, coarsely shredded |
| 2 | tablespoons raisins |
| 2 | teaspoons firmly packed brown sugar |
| 1/2 | teaspoon vanilla extract |
| 1/4 | teaspoon ground cinnamon |
| 1/8 | teaspoon almond extract |
| | Dash ground allspice |

Combine all ingredients in a bowl and mix well. Let stand at least 15 minutes.

Stir again and serve. Leftovers should be refrigerated and can be served cold.

---

Each serving provides:

**232 Calories**

| | | | |
|---|---|---|---|
| 1 | Bread Serving | 6 g | Protein |
| 2 | Fruit Servings | 2 g | Fat (6% of calories) |
| 1/2 | Milk Serving | 50 g | Carbohydrate |
| 16 | Additional Calories | 26 mg | Sodium |
| | | 1 mg | Cholesterol |
| | | 4 g | Fiber |

# Vegetables

Low in fat, high in fiber, and loaded with vitamins and minerals, vegetables are virtual powerhouses of nutrition. With health professionals recommending that vegetables play a major role in our daily meals, it is wise to include a wide variety of vegetables in your diet.

For the best flavor and nutritional value, cook vegetables until just tender-crisp and leave the skin on whenever possible. Fresh vegetables are best, with frozen vegetables being our second choice. Canned vegetables often contain high amounts of salt and also tend to be overcooked.

Our creative vegetable dishes are good enough for company, yet they are easy to prepare.

# BASIC COOKING DIRECTIONS
# FOR VEGETABLES

Steaming is a cooking method that preserves much of the flavor and texture of the vegetables and keeps vitamin loss to a minimum.

Always wash and trim vegetables before using. Place a steamer basket or rack in the bottom of a saucepan and add water almost up to, but not touching, the rack. Bring the water to a boil and add the vegetables. Cover and cook just until vegetables are tender-crisp. Our chart is a guideline; however, cooking times will vary, depending on the freshness and variety of the vegetables.

A word of caution: When removing the cover from a steaming pot, always open it away from you.

| Vegetable | Cooking Time | Suggested Spices |
|---|---|---|
| Asparagus spears | 8 minutes | lemon peel, basil, thyme, |
| Asparagus, 2-inch pieces | 3 to 5 minutes | sesame seed |
| Green beans, whole | 15 to 25 minutes | basil, oregano, dill weed, |
| Green beans, 2-inch pieces | 10 to 15 minutes | thyme, rosemary, tarragon |
| Broccoli spears | 10 to 15 minutes | dill weed, basil, thyme, |
| Broccoli, flowerets | 5 to 8 minutes | lemon peel, oregano, garlic |
| Brussels sprouts | 10 to 20 minutes | mace, garlic, lemon peel, dill weed |
| Cabbage wedges | 10 to 15 minutes | savory, fennel, dill seed, caraway seed |

*Vegetable Cooking Times, continued*

| Vegetable | Cooking Time | Suggested Spices |
|---|---|---|
| Carrots, whole | 20 minutes | basil, orange peel, |
| Carrots, sliced | 10 to 12 minutes | cinnamon, ginger, allspice, mint, savory, nutmeg |
| Cauliflower, whole | 10 to 15 minutes | dill weed, basil, thyme, |
| Cauliflower, flowerets | 5 to 8 minutes | tarragon, marjoram, paprika, rosemary |
| Parsnips, sliced | 10 to 15 minutes | allspice, orange peel, dill weed |
| Turnips, chunks | 20 minutes | bay leaves, oregano, allspice, rosemary |
| Yellow summer squash, sliced | 5 to 8 minutes | basil, marjoram, oregano, garlic, sage, thyme |
| Zucchini, sliced | | |

# Eggplant Supreme

*Everyone who tastes this delicious dish agrees that it is, indeed, supreme. It can be served as a side dish, either hot or cold, or on crackers or toast points as an elegant appetizer.*

*Makes 8 side-dish servings*

| | |
|---|---|
| 1 | tablespoon plus 1 teaspoon vegetable oil |
| 1 | small eggplant (about 3/4 pound), unpeeled, finely chopped (3 cups) |
| 1/2 | cup finely chopped onion |
| 1/2 | cup finely chopped green bell pepper |
| 1 | cup chopped mushrooms |
| 3 | cloves garlic, finely minced |
| 1 | 6-ounce can tomato paste |
| 1/2 | cup water |
| 2 | tablespoons red wine vinegar |
| 1 1/2 | teaspoons sugar |
| 1/2 | teaspoon dried oregano |
| 1/2 | teaspoon salt |
| 1/4 | teaspoon pepper |
| 10 | small, stuffed green olives, chopped |
| 3 | tablespoons sunflower seeds (raw or dry roasted) |

Heat oil in a large nonstick skillet over medium heat. Add eggplant, onion, green pepper, mushrooms, and garlic. Mix well. Cover and cook 10 minutes, stirring occasionally. Add small amounts of water if necessary (a few tablespoons at a time) to prevent sticking.

Add remaining ingredients, mixing well. Reduce heat to medium-low, cover, and simmer 30 minutes, stirring occasionally.

Serve hot, or chill and serve cold.

---

Each serving provides:

**86 Calories**

| | | | |
|---|---|---|---|
| 2 1/2 | Vegetable Servings | 2 g | Protein |
| 1/2 | Fat Serving | 5 g | Fat (45% of calories) |
| 25 | Additional Calories | 10 g | Carbohydrate |
| | | 393 mg | Sodium |
| | | 0 mg | Cholesterol |
| | | 2 g | Fiber |

# Ratatouille

*Fancy and delicious but easy to prepare, this is a classic dish. It's meant to be served hot, but the leftovers, along with a slice of reduced-fat cheese, make a great sandwich.*

*Makes 8 servings*

| | |
|---|---|
| 2 | teaspoons vegetable oil |
| 1 | cup sliced onion |
| 2 | large cloves garlic, finely chopped |
| 2 | cups eggplant, peeled, cut into 1/2-inch cubes |
| 2 | cups zucchini, unpeeled, sliced 1/2-inch thick |
| 1 | medium green bell pepper, cut into 1/4-inch strips |
| 1 | 1-pound can salt-free (or regular) tomatoes, chopped and drained (reserve juice) |
| 1 | teaspoon dried basil |
| 1 | teaspoon dried parsley flakes |
| 1 | teaspoon salt |
| 1/8 | teaspoon pepper |

Heat oil in a large saucepan over medium heat. Add onion and garlic. Cook, stirring frequently, 3 minutes.

Add remaining ingredients. Cover and simmer 20 minutes, or until vegetables are tender. Add the reserved tomato juice as necessary to prevent drying. (Mixture should be moist, but not soupy.)

---

Each serving provides:

**46 Calories**

| | | | |
|---|---|---|---|
| 2 | Vegetable Servings | 2 g | Protein |
| 1/4 | Fat Serving | 1 g | Fat (25% of calories) |
| | | 8 g | Carbohydrate |
| | | 285 mg | Sodium |
| | | 0 mg | Cholesterol |
| | | 2 g | Fiber |

# Warm Eggplant Salad

*We call this a salad because the eggplant is served in an oil and vinegar dressing; however, we really consider it a side dish. It's a nice complement to a chicken or fish dinner.*

*Makes 6 servings*

| | |
|---|---|
| 1/4 | cup red wine vinegar |
| 1 | tablespoon plus 1 1/2 teaspoons vegetable oil |
| 1 1/2 | tablespoons water |
| 1 | tablespoon plus 1 teaspoon sugar |
| 1 | teaspoon dried parsley flakes |
| 1 | teaspoon dried basil |
| 1/2 | teaspoon dried mint |
| 1 | large eggplant (about 1 1/4 pounds), unpeeled, sliced crosswise into 1/2-inch slices |
| | Salt and pepper to taste |

Preheat broiler.

In a small bowl, combine vinegar, oil, water, sugar, and herbs. Mix well and set aside.

Place eggplant slices on a nonstick baking sheet. Sprinkle them lightly with salt and pepper. Broil about 5 minutes on each side, or until browned. Sprinkle the other side with salt and pepper after turning slices over.

In the bottom of a deep bowl or soufflé dish, put one third of the warm eggplant slices. Top with about one third of the vinegar mixture. Top with another layer of the eggplant and more of the vinegar mixture. Top with remaining eggplant and remaining vinegar mixture.

Serve right away or cover until serving time and serve at room temperature.

---

Each serving provides:

**67 Calories**

| | | | |
|---|---|---|---|
| 1 3/4 | Vegetable Servings | 1 g | Protein |
| 3/4 | Fat Serving | 3 g | Fat (43% of calories) |
| 11 | Additional Calories | 9 g | Carbohydrate |
| | | 4 mg | Sodium |
| | | 0 mg | Cholesterol |
| | | 1 g | Fiber |

# Italian Spinach Bake

*This delectable dish combines the flavors of Italy in an easy side dish casserole. You can turn this into a filling meal by spooning the finished spinach over a baked potato. Accompanied by some sliced fresh tomatoes and cucumbers, that's all you need for a healthful, delicious dinner.*

*Makes 6 servings*

| | |
|---|---|
| 2 | teaspoons olive oil |
| 1/2 | cup chopped onion |
| 2 | 10-ounce packages frozen, chopped spinach, thawed and drained well |
| 3/4 | cup part-skim ricotta cheese |
| 2 | tablespoons grated Parmesan cheese |
| 1/4 | teaspoon ground nutmeg |
| 1/4 | teaspoon garlic powder |
| | Salt and pepper to taste |
| 1 | 8-ounce can salt-free (or regular) tomato sauce |
| 1 | teaspoon dried basil |
| 1/2 | teaspoon dried oregano |

Heat oil in a large nonstick skillet over medium-high heat. Add onion. Cook, stirring frequently, until lightly browned, about 5 minutes. Remove from heat.

Preheat oven to 350°.

Spray a 9-inch pie pan or shallow casserole with nonstick cooking spray.

Add spinach, both cheeses, nutmeg, garlic powder, salt, and pepper to skillet. Mix well. Spoon mixture into prepared pan. Smooth the top with the back of a spoon.

Combine tomato sauce, basil, and oregano, and spread evenly over spinach mixture.

Bake, uncovered, 25 minutes.

Let stand 5 minutes before serving.

Each serving provides:

**107 Calories**

| | | | |
|---|---|---|---|
| $1/2$ | Protein Serving | 8 g | Protein |
| $2^{1}/4$ | Vegetable Servings | 5 g | Fat (39% of calories) |
| $1/4$ | Fat Serving | 10 g | Carbohydrate |
| 13 | Additional Calories | 148 mg | Sodium |
| | | 11 mg | Cholesterol |
| | | 3 g | Fiber |

# Dilled Carrots in Wine

*If ever there was a "comfort food" vegetable, this is it. Mild and sweet, with the subtle flavor of dill, these carrots enhance, yet never compete with, almost any entrée.*

*Makes 6 servings*

2       cups carrots, sliced crosswise into 1/4-inch slices
1       cup chopped onion
1/2     cup chopped celery
1/2     cup chopped celery leaves
1/3     cup dry white wine
1/2     teaspoon dill weed
        Salt and pepper to taste

Combine all ingredients *except* salt and pepper in a medium saucepan. Bring to a boil over medium heat, stirring occasionally.

Reduce heat slightly, cover, and simmer 15 to 20 minutes, or until carrots are just tender.

Sprinkle each serving with salt and pepper to taste.

| Each serving provides: | | | |
|---|---|---|---|
| | **38 Calories** | | |
| 1 1/4 | Vegetable Servings | 1 g | Protein |
| 11 | Additional Calories | trace | Fat (3% of calories) |
| | | 7 g | Carbohydrate |
| | | 25 mg | Sodium |
| | | 0 mg | Cholesterol |
| | | 2 g | Fiber |

# Golden Carrot Loaf

*This golden loaf is sweet, moist, and delicious. It provides an excellent way to get them to eat their vegetables.*

*Makes 6 servings*

| | |
|---|---|
| 1 | cup liquid egg substitute |
| 2 | tablespoons dry sherry |
| 1 | packet low-sodium instant chicken- or vegetable-flavored broth mix |
| 1/2 | cup plus 1 tablespoon all-purpose flour |
| 1 | 1-pound bag of carrots, grated or finely shredded (The food processor, using the steel blade, does the best job; cut the carrots into large chunks first.) |
| 1 | small onion, grated (or put it in the food processor with the carrots) |

Preheat oven to 350°.

Spray a 4 × 8-inch loaf pan with nonstick cooking spray.

Combine egg substitute, sherry, and broth mix in a large bowl. Stir in flour, using a wire whisk. Whisk until smooth. Add carrots and onion. Mix well.

Spoon mixture into prepared pan.

Bake, uncovered, 50 to 55 minutes, until set.

Cool in pan on a wire rack for 5 minutes, then invert onto a serving plate.

Cut into slices to serve.

---

Each serving provides:

**110 Calories**

| | | | |
|---|---|---|---|
| 1/2 | Protein Serving | 6 g | Protein |
| 1/2 | Bread Serving | trace | Fat (4% of calories) |
| 3/4 | Vegetable Serving | 19 g | Carbohydrate |
| 16 | Additional Calories | 95 mg | Sodium |
| | | 0 mg | Cholesterol |
| | | 3 g | Fiber |

# Apricot-Glazed Carrots

*This elegant dish combines the flavors of apricot, orange, and nutmeg. It looks so pretty and makes a nice accompaniment to chicken or turkey.*

*Makes 4 servings*

| | |
|---|---|
| 4 | cups carrots, sliced crosswise into $1/4$-inch slices |
| $1/4$ | cup fruit-only apricot spread |
| $1/2$ | teaspoon grated fresh orange peel |
| $1/4$ | teaspoon ground nutmeg |
| 2 | teaspoons lemon juice |

Place a steamer rack in the bottom of a medium saucepan. Add enough water to come almost up to the bottom of the rack. Place saucepan over medium heat. When water boils, add carrots, cover saucepan, and cook 10 minutes, or until carrots are tender. Drain.

While carrots are cooking, combine remaining ingredients in a small bowl. Mix well. Add a little water or orange juice (a teaspoon at a time) if sauce is too thick.

Place carrots in a serving bowl. Spoon sauce over carrots. Toss and serve.

---

Each serving provides:

**91 Calories**

| | | | |
|---|---|---|---|
| 2 | Vegetable Servings | 1 g | Protein |
| 1 | Fruit Serving | trace | Fat (2% of calories) |
| | | 22 g | Carbohydrate |
| | | 39 mg | Sodium |
| | | 0 mg | Cholesterol |
| | | 4 g | Fiber |

# Carrot and Apple Pudding

*This sweet-tasting dish is served warm, as a side dish for dinner or brunch.*
*The leftovers make a delicious cold side dish or snack.*

*Makes 4 servings*

| | |
|---|---|
| 1 | cup finely shredded carrots |
| 2 | small, sweet apples, unpeeled, shredded |
| 1/4 | cup raisins |
| 1/2 | cup liquid egg substitute |
| 1/4 | cup plus 2 tablespoons all-purpose flour |
| 1 | tablespoon plus 1 teaspoon firmly packed brown sugar |
| 2 | teaspoons lemon juice |
| 1 | teaspoon ground cinnamon |
| 3 | egg whites (Egg substitute will not work here.) |

Preheat oven to 350°.

Spray a 1 1/2-quart casserole with nonstick cooking spray.

In a medium bowl, combine carrots, apples, raisins, egg substitute, flour, brown sugar, lemon juice, and cinnamon. Mix well.

In another bowl, beat egg whites on high speed of an electric mixer until stiff. Fold into carrot mixture. Spoon mixture into prepared casserole. Spray the top lightly and evenly with nonstick cooking spray.

Bake, uncovered, 30 to 40 minutes, or until set and lightly browned.

---

Each serving provides:

**171 Calories**

| | | | |
|---|---|---|---|
| 3/4 | Protein Serving | 8 g | Protein |
| 1/2 | Bread Serving | 2 g | Fat (9% of calories) |
| 1/2 | Vegetable Serving | 33 g | Carbohydrate |
| 1 | Fruit Serving | 104 mg | Sodium |
| 16 | Additional Calories | 0 mg | Cholesterol |
| | | 3 g | Fiber |

# Orange-Glazed Green Beans

*So elegant, yet so easy to do, these green beans are at home with the family or with guests. The rich orange glaze, accented with basil, really turns a popular vegetable into a gourmet's delight.*

*Makes 6 servings*

| | |
|---|---|
| 3/4 | cup orange juice |
| 1 | tablespoon cornstarch |
| 1 | teaspoon dried basil |
| 1/2 | teaspoon lemon juice |
| | Salt and pepper to taste |
| 1 | pound green beans, ends trimmed and strings removed |

In a small saucepan, combine all ingredients *except* green beans. Mix well, stirring until cornstarch is dissolved. Set aside.

Place a steamer rack in the bottom of a medium saucepan. Add enough water to come almost up to the bottom of the rack. Place saucepan over medium heat. When water boils, add green beans, cover saucepan, and cook about 15 minutes, or until beans are tender. Drain.

When beans are almost done, heat orange juice mixture over medium heat, stirring constantly, until mixture boils. Continue to cook and stir for 1 minute.

Place green beans in a shallow serving bowl. Pour glaze evenly over beans.

---

Each serving provides:

**40 Calories**

| | | | |
|---|---|---|---|
| 3/4 | Vegetable Serving | 1 g | Protein |
| 1/4 | Fruit Serving | trace | Fat (2% of calories) |
| 5 | Additional Calories | 9 g | Carbohydrate |
| | | 5 mg | Sodium |
| | | 0 mg | Cholesterol |
| | | 1 g | Fiber |

# Green Beans and Tomatoes

*This colorful, tasty blend of vegetables and spices couldn't be easier. It goes with almost any entrée and also looks great on a buffet.*

*Makes 4 servings*

1      10-ounce package frozen cut green beans
1      1-pound can salt-free (or regular) tomatoes, chopped,
          undrained
1/2    teaspoon dried oregano
1/8    teaspoon garlic powder
       Salt and pepper to taste

Cook beans according to package directions. Drain. Return beans to saucepan and add remaining ingredients. Bring to a boil over medium heat, then reduce heat to medium-low and simmer 5 minutes, uncovered.

---

Each serving provides:

**47 Calories**

| 2 | Vegetable Servings | 2 g | Protein |
|---|---|---|---|
| | | trace | Fat (7% of calories) |
| | | 10 g | Carbohydrate |
| | | 17 mg | Sodium |
| | | 0 mg | Cholesterol |
| | | 2 g | Fiber |

# Baked Cabbage Packets

*Cabbage wedges wrapped in individual foil packages are an easy, delicious way to enjoy this often-neglected vegetable. The packets can also be cooked on a barbecue grill.*

*Makes 6 servings*

1      medium cabbage (about 1 1/4 pounds), cut vertically into 6 wedges
       Salt and pepper to taste
1/2    cup plus 1 tablespoon evaporated skim milk
1 1/2  teaspoons grated Parmesan cheese

Preheat oven to 350°.

Place each cabbage wedge on a 10-inch square of aluminum foil. Sprinkle each wedge lightly with salt and pepper on each side. Spoon 1 1/2 tablespoons of milk over each wedge. Bring the foil up around the sides of the cabbage and roll the edges together securely to seal the packets. Place packets directly on the middle oven rack.

Bake 45 minutes.

Sprinkle each wedge with 1/4 teaspoon of the Parmesan cheese just before serving.

---

Each serving provides:

**43 Calories**

| | | | |
|---|---|---|---|
| 1 | Vegetable Serving | 3 g | Protein |
| 19 | Additional Calories | trace | Fat (6% of calories) |
| | | 8 g | Carbohydrate |
| | | 52 mg | Sodium |
| | | 1 mg | Cholesterol |
| | | 2 g | Fiber |

# Cabbage with Mustard Sauce

*The horseradish adds a wonderful zip to this dish, turning cabbage into a special-event vegetable. In the original version, we used cream and butter, which we've learned we can replace with evaporated skim milk and reduced-calorie margarine.*

*Makes 6 servings*

| | |
|---|---|
| 1 | small head of cabbage, cut vertically into 6 wedges |
| 1 | tablespoon reduced-calorie margarine |
| 2 | tablespoons grated onion |
| 3 | tablespoons all-purpose flour |
| 3 | tablespoons water |
| 1 | cup evaporated skim milk |
| | Salt and pepper to taste |
| 1 | tablespoon prepared yellow mustard |
| 2 | teaspoons prepared horseradish |

Place a steamer rack in the bottom of a medium saucepan. Add enough water to come almost up to the bottom of the rack. Place saucepan over medium heat. When water boils, add cabbage, cover saucepan, and cook 10 to 15 minutes, or until cabbage is tender. Drain.

While cabbage is cooking, melt margarine in a small saucepan over medium heat. Stir in onion.

Place flour in a small bowl. Gradually stir in water, mixing briskly to avoid lumps. Then gradually stir in milk, salt, and pepper. Stir into margarine. Cook, stirring constantly, until mixture has thickened and is hot and bubbly. Remove from heat and stir in mustard and horseradish, mixing well.

Place cabbage into 6 individual serving bowls. Divide sauce evenly and spoon over cabbage.

---

Each serving provides:

**87 Calories**

| | | | |
|---|---|---|---|
| 3/4 | Vegetable Serving | 5 g | Protein |
| 1/4 | Fat Serving | 1 g | Fat (13% of calories) |
| 1/4 | Milk Serving | 14 g | Carbohydrate |
| 23 | Additional Calories | 126 mg | Sodium |
| | | 2 mg | Cholesterol |
| | | 3 g | Fiber |

# Cheese Herbed Onions

*If you keep a few jars of these little onions in the pantry, they'll always be available to add to soups and stews and for making easy side dishes like this one.*

*Makes 6 servings*

| | |
|---|---|
| 2 | 1-pound jars pearl onions, drained |
| 1 | cup lowfat (1%) cottage cheese |
| 1 | tablespoon grated Parmesan cheese |
| 1 | tablespoon all-purpose flour |
| 1/2 | teaspoon dried marjoram |
| 1/2 | teaspoon dried basil |
| 1/2 | teaspoon dried oregano |
| 1/8 | teaspoon salt |
| 1/8 | teaspoon pepper |
| 1 | tablespoon dry bread crumbs |

Preheat oven to 375°.

Spray a 1-quart baking dish with nonstick cooking spray.

Place onions in prepared baking dish.

In a small bowl, combine cottage cheese, Parmesan cheese, flour, herbs, salt, and pepper. Mix well and spoon over onions, spreading evenly. Sprinkle with bread crumbs.

Bake, uncovered, 25 minutes, or until lightly browned.

---

Each serving provides:

**74 Calories**

| | | | |
|---|---|---|---|
| 1/2 | Protein Serving | 7 g | Protein |
| 1 1/4 | Vegetable Servings | 1 g | Fat (10% of calories) |
| 15 | Additional Calories | 11 g | Carbohydrate |
| | | 754 mg | Sodium |
| | | 2 mg | Cholesterol |
| | | 1 g | Fiber |

# Sweet and Sour Braised Onions

*Hot or cold, this unique blend of flavors adds a spark to any meal. This is a great dish for a buffet or summer cookout.*

*Makes 6 servings*

| | |
|---|---|
| 2 | cups small white pearl onions, peeled* |
| 1 | 1-pound can salt-free (or regular) tomatoes, chopped and drained |
| 1 | cup water |
| 1/4 | cup raisins |
| 1 | tablespoon plus 1 1/2 teaspoons red wine vinegar |
| 1 | tablespoon plus 1 teaspoon sugar |
| 1 | clove garlic, crushed |
| 1 | packet low-sodium instant chicken-flavored broth mix |
| 1 | teaspoon dry mustard |
| 1/4 | teaspoon dried thyme |
| 1/4 | teaspoon salt |
| 1/8 | teaspoon pepper |
| 1 | bay leaf |

Combine all ingredients in a medium saucepan. Bring to a boil over medium heat, stirring occasionally. Reduce heat to medium-low, cover, and simmer 1 hour or until onions are tender.

Remove and discard bay leaf before serving.

Serve hot or cold.

*To make peeling onions easier, drop them into a saucepan of boiling water. Boil 1 minute to loosen skin. Drain and peel.

---

Each serving provides:

**72 Calories**

| | | | |
|---|---|---|---|
| 1 1/4 | Vegetable Servings | 2 g | Protein |
| 1/4 | Fruit Serving | trace | Fat (4% of calories) |
| 17 | Additional Calories | 17 g | Carbohydrate |
| | | 108 mg | Sodium |
| | | 0 mg | Cholesterol |
| | | 1 g | Fiber |

# Baked Onions

*Our favorite onions for this recipe are the wonderful, sweet Vidalia onions. If they're not available, then any large onion will do. You'll find that baking makes the onions taste sweeter. This makes a nice, extra accompaniment to almost any entrée, especially dishes like oven-fried chicken and fish.*

*Makes 4 servings*

4      medium onions, unpeeled
       Freshly ground black pepper

Preheat oven to 350°.
Place onions directly on oven rack.
Bake 1 hour, or until onions are fork-tender.
Cut each onion into 4 wedges and sprinkle with pepper before serving.

---

Each serving provides:

**35 Calories**

| 1 | Vegetable Serving | 1 g | Protein |
|---|---|---|---|
| | | trace | Fat (3% of calories) |
| | | 8 g | Carbohydrate |
| | | 9 mg | Sodium |
| | | 0 mg | Cholesterol |
| | | 1 g | Fiber |

# Broiled Peppers

*Have you seen the long, thin, light green peppers called* cubanelle *or* cubanella *in the grocery store and wondered what to do with them? Here's a nice, easy way to prepare them, making a delicious addition to any meal, especially one with an Italian or Mexican theme.*

*Makes 4 servings*

4      medium cubanelle peppers

Preheat broiler.
Place whole peppers on a broiler pan or baking sheet.
Broil until peppers are charred on both sides, turning once.
Serve hot.

---

Each serving provides:
### 25 Calories

| 1 | Vegetable Serving | 1 g | Protein |
|---|---|---|---|
| | | trace | Fat (5% of calories) |
| | | 6 g | Carbohydrate |
| | | 2 mg | Sodium |
| | | 0 mg | Cholesterol |
| | | 1 g | Fiber |

# Beets à l'Orange

*Serve these delicious beets hot as a side dish, then refrigerate the leftovers and enjoy them cold. Either way, they're sure to please the beet lovers in the family.*

*Makes 8 servings*

2       1-pound cans small whole beets, undrained
1       cup orange juice
2       tablespoons cornstarch
1       tablespoon lemon juice
2       teaspoons vinegar
1       teaspoon grated fresh orange peel
1/8     teaspoon ground nutmeg
        Dash salt and pepper

Drain beets, reserving 1/2 cup liquid. Place liquid in a medium saucepan. Add remaining ingredients *except* beets. Stir to dissolve cornstarch. Bring mixture to a boil over medium heat, stirring constantly. Continue to cook, stirring, 1 minute.

Add beets. Heat through.

Serve hot or cold.

---

Each serving provides:

**51 Calories**

| | | | |
|---|---|---|---|
| 1 | Vegetable Serving | 1 g | Protein |
| 1/4 | Fruit Serving | trace | Fat (2% of calories) |
| 8 | Additional Calories | 12 g | Carbohydrate |
| | | 254 mg | Sodium |
| | | 0 mg | Cholesterol |
| | | 1 g | Fiber |

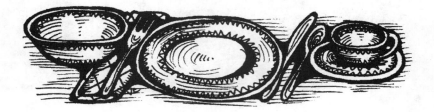

# Mushrooms, Onions, and Peppers

*This delectable medley can be served as a side dish or used as a topping for baked chicken, fish, or omelets. It also makes a great addition to a sandwich. Enjoy the wonderful natural flavors the vegetables have to offer.*

*Makes 4 servings*

| | |
|---|---|
| 2 | teaspoons vegetable oil |
| 1 | large green bell pepper, thinly sliced |
| 1 | large onion, thinly sliced |
| 2 | cups sliced mushrooms |
| | Salt and pepper to taste |

Heat oil in a large nonstick skillet over medium-high heat. Add vegetables. Cook, stirring frequently, until vegetables begin to brown, about 5 minutes.

Sprinkle with salt and pepper to taste.

Each serving provides:

**49 Calories**

| 1 1/2 | Vegetable Servings | 1 g | Protein |
|---|---|---|---|
| 1/2 | Fat Serving | 3 g | Fat (42% of calories) |
| | | 6 g | Carbohydrate |
| | | 3 mg | Sodium |
| | | 0 mg | Cholesterol |
| | | 1 g | Fiber |

# Snow Peas Surprise

*The surprise is that the often-neglected snow peas make an unusual, and very tasty, side dish.*

*Makes 4 servings*

| | |
|---|---|
| 1 | tablespoon reduced-sodium soy sauce |
| 1/8 | teaspoon garlic powder |
| 1/8 | teaspoon ground ginger |
| 1/2 | teaspoon vegetable oil |
| 1/2 | teaspoon sesame oil |
| 1/2 | cup chopped onion |
| 3 | cups fresh snow peas |

In a small bowl or custard cup, combine soy sauce, garlic powder, and ginger. Set aside.

Heat both oils in a large nonstick skillet over medium-high heat. Add onion. Cook, stirring frequently, 1 minute. Add snow peas and soy sauce mixture. Cook, stirring, 1 minute more.

---

Each serving provides:

**66 Calories**

| | | | |
|---|---|---|---|
| 1 3/4 | Vegetable Servings | 3 g | Protein |
| 1/4 | Fat Serving | 1 g | Fat (18% of calories) |
| | | 10 g | Carbohydrate |
| | | 155 mg | Sodium |
| | | 0 mg | Cholesterol |
| | | 3 g | Fiber |

# Tomatoes Provençal

*A delicious and colorful side dish, this one is great for a party. We usually make it in the summer when fresh, vine-ripened tomatoes are plentiful.*

*Makes 6 servings*

| | |
|---|---|
| 1 | teaspoon olive oil |
| 1 | cup chopped onion |
| 1 | cup sliced mushrooms |
| 1/8 | teaspoon garlic powder |
| 1/2 | teaspoon seasoned salt |
| | Pepper to taste |
| 1 | tablespoon imitation bacon bits |
| 2 | pounds fresh, ripe tomatoes, sliced crosswise into 1/2-inch slices (6 medium tomatoes) |
| 2 | tablespoons grated Parmesan cheese |

Preheat oven to 350°.

Spray a 9-inch round or square baking dish with nonstick cooking spray.

Heat oil in a large nonstick skillet over medium heat. Add onion and mushrooms. Cook, stirring frequently, until onion is tender, about 5 minutes. Remove from heat and stir in garlic powder, seasoned salt, pepper, and bacon bits.

Place *half* of the tomato slices in the bottom of the prepared baking dish. Spread onion mixture evenly over tomatoes. Sprinkle with *half* of the Parmesan cheese, then top with remaining tomatoes. Sprinkle with remaining cheese.

Cover tightly and bake 34 to 40 minutes.

---

Each serving provides:

**65 Calories**

| | | | |
|---|---|---|---|
| 2 3/4 | Vegetable Servings | 3 g | Protein |
| 22 | Additional Calories | 2 g | Fat (26% of calories) |
| | | 10 g | Carbohydrate |
| | | 98 mg | Sodium |
| | | 1 mg | Cholesterol |
| | | 3 g | Fiber |

# Best Stewed Tomatoes

*If you like, you can add bread cubes, plain or toasted, to the stewed tomatoes just before serving. The tomatoes are also delicious served over rice.*

*Makes 6 servings*

| | |
|---|---|
| 2 | 1-pounds can salt-free (or regular) tomatoes, chopped, undrained |
| 1/4 | cup very finely minced celery |
| 1 | tablespoon minced onion flakes |
| 1 | tablespoon sugar |
| 1/2 | teaspoon salt |
| 1/2 | teaspoon dried oregano |
| 1/4 | teaspoon dried basil |
| | Pepper to taste |
| 1 | tablespoon cornstarch dissolved in 1 tablespoon water |

Combine all ingredients *except* dissolved cornstarch in a medium saucepan. Bring to a boil over medium heat, stirring occasionally. Reduce heat to medium-low and simmer, uncovered, 15 minutes.

Stir in cornstarch and water mixture. Continue to cook, stirring constantly, 2 to 3 more minutes.

---

Each serving provides:

**47 Calories**

| | | | |
|---|---|---|---|
| 1 1/2 | Vegetable Servings | 1 g | Protein |
| 13 | Additional Calories | trace | Fat (6% of calories) |
| | | 11 g | Carbohydrate |
| | | 207 mg | Sodium |
| | | 0 mg | Cholesterol |
| | | 1 g | Fiber |

# Savory Sprouts

*Fresh Brussels sprouts also work in this easy recipe. Steam them first over boiling water until they are just tender-crisp, about 10 to 15 minutes, and proceed with the rest of the recipe. You may find that your family does like this often-neglected vegetable after all.*

*Makes 4 servings*

| | |
|---|---|
| 1 | 10-ounce package frozen Brussels sprouts |
| 2 | teaspoons margarine |
| 1 | packet low-sodium instant chicken- or vegetable-flavored broth mix |
| 1/4 | teaspoon dried basil |
| 1/8 | teaspoon ground savory |
| 1/8 | teaspoon pepper |
| | Dash nutmeg |
| | Salt to taste |

Cook Brussels sprouts according to package directions. Drain. Place sprouts in a serving bowl. Add remaining ingredients. Toss and serve.

---

Each serving provides:

**50 Calories**

| | | | |
|---|---|---|---|
| 1 | Vegetable Serving | 3 g | Protein |
| 1/2 | Fat Serving | 2 g | Fat (35% of calories) |
| 3 | Additional Calories | 6 g | Carbohydrate |
| | | 31 mg | Sodium |
| | | 0 mg | Cholesterol |
| | | 2 g | Fiber |

# Simmered Sauerkraut

*Sauerkraut is extremely high in sodium, so we always rinse it several times and eat very small portions. This dish provides a nice accent to a simple entrée of baked chicken or fish.*

*Makes 6 servings*

| | |
|---|---|
| 1 | 1-pound can sauerkraut, rinsed several times and drained |
| 1 | 1-pound can salt-free (or regular) tomatoes, chopped, undrained |
| 1 | small apple, peeled and coarsely shredded |
| 1/4 | cup very finely minced onion |
| 1 | packet low-sodium instant beef-flavored broth mix |
| 1 | tablespoon plus 1 teaspoon firmly packed brown sugar |

Combine all ingredients in a medium saucepan. Bring to a boil over medium heat, stirring occasionally. Then reduce heat to medium-low, cover, and simmer 30 minutes.

Each serving provides:

**62 Calories**

| | | | |
|---|---|---|---|
| 1 1/2 | Vegetable Servings | 2 g | Protein |
| 22 | Additional Calories | trace | Fat (6% of calories) |
| | | 14 g | Carbohydrate |
| | | 192 mg | Sodium |
| | | 0 mg | Cholesterol |
| | | 3 g | Fiber |

# Cauliflower Puree

*This scrumptious way of serving cauliflower tastes amazingly like mashed potatoes. Fresh cauliflower also works well. Just steam it over boiling water until it is tender enough to puree.*

*Makes 4 servings*

| | |
|---|---|
| 2 | 10-ounce packages frozen cauliflower |
| 1 | tablespoon plus 1 teaspoon reduced-calorie margarine |
| 1 | tablespoon minced onion flakes |
| 1 | packet low-sodium instant beef-flavored broth mix |
| 1/8 | teaspoon pepper |

Cook cauliflower according to package directions. Continue to cook until cauliflower is very tender. Drain.

Preheat oven to 375°.

Spray a 1-quart baking dish with nonstick cooking spray.

Combine cauliflower and remaining ingredients in a food processor or blender. Process until mixture is pureed. Spoon into prepared baking dish.

Bake, uncovered, 10 minutes, or until hot.

---

Each serving provides:

**58 Calories**

| | | | |
|---|---|---|---|
| 2 | Vegetable Servings | 3 g | Protein |
| 1/4 | Fat Serving | 2 g | Fat (34% of calories) |
| 3 | Additional Calories | 8 g | Carbohydrate |
| | | 82 mg | Sodium |
| | | 0 mg | Cholesterol |
| | | 4 g | Fiber |

# Lemon Broccoli

*Lemon makes a great accent for broccoli, enhancing its deep flavor and making it a very special vegetable. Fresh broccoli works just as well in this recipe. Steam it over boiling water until tender-crisp, about 10 to 15 minutes.*

*Makes 4 servings*

| | |
|---|---|
| 1 | 10-ounce package frozen broccoli spears |
| 2 | tablespoons reduced-calorie margarine |
| 2 | teaspoons lemon juice |
| 2 | tablespoons thinly sliced green onions (green part only) |
| 1/4 | teaspoon grated fresh lemon peel |
| | Salt and pepper to taste |

Cook broccoli according to package directions. Drain.

While broccoli is cooking, heat margarine until almost melted. (Placing it in a custard cup in the microwave does it nicely.) Stir in lemon juice.

Place broccoli in a serving dish. Spoon margarine mixture over broccoli. Sprinkle with green onions, lemon peel, salt, and pepper.

---

Each serving provides:

**47 Calories**

| | | | |
|---|---|---|---|
| 1 | Vegetable Serving | 2 g | Protein |
| 3/4 | Fat Serving | 3 g | Fat (51% of calories) |
| | | 4 g | Carbohydrate |
| | | 81 mg | Sodium |
| | | 0 mg | Cholesterol |
| | | 2 g | Fiber |

# Italian Veggie Bake

*An easy way to prepare vegetables is to bake them. If you like them tender-crisp, bake them for less time, and if you like them softer, just bake them longer.*

*Makes 6 servings*

| | |
|---|---|
| 1 | cup zucchini, unpeeled, cut into 1-inch cubes |
| 1 | cup mushrooms, quartered |
| 1 | cup broccoli, cut into flowerets |
| 1/2 | cup yellow squash, unpeeled, cut into 1-inch cubes |
| 1/2 | cup cauliflower, cut into flowerets |
| 1/2 | cup chopped onion |
| 1/2 | medium green bell pepper, sliced |
| 1 | 1-pound can salt-free (or regular) tomatoes, chopped, undrained |
| 1 | teaspoon dried basil |
| 1/2 | teaspoon dried oregano |
| 1/2 | teaspoon garlic powder |
| 1/8 | teaspoon pepper |
| | Salt to taste |
| 6 | ounces shredded part-skim Mozzarella cheese (1 1/2 cups) |
| 2 | tablespoons grated Parmesan cheese |

Preheat oven to 375°.

Spray a 7 × 11-inch baking pan with nonstick cooking spray.

Combine vegetables and spices in a large bowl and mix well. Spoon into prepared pan.

Cover tightly and bake 45 minutes, or until vegetables are tender, stirring once halfway through cooking time.

Uncover vegetables and sprinkle with cheeses. Continue to bake, uncovered, 10 minutes, or until cheese is melted and begins to brown.

---

Each serving provides:

**120 Calories**

| | | | |
|---|---|---|---|
| 1 1/4 | Protein Servings | 10 g | Protein |
| 2 1/4 | Vegetable Servings | 6 g | Fat (39% of calories) |
| 15 | Additional Calories | 9 g | Carbohydrate |
| | | 180 mg | Sodium |
| | | 18 mg | Cholesterol |
| | | 2 g | Fiber |

# Zucchini Cheese Bake

*Cheese and oregano give new dimensions to zucchini in this easy dish. Although we usually serve it as a side dish for 6, it can also serve 4 as a nice, light luncheon entrée.*

*Makes 6 servings*

| | |
|---|---|
| 5 | cups zucchini, unpeeled, sliced crosswise into thin slices |
| 2/3 | cup lowfat (1%) cottage cheese |
| 2 | ounces shredded reduced-fat Cheddar cheese (1/2 cup) |
| 1 | tablespoon minced onion flakes |
| 1 | teaspoon dried oregano |
| | Salt and pepper to taste |

Preheat oven to 375°.

Spray a 1-quart baking dish with nonstick cooking spray.

Steam zucchini on a rack in a covered saucepan 5 minutes, or until just tender-crisp. Arrange in prepared baking dish.

In a blender container, combine remaining ingredients. Blend until smooth. Spoon evenly over zucchini.

Bake, uncovered, 20 minutes, or until hot and lightly browned.

---

Each serving provides:

**64 Calories**

| | | | |
|---|---|---|---|
| 3/4 | Protein Serving | 7 g | Protein |
| 1 3/4 | Vegetable Servings | 2 g | Fat (30% of calories) |
| 2 | Additional Calories | 4 g | Carbohydrate |
| | | 179 mg | Sodium |
| | | 8 mg | Cholesterol |
| | | 1 g | Fiber |

# Zucchini-Mozzarella Casserole

*The wonderful flavors of Italy, accented with a little Dijon mustard, make this delightful dish a favorite they'll ask for over and over again. The mild-mannered zucchini really shines here.*

*Makes 6 servings*

2      teaspoons olive oil
4      cups zucchini, unpeeled, sliced crosswise into thin slices
1/2    cup finely chopped onion
1      tablespoon dried parsley flakes
1/2    teaspoon dried oregano
1/4    teaspoon dried basil
1/8    teaspoon garlic powder
       Salt and pepper to taste
1/2    cup liquid egg substitute
4      ounces shredded part-skim Mozzarella cheese (1 cup)
1      teaspoon Dijon mustard

Heat oil in a large nonstick skillet over medium heat. Add zucchini and onion. Cook, stirring frequently, until vegetables are tender-crisp, about 5 minutes. Add small amounts of water if necessary (about a tablespoon at a time) to prevent sticking. Remove from heat.

Preheat oven to 350°.

Spray a 1-quart casserole with nonstick cooking spray.

Sprinkle parsley, oregano, basil, garlic powder, salt, and pepper over zucchini. Mix gently.

In a large bowl, combine egg substitute, Mozzarella cheese, and mustard. Mix well. Add zucchini and stir until mixture is combined. Spoon into prepared casserole.

Bake, uncovered, 35 minutes, until lightly browned.

---

Each serving provides:

**91 Calories**

| 1 | Protein Serving | 8 g | Protein |
| 1 1/2 | Vegetable Servings | 5 g | Fat (47% of calories) |
| 1/4 | Fat Serving | 5 g | Carbohydrate |
| 17 | Additional Calories | 145 mg | Sodium |
| | | 11 mg | Cholesterol |
| | | 1 g | Fiber |

# Savory Zucchini Fritters

*This versatile vegetable, with its mild flavor, can be used in so many recipes. It can be used to make delicious fritters that are either savory, as in this recipe, or sweet, as in the next recipe. Why not enjoy them both?*

*Makes 4 servings*
*(4 fritters each serving)*

| | |
|---|---|
| 1/2 | cup liquid egg substitute |
| 2/3 | cup lowfat (1%) cottage cheese |
| 1/4 | cup plus 2 tablespoons all-purpose flour |
| 1 | tablespoon minced onion flakes |
| 1/2 | teaspoon baking powder |
| 1/4 | teaspoon dried marjoram |
| 1/4 | teaspoon dried thyme |
| 1/8 | teaspoon salt |
| 1/8 | teaspoon pepper |
| 1/8 | teaspoon garlic powder |
| 1 | cup (packed) finely shredded zucchini, unpeeled |

In a blender container, combine all ingredients *except* zucchini. Blend until smooth. Spoon mixture into a bowl.

Drain zucchini in a strainer, pressing out liquid with the back of a spoon. Stir into first mixture.

Spray a large nonstick skillet or griddle with nonstick cooking spray. Preheat over medium-high heat. Drop batter into skillet, making 16 fritters, using about 2 tablespoons for each fritter. Turn fritters carefully and cook until nicely browned on both sides. (To make turning fritters easier, spray spatula lightly with nonstick cooking spray.)

---

Each serving provides:

**96 Calories**

| | | | |
|---|---|---|---|
| 1 | Protein Serving | 9 g | Protein |
| 1/2 | Bread Serving | 1 g | Fat (7% of calories) |
| 1/2 | Vegetable Serving | 13 g | Carbohydrate |
| | | 335 mg | Sodium |
| | | 2 mg | Cholesterol |
| | | 1 g | Fiber |

# Sweet Zucchini Fritters

*These tender fritters provide a great way to get the finicky eaters to eat their vegetables. They make a delicious side dish and can even be drizzled with maple syrup and served as a unique brunch dish.*

*Makes 4 servings*
*(4 fritters each serving)*

| | |
|---|---|
| 1/2 | cup liquid egg substitute |
| 2/3 | cup lowfat (1%) cottage cheese |
| 1/4 | cup plus 2 tablespoons all-purpose flour |
| 2 | tablespoons sugar |
| 1 | teaspoon vanilla extract |
| 1/2 | teaspoon baking powder |
| 1/2 | teaspoon ground cinnamon |
| 1/4 | teaspoon ground nutmeg |
| 1/8 | teaspoon ground allspice |
| 1 | cup (packed) finely shredded zucchini, unpeeled |
| 1/4 | cup raisins |

In a blender container, combine all ingredients *except* raisins and zucchini. Blend until smooth. Spoon mixture into a bowl.

Drain zucchini in a strainer, pressing out liquid with the back of a spoon. Stir zucchini and raisins into first mixture.

Spray a large nonstick skillet or griddle with nonstick cooking spray. Preheat over medium-high heat. Drop batter into skillet, making 16 fritters, using about 2 tablespoons for each fritter. Turn fritters carefully and cook until nicely browned on both sides. (To make turning fritters easier, spray spatula lightly with nonstick cooking spray.)

Each serving provides:

**149 Calories**

| | | | |
|---|---|---|---|
| 1 | Protein Serving | 10 g | Protein |
| 1/2 | Bread Serving | 1 g | Fat (5% of calories) |
| 1/2 | Vegetable Serving | 26 g | Carbohydrate |
| 1/2 | Fruit Serving | 267 mg | Sodium |
| 24 | Additional Calories | 2 mg | Cholesterol |
| | | 1 g | Fiber |

# Italian Baked Spaghetti Squash

*Kids love the spaghetti-like strands of this unique vegetable. This easy casserole can be assembled ahead, refrigerated, and baked when needed. If you have a large squash, you can easily double the recipe.*

*Makes 4 servings*

2      cups cooked spaghetti squash*
1      8-ounce can salt-free (or regular) tomato sauce
1/2    teaspoon dried oregano
1/8    teaspoon garlic powder
       Pepper to taste
1      tablespoon plus 1 teaspoon grated Parmesan cheese

Preheat oven to 375°.

Spray a 1-quart baking dish with nonstick cooking spray.

Place spaghetti squash in prepared baking dish. Combine tomato sauce, oregano, garlic powder, and pepper. Spoon evenly over squash.

Sprinkle with Parmesan cheese.

Bake, uncovered, 20 minutes, until hot and bubbly.

*To cook spaghetti squash, cut squash in half lengthwise. Remove seeds. Bake cut-side down in a baking pan containing 1 inch of water at 350° for 45 minutes, or until tender. Remove squash from pan and drain cut-side down. Pull strands free with a fork.

---

Each serving provides:

**53 Calories**

| | | | |
|---|---|---|---|
| 2 | Vegetable Servings | 2 g | Protein |
| 10 | Additional Calories | 1 g | Fat (19% of calories) |
| | | 10 g | Carbohydrate |
| | | 57 mg | Sodium |
| | | 1 mg | Cholesterol |
| | | 1 g | Fiber |

# Dilled Yellow Squash

*This simple, herbed dish makes a delicious complement to almost any meal. For the best flavor, let the onions get nice and brown before adding the squash.*

*Makes 6 servings*

| | |
|---|---|
| 2 | teaspoons olive oil |
| 1 | cup chopped onion |
| 3 | cloves garlic, finely chopped |
| 4 | cups yellow summer squash, unpeeled, slice crosswise into $1/2$-inch slices |
| 1 | teaspoon dill weed |
| $1/2$ | teaspoon salt |
| $1/8$ | teaspoon pepper |

Heat oil in a large nonstick skillet over medium heat. Add onion and garlic. Cook, stirring frequently, until onion is lightly browned, 8 to 10 minutes.

Add squash. Sprinkle evenly with dill, salt, and pepper.

Cover and cook until squash is lightly browned and tender-crisp, about 5 to 7 minutes. Turn squash several times while cooking to brown both sides.

---

Each serving provides:

**44 Calories**

| $1^3/4$ | Vegetable Servings | 1 g | Protein |
|---|---|---|---|
| $1/4$ | Fat Serving | 2 g | Fat (32% of calories) |
| 3 | Additional Calories | 7 g | Carbohydrate |
| | | 185 mg | Sodium |
| | | 0 mg | Cholesterol |
| | | 1 g | Fiber |

# Baked Squash Southern Style

*An adaptation of an old Southern recipe, this dish has been a family favorite for years.*

*Makes 6 servings*

| | |
|---|---|
| 2 | 10-ounce packages frozen yellow summer squash |
| 1 | tablespoon minced onion flakes |
| 2 | tablespoons reduced-calorie margarine |
| 2 | egg whites |
| 1 1/2 | teaspoons sugar |
| 1/2 | teaspoon salt |
| 1/8 | teaspoon pepper |
| 3 | tablespoons Italian-seasoned bread crumbs |

Cook squash according to package directions, cooking until it is very tender. Drain.

Preheat oven to 350°.

Spray a 1-quart baking dish with nonstick cooking spray.

Place squash in a large bowl. Mash well, using a fork or a potato masher. Add onion flakes, *half* of the margarine, egg whites, sugar, salt, pepper, and *half* of the bread crumbs. Mix well.

Spoon mixture into prepared baking dish. Sprinkle with remaining crumbs. Dot with remaining margarine.

Bake, uncovered, 45 minutes, or until set and lightly browned.

---

Each serving provides:

**61 Calories**

| | | | |
|---|---|---|---|
| 1 1/4 | Vegetable Servings | 3 g | Protein |
| 1/2 | Fat Serving | 2 g | Fat (32% of calories) |
| 26 | Additional Calories | 8 g | Carbohydrate |
| | | 347 mg | Sodium |
| | | 0 mg | Cholesterol |
| | | 1 g | Fiber |

# Italian Stuffed Squash

*Zucchini or yellow summer squash will work in this elegant dish. It's so easy to prepare, yet it looks—and tastes—like you've worked for hours. For extra servings, it's easy to double the recipe.*

*Makes 4 servings*

| | |
|---|---|
| 2 | zucchini or yellow summer squash, about 8 ounces each |
| 2 | teaspoons olive oil |
| 1/2 | cup chopped onion |
| 1 | tablespoon Italian-seasoned bread crumbs |
| 2 | teaspoons grated Parmesan cheese |
| 1/2 | teaspoon dried oregano |
| 1/4 | teaspoon dried basil |
| | Dash garlic powder |
| | Dash pepper |

Steam whole squash in 1 inch of boiling water for 5 minutes. Drain.

Cut squash in half lengthwise. Carefully scoop out pulp, using a spoon or melon ball scoop, leaving a 1/4- to 1/2-inch shell. Save squash shells. Chop pulp.

Preheat oven to 350°.

Spray a shallow baking pan with nonstick cooking spray.

Heat oil in a small nonstick skillet over medium heat. Add onion. Cook, stirring frequently, until lightly browned, about 4 minutes. Remove from heat and stir in squash pulp, bread crumbs, Parmesan cheese, and spices. Mix well.

Pile mixture into squash shells. Place in prepared pan.

Bake, uncovered, 30 minutes, or until lightly browned.

---

Each serving provides:

**57 Calories**

| | | | |
|---|---|---|---|
| 1 1/4 | Vegetable Servings | 2 g | Protein |
| 1/2 | Fat Serving | 3 g | Fat (43% of calories) |
| 13 | Additional Calories | 7 g | Carbohydrate |
| | | 69 mg | Sodium |
| | | 1 mg | Cholesterol |
| | | 1 g | Fiber |

# *Starchy Vegetables*

The starchy vegetables include white potatoes, sweet potatoes, corn, peas, parsnips, and all varieties of winter squash. These vegetables are higher in carbohydrates than other vegetables, and many weight-reduction organizations consider one serving of a starchy vegetable to be nutritionally equivalent to one serving of bread. Starchy vegetables, like other vegetables, are packed with vitamins, minerals, and fiber.

We always recommend leaving the skin on potatoes whenever possible, which provides extra nutrients and fiber. And remember that contrary to what our mothers may have told us, it's not the potato that is fattening but the fatty toppings and deep-frying!

# Baked Orange Squash

*The complementary flavors of orange and cinnamon really enhance the squash in this delicious casserole. It's good for holidays or any day.*

*Makes 4 servings*

| | |
|---|---|
| 2 | cups mashed, cooked butternut or acorn squash* |
| 1/4 | cup frozen orange juice concentrate, thawed |
| 1 | tablespoon plus 1 teaspoon firmly packed brown sugar |
| 1/2 | teaspoon grated fresh orange peel |
| 1/8 | teaspoon ground cinnamon |
| | Dash ground ginger |

Preheat oven to 375°.

Spray a 1-quart baking dish with nonstick cooking spray.

Combine all ingredients in a medium bowl. Mix well. Spoon into prepared baking dish.

Bake, uncovered, 20 minutes.

*To cook winter squash, cut squash into halves or quarters and remove the seeds. Place squash, cut-side down, in a shallow baking pan. Cover with foil and bake at 350° for 30 minutes. Then turn squash cut-side up and continue to bake until tender, about 30 minutes. Remove peel.

---

Each serving provides:

**96 Calories**

| | | | |
|---|---|---|---|
| 1/2 | Bread Serving | 2 g | Protein |
| 1/2 | Fruit Serving | trace | Fat (3% of calories) |
| 16 | Additional Calories | 24 g | Carbohydrate |
| | | 7 mg | Sodium |
| | | 0 mg | Cholesterol |
| | | 4 g | Fiber |

# Pineapple-Filled Acorn Squash

*Acorn squash cut in half makes a perfect "basket" for fruits or other vegetables. In this dish, we've filled the squash halves with pineapple, making a deliciously sweet side dish. You can turn this into a nice light lunch by topping each half with a scoop of cottage cheese just before serving.*

*Makes 4 servings*

| | |
|---|---|
| 2 | acorn squash (about 10 ounces each) |
| 1 | 8-ounce can crushed pineapple (packed in juice), drained slightly |
| 1 | tablespoon plus 1 teaspoon firmly packed brown sugar |
| 1 | teaspoon ground cinnamon |
| 1/2 | teaspoon vanilla extract |
| 1/4 | teaspoon rum extract |

Preheat oven to 400°.

Cut squash in half lengthwise and remove seeds. Place squash cut-side down in a shallow baking pan. Pour hot water around squash to a depth of 1/2 inch.

Bake, uncovered, 30 to 40 minutes, or until squash is tender.

Carefully remove pulp from squash using a spoon, and leave a 1/2-inch shell. Place pulp in a small bowl and mash with remaining ingredients. Pile mixture back into shells. Return squash to pan.

Bake, uncovered, 10 minutes, or until heated through.

---

Each serving provides:

**99 Calories**

| | | | |
|---|---|---|---|
| 1/2 | Bread Serving | 1 g | Protein |
| 1/2 | Fruit Serving | trace | Fat (1% of calories) |
| 16 | Additional Calories | 25 g | Carbohydrate |
| | | 6 mg | Sodium |
| | | 0 mg | Cholesterol |
| | | 4 g | Fiber |

# Butternut Squash with Apples and Leeks

*This recipe can be made with any type of winter squash, such as hubbard, turban, or pumpkin. It seems like an unusual combination of ingredients, but it's a very tasty one.*

*Makes 6 servings*

| | |
|---|---|
| 1 | teaspoon vegetable oil |
| 1 | large leek, white part only, chopped (1 cup) |
| 2 | cloves garlic, crushed |
| 1 | 2-pound butternut squash, cut into wedges, peeled, seeded, then sliced into 1/8-inch slices |
| 1/4 | cup water |
| 2 | small Granny Smith apples, unpeeled, cut into wedges, and sliced into 1/8-inch slices |
| 2 | tablespoons honey |
| 1/4 | teaspoon salt |
| 1/4 | teaspoon ground nutmeg |
| 1/8 | teaspoon ground allspice |
| | Freshly ground black pepper |

Heat oil in a large nonstick skillet over medium heat. Add leek and garlic. Cook, stirring frequently, 2 minutes. Add squash and water. Mix well. Cover, reduce heat slightly, and cook 6 to 7 minutes, until squash is tender-crisp. Stir once while cooking.

Add remaining ingredients *except* pepper. Mix well. Cover and cook 5 minutes, until squash and apples are tender. Spoon into a serving bowl and sprinkle with freshly ground pepper to taste.

---

Each serving provides:

**119 Calories**

| | | | |
|---|---|---|---|
| 3/4 | Bread Serving | 2 g | Protein |
| 1/4 | Vegetable Serving | 1 g | Fat (7% of calories) |
| 1/4 | Fruit Serving | 29 g | Carbohydrate |
| 32 | Additional Calories | 99 mg | Sodium |
| | | 0 mg | Cholesterol |
| | | 5 g | Fiber |

# Whipped Spiced Parsnips

*An often-forgotten vegetable, parsnips have a wonderful flavor and texture and make a delicious side dish. They look like white carrots and can also be chopped and added to soups and stews.*

*Makes 4 servings*

12      ounces parsnips, peeled and sliced crosswise into 1/8-inch slices
2       teaspoons firmly packed brown sugar
1       teaspoon margarine
1/4     teaspoon grated fresh orange peel
        Dash ground nutmeg *or* allspice
        Dash salt
1/4     cup orange juice
1/4     cup canned crushed pineapple (packed in juice), drained
            slightly

Place a steamer rack in the bottom of a medium saucepan. Add enough water to come almost up to the bottom of the rack. Place saucepan over medium heat. When water boils, add parsnips, cover saucepan, and cook 15 to 20 minutes, or until parsnips are very tender. Drain.

Preheat oven to 350°.

Spray a 1-quart baking dish with nonstick cooking spray.

Place parsnips in a large bowl. Add brown sugar, margarine, orange peel, nutmeg, salt, and *half* of the orange juice. Mash with a fork or potato masher, then beat on medium speed of an electric mixer until smooth. Add remaining orange juice as needed, until desired consistency is reached. Stir in pineapple.

Spoon mixture into prepared baking dish.

Bake, uncovered, 15 minutes, or until hot.

---

Each serving provides:
### 90 Calories

| | | | |
|---|---|---|---|
| 1 | Bread Serving | 1 g | Protein |
| 1/4 | Fat Serving | 1 g | Fat (14% of calories) |
| 1/4 | Fruit Serving | 19 g | Carbohydrate |
| 8 | Additional Calories | 53 mg | Sodium |
| | | 0 mg | Cholesterol |
| | | 3 g | Fiber |

# Peas New Orleans

*As colorful as Mardi Gras, this easy recipe turns ordinary peas into a gourmet side dish. It makes a lovely dish for a buffet.*

*Makes 4 servings*

| | |
|---|---|
| 1 | 10-ounce package frozen peas |
| 2 | teaspoons vegetable oil |
| 1/4 | cup chopped onion |
| 1/4 | cup chopped green bell pepper |
| 1 | 1-pound can salt-free (or regular) tomatoes, chopped and drained (reserve liquid) |
| 1 | teaspoon sugar |
| | Salt and pepper to taste |
| 2 | teaspoons cornstarch |

Cook peas according to package directions. Drain.

Heat oil in a small saucepan over medium heat. Add onion and green pepper. Cook, stirring frequently, until tender. Add small amounts of water as necessary (about a tablespoon at a time) to prevent sticking.

Add peas, tomatoes, sugar, salt, and pepper to saucepan.

In a small bowl, stir a few tablespoons of the tomato liquid into the cornstarch, stirring to dissolve the cornstarch. Add cornstarch mixture and remaining tomato liquid to saucepan.

Bring to a boil, stirring constantly, then continue to cook, stirring, 1 minute.

---

Each serving provides:

**112 Calories**

| | | | |
|---|---|---|---|
| 1 | Bread Serving | 5 g | Protein |
| 1 1/4 | Vegetable Servings | 3 g | Fat (22% of calories) |
| 1/2 | Fat Serving | 18 g | Carbohydrate |
| 9 | Additional Calories | 95 mg | Sodium |
| | | 0 mg | Cholesterol |
| | | 4 g | Fiber |

# Savory Peas and Mushrooms

*Here's a quick, easy way to dress up a package of peas.*

*Makes 4 servings*

| | |
|---|---|
| 1 | 10-ounce package frozen peas |
| 1 | 4-ounce can mushroom pieces, drained |
| 2 | teaspoons margarine |
| 1 | teaspoon onion powder |
| 1/8 | teaspoon ground savory |
| | Salt and pepper to taste |

Cook peas according to package directions, adding mushrooms during the last half of the cooking time. Drain.

Place peas in a serving bowl. Add remaining ingredients. Toss and serve.

---

Each serving provides:

**78 Calories**

| | | | |
|---|---|---|---|
| 1 | Bread Serving | 4 g | Protein |
| 1/4 | Vegetable Serving | 2 g | Fat (25% of calories) |
| 1/2 | Fat Serving | 11 g | Carbohydrate |
| | | 168 mg | Sodium |
| | | 0 mg | Cholesterol |
| | | 3 g | Fiber |

# Potato Kugel

*A dish our mothers always made, this potato pudding is moist and delicious. We like it with lots of pepper, but you can let your own tastebuds be your guide. It's a perfect side dish to serve with just about any entrée.*

*Makes 6 servings*

| | |
|---|---|
| 1¹/₂ | pounds potatoes, unpeeled (3 medium potatoes), grated or finely shredded |
| ¹/₂ | cup liquid egg substitute |
| 1 | small onion, grated |
| 3 | tablespoons all-purpose flour |
| 1 | tablespoon vegetable oil |
| ³/₄ | teaspoon salt, or to taste |
| ¹/₄ | teaspoon pepper, or to taste |
| ¹/₄ | teaspoon baking powder |

Preheat oven to 375°.

Spray a 1-quart baking pan with nonstick cooking spray.

Place the potatoes in a bowl and set aside for 10 minutes, then place them in a strainer and press out as much liquid as you can.

Return potatoes to bowl. Add remaining ingredients. Mix well. Spoon mixture into prepared pan.

Bake, uncovered, 1 hour and 10 minutes, until set and lightly browned.

---

Each serving provides:

**133 Calories**

| | | | |
|---|---|---|---|
| ¹/₄ | Protein Serving | 5 g | Protein |
| 1 | Bread Serving | 3 g | Fat (17% of calories) |
| ¹/₂ | Fat Serving | 23 g | Carbohydrate |
| 5 | Additional Calories | 336 mg | Sodium |
| | | 0 mg | Cholesterol |
| | | 2 g | Fiber |

# Buttermilk Mashed Potatoes

*Mashed potatoes become a special dish when buttermilk, mushrooms, and herbs are added.*

*Makes 4 servings*

| | |
|---|---|
| 15 | ounces potatoes, unpeeled, quartered |
| 1/4 | cup buttermilk |
| 1 | tablespoon minced onion flakes |
| 1/4 | teaspoon dried thyme |
| 1/8 | teaspoon pepper |
| 1/8 | teaspoon garlic powder |
| | Salt to taste |
| 1 | 8-ounce can mushroom pieces, drained |
| 1 | tablespoon wheat germ *or* dry bread crumbs |
| 1 | tablespoon plus 1 teaspoon reduced-calorie margarine |

Place potatoes in 2 inches of boiling water, cover, and cook over medium heat 15 to 20 minutes, or until potatoes are tender. Drain potatoes and remove skin.

Preheat oven to 400°.

Spray a 1-quart casserole with nonstick cooking spray.

Place cooked potatoes in a large bowl and add buttermilk, onion flakes, thyme, pepper, garlic powder, and salt. Mash with a fork or potato masher. Beat on medium speed of an electric mixer until smooth. Add water or a little more buttermilk if potatoes are too dry. Stir in mushrooms.

Place mixture in prepared casserole. Sprinkle evenly with wheat germ. Dot with margarine.

Bake, uncovered, 15 minutes, until hot and lightly browned.

---

Each serving provides:

**132 Calories**

| | | | |
|---|---|---|---|
| 3/4 | Bread Serving | 4 g | Protein |
| 1/2 | Vegetable Serving | 2 g | Fat (15% of calories) |
| 1/2 | Fat Serving | 25 g | Carbohydrate |
| 13 | Additional Calories | 198 mg | Sodium |
| | | 1 mg | Cholesterol |
| | | 2 g | Fiber |

# Oven-Baked French "Fries"

*Can you believe it? These taste so much like the real thing, you'll make them over and over again. Just a spray of nonstick spray, and you still have all of the taste without the gobs of fat.*

*Makes 4 servings*

4      medium baking potatoes, unpeeled (about 5 ounces each)
       Salt and pepper to taste

Preheat oven to 450°.

Spray a baking sheet with nonstick cooking spray.

Cut potatoes into strips to resemble French fries. Place on prepared sheet in a single layer. Spray potatoes lightly with nonstick spray. Sprinkle with salt and pepper to taste.

Bake 10 minutes, then stir potatoes and bake 10 minutes more, or until desired crispness is reached.

---

Each serving provides:

**132 Calories**

| | | |
|---|---|---|
| 1 Bread Serving | 4 g | Protein |
| | 1 g | Fat (8% of calories) |
| | 28 g | Carbohydrate |
| | 12 mg | Sodium |
| | 0 mg | Cholesterol |
| | 3 g | Fiber |

# Potato Latkes (Pancakes)

*Top these tender delicacies with applesauce, and you create a side dish or brunch dish that's really special.*

*Makes 6 servings*
*(3 pancakes each serving)*

1¹/₂   pounds potatoes, unpeeled (3 medium potatoes), grated or
        finely shredded
¹/₂     cup liquid egg substitute
1       small onion, grated
2       tablespoons all-purpose flour
³/₄     teaspoon salt, or to taste
¹/₄     teaspoon pepper, or to taste

Place the potatoes in a bowl and set aside for 10 minutes, then place them in a strainer and press out as much liquid as you can.

Return potatoes to bowl. Add remaining ingredients. Mix well.

Spray a large nonstick skillet or griddle with nonstick cooking spray. Preheat over medium heat. Drop potato mixture onto skillet, making 18 pancakes, using about 2 tablespoons for each pancake. Flatten each one slightly with a spatula. Turn fritters carefully and cook until nicely browned on both sides.

---

Each serving provides:

**112 Calories**

| | | | |
|---|---|---|---|
| ¹/₄ | Protein Serving | 5 g | Protein |
| ³/₄ | Bread Serving | 1 g | Fat (6% of calories) |
| 19 | Additional Calories | 22 g | Carbohydrate |
| | | 316 mg | Sodium |
| | | 0 mg | Cholesterol |
| | | 2 g | Fiber |

# Sweet Potatoes and Apples

*Alternate slices of sweet potatoes and apples, baked in a spiced orange sauce, make a holiday favorite that you'll want to make throughout the year.*

*Makes 4 servings*

| | |
|---|---|
| 12 | ounces cooked sweet potatoes, peeled and sliced into thin slices (Bake the sweet potatoes in a 350° oven for about 1 hour, or microwave for 8 to 10 minutes, until tender, but not mushy.) |
| 2 | small, sweet apples, peeled and cored, cut in half, and cut into very thin slices |
| 1/4 | cup frozen orange juice concentrate, thawed |
| 1/4 | cup water |
| 2 | tablespoons firmly packed brown sugar |
| 1/4 | teaspoon ground cinnamon |
| 1/8 | teaspoon ground nutmeg |
| 1/8 | teaspoon ground ginger |
| 1 | tablespoon plus 1 teaspoon reduced-calorie margarine |

Preheat oven to 350°.

Spray a 1-quart baking dish with nonstick cooking spray.

Arrange alternate slices of sweet potatoes and apples in prepared baking dish.

Combine orange juice, water, brown sugar, and spices. Pour mixture evenly over sweet potatoes and apples. Dot with margarine.

Bake, covered, 1 hour. (If a crisper dish is desired, remove cover during last half of cooking time.)

---

Each serving provides:

**190 Calories**

| | | | |
|---|---|---|---|
| 1 | Bread Serving | 2 g | Protein |
| 1/2 | Fat Serving | 3 g | Fat (12% of calaories) |
| 1 | Fruit Serving | 41 g | Carbohydrate |
| 24 | Additional Calories | 60 mg | Sodium |
| | | 0 mg | Cholesterol |
| | | 4 g | Fiber |

# Island Sweet Potato Pudding

*The sweet, moist banana adds flavor and texture to this delicious casserole that's laced with the flavors of nutmeg and rum and baked until golden.*

*Makes 4 servings*

| | |
|---|---|
| 12 | ounces cooked sweet potatoes, peeled and cut into chunks (Bake the sweet potatoes in a 350° oven for about 1 hour, or microwave for about 8 to 10 minutes, until very tender.) |
| 1 | medium, very ripe banana, mashed |
| 1 | tablespoon firmly packed brown sugar |
| 1/4 | teaspoon ground nutmeg |
| 1 | teaspoon rum extract |
| 1 | egg white |

Preheat oven to 350°.

Spray a 1-quart casserole with nonstick cooking spray.

In a large bowl, combine sweet potatoes, banana, brown sugar, nutmeg, and rum extract. Beat on low speed of an electric mixer until smooth. Add small amounts of water or orange juice, if necessary, to get a smooth consistency.

In a separate bowl, using clean, dry beaters, beat egg white until stiff. Fold into sweet potato mixture. Spoon mixture into prepared casserole.

Bake, uncovered, 45 to 50 minutes, until lightly browned.

---

Each serving provides:

**138 Calories**

| | | | |
|---|---|---|---|
| 1 | Bread Serving | 3 g | Protein |
| 1/2 | Fruit Serving | 1 g | Fat (4% of calories) |
| 17 | Additional Calories | 31 g | Carbohydrate |
| | | 26 mg | Sodium |
| | | 0 mg | Cholesterol |
| | | 3 g | Fiber |

# Corn Soufflé

*This easy soufflé is so creamy and rich-tasting, you won't believe it's so low in fat.*

*Makes 4 servings*

| | |
|---|---|
| 1/4 | cup liquid egg substitute |
| 1 | 1-pound can salt-free (or regular) cream-style corn |
| 1/2 | cup skim milk |
| 3 | tablespoons all-purpose flour |
| 2 | teaspoons sugar |
| 1 | teaspoon minced onion flakes |
| 1/2 | teaspoon dry mustard |
| 2 | egg whites (Egg substitute will not work here.) |

Preheat oven to 350°.

Spray a 2-quart soufflé dish or baking dish with nonstick cooking spray.

In a medium bowl, combine all ingredients *except* egg whites. Beat with a fork or wire whisk until blended.

In another bowl, beat egg whites with an electric mixer until stiff. Fold into corn mixture. Pour mixture into prepared baking dish.

Bake, uncovered, 45 minutes, until puffed and lightly browned.

Serve right away.

---

Each serving provides:

**141 Calories**

| | | | |
|---|---|---|---|
| 1/4 | Protein Serving | 7 g | Protein |
| 1 1/4 | Bread Servings | 1 g | Fat (5% of calories) |
| 29 | Additional Calories | 29 g | Carbohydrate |
| | | 72 mg | Sodium |
| | | 1 mg | Cholesterol |
| | | 2 g | Fiber |

# Mexi-Corn

*The sprinkle of fresh cilantro at the end is optional, but we do hope you'll try it that way. Its unusual flavor really enhances the flavors of Mexican food. Look for cilantro in the produce section of most large grocery stores.*

*Makes 4 servings*

| | |
|---|---|
| 2 | teaspoons vegetable oil |
| 1/4 | cup finely chopped green bell pepper |
| 1/4 | cup finely chopped red bell pepper |
| 1/4 | cup finely chopped onion |
| 1/4 | cup water |
| 1 | 1-pound can salt-free (or regular) corn, drained |
| | Pepper to taste |
| 1 | tablespoon chopped fresh cilantro (optional) |

Heat oil in a small saucepan over medium heat. Add peppers and onion. Cook, stirring frequently, until vegetables are tender, about 8 minutes. Add small amounts of water if necessary (about a tablespoon at a time) to prevent sticking.

Add water and corn. Heat through and add pepper to taste.

Sprinkle with cilantro, if desired.

---

Each serving provides:

**97 Calories**

| | | | |
|---|---|---|---|
| 1 | Bread Serving | 2 g | Protein |
| 3/4 | Vegetable Serving | 3 g | Fat (23% of calories) |
| 1/2 | Fat Serving | 18 g | Carbohydrate |
| | | 4 mg | Sodium |
| | | 0 mg | Cholesterol |
| | | 2 g | Fiber |

# Breads and Muffins

Breads and muffins can be an excellent source of fiber in our diet. Versatile and delicious, they can be served with any meal and also make great snacks. While many bakeries sell breads and muffins, most commercial varieties are high in fat and low in fiber. Often made with white flour, butter, and whole eggs, they are often laden with fat and calories.

Most of the breads and muffins in this section are made with a combination of all-purpose flour and whole wheat flour. This, along with the addition of fruits and vegetables, adds vitamins, minerals, and fiber as well as a delectable texture to the recipes.

To keep the fat down, we use skim milk and lowfat buttermilk in our breads and muffins. To reduce the amount of cholesterol, we use egg whites or liquid egg substitute in place of whole eggs. We also use as little oil as possible and, instead, add moistness by using applesauce, yogurt, or fruits in place of most of the shortening. When we do use oil, we choose one that is mostly monounsaturated, such as canola oil.

All of our breads are quick breads. Our muffins are baked in standard muffin pans with 2 1/2-inch cups. We prefer nonstick pans for breads and muffins and spray them lightly with nonstick cooking spray. Remember that oven temperatures may vary slightly, so it is wise to test breads and muffins for doneness by inserting a toothpick in the center. It will come out clean when the breads or muffins are done.

Most breads and muffins taste best when served warm. If this is not possible, let them cool completely before wrapping. Because these homemade delicacies are not made with preservatives, they have a shorter shelf life than many commercially baked goods. Therefore, we advise refrigerating them on the second day and reheating them briefly before serving.

From Beer Bread to Banana Date-Nut Muffins, from sweet to savory, our wonderful variety of breads and muffins are all made "light" for you.

# Pumpkin Raisin Bread

*This special bread has a mild, spiced flavor and just a hint of orange. It's perfect for holiday gift-giving.*

*Makes 8 servings*

| | |
|---|---|
| ³/₄ | cup whole wheat flour |
| ³/₄ | cup all-purpose flour |
| 1¹/₂ | teaspoons baking powder |
| ¹/₂ | baking soda |
| 1 | teaspoon pumpkin pie spice |
| ¹/₄ | cup plus 2 tablespoons raisins |
| 2 | egg whites |
| 1 | cup canned pumpkin |
| ¹/₃ | cup sugar |
| ¹/₄ | cup plus 2 tablespoons skim milk |
| 2 | tablespoons vegetable oil |
| 1 | teaspoon vanilla extract |
| ¹/₂ | teaspoon orange extract |

Preheat oven to 350°.

Spray a 4 × 8-inch loaf pan with nonstick cooking spray.

In a large bowl, combine both types of flour, baking powder, baking soda, and pumpkin pie spice. Mix well. Stir in raisins.

In another bowl, combine remaining ingredients. Beat with a fork or wire whisk until blended. Add to dry mixture, mixing until all ingredients are moistened.

Spoon batter into prepared pan.

Bake 40 to 50 minutes, until a toothpick inserted in the center of the bread comes out clean.

Cool in pan on a wire rack 5 minutes, then turn out onto rack to finish cooling.

---

Each serving provides:

**188 Calories**

| | | | |
|---|---|---|---|
| 1 | Bread Serving | 5 g | Protein |
| ¹/₄ | Vegetable Serving | 4 g | Fat (19% of calories) |
| ³/₄ | Fat Serving | 34 g | Carbohydrate |
| ¹/₄ | Fruit Serving | 193 mg | Sodium |
| 49 | Additional Calories | 0 mg | Cholesterol |
| | | 3 g | Fiber |

# Irish Soda Bread

*This bumpy, crusty bread is traditionally made in a round shape and sliced into thin wedges to serve. Its nice texture and mild caraway flavor make it a perfect accompaniment to any meal.*

*Makes 16 servings*

| | |
|---|---|
| 3 | cups all-purpose flour |
| 2 | tablespoons sugar |
| 1 | tablespoon caraway seeds |
| 1 | teaspoon baking soda |
| 1 | teaspoon baking powder |
| 1 | teaspoon salt |
| 1/2 | cup raisins |
| 1 1/4 | cups plus 2 tablespoons skim milk |
| 1 | tablespoon vinegar |
| 2 | tablespoons plus 2 teaspoons vegetable oil |

Preheat oven to 375°.

Spray an 8-inch cake pan with nonstick cooking spray.

In a large bowl, combine flour, sugar, caraway seeds, baking soda, baking powder, and salt. Mix well. Stir in raisins.

In a small bowl, combine milk and vinegar. Let stand 3 to 5 minutes. Stir in oil.

Add to flour mixture, mixing until all ingredients are moistened. Place dough in prepared pan and, with lightly floured hands, spread dough in pan.

Bake 30 minutes, until golden brown.

Transfer the bread to a wire rack, cover with a clean dish towel, and let cool.

---

Each serving provides:

**135 Calories**

| | | | |
|---|---|---|---|
| 1 | Bread Serving | 3 g | Protein |
| 1/2 | Fat Serving | 3 g | Fat (18% of calories) |
| 1/4 | Fruit Serving | 24 g | Carbohydrate |
| 17 | Additional Calories | 259 mg | Sodium |
| | | 0 mg | Cholesterol |
| | | 1 g | Fiber |

# Orange-Raisin Tea Loaf

*The chopped orange and raisins give this bread a delicate flavor and moistness you'll love. Be sure to discard the white membrane of the orange, since it is quite bitter.*

*Makes 10 servings*

| | |
|---|---|
| 1/2 | cup boiling water |
| 1/2 | cup raisins |
| 1 | small orange |
| 1/4 | cup plus 2 tablespoons sugar |
| 2 | egg whites |
| 1 | plus 2 teaspoons vegetable oil |
| 1 | teaspoon vanilla extract |
| 1 | cup minus 2 tablespoons all-purpose flour |
| 1 | cup whole wheat flour |
| 1 | teaspoon baking powder |
| 1 | teaspoon baking soda |
| 1 | teaspoon ground cinnamon |
| 1/2 | teaspoon ground nutmeg |
| 1/2 | teaspoon ground ginger |

Preheat oven to 350°.

Spray a 4 × 8-inch loaf pan with nonstick cooking spray.

Pour boiling water over raisins in a small bowl. Set aside.

Grate the orange, saving the peel. Peel orange, discarding the white membrane. Cut up the orange pulp. Place the orange pulp, raisins, and water in a blender container. Blend for a few seconds, until raisins are just chopped. Do not puree.

In a large bowl, combine raisin mixture, orange peel, sugar, egg whites, oil, and vanilla. Mix well.

In another bowl, combine remaining ingredients. Mix well. Add to orange mixture, mixing until all ingredients are moistened. Spoon batter into prepared pan.

Bake 40 to 45 minutes, until a toothpick inserted in the center of the bread comes out clean. Cool in pan on a wire rack for 5 minutes, then turn out onto rack to finish cooling.

Each serving provides:

**165 Calories**

| | | | |
|---|---|---|---|
| 1 | Bread Serving | 4 g | Protein |
| 1/2 | Fat Serving | 3 g | Fat (15% of calories) |
| 1/2 | Fruit Serving | 32 g | Carbohydrate |
| 33 | Additional Calories | 188 mg | Sodium |
| | | 0 mg | Cholesterol |
| | | 2 g | Fiber |

# Skillet Cheese Corn Bread

*You can bake and serve this delicious corn bread right in the skillet. For a
Mexican flavor, add some chopped chilies, either fresh, dried, or canned, to
the wet ingredients.*

*Makes 12 servings*

| | |
|---|---|
| 2 | cups yellow cornmeal (12 ounces) |
| 2 | teaspoons baking powder |
| 1/2 | teaspoon baking soda |
| 1/4 | teaspoon salt |
| 1 1/4 | cups buttermilk |
| 1 | 1-pound can salt-free (or regular) cream-style corn |
| 3 | egg whites |
| 1/4 | cup honey |
| 2 | tablespoons vegetable oil |
| 1 | cup shredded reduced-fat Cheddar cheese (4 ounces) |

Preheat oven to 400°.

Spray a 10-inch cast-iron skillet with nonstick cooking spray.

In a large bowl, combine cornmeal, baking powder, baking soda,
and salt. Mix well.

In another bowl, combine buttermilk, corn, egg whites, honey, and
oil. Beat with a fork or wire whisk until blended. Stir in cheese. Add
to dry mixture, stirring until all ingredients are moistened.

Heat skillet in oven for 3 minutes. Remove from oven and immedi-
ately pour in batter.

Bake 30 to 35 minutes, until a toothpick inserted in the center of the
bread comes out clean.

Cut into wedges and serve hot.

Each serving provides:
**215 Calories**

| | | | |
|---|---|---|---|
| 1/2 | Protein Serving | 8 g | Protein |
| 1 1/2 | Bread Servings | 5 g | Fat (20% of calories) |
| 1/2 | Fat Serving | 36 g | Carbohydrate |
| 44 | Additional Calories | 295 mg | Sodium |
| | | 8 mg | Cholesterol |
| | | 2 g | Fiber |

# Beer Bread

*This bread is so quick and easy, you'll make it time and again. It tastes wonderful and the texture is divine! What more could you ask for?*

*Makes 12 servings*

1¼    cups all-purpose flour
1      cup whole wheat flour
2      tablespoons sugar
2¼    teaspoons baking powder
½      teaspoon salt
1      12-ounce can light beer, at room temperature

Preheat oven to 375°.

Spray a 4 × 8-inch loaf pan with nonstick cooking spray.

In a large bowl, combine both types of flour, sugar, baking powder, and salt. Mix well. Add beer. Stir until foam subsides and all ingredients are moistened.

Pour batter into prepared pan.

Bake 45 to 50 minutes, until a toothpick inserted in the center of the bread comes out clean.

Cool in pan on a wire rack for 5 minutes, then turn out onto rack to finish cooling.

For a delicious variation that tastes like rye bread, add ⅛ teaspoon garlic powder and 1 teaspoon caraway seeds to the dry ingredients.

---

Each serving provides:

### 99 Calories

| | | | |
|---|---|---|---|
| 1 | Bread Serving | 3 g | Protein |
| 16 | Additional Calories | trace | Fat (4% of calories) |
| | | 20 g | Carbohydrate |
| | | 184 mg | Sodium |
| | | 0 mg | Cholesterol |
| | | 2 g | Fiber |

# Scones

*A popular English treat, these pie-shaped rolls taste great with strawberry jam. Served warm with a cup of tea, they're such a friendly treat.*

*Makes 8 scones*

| | |
|---|---|
| 3/4 | cup all-purpose flour |
| 3/4 | cup whole wheat flour |
| 1 1/2 | teaspoons baking powder |
| 1/4 | teaspoon salt |
| 1 | tablespoon sugar |
| 2 | tablespoons plus 2 teaspoons margarine |
| 1/4 | cup raisins |
| 1/2 | cup skim milk |
| 2 | teaspoons vinegar |
| 2 | egg whites |
| 1 | teaspoon grated fresh lemon peel |

Preheat oven to 400°.

Spray a baking sheet with nonstick cooking spray.

In a large bowl, combine both types of flour, baking powder, salt, and sugar. Mix well.

Add margarine. Mix with a fork or pastry blender until mixture resembles coarse crumbs. Stir in raisins. ·

Place milk in a small bowl. Add vinegar and let stand 1 minute. Add egg whites and lemon peel. Beat with a fork or wire whisk until blended. Add to dry mixture, mixing until all ingredients are moistened.

Turn dough out onto prepared baking sheet. Flatten dough into an 8-inch circle, wetting your hands lightly to prevent sticking. With a sharp knife, score the dough, marking 8 pie-shaped wedges.

Bake 15 minutes, until bottom of bread is lightly browned.

Transfer to a wire rack and serve warm for best flavor.

---

Each scone provides:

**146 Calories**

| | | | |
|---|---|---|---|
| 1 | Bread Serving | 4 g | Protein |
| 1 | Fat Serving | 4 g | Fat (26% of calories) |
| 1/4 | Fruit Serving | 23 g | Carbohydrate |
| 17 | Additional Calories | 227 mg | Sodium |
| | | 0 mg | Cholesterol |
| | | 2 g | Fiber |

# Quick Onion Biscuits

*Turn refrigerator biscuits into hot onion rolls with just 2 extra ingredients.*

*Makes 5 biscuits*

2¹/₂    teaspoons margarine, melted
2¹/₂    teaspoons minced onion flakes
1       5-ounce package refrigerator biscuits

Preheat oven to 450°.

Combine margarine and onion flakes in a small bowl or custard cup.

Place biscuits on a nonstick baking sheet. With your finger, make a large dent in the center of each biscuit. Divide the margarine mixture evenly and fill the dents in the biscuits.

Bake 8 to 10 minutes, until biscuits are golden.

Remove from pan right away and serve hot.

---

Each biscuit provides:

**99 Calories**

|       |                |         |                       |
| ----: | -------------- | ------: | --------------------- |
| 1     | Bread Serving  | 2 g     | Protein               |
| 1¹/₂  | Fat Servings   | 6 g     | Fat (48% of calories) |
|       |                | 13 g    | Carbohydrates         |
|       |                | 322 mg  | Sodium                |
|       |                | 0 mg    | Cholesterol           |
|       |                | 0 g     | Fiber                 |

# Sweet Potato "Ruffins"

*Unique and delicious, these bumpy, crusty rolls are a cross between a roll and a muffin. We enjoy them all year long, and they always make an appearance at our holiday tables.*

*Makes 12 muffins*

| | |
|---|---|
| 1 1/2 | cups whole wheat flour |
| 3/4 | cup all-purpose flour |
| 2 | teaspoons baking powder |
| 1 | teaspoon baking soda |
| 3 | tablespoons dried chives |
| 1 | teaspoon dried basil |
| 1/2 | teaspoon dried thyme |
| 2 | egg whites |
| 1 | teaspoon grated fresh lemon peel |
| 1 | cup plain nonfat yogurt |
| 2 | tablespoons vegetable oil |
| 12 | ounces finely shredded sweet potato, unpeeled (1 1/2 cups packed) |

Preheat oven to 400°.

Spray 12 muffin cups with nonstick cooking spray.

In a large bowl, combine both types of flour, baking powder, baking soda, and herbs. Mix well.

In another bowl, combine remaining ingredients *except* sweet potato. Mix well. Stir in sweet potato. Add to dry mixture, mixing until all ingredients are moistened.

Divide dough evenly into prepared muffin cups.

Bake 15 to 18 minutes, until a toothpick inserted in the center of a muffin comes out clean.

Remove muffins to a wire rack and serve warm for best flavor.

---

Each muffin provides:

**145 Calories**

| | | | |
|---|---|---|---|
| 1 1/4 | Bread Servings | 5 g | Protein |
| 1/2 | Fat Serving | 3 g | Fat (18% of calories) |
| 13 | Additional Calories | 26 g | Carbohydrate |
| | | 215 mg | Sodium |
| | | 0 mg | Cholesterol |
| | | 3 g | Fiber |

# Yogurt Biscuits

*Try 'em while they're hot! Topped with jam or made into little sandwiches, you'll love the moist texture of these delectable biscuits.*

*Makes 6 biscuits*

| | |
|---|---|
| 1/2 | cup plus 2 tablespoons all-purpose flour |
| 1/2 | cup whole wheat flour |
| 1 1/2 | teaspoons baking powder |
| 1/4 | teaspoon baking soda |
| 1 | teaspoon sugar |
| 1/4 | teaspoon salt |
| 2 | tablespoons margarine |
| 1/2 | cup plain nonfat yogurt |
| 1/2 | teaspoon skim milk |

Preheat oven to 425°.

Have a nonstick baking sheet ready.

In a large bowl, combine both types of flour, baking powder, baking soda, sugar, and salt. Add margarine. Using a fork or pastry blender, mix until mixture resembles coarse crumbs.

Add yogurt, mixing until all ingredients are moistened. Add a little skim milk if necessary (about a tablespoon at a time) to form a soft dough. Place dough on a lightly floured surface and knead gently to form a ball.

Place dough on baking sheet and roll or pat into a rectangle, about 1/2-inch thick. With a sharp knife, cut the dough, forming 6 even biscuits, but do not separate them.

With your finger, "paint" the top of the biscuits with the milk.

Bake 10 to 12 minutes, until biscuits are golden.

Remove to a wire rack and serve warm for best flavor.

---

Each biscuit provides:

**129 Calories**

| | | | |
|---|---|---|---|
| 1 | Bread Serving | 4 g | Protein |
| 1 | Fat Serving | 4 g | Fat (28% of calories) |
| 13 | Additional Calories | 20 g | Carbohydrate |
| | | 323 mg | Sodium |
| | | 0 mg | Cholesterol |
| | | 2 g | Fiber |

# Cheese Pinwheels

*Biscuits rolled with cheese make pretty pinwheels that add a spark to any meal.*

*Makes 9 servings*
*(2 pinwheels each serving)*

1      recipe Yogurt Biscuits (see page 304)
3      ounces shredded reduced-fat Cheddar cheese (³/₄ cup)

Prepare dough for Yogurt Biscuits as directed.

Preheat oven to 425°.

Have a nonstick baking sheet ready.

Place dough on a lightly floured surface and roll or pat into a rectangle about ¹/₄-inch thick. Sprinkle evenly with cheese.

Starting with 1 long side, roll dough tightly into a log. Cut into 18 even slices. Place slices on baking sheet.

Bake 12 minutes, until lightly browned.

Remove pinwheels to a wire rack and serve warm for best flavor.

---

Each serving provides:

**113 Calories**

| | | | |
|---|---|---|---|
| ¹/₄ | Protein Serving | 6 g | Protein |
| ¹/₂ | Bread Serving | 4 g | Fat (35% of calories) |
| ¹/₂ | Fat Serving | 13 g | Carbohydrate |
| 40 | Additional Calories | 289 mg | Sodium |
| | | 7 mg | Cholesterol |
| | | 1 g | Fiber |

# Jelly Muffins

*These tender, egg-free muffins have a surprise burst of flavor in the center.*
*We prefer the taste of raspberry or blackberry jam, but any flavor will work.*

*Makes 12 muffins*

### Topping
2¹/₂      teaspoons sugar
¹/₄       teaspoon ground cinnamon

### Muffins
1¹/₄     cups all-purpose flour
1          cup whole wheat flour
1¹/₂     teaspoons baking powder
1          teaspoon baking soda
³/₄       teaspoon ground cinnamon
2          cups skim milk
¹/₃       cup honey
2          tablespoons vegetable oil
1¹/₂     teaspoons vanilla extract
¹/₂       teaspoon almond extract
¹/₄       cup fruit-only raspberry *or* blackberry spread

Preheat oven to 400°.

Spray 12 muffin cups with nonstick cooking spray.

Combine topping ingredients in a small bowl and set aside.

In a large bowl, combine both types of flour, baking powder, baking soda, and cinnamon. Mix well.

In another bowl, combine milk, honey, oil, and extracts. Beat with a fork or wire whisk until blended. Add to dry mixture. Mix until all ingredients are moistened. (Batter will be loose.) Divide mixture evenly

into prepared muffin cups. Place a teaspoon of the jam on the top center of each muffin. Sprinkle evenly with topping.

Bake 18 to 20 minutes, until a toothpick near the center of each muffin (not in the jam) comes out clean.

Remove muffins to a rack and serve warm for best flavor.

---

Each muffin provides:

**166 Calories**

| | | | |
|---|---|---|---|
| 1 | Bread Serving | 4 g | Protein |
| 1/2 | Fat Serving | 3 g | Fat (15% of calories) |
| 1/4 | Fruit Serving | 32 g | Carbohydrate |
| 50 | Additional Calories | 188 mg | Sodium |
| | | 1 mg | Cholesterol |
| | | 2 g | Fiber |

# Cinnamon Yogurt Muffins

*Mmm . . . a hot cup of tea and a warm, moist cinnamon-flavored muffin. What better way to enrich a friendship?*

*Makes 12 muffins*

### Topping

| | |
|---|---|
| 2 | teaspoons sugar |
| 1/4 | teaspoon ground cinnamon |
| 1/8 | teaspoon ground nutmeg |

### Muffins

| | |
|---|---|
| 1 1/4 | cups whole wheat four |
| 1 | cup all-purpose flour |
| 1 1/2 | teaspoons baking powder |
| 1 1/2 | teaspoons baking soda |
| 2 1/4 | teaspoons ground cinnamon |
| 1/4 | teaspoon ground nutmeg |
| 2 | egg whites |
| 1 1/2 | cups vanilla nonfat yogurt |
| 1/4 | cup plus 2 tablespoons sugar |
| 2 | tablespoons vegetable oil |
| 2 | teaspoons vanilla extract |

Preheat oven to 400°.

Spray 12 muffin cups with nonstick cooking spray.

In a small bowl or custard cup, combine topping ingredients. Set aside.

In a large bowl, combine both types of flour, baking powder, baking soda, cinnamon, and nutmeg. Mix well.

In another bowl, combine remaining ingredients. Beat with a fork or wire whisk until blended. Add to dry mixture, mixing until all

ingredients are moistened. Divide mixture evenly into prepared muffin cups. Sprinkle evenly with topping.

Bake 15 minutes, until a toothpick inserted in the center of a muffin comes out clean.

Remove muffins to a wire rack and serve warm for best flavor.

Each muffin provides:

**161 Calories**

| | | | |
|---|---|---|---|
| 1 | Bread Serving | 5 g | Protein |
| 1/2 | Fat Serving | 3 g | Fat (16% of calories) |
| 54 | Additional Calories | 29 g | Carbohydrate |
| | | 248 mg | Sodium |
| | | 1 mg | Cholesterol |
| | | 2 g | Fiber |

# Maple Bran Muffins

*Serving these muffins warm, right out of the oven, really accentuates the sweet, maple flavor. You won't believe that a muffin so low in fat and high in fiber can taste so good.*

*Makes 12 muffins*

| | |
|---|---|
| 3/4 | cup all-purpose flour |
| 3/4 | cup whole wheat flour |
| 1 1/2 | cups bran (3 ounces) (This is wheat bran, not bran cereal, and it's found in the cereal section of most large grocery stores.) |
| 2 | teaspoons baking powder |
| 1 | teaspoon baking soda |
| 1/2 | teaspoon ground cinnamon |
| 1/2 | cup raisins |
| 1 1/2 | cups skim milk |
| 1/4 | cup plus 2 tablespoons maple syrup |
| 2 | tablespoons vegetable oil |
| 2 | tablespoons firmly packed brown sugar |
| 2 | egg whites |
| 1 1/4 | teaspoons maple extract |
| 1 | teaspoon vanilla extract |

Preheat oven to 400°.

Spray 12 muffin cups with nonstick cooking spray.

In a large bowl, combine both types of flour, bran, baking powder, baking soda, and cinnamon. Mix well. Stir in raisins.

In another bowl, combine remaining ingredients. Beat with a fork or wire whisk until blended. Add to dry mixture, mixing until all

ingredients are moistened. Divide mixture evenly into prepared muffin cups.

Bake 15 minutes, until a toothpick inserted in the center of a muffin comes out clean.

Remove muffins to a wire rack and serve warm for best flavor.

Each muffin provides:

**159 Calories**

| | | | |
|---|---|---|---|
| 1 | Bread Serving | 5 g | Protein |
| 1/2 | Fat Serving | 3 g | Fat (16% of calories) |
| 1/4 | Fruit Serving | 32 g | Carbohydrate |
| 50 | Additional Calories | 215 mg | Sodium |
| | | 1 mg | Cholesterol |
| | | 4 g | Fiber |

# Pumpkin Apple Muffins

*Moist, tender, and filled with fruit and spices, these muffins will grace your holiday table or please your family all year long.*

*Makes 12 muffins*

| | |
|---|---|
| 1¹/₄ | cups all-purpose flour |
| 1 | cup whole wheat flour |
| 2 | teaspoons baking powder |
| ¹/₂ | teaspoon baking soda |
| 1 | teaspoon ground cinnamon |
| ¹/₂ | teaspoon ground nutmeg |
| ¹/₄ | teaspoon ground cloves |
| ¹/₄ | teaspoon ground ginger |
| ¹/₄ | cup plus 2 tablespoons raisins |
| 2 | egg whites |
| 2 | tablespoons vegetable oil |
| ¹/₂ | cup sugar |
| ¹/₂ | cup orange juice |
| 1 | teaspoon vanilla extract |
| 1 | cup canned pumpkin |
| 2 | small apples, unpeeled, coarsely shredded (1 cup) |

Preheat oven to 400°.

Spray 12 muffin cups with nonstick cooking spray.

In a large bowl, combine both types of flour, baking powder, baking soda, and spices. Mix well. Stir in raisins.

In another bowl, combine egg whites, oil, sugar, orange juice, and vanilla. Beat with a fork or wire whisk until blended. Add pumpkin and apples and whisk until blended.

Add to dry mixture, mixing until all ingredients are moistened.

Divide mixture evenly into prepared muffin cups.

Bake 15 to 18 minutes, until a toothpick inserted in the center of a muffin comes out clean.

Remove muffins to a wire rack and serve warm for best flavor.

Each muffin provides:

**172 Calories**

| | | | |
|---|---|---|---|
| 1 | Bread Serving | 4 g | Protein |
| 1/4 | Vegetable Serving | 3 g | Fat (15% of calories) |
| 1/2 | Fat Serving | 34 g | Carbohydrate |
| 1/2 | Fruit Serving | 145 mg | Sodium |
| 35 | Additional Calories | 0 mg | Cholesterol |
| | | 2 g | Fiber |

# Banana Date-Nut Muffins

*The sweetness of the bananas, teamed up with the chewy dates and crunchy nuts, makes a special combination. For the sweetest muffins, make sure the bananas are super-ripe.*

*Makes 12 muffins*

| | |
|---|---|
| 1¼ | cups whole wheat flour |
| 1 | cup all-purpose flour |
| 1½ | teaspoons baking powder |
| 1 | teaspoon baking soda |
| 4 | dates, chopped (1½ ounces) |
| 2 | tablespoons chopped walnuts (½ ounce) |
| 2 | egg whites |
| ¾ | cup skim milk |
| ⅓ | cup firmly packed brown sugar |
| 2 | tablespoons vegetable oil |
| 2 | teaspoons vanilla extract |
| 2 | medium, very ripe bananas, mashed (1 cup) |

Preheat oven to 400°.

Spray 12 muffin cups with nonstick cooking spray.

In a large bowl, combine both types of flour, baking powder, and baking soda. Mix well. Stir in dates and nuts.

In another bowl, combine egg whites, milk, brown sugar, oil, and vanilla. Beat with a fork or wire whisk until blended. Whisk in bananas. Add to dry mixture, mixing until all ingredients are moistened. Divide mixture evenly into prepared muffin cups.

Bake 15 to 18 minutes, until a toothpick inserted in the center of a muffin comes out clean.

Remove muffins to a wire rack and serve warm for best flavor.

---

Each muffin provides:

**170 Calories**

| | | | |
|---|---|---|---|
| 1 | Bread Serving | 4 g | Protein |
| ½ | Fat Serving | 4 g | Fat (19% of calories) |
| ½ | Fruit Serving | 31 g | Carbohydrate |
| 36 | Additional Calories | 187 mg | Sodium |
| | | 0 mg | Cholesterol |
| | | 2 g | Fiber |

# Zucchini Muffins

*Everyone's favorite made light, these delicious muffins are an ideal way to take advantage of the abundant garden zucchini. The muffins freeze well, so you can make lots.*

*Makes 12 muffins*

| | |
|---|---|
| 1 1/4 | cups all-purpose flour |
| 1 | cup whole wheat flour |
| 1 1/2 | teaspoons baking powder |
| 1 | teaspoon baking soda |
| 1 1/2 | teaspoons ground cinnamon |
| 3/4 | teaspoon ground nutmeg |
| 1/4 | cup plus 2 tablespoons raisins |
| 2 | egg whites |
| 1/2 | cup skim milk |
| 1/2 | cup sugar |
| 2 | tablespoons vegetable oil |
| 1 | teaspoon vanilla extract |
| 1/2 | teaspoon lemon extract |
| 1 1/2 | cups zucchini (packed), unpeeled, finely shredded |

Preheat oven to 400°.

Spray 12 muffin cups with nonstick cooking spray.

In a large bowl, combine both types of flour, baking powder, baking soda, and spices. Mix well. Stir in raisins.

In another bowl, combine all ingredients *except* zucchini. Beat with a fork or wire whisk until blended. Stir in zucchini. Add to dry mixture, mixing until all ingredients are moistened.

Divide mixture evenly into prepared muffin cups.

Bake 15 to 18 minutes, until a toothpick inserted in the center of a muffin comes out clean.

Remove muffins to a wire rack and serve warm for best flavor.

---

Each muffin provides:

**163 Calories**

| | | | |
|---|---|---|---|
| 1 | Bread Serving | 4 g | Protein |
| 1/4 | Vegetable Serving | 3 g | Fat (16% of calories) |
| 1/2 | Fat Serving | 31 g | Carbohydrate |
| 1/4 | Fruit Serving | 183 mg | Sodium |
| 39 | Additional Calories | 0 mg | Cholesterol |
| | | 2 g | Fiber |

# Cheddar 'n' Onion Muffins

*A perfect accompaniment to a bowl of thick soup or stew, these muffins are best when served hot, right out of the oven.*

*Makes 12 muffins*

| | |
|---|---|
| 1 1/2 | cups all-purpose flour |
| 3/4 | cup whole wheat flour |
| 1 1/2 | teaspoons baking powder |
| 1 1/2 | teaspoons baking soda |
| 1 | tablespoon plus 1 teaspoon dried chives |
| 2 | teaspoons onion powder |
| 1/8 | teaspoon salt |
| 2 | egg whites |
| 2 | tablespoons vegetable oil |
| 2 | tablespoons grated onion |
| 1 1/2 | cups plain nonfat yogurt |
| 4 | ounces shredded reduced-fat Cheddar cheese (1 cup) |

Preheat oven to 400°.

Spray 12 muffin cups with nonstick cooking spray.

In a large bowl, combine both types of flour, baking powder, baking soda, chives, onion powder, and salt. Mix well.

In another bowl, combine all ingredients *except* Cheddar cheese. Beat with a fork or wire whisk until blended. Stir in cheese. Add to dry mixture, mixing until all ingredients are moistened.

Divide mixture evenly into prepared muffin cups.

Bake 15 to 18 minutes, until tops of muffins are light brown and a toothpick inserted in the center of a muffin comes out clean.

Remove muffins to a wire rack and serve right away for best flavor.

---

Each muffin provides:

**152 Calories**

| | | | |
|---|---|---|---|
| 1/4 | Protein Serving | 8 g | Protein |
| 1 | Bread Serving | 5 g | Fat (27% of calories) |
| 1/2 | Fat Serving | 20 g | Carbohydrate |
| 30 | Additional Calories | 346 mg | Sodium |
| | | 7 mg | Cholesterol |
| | | 1 g | Fiber |

# Savory Herbed Muffins

*The mellow herbs create an aroma and flavor that spells h-o-m-e. A basket of these golden muffins, with their bumpy, crusty appearance, will definitely grace any table.*

*Makes 12 muffins*

1<sup>1</sup>/2   cups all-purpose flour
3/4   cup whole wheat flour
1<sup>1</sup>/2   teaspoons baking soda
1   teaspoon baking powder
2   packets low-sodium instant chicken- or vegetable-flavored
      broth mix
2   tablespoons minced onion flakes
1/4   teaspoon dill weed
2   tablespoons vegetable oil
2   egg whites
1   tablespoon plus 1 teaspoon honey
1<sup>1</sup>/2   cups plain nonfat yogurt

Preheat oven to 400°.

Spray 12 muffin cups with nonstick cooking spray.

In a large bowl, combine both types of flour, baking soda, baking powder, broth mix, onion flakes, and dill. Mix well.

In another bowl, combine remaining ingredients. Beat with a fork or wire whisk until blended. Add to dry mixture, mixing until all ingredients are moistened. Divide mixture into prepared muffin cups.

Bake 15 to 18 minutes, until tops of muffins are golden and a toothpick inserted in the center of a muffin comes out clean.

Remove to a wire rack and serve warm for best flavor.

---

Each muffin provides:

**133 Calories**

| | | | |
|---|---|---|---|
| 1 | Bread Serving | 5 g | Protein |
| 1/2 | Fat Serving | 3 g | Fat (18% of calories) |
| 27 | Additional Calories | 22 g | Carbohydrate |
| | | 230 mg | Sodium |
| | | 1 mg | Cholesterol |
| | | 1 g | Fiber |

# *Fruits*

Fruits are sweet, natural gifts from Mother Nature. Their versatility is endless, whether used as appetizers, entrées, desserts, or as in-between-meals snacks. Most fruits are low in fat and high in carbohydrates, supplying our bodies with necessary vitamins, minerals, and fiber.

In preparing fruit recipes, always choose varieties of fruits that are naturally sweet. The sweeter the fruit, the less sugar you will need to use. Also, for added nutrition, leave the skin on whenever possible.

So, enjoy exploring the many culinary possibilities we've created here for you, and browse through our other sections, too, to find fruits uniquely combined with unusual ingredients and as an added bonus in many of our cakes and pies.

# Company Fruit Compote

*One of our quick and easy favorites, we adapted this recipe from one that we used to make with lots of butter. The delightful combination of extracts helps to create a unique and delicious flavor.*

*Makes 4 servings*

| | |
|---|---|
| 1/2 | cup canned, sliced peaches (packed in juice), drained (Reserve 2 tablespoons of the juice.) |
| 12 | large frozen dark, sweet cherries (unsweetened) |
| 1/2 | cup canned, sliced pears (packed in juice), drained (Reserve 2 tablespoons of the juice.) |
| 1/2 | cup canned pineapple chunks (packed in juice), drained (Reserve 2 tablespoons of the juice.) |
| 2 | tablespoons firmly packed brown sugar |
| 1/4 | teaspoon ground cinnamon |
| 1/2 | teaspoon vanilla extract |
| 1/4 | teaspoon maple extract |
| 1/4 | teaspoon lemon extract |
| 1 | tablespoon plus 1 teaspoon cornstarch |

Preheat oven to 350°.

Spray a 1-quart casserole with nonstick cooking spray.

Combine fruits in a large bowl. Sprinkle with brown sugar and cinnamon. Mix well. Place in prepared casserole.

In a small bowl, combine reserved fruit juices, extracts, and cornstarch. Stir to dissolve cornstarch. Pour mixture over fruit.

Bake, uncovered, 15 to 20 minutes, until hot and bubbly.

Serve warm for best flavor.

---

Each serving provides:

**111 Calories**

| | | | |
|---|---|---|---|
| 1 | Fruit Serving | 1 g | Protein |
| 34 | Additional Calories | 1 g | Fat (11% of calories) |
| | | 25 g | Carbohydrate |
| | | 6 mg | Sodium |
| | | 0 mg | Cholesterol |
| | | 1 g | Fiber |

# Fruit Salad in a Watermelon Basket

*Always a crowd pleaser, this elegant dish is really easy to prepare. Our fruits are just a suggestion. Feel free to fill the watermelon with whatever fresh fruits are available. Our amounts are also a suggestion, and they will vary according to the size of the watermelon.*

*Makes 16 servings*

| | |
|---|---|
| 1 | medium watermelon |
| 2 | cups watermelon balls |
| 1 | cup cantaloupe balls |
| 1 | cup honeydew melon balls |
| 1 | cup strawberries, halved |
| 1 | cup blueberries |
| 2 | medium peaches, peeled, pitted, cut into chunks |
| 24 | large seedless red grapes |
| 1/4 | medium, ripe pineapple, pared, cut into chunks |
| 3 | tablespoons orange juice |
| 1 | tablespoon lime juice (preferably fresh) |
| 2 | tablespoons confectioners' sugar |
| 1/2 | teaspoon rum extract |

To prepare basket, cut the watermelon in half lengthwise. Using a melon ball scoop, remove the pulp. Measure 2 cups of watermelon balls, reserving remaining watermelon balls for another use. Using a sharp knife, scallop the edges of the watermelon. Slice a very thin piece off the bottom of the melon to keep it from tipping over.

Chill prepared watermelon basket. Also chill watermelon balls and remaining fruits, keeping them all separate.

Just before serving, combine all fruits in a large bowl. Combine orange juice, lime juice, sugar, and rum extract. Pour over fruit and mix well. Spoon fruit into watermelon basket.

---

Each serving provides:

**40 Calories**

| | | | |
|---|---|---|---|
| 3/4 | Fruit Serving | 0 g | Protein |
| 9 | Additional Calories | trace | Fat (5% of calories) |
| | | 10 g | Carbohydrate |
| | | 3 mg | Sodium |
| | | 0 mg | Cholesterol |
| | | 1 g | Fiber |

# Tropical Fruits with Apricot-Rum Sauce

*These fruits are only a suggestion. The unique sauce can be served over any combination of fruits. It's great with peaches, melons, apricots, berries, etc. It's also good over lowfat vanilla ice cream and makes a delicious shortcake with angel food cake and any ripe, fresh fruit.*

*Makes 6 servings*

### Apricot-Rum Sauce

| | |
|---|---|
| 1 | cup apricot nectar |
| 1 | tablespoon cornstarch |
| 2 | teaspoons honey |
| 1 | teaspoon lime juice (or lemon juice) |
| 1/2 | teaspoon rum extract |
| 1/16 | teaspoon ground allspice |

### Fruits

| | |
|---|---|
| 1 | small mango, cut into chunks (A medium papaya can be substituted, if desired.) |
| 1 | medium, ripe banana, sliced |
| 1/4 | medium, ripe pineapple, pared and cut into chunks |

Combine all sauce ingredients in a small saucepan. Mix well to dissolve cornstarch. Cook over medium heat, stirring constantly, until mixture comes to a boil. Continue to cook, stirring, 1 to 2 minutes. Spoon into a bowl and chill thoroughly.

At serving time:

Combine fruit and divide evenly into 6 individual serving bowls. Stir chilled sauce, divide evenly, and spoon over fruit.

---

Each serving provides:

**84 Calories**

| | | | |
|---|---|---|---|
| 1 1/2 | Fruit Servings | 1 g | Protein |
| 12 | Additional Calories | trace | Fat (3% of calories) |
| | | 21 g | Carbohydrate |
| | | 3 mg | Sodium |
| | | 0 mg | Cholesterol |
| | | 1 g | Fiber |

# Fruit Yogurt

*Making your own fruit yogurt means lots more fruit and lots less sugar than most commercial varieties. Choose fruits that are packed in juice, and the possibilities are endless.*

*Makes 1 serving*

| | |
|---|---|
| 3/4 | cup plain nonfat yogurt |
| 2 | teaspoons sugar |
| 1/2 | teaspoon vanilla extract |
| 1/8 | teaspoon any other extract, such as orange, lemon, coconut, rum, *or* almond |
| 1/4 | cup canned sliced pears, *or* sliced peaches, *or* crushed pine apple, *or* blueberries |

In a small bowl, combine yogurt, sugar, and extracts. Stir in fruit. Enjoy!

Each serving provides:

**169 Calories**

| | | | |
|---|---|---|---|
| 1/2 | Fruit Serving | 10 g | Protein |
| 1 | Milk Serving | trace | Fat (2% of calories) |
| 32 | Additional Calories | 30 g | Carbohydrate |
| | | 132 mg | Sodium |
| | | 3 mg | Cholesterol |
| | | 1 g | Fiber |

# Quick Peach Melba

*Now you can enjoy a slimmed-down version of this classic dessert in no time.*

*Makes 2 servings*

| | |
|---|---|
| 1/4 | cup part-skim ricotta cheese |
| 2 | tablespoons nonfat vanilla yogurt |
| 2 | teaspoons sugar |
| 1 | teaspoon vanilla extract |
| 1/8 | teaspoon almond extract |
| 1 | medium, very ripe peach, peeled, cut in half, center pit removed *or* 2 canned peach halves (packed in juice), drained |
| 4 | teaspoons fruit-only raspberry spread |

In a small bowl, combine ricotta cheese, yogurt, sugar, and extracts. Mix well.

Place a peach half, cut-side up, in each of two small serving bowls. Fill peaches with cheese mixture. Top with raspberry spread.

Serve right away. (If you want to save for a later serving, refrigerate the peaches and cheese mixture separately and assemble just before serving.)

---

Each serving provides:

**135 Calories**

| | | | |
|---|---|---|---|
| 1/2 | Protein Serving | 5 g | Protein |
| 1 | Fruit Serving | 2 g | Fat (17% of calories) |
| 38 | Additional Calories | 23 g | Carbohydrate |
| | | 48 mg | Sodium |
| | | 10 mg | Cholesterol |
| | | 1 g | Fiber |

# Red, White, and Blueberry Parfaits

*This colorful, patriotic dessert is perfect for that Fourth of July picnic. Fresh summer berries are always delicious.*

*Makes 4 servings*

| | |
|---|---|
| 1 | cup strawberries, sliced |
| 1/2 | cup blueberries |
| 2 | tablespoons sugar |
| 1/2 | cup part-skim ricotta cheese |
| 1/2 | cup vanilla nonfat yogurt |
| 1/2 | teaspoon vanilla extract |
| 1/8 | teaspoon almond extract |
| 1/8 | teaspoon orange extract |

Place strawberries and blueberries each in a separate small bowl. Toss each with 1 teaspoon of the sugar.

In another bowl, combine ricotta cheese with remaining sugar, yogurt, and extracts. Mix well.

In each of 4 parfait glasses, place 2 tablespoons of the strawberries. Top each with 2 tablespoons of the ricotta mixture. Divide blueberries evenly over the parfaits. Divide remaining ricotta mixture over blueberries. Top with remaining strawberries.

Serve right away or chill for up to several hours before serving.

---

Each serving provides:

**116 Calories**

| | | | |
|---|---|---|---|
| 1/2 | Protein Serving | 5 g | Protein |
| 1/4 | Fruit Serving | 3 g | Fat (20% of calories) |
| 58 | Additional Calories | 18 g | Carbohydrate |
| | | 60 mg | Sodium |
| | | 10 mg | Cholesterol |
| | | 1 g | Fiber |

# Pears Belle Helene

*This is just a fancy way of saying "Chocolate-Topped Pears and Cheese."*
*However you say it, it's quick, easy, and delicious.*

*Makes 4 servings*

### Pears
| | |
|---|---|
| 1 | cup part-skim ricotta cheese |
| 1 | tablespoon plus 1 teaspoon sugar |
| 1¹/2 | teaspoons vanilla extract |
| 4 | canned pear halves (packed in juice), drained |

### Chocolate Topping
| | |
|---|---|
| 1 | tablespoon plus 1 teaspoon sugar |
| 1 | tablespoon cocoa (unsweetened) |
| 2 | teaspoons cornstarch |
| ¹/2 | cup evaporated skim milk |
| ¹/2 | teaspoon vanilla extract |

In a small bowl, combine ricotta cheese, sugar, and vanilla. Mix well.

Place a pear half, cut-side up, in each of 4 small serving bowls. Fill pears with cheese mixture.

Prepare topping:

In a small saucepan, combine sugar, cocoa, and cornstarch. Slowly stir in evaporated milk, mixing well. Cook over medium-low heat, stirring constantly, until sauce thickens. Remove from heat and stir in vanilla. Spoon over pears.

Serve right away. (If you wish, you can make the cheese filling ahead and refrigerate until you are ready to assemble the dessert.)

---

Each serving provides:

**220 Calories**

| | | | |
|---|---|---|---|
| 1 | Protein Serving | 10 g | Protein |
| ¹/2 | Fruit Serving | 5 g | Fat (21% of calories) |
| 52 | Additional Calories | 34 g | Carbohydrate |
| | | 119 mg | Sodium |
| | | 20 mg | Cholesterol |
| | | 2 g | Fiber |

# Baked Pears

*Bartlett pears work well for this crispy, spiced version of a fall fruit favorite. They can be served warm or cold and are delicious topped with a dollop of vanilla nonfat yogurt.*

*Makes 4 servings*

| | |
|---|---|
| 2 | large pears, peeled, cored, cut in half lengthwise |
| 1/2 | cup water |
| 2 | teaspoons lemon juice |
| 2 | teaspoons honey |
| 3 | tablespoons graham cracker crumbs |
| 1/4 | teaspoon ground cinnamon |
| 2 | teaspoons reduced-calorie margarine |

Preheat oven to 350°.

Place pears, cut-side down, in an 8-inch square baking pan. Pour water around pears. Drizzle pears with lemon juice and honey.

Cover and bake 45 minutes, or until pears are tender. Uncover.

Combine graham cracker crumbs and cinnamon. Sprinkle evenly over pears. Dot with margarine. Return to oven and bake, uncovered, 10 minutes more.

---

Each serving provides:

**135 Calories**

| | | | |
|---|---|---|---|
| 1/4 | Bread Serving | 1 g | Protein |
| 1/4 | Fat Serving | 2 g | Fat (12% of calories) |
| 1 | Fruit Serving | 31 g | Carbohydrate |
| 10 | Additional Calories | 57 mg | Sodium |
| | | 0 mg | Cholesterol |
| | | 4 g | Fiber |

# Brandy and Nut-Filled Pears

*Serve this elegant dish warm or at room temperature and, to make it extra special, top it with vanilla nonfat yogurt.*

*Makes 4 servings*

### Pears
2       tablespoons firmly packed brown sugar
1/4     cup water
1       teaspoon lemon juice
2       large pears, peeled, cut in half lengthwise

### Filling
2       tablespoons finely chopped walnuts (1/2 ounce)
1       tablespoon firmly packed brown sugar
1       tablespoon plain nonfat yogurt
1/4     teaspoon vanilla extract
1/2     teaspoon brandy extract

Preheat oven to 350°.

Combine brown sugar, water, and lemon juice in an 8-inch square baking pan. Mix until brown sugar is dissolved.

Cut a thin slice off the bottom of each pear half so it will not roll around when served. Scoop out the seeds, making a small "cup" in each pear half.

Place the pears, scooped-side down, in the baking pan. Baste with the liquid. Cover tightly and bake 45 minutes, or until pears are tender. (Length of cooking time will vary according to the variety and ripeness of the pears.) When pears are tender, place them, scooped-side up, in either 1 serving bowl or in 4 individual serving bowls. Spoon liquid from pan over pears. Let cool 10 minutes.

Combine filling ingredients in a small bowl or custard cup. Mix well. Spoon into pear cavities. Serve right away or let cool to luke-warm to serve.

Refrigerate leftovers and serve cold or reheat in a microwave.

Each serving provides:

**154 Calories**

| 1/4 | Fat Serving | 1 g | Protein |
| 1 | Fruit Serving | 2 g | Fat (13% of calories) |
| 45 | Additional Calories | 35 g | Carbohydrate |
| | | 7 mg | Sodium |
| | | 0 mg | Cholesterol |
| | | 4 g | Fiber |

# Apricot-Almond Cranberry Sauce

*Why open a can of cranberry sauce when you can make your own so easily? And this one is really special. It's laced with the flavors of apricot and almond and is tart and delicious, as cranberries should be. (If you don't like it as tart, you can add a little extra sugar.)*

*Makes 9 servings*
*(1/3 cup each serving)*

| | |
|---|---|
| 1 | cup sugar |
| 1 | cup water |
| 3 | cups cranberries |
| 1/3 | cup fruit-only apricot spread |
| 1/2 | teaspoon almond extract |

Combine sugar and water in a small saucepan. Bring to a boil over medium heat. Continue to boil, without stirring, 5 minutes.

Stir in cranberries and cook, stirring occasionally, until cranberries burst and mixture comes to a full boil. Continue to boil 5 minutes. Remove from heat and stir in apricot spread and almond extract.

Cool slightly, then chill.

---

Each serving provides:

**129 Calories**

| | | | |
|---|---|---|---|
| 3/4 | Fruit Serving | 0 g | Protein |
| 96 | Additional Calories | 0 g | Fat (0% of calories) |
| | | 33 g | Carbohydrate |
| | | 1 mg | Sodium |
| | | 0 mg | Cholesterol |
| | | 1 g | Fiber |

# Chewy Fruit Squares

*Made with pure fruit juice, here's a treat you can encourage the kids to eat.*

*Makes 4 squares*

3      envelopes unflavored gelatin
1      cup water
1/2    cup frozen orange juice concentrate, thawed

Sprinkle gelatin over water in a medium saucepan. Let soften a few minutes.

Heat over low heat, stirring frequently, until gelatin is completely dissolved. Remove from heat. Stir in orange juice.

Pour mixture into a 4 × 8-inch loaf pan.

Chill several hours.

Cut into squares to serve.

As a variation, substitute grape juice concentrate for the orange juice and count each square as 1 1/2 fruit servings.

---

Each square provides:

**74 Calories**

| 1 | Fruit Serving | | |
|---|---|---|---|
| | | 5 g | Protein |
| | | trace | Fat (1% of calories) |
| | | 14 g | Carbohydrate |
| | | 11 mg | Sodium |
| | | 0 mg | Cholesterol |
| | | 0 g | Fiber |

# Baked Pineapple Tapioca

*Serve this delicious dish warm or cold, topped with vanilla or lemon nonfat yogurt. It's soothing and delicious.*

*Makes 4 servings*

2      cups canned crushed pineapple (packed in juice), drained
            (Reserve juice.)
$3/4$    cup hot water
3      tablespoons sugar
2      tablespoons plus 2 teaspoons quick-cooking tapioca
$1/4$    teaspoon lemon extract
            Dash ground cinnamon

Preheat oven to 325°.

Spray a 1-quart casserole with nonstick cooking spray.

Add additional water to pineapple juice, if necessary, to equal $1/2$ cup. Add to prepared casserole, along with remaining ingredients. Mix well. Let stand 10 minutes.

Bake, uncovered, 40 minutes, or until tapioca granules are clear. Serve warm or cold.

---

Each serving provides:

**146 Calories**

| | | | |
|---|---|---|---|
| 1 | Fruit Serving | 1 g | Protein |
| 76 | Additional Calories | 1 g | Fat (7% of calories) |
| | | 35 g | Carbohydrate |
| | | 32 mg | Sodium |
| | | 0 mg | Cholesterol |
| | | 1 g | Fiber |

# Sautéed Pineapple

*This elegant dish makes a great appetizer as well as a luscious dessert.*

*Makes 4 servings*

2     teaspoons margarine
1/2   of a medium, ripe pineapple, sliced crosswise into 1-inch slices,
       skin removed
1     tablespoon plus 1 teaspoon sugar (You may need more or less,
       depending on the ripeness of the pineapple.)
1/2   teaspoon ground cinnamon

Melt margarine in a large nonstick skillet over medium-high heat.
Add pineapple. Cook, turning pineapple frequently, until lightly
browned on both sides.
   Combine sugar and cinnamon, mixing well.
   Place pineapple on serving plate and sprinkle with sugar mixture.
Serve hot.

---

Each serving provides:

**77 Calories**

| 1/2 | Fat Serving | 0 g | Protein |
| 1 | Fruit Serving | 2 g | Fat (25% of calories) |
| 16 | Additional Calories | 15 g | Carbohydrate |
| | | 23 mg | Sodium |
| | | 0 mg | Cholesterol |
| | | 1 g | Fiber |

# Baked Pineapple with Creamy Coconut Sauce

*Baking really brings out the flavor of fresh pineapple. Served warm, this easy, refreshing dish makes a great appetizer or dessert.*

*Makes 8 servings*

## Coconut Sauce

| | |
|---|---|
| 1¹/₃ | cups lowfat (1%) cottage cheese |
| ¹/₄ | cup firmly packed brown sugar |
| 3 | tablespoons skim milk |
| 1¹/₂ | teaspoons vanilla extract |
| ³/₄ | teaspoon coconut extract |

## Pineapple

| | |
|---|---|
| 1 | medium ripe pineapple |
| 4 | teaspoons firmly packed brown sugar |
| | Ground cinnamon |

To prepare sauce:

In a blender container, combine all sauce ingredients. Blend until smooth. Spoon into a bowl and chill several hours, or overnight.

To prepare pineapple:

Preheat oven to 375°.

Remove and discard top of pineapple. Cut pineapple lengthwise into quarters. Remove and discard center core. Cut each quarter into chunks, but leave the chunks resting in place in the shells.

Sprinkle brown sugar along the top ledge of each quarter. (It will run down during cooking.) Sprinkle liberally with cinnamon.

Wrap each quarter tightly in aluminum foil. Bake 1 hour.

Carefully unwrap pineapple, and sprinkle with additional cinnamon. Serve hot and top each serving with 3 tablespoons of the sauce.

---

Each serving provides:

**110 Calories**

| | | | |
|---|---|---|---|
| ¹/₂ | Protein Serving | 5 g | Protein |
| 1 | Fruit Serving | 1 g | Fat (6% of calories) |
| 34 | Additional Calories | 22 g | Carbohydrate |
| | | 160 mg | Sodium |
| | | 2 mg | Cholesterol |
| | | 1 g | Fiber |

# Pineapple-Grapefruit Combo

*Tart and tangy, yet so refreshing, this combination is a perfect marriage of flavors. Serve it as an appetizer, a dessert, or a delicious addition to breakfast.*

*Makes 4 servings*

| | |
|---|---|
| 1/4 | medium ripe pineapple, cut into bit-sized pieces, skin removed *or* 1 cup canned pineapple tidbits (packed in juice), drained |
| 1 | medium grapefruit, peeled and sectioned, then cut into bit-sized pieces, white membrane discarded |
| 1/2 | cup vanilla nonfat yogurt |
| 2 | tablespoons confectioners' sugar |
| 1 | teaspoon vanilla extract |

Combine all ingredients, mixing well.
Serve right away.

---

Each serving provides:

**83 Calories**

| 1 | Fruit Serving | 2 g | Protein |
|---|---|---|---|
| 48 | Additional Calories | trace | Fat (3% of calories) |
| | | 19 g | Carbohydrate |
| | | 20 mg | Sodium |
| | | 1 mg | Cholesterol |
| | | 1 g | Fiber |

# Broiled Grapefruit Delight

*Indeed, it is a delight. Hot and bubbly, this makes a wonderful and welcome morning treat.*

*Makes 4 servings*

2      medium, pink grapefruits, cut in half crosswise
2      teaspoons margarine, melted
1      teaspoon rum extract
1      tablespoon firmly packed brown sugar

Preheat broiler.

Place grapefruit on a broiler pan, cut-side up.

Combine margarine and rum extract and spread evenly over grapefruit. Sprinkle evenly with brown sugar.

Broil 6 inches from heat about 5 minutes, until grapefruit is hot and bubbly and edges just begin to brown.

Serve hot.

---

Each serving provides:

**68 Calories**

| | | | |
|---|---|---|---|
| 1/2 | Fat Serving | 1 g | Protein |
| 1 | Fruit Serving | 2 g | Fat (27% of calories) |
| 12 | Additional Calories | 12 g | Carbohydrate |
| | | 24 mg | Sodium |
| | | 0 mg | Cholesterol |
| | | 0 g | Fiber |

# Orange Fruit Cups

*These bright and cheery fruit cups can easily be varied by filling them with different fruits. Let your imagination and taste buds guide you.*

*Makes 4 servings*

2      small oranges, cut in half crosswise
$^1/_2$      cup blueberries, fresh or frozen (unsweetened)
$^1/_2$      cup canned crushed pineapple (packed in juice), drained
1      teaspoon confectioners' sugar

Carefully cut out orange pulp, using a small, sharp knife. Leave the shells intact. Remove and discard white membranes. (For a fancy touch, you can scallop the edges of the orange halves with a sharp knife.)

In a small bowl, combine orange sections with blueberries and pineapple. Chill at least 1 hour. Cover orange shells and chill them separately.

To serve, pile fruit mixture into orange shells. (If necessary, slice a very thin slice off the bottom of each orange half to keep it from tipping over.)

Sprinkle with confectioners' sugar and serve right away.

---

Each serving provides:

**60 Calories**

| | | | |
|---|---|---|---|
| 1 | Fruit Serving | 1 g | Protein |
| 4 | Additional Calories | trace | Fat (3% of calories) |
| | | 15 g | Carbohydrate |
| | | 1 mg | Sodium |
| | | 0 mg | Cholesterol |
| | | 2 g | Fiber |

# Bananas New Orleans

*One of our most popular dishes, this one can easily be prepared for dessert while the coffee is brewing. It's delicious by itself, or it really makes a statement when served over vanilla lowfat ice cream.*

*Makes 4 servings*

| | |
|---|---|
| 1 | teaspoon margarine |
| 1/2 | cup orange juice |
| 2 | tablespoons firmly packed brown sugar |
| 1/2 | teaspoon rum extract |
| 1/2 | teaspoon vanilla butternut flavor* |
| 2 | medium, ripe bananas, cut in half lengthwise, then each piece cut in half crosswise (Choose bananas that are ripe, yet firm.) |
| | Ground cinnamon |

Melt margarine in a medium nonstick skillet over medium heat. Stir in orange juice, brown sugar, and extracts.

Add bananas. Cook 2 to 3 minutes, then turn bananas carefully and cook another 1 to 2 minutes. Sprinkle with cinnamon.

Place 2 banana pieces in each of 4 individual serving bowls. Spoon sauce over bananas.

Serve right away.

*Often called "vanilla butter and nut flavor," it is found with the extracts in many large grocery stores. If you cannot locate this flavor, use 1/2 teaspoon vanilla extract plus 1/2 teaspoon butter-flavor extract in its place.

---

Each serving provides:
### 104 Calories

| | | | |
|---|---|---|---|
| 1/4 | Fat Serving | 1 g | Protein |
| 1 1/4 | Fruit Servings | 1 g | Fat (10% of calories) |
| 24 | Additional Calories | 23 g | Carbohydrate |
| | | 15 mg | Sodium |
| | | 0 mg | Cholesterol |
| | | 1 g | Fiber |

# Baked Banana Crumble

*Baked until crisp on the outside, bananas are still wonderfully moist and tender on the inside.*

*Makes 4 servings*

2        medium, ripe bananas, sliced in half lengthwise
1        teaspoon lemon juice
3        tablespoons graham cracker crumbs
1        tablespoon plus 1 teaspoon firmly packed brown sugar
1/2      teaspoon ground cinnamon
2        teaspoons reduced-calorie margarine

Preheat oven to 400°.

Spray a shallow baking pan with nonstick cooking spray.

Place banana halves in the prepared pan. Using your finger, "paint" them with lemon juice.

In a small bowl, combine graham cracker crumbs, brown sugar, and cinnamon. Sprinkle evenly over bananas. Dot with margarine.

Bake 10 minutes, or until bananas are lightly browned.

Serve right away.

---

Each serving provides:

**110 Calories**

| | | | |
|---|---|---|---|
| 1/4 | Bread Serving | 1 g | Protein |
| 1/4 | Fat Serving | 3 g | Fat (21% of calories) |
| 1 | Fruit Serving | 22 g | Carbohydrate |
| 16 | Additional Calories | 59 mg | Sodium |
| | | 0 mg | Cholesterol |
| | | 1 g | Fiber |

# Banana Toast

*This is an unbelievable eggless version of French toast that you're sure to love. Drizzled with maple syrup, it tastes absolutely decadent! (Be sure to use a nonstick skillet for this recipe, as it gets very sticky.)*

*Makes 2 servings*

| | |
|---|---|
| 1 | medium, very ripe banana |
| 1/4 | cup skim milk |
| 2 | teaspoons sugar |
| 1/2 | teaspoon vanilla extract |
| 2 | slices whole wheat bread (1-ounce slices) |
| 2 | teaspoons reduced-calorie margarine |
| | Ground cinnamon |

In a blender container, combine banana, milk, sugar, and vanilla. Blend until smooth.

Place bread in a shallow pan. Pour banana mixture over bread. Turn bread several times, until it has absorbed most of the banana mixture.

Melt *half* of the margarine in a large nonstick skillet over medium-low heat. Carefully place bread in skillet, using a spatula. Drizzle any remaining banana mixture over bread.

Brown toast on both sides, then turn carefully, adding remaining margarine.

Sprinkle with cinnamon and serve.

---

Each serving provides:

**168 Calories**

| | | | |
|---|---|---|---|
| 1 | Bread Serving | 4 g | Protein |
| 1/2 | Fat Serving | 3 g | Fat (17% of calories) |
| 1 | Fruit Serving | 32 g | Carbohydrate |
| 27 | Additional Calories | 211 mg | Sodium |
| | | 1 mg | Cholesterol |
| | | 3 g | Fiber |

# Russian Prune Pudding

*We modernized this old-fashioned dessert by using jarred baby food instead of cooking and mashing the prunes the way it is done in the more traditional version. This airy pudding is usually served warm and provides a light ending to any meal.*

*Makes 6 servings*

| | |
|---|---|
| 3 | tablespoons sugar |
| $1/16$ | teaspoon ground cinnamon |
| 2 | egg whites |
| 1 | teaspoon vanilla extract |
| 2 | 4-ounce jars baby food prunes |

Preheat oven to 300°.

Have a 1-quart baking dish ready. (Do not oil it.)

In a small bowl or custard cup, combine sugar and cinnamon. Mix well.

Place egg whites in a medium, deep bowl. Beat on high speed of an electric mixer until stiff. Beat in sugar and cinnamon mixture a few teaspoons at a time, beating well after each addition. Beat in vanilla.

Gently, but thoroughly, fold prunes into egg whites. Spoon into pan, smoothing top of pudding with the back of a spoon.

Bake 40 minutes.

Serve warm for best flavor. (Refrigerate leftovers and serve cold.)

---

Each serving provides:

**59 Calories**

| | | | |
|---|---|---|---|
| 1 | Fruit Serving | 1 g | Protein |
| 31 | Additional Calories | 0 g | Fat (0% of calories) |
| | | 14 g | Carbohydrate |
| | | 20 mg | Sodium |
| | | 0 mg | Cholesterol |
| | | 0 g | Fiber |

# Rhubarb and Pineapple

*This irresistible mixture is delicious by itself or it can be served as a sauce and spooned over angel food cake or lowfat ice cream.*

*Makes 8 servings*
*(1/3 cup each serving)*

| | |
|---|---|
| 1 | 1-pound bag frozen rhubarb, thawed partially (or 3 cups of fresh rhubarb, chopped, discarding leaves) |
| 1 | 8-ounce can crushed pineapple (packed in juice), drained (Reserve juice.) |
| 1/2 | cup firmly packed brown sugar |
| 1 | tablespoon granulated sugar |
| 1/2 | teaspoon lemon extract |
| 2 | tablespoons cornstarch |

In a medium saucepan, combine rhubarb, pineapple, both sugars, and lemon extract.

Place cornstarch in a small bowl or custard cup. Add 3 tablespoons of the reserved pineapple juice and stir to dissolve cornstarch. Set aside.

Add remaining pineapple juice to saucepan. Bring mixture to a boil over medium heat, stirring occasionally. Reduce heat to medium-low, cover, and simmer 10 minutes, until rhubarb begins to fall apart. Stir in cornstarch mixture. When mixture returns to a boil, cook, stirring constantly, 2 minutes, until mixture is thick and bubbly.

Serve warm or cold.

---

Each serving provides:

**96 Calories**

| | | | |
|---|---|---|---|
| 3/4 | Vegetable Serving | 0 g | Protein |
| 1/4 | Fruit Serving | trace | Fat (1% of calories) |
| 62 | Additional Calories | 24 g | Carbohydrate |
| | | 7 mg | Sodium |
| | | 0 mg | Cholesterol |
| | | 0 g | Fiber |

# Sautéed Maple Peaches

*Fresh or frozen peaches will work in this delicious hot dish. It makes a great dessert, either by itself or topped with vanilla nonfat yogurt, and it is also a delectable addition to your morning oatmeal.*

*Makes 4 servings*

| | |
|---|---|
| 2 | teaspoons margarine |
| 1/2 | cup orange juice |
| 1 | tablespoon plus 1 teaspoon firmly packed brown sugar |
| 1/2 | teaspoon maple extract |
| 1/4 | teaspoon ground cinnamon |
| 4 | medium, ripe peaches, peeled, sliced 1/4-inch thick (If using frozen peaches, choose the unsweetened ones and thaw them first.) |

Melt margarine in a large nonstick skillet over medium heat. Stir in orange juice, brown sugar, maple extract, and cinnamon.

Add peaches. Cook, turning peaches frequently, until tender, about 5 minutes.

Serve warm.

---

Each serving provides:

**105 Calories**

| | | | |
|---|---|---|---|
| 1/2 | Fat Serving | 1 g | Protein |
| 1 1/4 | Fruit Servings | 2 g | Fat (16% of calories) |
| 16 | Additional Calories | 22 g | Carbohydrate |
| | | 24 mg | Sodium |
| | | 0 mg | Cholesterol |
| | | 2 g | Fiber |

# Snowcapped Peaches

*Peach halves, filled with raspberry jam and topped with meringue, make a truly elegant finale to any meal. And, best of all, they contain no fat at all.*

*Makes 4 servings*

| | |
|---|---|
| 8 | canned peach halves (packed in juice), drained |
| 2 | tablespoons plus 2 teaspoons fruit-only raspberry spread |
| 2 | egg whites |
| 1/4 | teaspoon cream of tartar |
| 2 | tablespoons sugar |

Preheat oven to 350°.

Have a shallow nonstick baking pan ready.

Drain peaches well on towels. Place, cut-side up, in prepared pan. If necessary, slice a very thin sliver off the bottom of each peach to keep them from rolling around. Spoon 1 teaspoon of jam into the center of each peach.

In a small, deep bowl, beat egg whites on high speed of an electric mixer until soft peaks form. Add cream of tartar and beat until stiff. Beat in sugar.

Spread the meringue evenly over the peaches, covering the fruit spread.

Bake 10 to 15 minutes, or until meringue is golden.

Serve right away.

---

Each serving provides:

**118 Calories**

| | | | |
|---|---|---|---|
| 1 1/2 | Fruit Servings | 3 g | Protein |
| 44 | Additional Calories | 0 g | Fat (0% of calories) |
| | | 28 g | Carbohydrate |
| | | 33 mg | Sodium |
| | | 0 mg | Cholesterol |
| | | 1 g | Fiber |

# Sautéed Apples

*Any variety of apples will work in this easy dish; however, the length of cooking time may vary. It tastes best when the apples are cooked until just tender, so be careful not to let them get mushy.*

*Makes 4 servings*

| | |
|---|---|
| 2 | teaspoons margarine |
| 4 | small, sweet apples, unpeeled, cored, and cut into rings 1/4-inch thick |
| 2 | tablespoons firmly packed brown sugar |
| 1 | teaspoon vanilla extract |
| 1/2 | teaspoon ground cinnamon |
| 1/4 | teaspoon ground nutmeg |

Melt margarine in a large nonstick skillet over medium heat. Add apples. Cook, stirring and turning apples frequently, until tender, about 10 minutes. Add small amounts of water if necessary, to prevent sticking.

Sprinkle apples with remaining ingredients. Toss to melt the sugar and coat the apples evenly.

Serve warm.

---

Each serving provides:

**110 Calories**

| | | | |
|---|---|---|---|
| 1/2 | Fat Serving | 0 g | Protein |
| 1 | Fruit Serving | 2 g | Fat (18% of calories) |
| 24 | Additional Calories | 23 g | Carbohydrate |
| | | 25 mg | Sodium |
| | | 0 mg | Cholesterol |
| | | 2 g | Fiber |

# Baked Apple Alaska

*Baked apples are taken one step further in this unusual presentation. Frosted with meringue, they look and taste luscious.*

*Makes 4 servings*

| | |
|---|---|
| 4 | small sweet apples, peeled, cored, and cut in half lengthwise (McIntosh, Rome, or Jonathan are good choices for this dish.) |
| 2 | tablespoons firmly packed brown sugar |
| 1/4 | teaspoon ground cinnamon |

### Meringue

| | |
|---|---|
| 2 | egg whites |
| 1/4 | teaspoon cream of tartar |
| 2 | tablespoons sugar |

Preheat oven to 350°.

Place apples, cut-side down, in a shallow baking pan. Sprinkle evenly with brown sugar and cinnamon. Pour water around apples to a depth of 1/2 inch. Cover and bake 30 minutes, or until apples are tender. (Length of cooking time will depend on variety and ripeness of apples.)

Let apples cool. (Or you can chill them and complete the dessert at a later time.)

Just before serving:

Preheat oven to 350°.

In a small, deep bowl, beat egg whites on high speed of an electric mixer until soft peaks form. Add cream of tartar and beat until stiff. Beat in sugar.

Place apples, cut-side down, on a nonstick cookie sheet. Frost with meringue.

Bake 10 to 15 minutes, or until meringue is golden.

Serve right away.

---

Each serving provides:

**114 Calories**

| | | | |
|---|---|---|---|
| 1 | Fruit Serving | 2 g | Protein |
| 58 | Additional Calories | trace | Fat (2% of calories) |
| | | 28 g | Carbohydrate |
| | | 30 mg | Sodium |
| | | 0 mg | Cholesterol |
| | | 2 g | Fiber |

# Quick and Creamy Applesauce Dessert

*Toast a slice of angel food cake or fat-free pound cake and top it with this delicious applesauce combo for a quick and easy dessert.*

*Makes 2 servings*

| | |
|---|---|
| 1 | cup applesauce (unsweetened) |
| 3/4 | cup vanilla nonfat yogurt |
| 1 | tablespoon sugar |
| 1/2 | teaspoon vanilla extract |
| 1/2 | teaspoon apple pie spice *or* 1/4 teaspoon *each* ground cinnamon and nutmeg and a pinch of ground cloves |

Combine all ingredients in a small bowl. Mix thoroughly.
Serve right away or chill for a later serving.

---

Each serving provides:

**158 Calories**

| | | | |
|---|---|---|---|
| 1 | Fruit Serving | 5 g | Protein |
| 95 | Additional Calories | trace | Fat (1% of calories) |
| | | 35 g | Carbohydrate |
| | | 63 mg | Sodium |
| | | 3 mg | Cholesterol |
| | | 2 g | Fiber |

# Applesauce Raisin Supreme

*Whipped topping folded into applesauce makes it creamy and smooth.*

*Makes 6 servings*

| | |
|---|---|
| 2 | cups applesauce (unsweetened) |
| 1/4 | cup raisins |
| 1 | tablespoon confectioners' sugar |
| 1/2 | teaspoon grated fresh orange peel |
| 1/2 | teaspoon vanilla extract |
| 1 | cup reduced-fat frozen whipped topping, thawed |
| | Ground cinnamon |

In a medium bowl, combine applesauce, raisins, sugar, orange peel, and vanilla. Mix well. Fold in whipped topping. Spoon mixture into a shallow bowl.

Chill at least 1 hour.

Just before serving, fold mixture again gently and sprinkle with cinnamon.

---

Each serving provides:

**86 Calories**

|   |                    |       |                        |
|---|--------------------|-------|------------------------|
| 1 | Fruit Serving      | 0 g   | Protein                |
| 29| Additional Calories | 1 g   | Fat (15% of calories)  |
|   |                    | 18 g  | Carbohydrate           |
|   |                    | 2 mg  | Sodium                 |
|   |                    | 0 mg  | Cholesterol            |
|   |                    | 2 g   | Fiber                  |

# *Desserts*

You've heard it said before, but now you can truly have your cake and eat it, too. In this section, we've created a special grouping of luscious desserts in which the taste has been heightened, while the calories and fat have been lightened. Our secret? Substituting high-fat ingredients with their lowfat counterparts. Try this:

| In place of: | Use: |
| --- | --- |
| whole milk | skim milk |
| sour cream | nonfat yogurt |
| cream | evaporated skim milk |
| baking chocolate | cocoa |
| whole eggs | egg whites or egg substitute |
| sugar | *half* the amount called for |
| chopped nuts | *half* the amount called for |
| coconut | *a quarter* of the amount called for |
| cream cheese | fat-free cream cheese |
| cottage cheese | lowfat (1%) cottage cheese |
| ricotta cheese | part-skim or fat-free ricotta cheese |
| pie with double crust | pie with one crust |
| vegetable oil in cakes and muffins | replace at least half with apple-sauce or yogurt |
| icing | sprinkling of sugar and cinnamon |

Add fiber to cakes by replacing half of the flour with whole wheat flour and using wheat germ as a topping for cakes and also as a substitute for ground nuts. Fruit also adds fiber in addition to adding flavor, moistness, and important vitamins.

And don't forget our favorite fat-free addition: extracts. Vanilla adds a sweet, rich flavor to desserts, tricking your taste buds into thinking foods are sweeter than they really are. Other extracts can also add delectable flavors without adding unnecessary calories and fat.

Our dessert cart is overflowing with puddings, molds, frozen desserts, cakes, pies, cobblers, crisps, cookies, and candies. Yes, desserts *can* be both lean and luscious.

Enjoy! Enjoy! Enjoy!

# PUDDINGS, MOLDS, AND FROZEN DESSERTS

## Floating Islands

*Picture a mound of lemon-flavored pudding floating on a bed of blueberries. Now indulge!*

*Makes 4 servings*

| | |
|---|---|
| 1 | cup water |
| 1 | envelope unflavored gelatin |
| 1 | cup lemon nonfat yogurt |
| 2 | tablespoons sugar |
| 1 | teaspoon vanilla extract |
| 1/4 | teaspoon lemon extract |
| 1/4 | teaspoon almond extract |
| 2 | tablespoons orange juice |
| 2 | cups frozen blueberries (unsweetened), thawed, undrained |

Place water in a small saucepan. Sprinkle gelatin over water and let soften a few minutes. Heat, stirring frequently, over low heat, until gelatin is completely dissolved. Remove from heat.

In a blender container, combine yogurt, sugar, and extracts. Add gelatin mixture and blend until smooth.

Pour mixture into 4 custard cups. Chill until firm.

Add orange juice to blueberries and chill until serving time.

To serve, place 1/2 cup blueberries in each of 4 serving bowls. Unmold a pudding into the center of each. Spoon a few berries over the top of each pudding. Spoon any remaining liquid over the puddings.

*Note:* To unmold, dip each cup in a bowl of hot water for 10 seconds, carefully run a knife around the edge, and invert.

---

Each serving provides:

**104 Calories**

| | | | |
|---|---|---|---|
| 1/2 | Fruit Serving | 4 g | Protein |
| 1/4 | Milk Serving | trace | Fat (5% of calories) |
| 63 | Additional Calories | 18 g | Carbohydrate |
| | | 34 mg | Sodium |
| | | 0 mg | Cholesterol |
| | | 2 g | Fiber |

# Piña Colada Fluff

*This fluffy dessert contains all of the flavors of the tropics. It works best if the pineapple is cold, so place it in the refrigerator at least an hour before making the pudding.*

*Makes 4 servings*

| | |
|---|---|
| 3/4 | cup water |
| 1 | envelope unflavored gelatin |
| 2/3 | cup nonfat dry milk |
| 2 | tablespoons sugar |
| 1 | teaspoon vanilla extract |
| 1/2 | teaspoon coconut extract |
| 1/4 | teaspoon rum extract |
| 1 | cup canned crushed pineapple (packed in juice), drained |
| 7 | large ice cubes |

Place water in a small saucepan. Sprinkle gelatin over water and let soften a few minutes. Heat over low heat, stirring frequently, until gelatin is completely dissolved. Remove from heat.

In a blender container, combine dry milk, sugar, extracts, and pineapple. Add gelatin mixture. Turn blender on and carefully add ice cubes, one at a time, while blending. Blend 1 minute, or until ice is gone.

Pudding may be divided into 4 serving bowls and eaten right away or, if a slightly firmer texture is desired, chilled for at least 15 minutes before serving.

---

Each serving provides:

**114 Calories**

| | | | |
|---|---|---|---|
| 1/2 | Fruit Serving | 6 g | Protein |
| 1/2 | Milk Serving | trace | Fat (1% of calories) |
| 24 | Additional Calories | 23 g | Carbohydrate |
| | | 67 mg | Sodium |
| | | 2 mg | Cholesterol |
| | | 0 g | Fiber |

# Mocha Fluff

*Light as a feather, this fluffy pudding is an ideal quick dessert or after-school snack. To make Chocolate Fluff, simply eliminate the coffee.*

*Makes 4 servings*

| | |
|---|---|
| 3/4 | cup water |
| 1 | envelope unflavored gelatin |
| 2/3 | cup nonfat dry milk |
| 3 | tablespoons sugar |
| 1 | tablespoon plus 1 teaspoon cocoa (unsweetened) |
| 1 1/2 | teaspoons vanilla extract |
| 1/4 | teaspoon rum *or* almond extract |
| 1 1/2 | teaspoons instant coffee granules (regular or decaffeinated) |
| 7 | large ice cubes |

Place water in a small saucepan. Sprinkle gelatin over water and let soften a few minutes. Heat over low heat, stirring frequently, until gelatin is completely dissolved. Remove from heat.

In a blender container, combine dry milk, sugar, cocoa, extracts, and coffee granules. Add gelatin mixture. Turn blender on and carefully add ice cubes, one at a time, while blending. Blend 1 minute, or until ice is gone.

Pudding may be divided into 4 serving bowls and eaten right away or, if a slightly firmer texture is desired, chilled for at least 15 minutes before serving.

---

Each serving provides:

**95 Calories**

| | | | |
|---|---|---|---|
| 1/2 | Milk Serving | 6 g | Protein |
| 41 | Additional Calories | trace | Fat (3% of calories) |
| | | 17 g | Carbohydrate |
| | | 67 mg | Sodium |
| | | 2 mg | Cholesterol |
| | | 1 g | Fiber |

# Creamy Chocolate Pudding

*By adding your favorite extract to this creamy pudding, you can create chocolate-almond, chocolate-rum, chocolate-coconut, or any other combination you can imagine.*

*Makes 2 servings*

| | |
|---|---|
| 1/2 | cup water |
| 1 | envelope unflavored gelatin |
| 1 | cup evaporated skim milk |
| 2 | tablespoons cocoa (unsweetened) |
| 1 | teaspoon vanilla extract |
| 1/4 | teaspoon any other extract (optional) |
| 2 | tablespoons plus 1 1/2 teaspoons sugar |

Place water in a small saucepan. Sprinkle gelatin over water and let soften a few minutes. Heat over low heat, stirring frequently, until gelatin is completely dissolved.

In a blender container, combine remaining ingredients. Add gelatin mixture. Blend until smooth.

Pour pudding into a bowl and chill until set, about 20 minutes.

Just before serving, beat chilled pudding on high speed of an electric mixer until creamy.

---

Each serving provides:

**192 Calories**

| | | | |
|---|---|---|---|
| 1 | Milk Serving | 14 g | Protein |
| 75 | Additional Calories | 1 g | Fat (4% of calories) |
| | | 34 g | Carbohydrate |
| | | 155 mg | Sodium |
| | | 5 mg | Cholesterol |
| | | 2 g | Fiber |

# Banana Bavarian

*The riper the bananas, the sweeter this easy pudding will be.*

*Makes 4 servings*

| | |
|---|---|
| 1/2 | cup water |
| 2 | envelopes unflavored gelatin |
| 2 | cups evaporated skim milk |
| 2 | medium, very ripe bananas |
| 2 | tablespoons sugar |
| 1/8 | teaspoon ground cinnamon |
| | Pinch ground nutmeg |
| 1 | teaspoon vanilla extract |
| 1/4 | teaspoon banana extract |

Place water in a small saucepan. Sprinkle gelatin over water and let soften a few minutes. Heat over low heat, stirring frequently, until gelatin is completely dissolved.

In a blender container, combine remaining ingredients. Add gelatin mixture. Blend until smooth.

Pour into 4 individual serving bowls and chill until set.

---

Each serving provides:

**191 Calories**

| | | | |
|---|---|---|---|
| 1 | Fruit Serving | 13 g | Protein |
| 1 | Milk Serving | 1 g | Fat (2% of calories) |
| 24 | Additional Calories | 34 g | Carbohydrate |
| | | 154 mg | Sodium |
| | | 5 mg | Cholesterol |
| | | 1 g | Fiber |

# Vanilla Tapioca Pudding

*The wonderful texture of the tapioca adds a special old-time note to this popular dessert.*

*Makes 4 servings*

| | |
|---|---|
| 2 | cups skim milk |
| 2 | tablespoons sugar |
| 3 | tablespoons quick-cooking tapioca |
| 1 | teaspoon vanilla extract |

Place milk and sugar in a small saucepan. Sprinkle tapioca over milk and let it stand to soften for 5 minutes.

Cook over medium heat, stirring constantly, until mixture comes to a boil. Boil, stirring, 2 minutes. Remove from heat and stir in vanilla.

Divide mixture into 4 custard cups.

Chill.

Each serving provides:

**97 Calories**

| | | | |
|---|---|---|---|
| 1/2 | Milk Serving | 4 g | Protein |
| 69 | Additional Calories | trace | Fat (2% of calories) |
| | | 19 g | Carbohydrate |
| | | 98 mg | Sodium |
| | | 2 mg | Cholesterol |
| | | 0 g | Fiber |

# Orange Tapioca Pudding

*Fruit juices cooked with tapioca make wonderful puddings. This one makes a great dessert or after-school snack.*

*Makes 4 servings*

2        cups orange juice
3        tablespoons quick-cooking tapioca
1        tablespoon plus 1 teaspoon firmly packed brown sugar
$1/4$    teaspoon lemon extract
$1/16$   teaspoon ground cinnamon

Combine all ingredients *except* cinnamon in a small saucepan. Mix and let stand 5 minutes.

Bring mixture to a boil over medium heat, stirring frequently. Remove from heat and stir in cinnamon.

Cool mixture in pan 20 minutes, then stir and spoon into 4 custard cups.

Chill.

---

Each serving provides:

**101 Calories**

| 1 | Fruit Serving | 1 g | Protein |
|---|---|---|---|
| 61 | Additional Calories | trace | Fat (1% of calories) |
| | | 25 g | Carbohydrate |
| | | 37 mg | Sodium |
| | | 0 mg | Cholesterol |
| | | 0 g | Fiber |

# Creamy Rice and Raisin Pudding

*Unlike most rice puddings, which are made with eggs, this one is made with cornstarch. The result is a creamy, rich pudding with just a trace of fat and lots of flavor. The servings are generous, and this dessert doubles as a filling, nutritious breakfast.*

*Makes 4 servings*

| | |
|---|---|
| 2 | cups skim milk |
| 2 | tablespoons sugar |
| 1 | tablespoon cornstarch |
| 2 | cups cooked brown (or white) rice |
| 2 | teaspoons vanilla extract |
| 1/4 | teaspoon ground cinnamon |
| 1/4 | cup raisins |
| | Ground nutmeg |

In a medium saucepan, combine milk, sugar, and cornstarch. Stir to dissolve cornstarch. Add rice. Heat over medium heat, stirring constantly, until mixture comes to a boil. Continue to cook and stir 1 minute. Remove from heat and stir in vanilla, cinnamon, and raisins.

Spoon mixture into a shallow bowl. Sprinkle with nutmeg. Chill.

---

Each serving provides:

**218 Calories**

| 1 | Bread Serving | 7 g | Protein |
|---|---|---|---|
| 1/2 | Fruit Serving | 1 g | Fat (5% of calories) |
| 1/2 | Milk Serving | 44 g | Carbohydrate |
| 32 | Additional Calories | 70 mg | Sodium |
| | | 2 mg | Cholesterol |
| | | 2 g | Fiber |

# Grape Gelatin Dessert

*As simple to prepare as the commercial product, but with real fruit juice and a lot less sugar, this tasty treat is fun for the kids to make. It's great all year round and is a refreshing, fat-free dessert or snack.*

*Makes 4 servings*

2      cups grape juice
2      tablespoons sugar
1      envelope unflavored gelatin

Place grape juice and sugar in a small saucepan. Sprinkle with gelatin. Let soften a few minutes. Heat over low heat, stirring frequently, until gelatin is completely dissolved. Divide mixture evenly into 6 custard cups.

Chill until firm.

---

Each serving provides:

**94 Calories**

| | | | |
|---|---|---|---|
| 1 1/2 | Fruit Servings | 2 g | Protein |
| 24 | Additional Calories | trace | Fat (1% of calories) |
| | | 22 g | Carbohydrate |
| | | 6 mg | Sodium |
| | | 0 mg | Cholesterol |
| | | 0 g | Fiber |

# Grape Nuts Raisin Pudding

*Incredibly thick and rich, this warm, satisfying, and quite unusual pudding doubles as a nutritious breakfast. What a nice way to start the day!*

*Makes 2 servings*

| | |
|---|---|
| 1 | cup water |
| 1/3 | cup Grape Nuts cereal (1 1/2 ounces) |
| 1/4 | cup raisins |
| 2 | tablespoons firmly packed brown sugar |
| 1 | tablespoon plus 1 teaspoon quick-cooking tapioca |
| 1 | teaspoon vanilla extract |
| 1/4 | teaspoon maple extract |
| | Ground cinnamon |

Bring about 3 inches of water to a boil in the bottom of a double boiler over medium-high heat. Combine all ingredients *except* cinnamon in the top of the double boiler. Cook, stirring frequently, until mixture thickens slightly, about 5 minutes. Continue to cook, stirring constantly, until mixture is very thick, about 4 minutes more.

Spoon into 2 serving bowls.

Sprinkle with cinnamon.

Serve right away.

---

Each serving provides:

**217 Calories**

| | | | |
|---|---|---|---|
| 1 | Bread Serving | 3 g | Protein |
| 1 | Fruit Serving | trace | Fat (1% of calories) |
| 88 | Additional Calories | 52 g | Carbohydrate |
| | | 162 mg | Sodium |
| | | 0 mg | Cholesterol |
| | | 2 g | Fiber |

# Pineapple Cheese Bread Pudding

*This moist pudding tastes almost like cheesecake. Why not have it for break-*
*fast? It's sweet and satisfying and much more nutritious than a doughnut.*

*Makes 8 servings*

| | |
|---|---|
| 4 | slices whole wheat bread (1-ounce slices), cut into cubes |
| 1 | cup canned crushed pineapple (packed in juice), drained slightly |
| 2 | cups skim milk |
| 1/2 | cup liquid egg substitute |
| 1/2 | cup part-skim ricotta cheese |
| 3 | tablespoons sugar |
| 2 | teaspoons vanilla extract |
| 1 | teaspoon lemon extract |
| 1/2 | teaspoon ground cinnamon |

Preheat oven to 350°.

Spray an 8-inch square baking pan with nonstick cooking spray.

Place bread cubes in prepared pan. Spread pineapple evenly over the bread.

In a blender container, combine remaining ingredients. Blend until smooth. Pour mixture evenly over bread and pineapple. Let stand 10 minutes.

Bake, uncovered, 35 to 40 minutes, until set.

Serve warm or cold.

---

Each serving provides:

**134 Calories**

| | | | |
|---|---|---|---|
| 1/2 | Protein Serving | 7 g | Protein |
| 1/2 | Bread Serving | 2 g | Fat (17% of calories) |
| 1/4 | Fruit Serving | 21 g | Carbohydrate |
| 1/4 | Milk Serving | 151 mg | Sodium |
| 18 | Additional Calories | 6 mg | Cholesterol |
| | | 1 g | Fiber |

# Blueberry Bread 'n' Butter Pudding

*Originally made with butter, this delectable, molded bread pudding can be served by itself or topped with vanilla nonfat yogurt. It's really an artistic creation.*

*Makes 4 servings*

| | |
|---|---|
| 2 | cups blueberries, fresh or frozen (unsweetened) |
| 1/4 | cup plus 2 tablespoons water |
| 3 | tablespoons sugar |
| 1/4 | teaspoon ground cinnamon |
| 2 | tablespoons plus 2 teaspoons reduced-calorie margarine |
| 8 | slices thin-sliced whole wheat bread (1/2-ounce slices) |

Combine blueberries, water, sugar, and cinnamon in a small saucepan. Bring to a boil over medium heat. Reduce heat to medium-low and simmer 5 minutes. Remove from heat.

Spread margarine on both sides of each bread slice, using 1/2 teaspoon of margarine per side. Cut each slice of bread into 5 or 6 triangular-shaped pieces.

Line the bottom of a 9-inch cake pan with *half* of the bread, arranging the pieces to fit like a jigsaw puzzle. Pour about 3/4 of the berries evenly over the bread.

Arrange remaining bread over berries and top evenly with remaining berries.

Cover pan with plastic wrap and top with a dish or paper plate. Place weights, such as several 1-pound cans of food, on top of plate. Refrigerate overnight.

To serve, loosen pudding with a spatula and unmold onto a serving platter.

---

Each serving provides:

**180 Calories**

| | | | |
|---|---|---|---|
| 1 | Bread Serving | 3 g | Protein |
| 1 | Fat Serving | 5 g | Fat (24% of calories) |
| 1/2 | Fruit Serving | 33 g | Carbohydrate |
| 46 | Additional Calories | 245 mg | Sodium |
| | | 0 mg | Cholesterol |
| | | 4 g | Fiber |

# Tofu Rice Pudding

*Look for silken tofu in small boxes in the produce section of health food stores and most large grocery stores. It adds a thickness and richness to puddings and pies.*

*Makes 4 servings*

| | |
|---|---|
| 1 | cup water |
| 1 | envelope unflavored gelatin |
| 1 | 10-ounce package silken (or soft) tofu |
| 1/4 | cup sugar |
| 1/2 | teaspoon ground cinnamon |
| 1 | teaspoon vanilla extract |
| 1/8 | teaspoon lemon extract |
| 1/8 | teaspoon almond extract |
| 2/3 | cup nonfat dry milk |
| 1 | cup cooked brown (or white) rice |
| 1/4 | cup raisins |
| | Ground cinnamon |
| | Dash ground nutmeg |

Place water in a small saucepan. Sprinkle gelatin over water and let soften a few minutes. Heat over low heat, stirring frequently, until gelatin is completely dissolved.

In a blender container, combine gelatin mixture, tofu, sugar, cinnamon, extracts, and dry milk. Blend until smooth. Pour into a bowl and chill until firm, about 45 minutes.

Beat chilled pudding on low speed of an electric mixer until smooth. Stir in rice and raisins. Spoon pudding into a serving bowl and sprinkle with cinnamon and a dash of nutmeg.

Chill thoroughly.

---

Each serving provides:

**227 Calories**

| | | | |
|---|---|---|---|
| 3/4 | Protein Serving | 13 g | Protein |
| 1/2 | Bread Serving | 2 g | Fat (8% of calories) |
| 1/2 | Fruit Serving | 39 g | Carbohydrate |
| 1/2 | Milk Serving | 117 mg | Sodium |
| 53 | Additional Calories | 2 mg | Cholesterol |
| | | 1 g | Fiber |

# Tofu Chocolate Pudding

*A delicious way to serve this creamy pudding is to top each serving with a dollop of raspberry jam.*

*Makes 4 servings*

| | |
|---|---|
| 1 | cup water |
| 1 | envelope unflavored gelatin |
| 1 | 10-ounce package silken (or soft) tofu |
| 2/3 | cup nonfat dry milk |
| 1/4 | cup confectioners' sugar |
| 2 | tablespoons cocoa (unsweetened) |
| 1 | teaspoon vanilla extract |
| 1/8 | teaspoon almond extract |

Place water in a small saucepan. Sprinkle gelatin over water and let soften a few minutes. Heat over low heat, stirring frequently, until gelatin is completely dissolved.

In a blender container, combine gelatin mixture with remaining ingredients. Blend until smooth.

Chill thoroughly.

*Note:* For a creamier texture, beat pudding on low speed of an electric mixer just before serving.

---

Each serving provides:

**131 Calories**

| | | | |
|---|---|---|---|
| 3/4 | Protein Serving | 12 g | Protein |
| 1/2 | Milk Serving | 2 g | Fat (13% of calories) |
| 61 | Additional Calories | 17 g | Carbohydrate |
| | | 114 mg | Sodium |
| | | 2 mg | Cholesterol |
| | | 1 g | Fiber |

# Pineapple-Banana Cheese Pudding

*The exotic island flavors of pineapple and banana are heightened by the addition of the rich-tasting coconut extract in this delectable pudding.*

*Makes 4 servings*

| | |
|---|---|
| 3/4 | cup water |
| 1 | envelope unflavored gelatin |
| 1 1/3 | cups lowfat (1%) cottage cheese |
| 2 | tablespoons sugar |
| 1 | teaspoon vanilla extract |
| 1/2 | teaspoon coconut extract |
| 1/2 | medium, very ripe banana |
| 1/2 | cup canned crushed pineapple (packed in juice), undrained |

Place water in a small saucepan. Sprinkle gelatin over water and let soften a few minutes. Heat over low heat, stirring frequently, until gelatin is completely dissolved.

In a blender container, combine gelatin mixture with remaining ingredients *except* pineapple. Blend until smooth. Stir in pineapple.

Pour into 1 large bowl or 4 individual serving bowls.

Chill until firm.

---

Each serving provides:

**120 Calories**

| | | | |
|---|---|---|---|
| 1 | Protein Serving | 11 g | Protein |
| 1/2 | Fruit Serving | 1 g | Fat (6% of calories) |
| 24 | Additional Calories | 17 g | Carbohydrate |
| | | 309 mg | Sodium |
| | | 3 mg | Cholesterol |
| | | 1 g | Fiber |

# Rum Raisin Pudding

*So elegant, yet so easy, this rich pudding with its delectable combination of flavors can dress up any dinner party.*

*Makes 4 servings*

| | |
|---|---|
| 3/4 | cup water |
| 1 | envelope unflavored gelatin |
| 1 | cup part-skim ricotta cheese |
| 1/3 | cup nonfat dry milk |
| 3 | tablespoons sugar |
| 1 | teaspoon vanilla extract |
| 1 | teaspoon rum extract |
| 1/4 | cup raisins |
| | Ground nutmeg |

Place water in a small saucepan. Sprinkle gelatin over water and let soften a few minutes. Heat over low heat, stirring frequently, until gelatin is completely dissolved.

In a blender container, combine gelatin mixture with remaining ingredients *except* raisins and nutmeg. Blend until smooth. Stir in raisins.

Pour pudding into 1 large bowl or 4 individual serving bowls. Sprinkle with nutmeg.

Chill until firm.

---

Each serving provides:

**182 Calories**

| | | | |
|---|---|---|---|
| 1 | Protein Serving | 11 g | Protein |
| 1/2 | Fruit Serving | 5 g | Fat (25% of calories) |
| 1/4 | Milk Serving | 23 g | Carbohydrate |
| 36 | Additional Calories | 112 mg | Sodium |
| | | 20 mg | Cholesterol |
| | | 1 g | Fiber |

# Cottage Apple Pudding

*What could taste better than apples laced with cinnamon and nutmeg and baked in a thick cheese custard? Served warm or cold, it's a real winner.*

*Makes 6 servings*

| | |
|---|---|
| 6 | small sweet apples, peeled, sliced very thin |
| 1/4 | cup water |
| 1 | teaspoon ground cinnamon |
| 1/2 | teaspoon ground nutmeg |
| 1 1/3 | cups lowfat (1%) cottage cheese |
| 3/4 | cup liquid egg substitute |
| 1/3 | cup nonfat dry milk |
| 1/4 | cup sugar |
| 2 | teaspoons vanilla extract |
| 1/2 | teaspoon almond extract |

Place apples and water in a large nonstick skillet or saucepan. Sprinkle with *half* of the cinnamon and *half* of the nutmeg. Simmer over medium heat 10 minutes, or until apples are slightly tender. Remove from heat.

Preheat oven to 350°.

Spray an 8-inch square baking pan with nonstick cooking spray.

In a blender container, combine cottage cheese with remaining ingredients, including remaining cinnamon and nutmeg. Blend until smooth.

Spread apples evenly in prepared pan. Pour cheese mixture over apples. Sprinkle lightly with additional cinnamon.

Bake, uncovered, 25 to 30 minutes, or until set.

---

Each serving provides:

**166 Calories**

| | | | |
|---|---|---|---|
| 1 | Protein Serving | 11 g | Protein |
| 1 | Fruit Serving | 2 g | Fat (9% of calories) |
| 57 | Additional Calories | 27 g | Carbohydrate |
| | | 274 mg | Sodium |
| | | 3 mg | Cholesterol |
| | | 2 g | Fiber |

# Applesauce Cheese Pudding

*This delicious blend of applesauce, cottage cheese, and spices makes a hearty and nutritious breakfast as well as a creamy dessert.*

*Makes 4 servings*

| | |
|---|---|
| $2/3$ | cup lowfat (1%) cottage cheese |
| 2 | tablespoons sugar |
| 1 | teaspoon vanilla extract |
| $1/2$ | teaspoon maple extract |
| $1/2$ | teaspoon grated fresh orange peel |
| $1/2$ | teaspoon ground cinnamon |
| $1/8$ | teaspoon ground nutmeg |
| 1 | cup applesauce (unsweetened) |
| 1 | cup orange juice |
| 2 | tablespoons cornstarch |

In a blender container, combine cottage cheese, sugar, extracts, orange peel, cinnamon, and nutmeg. Blend until smooth. Spoon into a medium saucepan. Stir in applesauce.

In a small bowl, combine orange juice and cornstarch. Stir to dissolve cornstarch.

Add to saucepan, mixing well.

Bring mixture to a boil over medium heat, stirring frequently. Continue to cook, stirring constantly, 2 minutes. Spoon into a shallow bowl.

Chill thoroughly.

---

Each serving provides:

**127 Calories**

| | | | |
|---|---|---|---|
| $1/2$ | Protein Serving | 5 g | Protein |
| 1 | Fruit Serving | trace | Fat (3% of calories) |
| 39 | Additional Calories | 25 g | Carbohydrate |
| | | 156 mg | Sodium |
| | | 2 mg | Cholesterol |
| | | 1 g | Fiber |

# Baked Custard

*This old-time favorite can easily be varied with the addition of another extract. Try lemon, orange, almond, or coconut and enjoy the many delights of a real comfort food.*

*Makes 4 servings*

1/2    cup liquid egg substitute
2    tablespoons sugar
2    cups skim milk
1    teaspoon vanilla extract
1/2    teaspoon another flavored extract (optional)
    Ground nutmeg

Preheat oven to 350°.

Spray 4 custard cups with nonstick cooking spray.

In a medium bowl, combine egg substitute and sugar. Add milk slowly, stirring constantly. Stir in vanilla. (Add optional extract, if desired.)

Pour mixture into prepared cups. Sprinkle with nutmeg.

Place cups in a shallow baking pan. Pour enough hot water in the larger pan to come halfway up the sides of the cups.

Bake 30 to 40 minutes, until a knife inserted near the center comes out clean.

Cool slightly, then chill.

---

Each serving provides:

**96 Calories**

| | | | |
|---|---|---|---|
| 1/2 | Protein Serving | 7 g | Protein |
| 1/2 | Milk Serving | 1 g | Fat (13% of calories) |
| 24 | Additional Calories | 13 g | Carbohydrate |
| | | 114 mg | Sodium |
| | | 2 mg | Cholesterol |
| | | 0 g | Fiber |

# Pineapple Bavarian Cream

*Cool and creamy, this refreshing mold is usually served as a dessert. However, we've also made individual molds and served them on a bed of lettuce for a delicious light lunch.*

*Makes 4 servings*

| | |
|---|---|
| 1/2 | cup water |
| 1 | cup canned crushed pineapple (packed in juice), drained (Reserve juice.) |
| 1 | envelope unflavored gelatin |
| 1 1/3 | cups lowfat (1%) cottage cheese |
| 2 | tablespoons sugar |
| 1 | teaspoon vanilla extract |
| 1/4 | teaspoon lemon extract |

In a small saucepan, combine water and 1/4 cup of the pineapple juice. Sprinkle with gelatin and let soften a few minutes. Heat over low heat, stirring frequently, until gelatin is completely dissolved.

In a blender container, combine gelatin mixture, cottage cheese, sugar, and extracts. Blend until smooth. Pour into a bowl and chill until slightly set, about 15 minutes. Stir in pineapple.

Place mixture in a 3-cup mold, or divide into 4 individual molds or parfait glasses.

Chill until firm.

---

Each serving provides:

**127 Calories**

| | | | |
|---|---|---|---|
| 4 | Protein Serving | 11 g | Protein |
| 1/2 | Fruit Serving | 1 g | Fat (6% of calories) |
| 24 | Additional Calories | 18 g | Carbohydrate |
| | | 309 mg | Sodium |
| | | 3 mg | Cholesterol |
| | | 0 g | Fiber |

# Peaches 'n' Creme Mold

*This delicious dessert makes great use of summer's fresh peaches. It has a nice, creamy texture and delicate flavor. Top each serving with a light sprinkling of cinnamon or freshly grated nutmeg.*

*Makes 6 servings*

| | |
|---|---|
| 6 | medium, very ripe peaches, peeled, pits removed, *or* 12 halves of canned, unsweetened peaches |
| 1/3 | cup sugar |
| 2 | cups water |
| 2 | envelopes unflavored gelatin |
| 1 1/2 | cups vanilla nonfat yogurt |
| 1 | teaspoon vanilla extract |
| 1/4 | teaspoon orange or lemon extract |
| 1/8 | teaspoon almond extract |
| | Ground cinnamon or nutmeg |

Slice 2 of the peaches into very thin slices. Sprinkle with 1 tablespoon of the sugar, mix, and set aside.

Place 1 cup of the water in a small saucepan. Sprinkle gelatin over water and let it soften a few minutes. Heat over low heat, stirring frequently, until gelatin is completely dissolved. Remove from heat.

In a blender container, combine yogurt and remaining unsliced peaches. Blend until smooth. Add gelatin mixture, remaining 1 cup of water, remaining sugar, and extracts. Blend until smooth. Stir in reserved sliced peaches.

Pour mixture into a 9-cup mold and chill until firm. Unmold to serve.

Top each serving with a little cinnamon or nutmeg. (If using nutmeg, try grating it fresh for the best flavor.)

---

Each serving provides:

**160 Calories**

| | | | |
|---|---|---|---|
| 1 | Fruit Serving | 6 g | Protein |
| 1/4 | Milk Serving | trace | Fat (1% of calories) |
| 68 | Additional Calories | 35 g | Carbohydrate |
| | | 45 mg | Sodium |
| | | 2 mg | Cholesterol |
| | | 2 g | Fiber |

# Tropical Fruit Mold

*A delectable blend of flavors awaits you in this fruit-flavored dessert. It's refreshing on a hot summer day.*

*Makes 4 servings*

3/4     cup water
2       envelopes unflavored gelatin
3/4     cup plain nonfat yogurt
1       cup strawberries, fresh or frozen (If frozen berries are used, there is no need to thaw them.)
1/2     cup canned crushed pineapple (packed in juice), drained (Reserve 2 tablespoons of juice.)
1/4     cup sugar
1       teaspoon vanilla extract
1/4     teaspoon *each* orange, lemon, and rum extracts

Place water in a small saucepan. Sprinkle gelatin over water and let soften a few minutes. Heat over low heat, stirring frequently, until gelatin is completely dissolved. Remove from heat.

In a blender container, combine yogurt, strawberries, pineapple, reserved pineapple juice, and sugar. Blend until fruit is in small pieces. Add gelatin mixture and extracts. Blend until smooth.

Pour mixture into a 3-cup mold or a small bowl.

Chill until firm. Unmold to serve.

Each serving provides:

**122 Calories**

| | | | |
|---|---|---|---|
| 1/2 | Fruit Serving | 6 g | Protein |
| 1/4 | Milk Serving | trace | Fat (2% of calories) |
| 48 | Additional Calories | 24 g | Carbohydrate |
| | | 40 mg | Sodium |
| | | 1 mg | Cholesterol |
| | | 1 g | Fiber |

# Mixed Fruit Sherbet

*This refreshing sherbet, with its delicious, fresh taste, makes a perfect, light ending to any meal.*

*Makes 4 servings*

1¹/₂ cups lemon nonfat yogurt
¹/₂ cup orange juice
1 cup strawberries, fresh or frozen
1 cup canned crushed pineapple (packed in juice), drained
1 tablespoon plus 1 teaspoon honey
1 tablespoon plus 1 teaspoon sugar

In a blender container or food processor, combine all ingredients. Blend until smooth. Pour mixture into a 7 × 11-inch glass baking dish. Freeze 1 hour, until partially frozen. While mixture is chilling, place a large bowl in the refrigerator to chill.

Place partially frozen sherbet into chilled bowl. Beat on low speed of an electric mixer 30 seconds. Place mixture in a 1-quart container. Cover tightly.

Freeze until serving time.

---

Each serving provides:

**138 Calories**

| | | | |
|---|---|---|---|
| 1 | Fruit Serving | 4 g | Protein |
| ¹/₄ | Milk Serving | trace | Fat (1% of calories) |
| 85 | Additional Calories | 28 g | Carbohydrate |
| | | 47 mg | Sodium |
| | | 2 mg | Cholesterol |
| | | 2 g | Fiber |

# Strawberry Ice Cream in a Flash

*There's just a trace of fat in a frosty, cold dish of this easy, ice cream-type dessert. Just throw a few ingredients in the blender and enjoy.*

*Makes 2 servings*

| | |
|---|---|
| 1/3 | cup nonfat dry milk |
| 2 | tablespoons sugar |
| 1/2 | cup ice water |
| 1/2 | teaspoon vanilla extract |
| 2 | cups frozen strawberries (unsweetened), still frozen |

In a blender container, combine dry milk, sugar, water, vanilla, and 1 cup of the strawberries. Blend just until berries are chopped into small pieces.

Add remaining berries. Blend until smooth.

Spoon into 2 serving bowls.

Serve right away.

---

Each serving provides:

**146 Calories**

| 1 | Fruit Serving | 5 g | Protein |
|---|---|---|---|
| 1/2 | Milk Serving | trace | Fat (1% of calories) |
| 48 | Additional Calories | 33 g | Carbohydrate |
| | | 65 mg | Sodium |
| | | 2 mg | Cholesterol |
| | | 0 g | Fiber |

# Orange Dreamsicle Freeze

*Reminiscent of the frozen confection we enjoyed as kids, this frozen dessert will be loved by all. Not only will they adore it, but they'll be eating a nutritious dessert as well. And you don't need an ice cream machine or any fancy equipment to make it.*

*Makes 4 servings*

| | |
|---|---|
| 1/2 | cup frozen orange juice concentrate, thawed |
| 1 | cup skim milk |
| 1/4 | cup ice water |
| 1/3 | cup nonfat dry milk |
| 1 | tablespoon lemon juice |
| 3 | tablespoons sugar |

In a large bowl, mix orange juice concentrate with skim milk. Set aside.

In a medium bowl, beat water and dry milk on medium speed of an electric mixer for 2 minutes. Beat on high speed until soft peaks form. Add lemon juice and continue beating on high speed until stiff. Gradually beat in sugar.

Fold fluffy mixture into orange mixture gently but thoroughly. Pour mixture into a 7 × 11-inch pan and place in the freezer for 1 hour, or until firm but not solid.

Spoon mixture into a bowl and beat on low speed of an electric mixer until smooth. Return mixture to pan.

Cover and freeze until firm.

Let stand at room temperature for 10 minutes before serving.

---

Each serving provides:

**135 Calories**

| | | | |
|---|---|---|---|
| 1 | Fruit Serving | 5 g | Protein |
| 1/2 | Milk Serving | trace | Fat (2% of calories) |
| 36 | Additional Calories | 29 g | Carbohydrate |
| | | 65 mg | Sodium |
| | | 2 mg | Cholesterol |
| | | 0 g | Fiber |

# Tortoni

*A traditional Italian dessert that is usually made with whipped cream, this version is just as refreshing as the original. And it's so creamy that you won't believe it isn't made with real cream.*

*Makes 4 servings*

| | |
|---|---|
| 1/3 | cup ice water |
| 1/3 | cup nonfat dry milk |
| 2 | tablespoons sugar |
| 1/2 | teaspoon almond extract |
| 1/2 | teaspoon rum extract |
| 1 | tablespoon graham cracker crumbs (one 2 1/2-inch square, crushed) |

Place ice water and dry milk in a deep bowl. Beat on medium speed of an electric mixer for 2 minutes. Increase speed to high and continue to beat for 2 more minutes.

Add sugar and beat 2 minutes on high speed, or until mixture is thick and forms soft peaks. Add extracts, beating well.

Divide mixture evenly into 4 custard cups. Sprinkle with crumbs. Place cups in freezer until set, at least 1 hour.

Let cups sit at room temperature for about 3 minutes before serving.

---

Each serving provides:

**56 Calories**

| | | | |
|---|---|---|---|
| 1/4 | Milk Serving | 2 g | Protein |
| 31 | Additional Calories | trace | Fat (3% of calories) |
| | | 11 g | Carbohydrate |
| | | 42 mg | Sodium |
| | | 1 mg | Cholesterol |
| | | 0 g | Fiber |

# Cherry-Berry Sorbet

*Unbelievably easy and delicious, this practically fat-free dessert can be made in no time. Just keep frozen cherries in your freezer so they'll be handy when you crave something sweet and cold.*

*Makes 2 servings*

| | |
|---|---|
| 2 | cups frozen pitted dark sweet cherries (unsweetened), still frozen (12 ounces) |
| 1/4 | cup water |
| 1 | tablespoon plus 1 teaspoon sugar |
| 1 | teaspoon strawberry extract |
| | Few drops almond extract |

In a blender container, combine all ingredients. Blend just until smooth. (You will need to turn the blender on and off and rearrange the cherries several times in order for them all to blend.)

Serve right away.

---

Each serving provides:

**123 Calories**

| | | | |
|---|---|---|---|
| 2 | Fruit Servings | 1 g | Protein |
| 16 | Additional Calories | trace | Fat (2% of calories) |
| | | 28 g | Carbohydrate |
| | | 2 mg | Sodium |
| | | 0 mg | Cholesterol |
| | | 0 g | Fiber |

## CAKES, PIES, COBBLERS, AND CRISPS

# Rum Fruit Cake

*Instead of flour, this super-moist cake gets its luscious taste and texture from graham cracker crumbs. It's unusual and delicious.*

*Makes 6 servings*

| | |
|---|---|
| 1 | cup plus 2 tablespoons graham cracker crumbs |
| 1/3 | cup sugar |
| 1/8 | teaspoon *each* ground cinnamon, cloves, nutmeg, and allspice |
| 1 | teaspoon baking powder |
| 2 | egg whites |
| 1 | teaspoon rum extract |
| 1/2 | teaspoon grated fresh orange peel |
| 1 | 1-pound can fruit cocktail (packed in juice), drained well (Reserve 1/4 cup plus 2 tablespoons juice.) |
| 3 | tablespoons raisins |

Preheat oven to 350°.

Spray a 4 × 8-inch loaf pan with nonstick cooking spray.

In a large bowl, combine graham cracker crumbs, sugar, spices, and baking powder. Mix well.

In a small bowl, combine egg whites, rum extract, orange peel, and reserved juice.

Beat with a fork or wire whisk until blended. Stir in fruit cocktail and raisins. Add to dry mixture, mixing until all ingredients are moistened. Spoon mixture into prepared pan. Smooth the top slightly with the back of a spoon.

Bake 45 minutes, until cake is firm.

Cool in pan on a wire rack.

---

Each serving provides:

**192 Calories**

| | | | |
|---|---|---|---|
| 1 | Bread Serving | 3 g | Protein |
| 3/4 | Fruit Serving | 2 g | Fat (8% of calories) |
| 59 | Additional Calories | 40 g | Carbohydrate |
| | | 238 mg | Sodium |
| | | 0 mg | Cholesterol |
| | | 1 g | Fiber |

# Surprise Apple Cake

*The surprise? The wonderful texture and moistness comes from beans! Don't tell them it's good for them, and they'll never guess!*

*Makes 16 servings*

| | |
|---|---|
| 3/4 | cup all-purpose flour |
| 3/4 | cup whole wheat flour |
| 2 | teaspoons baking powder |
| 1 1/2 | teaspoons ground cinnamon |
| 1/2 | teaspoon ground nutmeg |
| 1/4 | teaspoon ground cloves |
| 1/4 | teaspoon ground allspice |
| 1 | cup (6 ounces) canned pinto beans, rinsed and drained |
| 1/2 | cup applesauce, unsweetened |
| 1/2 | cup sugar |
| 1/4 | cup vegetable oil |
| 2 | egg whites |
| 2 | teaspoons vanilla extract |
| 1 | small, sweet apple, unpeeled, diced into 1/4-inch pieces |
| 1/4 | cup raisins |

Preheat oven to 350°.

Spray a Bundt pan with nonstick cooking spray.

In a large bowl, combine both types of flour, baking powder, and spices. Mix well.

In a blender container, combine beans, applesauce, sugar, oil, egg whites, and vanilla. Blend until smooth. Add to dry ingredients along with apple and raisins. Mix until all ingredients are moistened. Spoon mixture into prepared pan.

Bake 35 to 40 minutes, until a toothpick inserted in the cake comes out clean.

Cool in pan on a wire rack 5 minutes, then invert cake onto rack to finish cooling.

Each serving provides:

**125 Calories**

| | | | |
|---|---|---|---|
| 1/2 | Bread Serving | 3 g | Protein |
| 3/4 | Fat Serving | 4 g | Fat (26% of calories) |
| 1/4 | Fruit Serving | 21 g | Carbohydrate |
| 38 | Additional Calories | 100 mg | Sodium |
| | | 0 mg | Cholesterol |
| | | 2 g | Fiber |

# Pumpkin-Graham Cake

*It's hard to believe that a cake can be light and airy yet moist at the same time. This unusual cake is just that. It's a luscious taste treat.*

*Makes 8 servings*

| | |
|---|---|
| 1 | cup plus 2 tablespoons graham cracker crumbs (4 1/2 ounces) |
| 1 | cup canned pumpkin |
| 3/4 | cup liquid egg substitute |
| 1/4 | cup honey |
| 2 | teaspoons vanilla extract |
| 4 | egg whites (Egg substitute will not work here.) |
| 1/3 | cup sugar |

Preheat oven to 325°.

Spray a 9-inch cake pan with nonstick cooking spray. Line the bottom of the pan with wax paper and spray again.

In a large bowl, combine graham cracker crumbs, pumpkin, egg substitute, honey, and vanilla. Mix well.

Place egg whites in another large bowl. Beat on medium speed of an electric mixer until foamy, then beat on high speed until stiff. Gradually add sugar, beating well after each addition.

Stir about one fourth of the egg whites into pumpkin mixture. Fold in remaining egg whites, gently yet thoroughly. Spoon batter into prepared pan and smooth the top.

Bake 55 minutes, until a toothpick inserted in the center of the cake comes out clean.

Cool in pan on a wire rack for 10 minutes, then turn out onto rack to finish cooling.

Remove wax paper.

For a pretty effect, just before serving, place about 1/2 teaspoon of confectioners' sugar in a small strainer and shake evenly over cake.

---

Each serving provides:

**165 Calories**

| | | | |
|---|---|---|---|
| 1/2 | Protein Serving | 5 g | Protein |
| 3/4 | Bread Serving | 1 g | Fat (7% of calories) |
| 1/4 | Vegetable Serving | 33 g | Carbohydrate |
| 45 | Additional Calories | 168 mg | Sodium |
| | | 0 mg | Cholesterol |
| | | 1 g | Fiber |

# Banana Cake

*Everyone's favorite, this delectable cake is perfect with a cup of coffee or tea. For a pretty presentation, dust the top of the cake lightly with confectioners' sugar just before serving.*

*Makes 18 servings*

| | |
|---|---|
| 1³/₄ | cup plus 2 tablespoons all-purpose flour |
| 1¹/₂ | cups whole wheat flour |
| 2 | teaspoons baking powder |
| 1¹/₂ | teaspoons baking soda |
| ³/₄ | cup sugar |
| ¹/₂ | cup skim milk |
| 3 | tablespoons vegetable oil |
| 3 | egg whites |
| 1 | tablespoon vanilla extract |
| ¹/₄ | teaspoon banana extract (This is optional and adds flavor if the bananas are not very ripe and sweet.) |
| 2¹/₄ | cups mashed, very ripe bananas (4¹/₂ medium bananas) |

Preheat oven to 350°.

Spray a 10-inch tube pan with nonstick cooking spray.

In a large bowl, combine both types of flour, baking powder, and baking soda. Mix well.

In another bowl, combine remaining ingredients *except* bananas. Beat with a fork or wire whisk until blended. Add bananas. Whisk again. Add to dry mixture, mixing until all ingredients are moistened. Spoon batter into prepared pan. Smooth the top slightly with the back of a spoon.

Bake 40 to 45 minutes, or until a toothpick inserted in the center of the cake comes out clean.

Cool in pan on a wire rack for 5 minutes, then remove cake to rack. Serve warm for best flavor.

Each serving provides:

**167 Calories**

| | | | |
|---|---|---|---|
| 1 | Bread Serving | 4 g | Protein |
| 1/2 | Fat Serving | 3 g | Fat (15% of calories) |
| 1/2 | Fruit Serving | 33 g | Carbohydrate |
| 38 | Additional Calories | 173 mg | Sodium |
| | | 0 mg | Cholesterol |
| | | 2 g | Fiber |

# Heavenly Chocolate Cake

*Replacing part of the sugar with corn syrup adds moistness to this chocolatey cake. Yes, you can indulge in a heavenly dessert without a lot of fat.*

*Makes 8 servings*

| | |
|---|---|
| 1 | cup all-purpose flour |
| 1/2 | cup whole wheat flour |
| 1/3 | cup cocoa (unsweetened) |
| 1 | teaspoon baking powder |
| 1/2 | teaspoon baking soda |
| 1 | cup evaporated skim milk |
| 1/4 | cup firmly packed brown sugar |
| 1/4 | cup plus 2 tablespoons light corn syrup |
| 1 | tablespoon plus 1 teaspoon vegetable oil |
| 3 | egg whites |
| 1 | teaspoon vanilla extract |
| 1/4 | teaspoon almond extract |
| 2 | tablespoons fruit-only raspberry spread (optional) |
| 1 | teaspoon confectioners' sugar (optional) |

Preheat oven to 350°.

Spray a 9-inch nonstick cake pan with nonstick cooking spray.

In a large bowl, combine both types of flour, cocoa, baking powder, and baking soda. Mix well.

In another bowl, combine remaining ingredients *except* optional ingredients. Beat with a fork or wire whisk until blended. Add to dry mixture. Mix until all ingredients are moistened. Spoon into prepared pan.

Bake 20 to 25 minutes, until a toothpick inserted in the center of the cake comes out clean. Cool 5 minutes in pan on a wire rack, then invert onto rack to finish cooling.

If desired, cut cooled cake in half horizontally and spread raspberry spread over bottom half. Replace top. Just before serving, sprinkle with confectioners' sugar. (If optional ingredients are used, add 1/4 Fruit Serving and increase Additional Calories to 77.)

Each serving provides:

**214 Calories**

|   |   |   |   |
|---|---|---|---|
| 1 | Bread Serving | 7 g | Protein |
| 1/2 | Fat Serving | 3 g | Fat (13% of calories) |
| 1/4 | Milk Serving | 42 g | Carbohydrate |
| 75 | Additional Calories | 219 mg | Sodium |
|   |   | 1 mg | Cholesterol |
|   |   | 2 g | Fiber |

# Chocolate Zucchini Spice Cake

*Similar to brownies, this luscious cake is moist and tender and very rich-tasting. The versatile squash reigns again!*

*Makes 16 servings*

| | |
|---|---|
| 3/4 | cup whole wheat flour |
| 3/4 | cup all-purpose flour |
| 3 | tablespoons cocoa (unsweetened) |
| 1 | teaspoons baking powder |
| 1/2 | teaspoon baking soda |
| 1 | teaspoon ground cinnamon |
| 1/4 | teaspoon ground nutmeg |
| 1/8 | teaspoon ground allspice |
| 2/3 | cup sugar |
| 1/3 | cup skim milk |
| 2 | tablespoons vegetable oil |
| 2 | egg whites |
| 1 | teaspoon vanilla extract |
| 1/2 | teaspoon grated fresh orange peel |
| 1 | cup (packed) finely shredded zucchini, unpeeled |

Preheat oven to 350°.

Spray an 8-inch square baking pan with nonstick cooking spray.

In a large bowl, combine both types of flour, cocoa, baking powder, baking soda, and spices. Mix well.

In another bowl, combine remaining ingredients *except* zucchini. Beat with a fork or wire whisk until blended. Stir in zucchini. Add to

dry mixture, mixing until all ingredients are moistened. Spoon into prepared pan.

Bake 30 minutes, until a toothpick inserted in the center of the cake comes out clean.

Cool in pan on a wire rack. Cut into squares to serve.

Each serving provides:

**98 Calories**

| | | | |
|---|---|---|---|
| 1/2 | Bread Serving | 2 g | Protein |
| 1/4 | Vegetable Serving | 2 g | Fat (18% of calories) |
| 1/4 | Fat Serving | 18 g | Carbohydrate |
| 44 | Additional Calories | 80 mg | Sodium |
| | | 0 mg | Cholesterol |
| | | 1 g | Fiber |

# Tropical Pineapple Banana Cake

*With its tender chunks of pineapple and banana, the flavor is reminiscent of the tropics.*

*Makes 8 servings*

## Cake

| | |
|---|---|
| 3/4 | cup whole wheat flour |
| 3/4 | cup all-purpose flour |
| 1 1/2 | teaspoons baking powder |
| 1/4 | teaspoon baking soda |
| 1/2 | teaspoon ground cinnamon |
| 1 | cup skim milk |
| 1 | tablespoon vinegar |
| 2/3 | cup sugar |
| 2 | egg whites |
| 2 | tablespoons vegetable oil |
| 1 | teaspoon vanilla extract |
| 1/2 | teaspoon lemon extract |
| 1 | 8-ounce can crushed pineapple (packed in juice), drained very well |
| 1 | medium, ripe banana, diced into 1/2-inch pieces |

## Topping

| | |
|---|---|
| 2 | teaspoons sugar |
| 1/4 | teaspoon ground cinnamon |

Preheat oven to 350°.

Spray a 9-inch nonstick cake pan with nonstick cooking spray.

In a large bowl, combine both types of flour, baking powder, baking soda, and cinnamon. Mix well.

Combine milk and vinegar in a medium bowl. Let stand a few minutes. Add sugar, egg whites, oil, and extracts. Beat with a fork or wire whisk until blended. Gently stir in pineapple and banana. Add to dry mixture, stirring until all ingredients are moistened. Spoon into prepared pan.

For topping, combine sugar and cinnamon and sprinkle evenly over top of cake.

Bake 35 minutes, until a toothpick inserted in the center of the cake comes out clean.

Cool 10 minutes in pan on a wire rack, then either serve warm right from the pan, or remove cake to rack (topping-side up) to finish cooling.

Each serving provides:

**230 Calories**

| | | | |
|---|---|---|---|
| 1 | Bread Serving | 5 g | Protein |
| 3/4 | Fat Serving | 4 g | Fat (15% of calories) |
| 1/2 | Fruit Serving | 45 g | Carbohydrate |
| 84 | Additional Calories | 161 mg | Sodium |
| | | 1 mg | Cholesterol |
| | | 2 g | Fiber |

# Carrot Cake

*Unlike most carrot cakes that get their moistness from lots of oil, this one owes its wonderful, moist texture to applesauce.*

*Makes 8 servings*

### Cake
| | |
|---|---|
| ³/₄ | cup whole wheat flour |
| ³/₄ | cup all-purpose flour |
| 1¹/₂ | teaspoons baking powder |
| 1¹/₂ | teaspoons ground cinnamon |
| ¹/₄ | teaspoon ground nutmeg |
| ¹/₈ | teaspoon ground allspice |
| ¹/₄ | cup raisins |
| 1 | cup applesauce (unsweetened) |
| 2 | egg whites |
| ¹/₂ | cup firmly packed brown sugar |
| 2 | tablespoons plus 2 teaspoons vegetable oil |
| 1 | teaspoon vanilla extract |
| 1 | cup finely shredded carrots |
| 1 | 8-ounce can crushed pineapple (packed in juice), drained well |

### Topping
| | |
|---|---|
| ¹/₄ | cup plus 1 tablespoon tub-style fat-free cream cheese |
| 1 | teaspoon vanilla extract |
| 1 | tablespoon plus 1 teaspoon confectioners' sugar |

Preheat oven to 350°.

Spray an 8-inch square baking pan with nonstick cooking spray.

In a large bowl, combine both types of flour, baking powder, and spices. Mix well and stir in raisins.

In another bowl, combine applesauce, egg whites, brown sugar, oil, and vanilla. Beat with a fork or wire whisk until blended. Stir in

carrots and pineapple. Add to dry mixture, mixing until all ingredients are moistened. Place in prepared pan.

Bake 40 to 45 minutes, until a toothpick inserted in the center of the cake comes out clean. Cool in pan on a wire rack.

Combine topping ingredients in a small bowl. Mix well. Refrigerate until needed.

Just before serving, spread topping on cake. Refrigerate leftover cake.

Each serving provides:

**247 Calories**

| | | | |
|---|---|---|---|
| 1 | Bread Serving | 6 g | Protein |
| 1/4 | Vegetable Serving | 5 g | Fat (18% of calories) |
| 1 | Fat Serving | 46 g | Carbohydrate |
| 3/4 | Fruit Serving | 168 mg | Sodium |
| 70 | Additional Calories | 1 mg | Cholesterol |
| | | 3 g | Fiber |

# Apple Pudding Cake

*Lots of chopped apples fill this super-moist cake.*

*Makes 8 servings*

## Cake

| | |
|---|---|
| 4 | small sweet apples, peeled, chopped into 1/4-inch pieces |
| 1 | cup liquid egg substitute |
| 1 | cup part-skim ricotta cheese |
| 3/4 | cup all-purpose flour |
| 2/3 | cup nonfat dry milk |
| 1/3 | cup sugar |
| 1 | teaspoon baking powder |
| 1/2 | teaspoon baking soda |
| 2 | teaspoons vanilla extract |
| 1 | teaspoon ground cinnamon |

## Topping

| | |
|---|---|
| 1 | tablespoon sugar |
| 1/4 | teaspoon ground cinnamon |

Preheat oven to 350°.

Spray an 8-inch square baking pan with nonstick cooking spray.

Place apples in a large bowl.

In a blender container, combine remaining cake ingredients. Blend until smooth. Spoon over apples and stir gently. Spoon mixture into prepared pan.

Combine topping ingredients and sprinkle evenly over cake.

Bake 50 to 55 minutes, until cake is firm and nicely browned.

Remove pan to a wire rack. Serve warm for best flavor. Refrigerate leftovers and reheat or serve cold.

---

Each serving provides:

**192 Calories**

| | | | |
|---|---|---|---|
| 1 | Protein Serving | 10 g | Protein |
| 1/2 | Bread Serving | 3 g | Fat (13% of calories) |
| 1/2 | Fruit Serving | 32 g | Carbohydrate |
| 1/4 | Milk Serving | 259 mg | Sodium |
| 38 | Additional Calories | 11 mg | Cholesterol |
| | | 1 g | Fiber |

# Peach Kuchen

*This is an easy version of an old-time favorite. It's low in fat, but it sure is high in flavor.*

*Makes 8 servings*

## Cake
4       slices whole wheat bread (1-ounce slices), crumbled
2/3     cup nonfat dry milk
2       tablespoons sugar
2       tablespoons plus 2 teaspoons reduced-calorie margarine
1       teaspoon baking powder
1/2     teaspoon ground cinnamon
1 1/2   teaspoons vanilla extract
1       1-pound can sliced peaches (packed in juice), drained

## Topping
1       cup liquid egg substitute
1       cup vanilla nonfat yogurt
1/2     teaspoon almond extract
2       tablespoons sugar

Preheat oven to 350°.

Spray a 7 × 11-inch baking pan with nonstick cooking spray.

In a large bowl, combine bread, dry milk, sugar, margarine, baking powder, cinnamon, and vanilla. Mix with a fork until mixture is in the form of coarse crumbs. Press crumbs firmly into prepared pan. Bake 10 minutes.

Slice peaches in half lengthwise and arrange them on crust.

Combine topping ingredients in a medium bowl. Beat with a fork or wire whisk until blended. Pour over peaches.

Bake 30 minutes, until topping is set.

Cool slightly. Cut into squares and serve lukewarm.

---

Each serving provides:

**166 Calories**

| | | | |
|---|---|---|---|
| 1/2 | Protein Serving | 8 g | Protein |
| 1/2 | Bread Serving | 3 g | Fat (14% of calories) |
| 1/2 | Fat Serving | 28 g | Carbohydrate |
| 1/2 | Fruit Serving | 285 mg | Sodium |
| 1/4 | Milk Serving | 2 mg | Cholesterol |
| 48 | Additional Calories | 1 g | Fiber |

# Cinnamon Orange Coffee Cake

*Orange juice concentrate gives this delicious cake a rich flavor and moist texture. It's delicious served warm and tastes great alongside a scoop of vanilla nonfat ice cream or frozen yogurt.*

*Makes 8 servings*

## Cake

| | |
|---|---|
| 1 | cup all-purpose flour |
| $1/2$ | cup whole wheat flour |
| $1 1/2$ | teaspoons baking powder |
| $1/4$ | teaspoon baking soda |
| 1 | teaspoon ground cinnamon |
| 2 | egg whites |
| $1/2$ | cup sugar |
| $1/4$ | cup plus 2 tablespoons frozen orange juice concentrate, thawed |
| $2/3$ | cup skim milk |
| 2 | tablespoons vegetable oil |
| 1 | teaspoon vanilla extract |
| $1/2$ | teaspoon orange extract |

## Topping

| | |
|---|---|
| 2 | tablespoons frozen orange juice concentrate, thawed |
| 1 | teaspoon sugar |
| $1/4$ | teaspoon ground cinnamon |

Preheat oven to 350°.

Spray a 9-inch nonstick cake pan with nonstick cooking spray.

In a large bowl, combine both types of flour, baking powder, baking soda, and cinnamon. Mix well.

In another bowl, combine remaining cake ingredients. Beat with a fork or wire whisk until blended. Add to dry mixture, mixing until all ingredients are moistened. Place mixture in prepared pan.

Bake 30 minutes, until a toothpick inserted in the center of the cake comes out clean.

Place pan on a wire rack.

For topping, spread orange juice concentrate evenly over hot cake. Combine sugar and cinnamon and sprinkle evenly over cake.

Each serving provides:

**208 Calories**

| | | | |
|---|---|---|---|
| 1 | Bread Serving | 5 g | Protein |
| 3/4 | Fat Serving | 4 g | Fat (17% of calories) |
| 1/2 | Fruit Serving | 39 g | Carbohydrate |
| 63 | Additional Calories | 156 mg | Sodium |
| | | 0 mg | Cholesterol |
| | | 1 g | Fiber |

# Apricot Coffee Cake

*The delicate flavor of the apricots is highlighted by the flavors of almond and orange in this delicious cake. Served warm along with a cup of coffee or tea, it makes a perfect dessert or snack.*

*Makes 8 servings*

## Cake

| | |
|---|---|
| 1 | cup all-purpose flour |
| 1/2 | cup whole wheat flour |
| 1 1/2 | teaspoons baking powder |
| 1/2 | teaspoon baking soda |
| 1 | 1-pound can apricots (packed in juice), drained (Reserve juice.) |
| 2 | egg whites |
| 1/3 | cup sugar |
| 2 | tablespoons vegetable oil |
| 1 1/2 | teaspoons vanilla extract |
| 1 | teaspoon almond extract |
| 1/4 | teaspoon orange extract |

## Topping

| | |
|---|---|
| 2 | teaspoons sugar |
| 1/4 | teaspoon ground cinnamon |

Preheat oven to 350°.

Spray a 9-inch nonstick cake pan with nonstick cooking spray.

In a large bowl, combine both types of flour, baking powder, and baking soda. Mix well.

Place drained apricots in a blender container. Blend until smooth. Pour into a measuring cup and add reserved liquid, if necessary, to equal 1 cup. Place in a small bowl. Add remaining cake ingredients. Beat with a fork or wire whisk until blended. Add to dry ingredients,

mixing until all ingredients are moistened. Beat with a spoon for 30 seconds. Spoon mixture into prepared pan.

Combine sugar and cinnamon and sprinkle evenly over cake.

Bake 30 minutes, until a toothpick inserted in the center of the cake comes out clean.

Place pan on a wire rack. Serve cake warm for best flavor.

---

Each serving provides:

**187 Calories**

| | | | |
|---|---|---|---|
| 1 | Bread Serving | 4 g | Protein |
| 3/4 | Fat Serving | 4 g | Fat (18% of calories) |
| 1/2 | Fruit Serving | 34 g | Carbohydrate |
| 41 | Additional Calories | 186 mg | Sodium |
| | | 0 mg | Cholesterol |
| | | 2 g | Fiber |

# Cinnamon Streusel Coffee Cake

*So good with coffee or tea, this tender cake is at its best when served warm.*
*For a special treat, serve it alongside a scoop of vanilla nonfat frozen yogurt.*

*Makes 8 servings*

### Cake

| | |
|---|---|
| 1 | cup all-purpose flour |
| 1/2 | cup whole wheat flour |
| 2 | teaspoons baking powder |
| 1 | teaspoon baking soda |
| 2 | egg whites |
| 1 | cup vanilla nonfat yogurt |
| 1/3 | cup firmly packed brown sugar |
| 1 | tablespoon plus 1 teaspoon vegetable oil |
| 1 | tablespoon vanilla extract |

### Topping

| | |
|---|---|
| 1 | tablespoon firmly packed brown sugar |
| 1 | tablespoon wheat germ |
| 1/2 | teaspoon ground cinnamon |

Preheat oven to 350°.

Spray an 8-inch square baking pan with nonstick cooking spray.

In a large bowl, combine both types of flour, baking powder, and baking soda. Mix well.

In another bowl, combine remaining cake ingredients. Beat with a fork or wire whisk until blended. Add to dry mixture, mixing until all ingredients are moistened. Spoon into prepared pan.

In a small bowl or custard cup, combine topping ingredients, mixing well. Sprinkle evenly over cake.

Bake 25 to 30 minutes, until a toothpick inserted in the center of the cake comes out clean. Place pan on a wire rack and spray the top of the hot cake lightly with nonstick cooking spray.

Serve warm for best flavor.

---

Each serving provides:

**183 Calories**

|   |   |   |   |
|---|---|---|---|
| 1 | Bread Serving | 5 g | Protein |
| 1/2 | Fat Serving | 3 g | Fat (14% of calories) |
| 71 | Additional Calories | 34 g | Carbohydrate |
|   |   | 318 mg | Sodium |
|   |   | 1 mg | Cholesterol |
|   |   | 1 g | Fiber |

# Pumpkin Log

*This elegant dessert makes a perfect ending for any special meal. What a treat!*

*Makes 8 servings*

## Cake

| | |
|---|---|
| 3/4 | cup all-purpose flour |
| 1 | teaspoon baking powder |
| 2 | teaspoons ground cinnamon |
| 1/2 | teaspoon ground nutmeg |
| 1/8 | teaspoon *each* ground allspice and ground ginger |
| 3/4 | cup liquid egg substitute |
| 1/3 | cup sugar |
| 1/4 | cup water |
| 1 | tablespoon plus 1 teaspoon vegetable oil |
| 1 | teaspoon vanilla extract |
| 1/2 | cup canned pumpkin |

## Filling

| | |
|---|---|
| 1 1/4 | cups part-skim ricotta cheese |
| 2 | tablespoons sugar |
| 2 | teaspoons vanilla extract |
| 1/4 | teaspoon rum extract |

Preheat oven to 375°.

Spray a 10 × 15-inch nonstick jelly roll pan with nonstick cooking spray.

Into a small bowl, sift flour, baking powder, and spices.

In another bowl, beat egg substitute on medium speed of an electric mixer for 2 minutes. Reduce speed to low and beat in sugar, water, oil, and vanilla. Add pumpkin and beat until blended. Gradually add dry mixture, beating well after each addition. Spread batter evenly in prepared pan.

Bake 10 minutes. Let cake cool in pan 3 minutes, then loosen sides with a spatula. Run the spatula under the sides of the cake, loosening the entire cake. Turn cake out onto a towel. Roll the cake and the towel into a log, starting with one short side. Cool completely.

In a medium bowl, combine all filling ingredients, mixing well.

Gently unroll cooled cake. Spread filling evenly over cake. Roll up carefully.

Chill thoroughly.

---

Each serving provides:

**181 Calories**

| | | | |
|---|---|---|---|
| 1 | Protein Serving | 8 g | Protein |
| 1/2 | Bread Serving | 6 g | Fat (28% of calories) |
| 1/4 | Vegetable Serving | 24 g | Carbohydrate |
| 1/2 | Fat Serving | 147 mg | Sodium |
| 44 | Additional Calories | 12 mg | Cholesterol |
| | | 0 g | Fiber |

# Honey Sweet Sticky Buns

*Yes, you can indulge in this sticky treat! And, with refrigerator biscuits, nothing could be easier.*

*Makes 10 servings*

3    tablespoons plus 1 teaspoon soft, tub-style (not diet) margarine, melted
2    tablespoons firmly packed brown sugar
1    tablespoon honey
1/4  cup plus 1 tablespoon raisins
1    10-ounce package refrigerator biscuits (10 biscuits)

Preheat oven to 350°.

Combine margarine, brown sugar, and honey in the bottom of a 9-inch pie pan. Mix well and spread mixture evenly in pan. Sprinkle with raisins.

Arrange biscuits evenly in pan. Press them down slightly with the palm of your hand.

Bake 20 minutes, until biscuits are lightly browned. Remove from oven and let stand 1 minute, then invert onto a serving plate.

Serve warm.

---

Each serving provides:

**124 Calories**

| | | | |
|---|---|---|---|
| 1 | Bread Serving | 2 g | Protein |
| 2 | Fat Servings | 6 g | Fat (36% of calories) |
| 1/4 | Fruit Serving | 20 g | Carbohydrates |
| 16 | Additional Calories | 322 mg | Sodium |
| | | 0 mg | Cholesterol |
| | | 1 g | Fiber |

# Almond Oatmeal Breakfast Bars

*These quick, easy bars make a great dessert or a unique and nutritious break-fast-on-the-go. Imagine having your cereal, milk, and fruit all rolled into one delicious bar.*

*Makes 8 servings*

| | |
|---|---|
| 1 | cup rolled oats, uncooked (3 ounces) |
| 2/3 | cup nonfat dry milk |
| 1/2 | teaspoon baking powder |
| 1/2 | teaspoon baking soda |
| 1/2 | teaspoon ground cinnamon |
| 1/4 | teaspoon ground nutmeg |
| | Dash ground allspice |
| 1/4 | cup raisins |
| 1 | cup applesauce (unsweetened) |
| 3 | tablespoons sugar |
| 1 | teaspoon vanilla extract |
| 3/4 | teaspoon almond extract |

Preheat oven to 350°.

Spray an 8-inch square baking pan with nonstick cooking spray.

In a large bowl, combine oats, dry milk, baking powder, baking soda, and spices. Mix well. Stir in raisins.

In a small bowl, combine remaining ingredients, mixing well. Add to dry mixture, mixing until all ingredients are moistened. Spoon into prepared pan. Smooth the top with the back of a spoon.

Bake 30 minutes, until lightly browned.

Cool in pan on a wire rack. Cut into bars.

---

Each serving provides:

**111 Calories**

| | | | |
|---|---|---|---|
| 1/2 | Bread Serving | 4 g | Protein |
| 1/2 | Fruit Serving | 1 g | Fat (7% of calories) |
| 1/4 | Milk Serving | 22 g | Carbohydrate |
| 18 | Additional Calories | 142 mg | Sodium |
| | | 1 mg | Cholesterol |
| | | 2 g | Fiber |

# Pink Bean "Pumpkin" Pie

*This delectable pie is so unusual that you'll just have to try it to believe it. Close your eyes, and you'll think it's pumpkin pie! (Thanks for this one, Bubbie!)*

*Makes 8 servings*

### Crust

| | |
|---|---|
| 1/2 | cup all-purpose flour |
| 1/4 | cup whole wheat flour |
| 1/4 | teaspoon baking powder |
| 2 | tablespoons plus 2 teaspoons margarine |
| 3 | tablespoons plus 2 teaspoons ice water |

### Filling

| | |
|---|---|
| 1 | 19-ounce can pinto beans, rinsed and drained (This will yield approximately 12 ounces of beans.) |
| 1 1/2 | cups evaporated skim milk |
| 1/2 | cup liquid egg substitute |
| 1/2 | cup sugar |
| 1 1/4 | teaspoons ground cinnamon |
| 1/2 | teaspoon ground nutmeg |
| 1/2 | teaspoon ground cloves |
| 1/8 | teaspoon ground ginger |

Preheat oven to 400°.

Have a 9-inch pie pan ready.

In a medium bowl, combine both types of flour and baking powder, mixing well. Add margarine. Mix with a fork or pastry blender until mixture resembles coarse crumbs.

Add water. Mix with a fork until all ingredients are moistened. Work dough into a ball, using your hands. (Add a little more flour if dough is sticky, or a little more water if dough is too dry.) Roll dough between 2 sheets of wax paper into an 11-inch circle. Remove top sheet of wax paper and invert crust into prepared pan. Fit crust into pan, leaving an overhang. Carefully remove remaining wax paper. Bend edges of crust under and flute dough with your fingers or a fork. Prick the bottom and sides of crust about 30 times with a fork. Bake 10 minutes. Remove from oven. Reduce oven to 375°.

In a blender container, combine all filling ingredients. Blend until smooth. Pour mixture into crust. Bake 30 minutes, until set. Cool slightly, then chill.

---

Each serving provides:

**208 Calories**

| | | | |
|---|---|---|---|
| 1 | Protein Serving | 9 g | Protein |
| 1/2 | Bread Serving | 4 g | Fat (19% of calories) |
| 1 | Fat Serving | 34 g | Carbohydrate |
| 1/4 | Milk Serving | 249 mg | Sodium |
| 59 | Additional Calories | 2 mg | Cholesterol |
| | | 3 g | Fiber |

# Chocolate Tofu Cheese Pie

*Tofu adds just the right creamy texture to this luscious, rich pie. No one will ever guess what's in it!*

*Makes 8 servings*

### Crust

| | |
|---|---|
| 1 | tablespoon plus 1 1/2 teaspoons margarine, melted |
| 1 | tablespoon plus 1 1/2 teaspoons honey |
| 3/4 | cup graham cracker crumbs |

### Filling

| | |
|---|---|
| 1 1/2 | envelopes unflavored gelatin |
| 1 1/2 | cups water |
| 9 | ounces soft or medium tofu, sliced and drained well between layers of towels |
| 1 | cup nonfat dry milk |
| 3/4 | cup part-skim ricotta cheese |
| 1/3 | cup sugar |
| 2 | tablespoons cocoa (unsweetened) |
| 1 | teaspoon vanilla extract |
| 1 | teaspoon almond extract |
| 1/4 | teaspoon rum extract |

Preheat oven to 350°.

Combine margarine and honey in a 9-inch pie pan. Add graham cracker crumbs and mix until crumbs are moistened. Press crumbs into bottom and sides of pan to form a crust. Bake 5 minutes. Cool completely.

In a small saucepan, sprinkle gelatin over water and let soften a few minutes. Heat over low heat, stirring frequently, until gelatin is completely dissolved.

In a blender container, combine gelatin mixture with remaining ingredients. Blend until smooth. Pour mixture into cooled crust.

Chill until firm.

Each serving provides:

**199 Calories**

| | | | |
|---|---|---|---|
| 3/4 | Protein Serving | 9 g | Protein |
| 1/2 | Bread Serving | 6 g | Fat (26% of calories) |
| 1/2 | Fat Serving | 27 g | Carbohydrate |
| 1/4 | Milk Serving | 173 mg | Sodium |
| 61 | Additional Calories | 9 mg | Cholesterol |
| | | 1 g | Fiber |

# Banana Tofu Cream Pie

*Adding banana extract to this pie really deepens the rich flavor. And the riper the bananas, the sweeter this delectable pie will be.*

*Makes 8 servings*

### Crust

| | |
|---|---|
| 1 | tablespoon plus 1 1/2 teaspoons margarine, melted |
| 1 | tablespoon plus 1 1/2 teaspoons honey |
| 3/4 | cup graham cracker crumbs |

### Filling

| | |
|---|---|
| 9 | ounces soft or medium tofu, sliced and drained well between layers of towels |
| 3/4 | cup liquid egg substitue |
| 1 1/2 | medium, ripe bananas, cut into chunks |
| 1 | cup lowfat (1%) cottage cheese |
| 1/3 | cup sugar |
| 1 | tablespoon all-purpose flour |
| 1 | teaspoon vanilla extract |
| 1 | teaspoon banana extract |
| | Ground nutmeg |

Preheat oven to 350°.

Combine margarine and honey in a 9-inch pie pan. Add graham cracker crumbs and mix until crumbs are moistened. Press crumbs into bottom and sides of pan to form a crust. Bake 5 minutes.

In a blender container, combine all filling ingredients *except* nutmeg. Blend until smooth. Pour into crust. Sprinkle very lightly with nutmeg, preferably freshly ground.

Bake 30 to 35 minutes, until set.

Cool slightly, then chill.

Each serving provides:

**182 Calories**

| | | | |
|---|---|---|---|
| 1 | Protein Serving | 8 g | Protein |
| 1/2 | Bread Serving | 4 g | Fat (20% of calories) |
| 1/2 | Fat Serving | 28 g | Carbohydrate |
| 1/4 | Fruit Serving | 247 mg | Sodium |
| 65 | Additional Calories | 1 mg | Cholesterol |
| | | 1 g | Fiber |

# Orange Sponge Pie

*Our version of a Pennsylvania Dutch dessert, this fluffy pie is light-tasting and delicious.*

*Makes 8 servings*

## Crust

| | |
|---|---|
| 1 | tablespoon plus 1 1/2 teaspoons margarine, melted |
| 1 | tablespoon plus 1 1/2 teaspoons honey |
| 3/4 | cup graham cracker crumbs |
| 1/4 | teaspoon ground cinnamon |

## Filling

| | |
|---|---|
| 1/2 | cup sugar |
| 2/3 | cup nonfat dry milk |
| 1/2 | cup liquid egg substitute |
| 1/2 | cup frozen orange juice concentrate, thawed |
| 1/3 | cup water |
| 2 | tablespoons all-purpose flour |
| 1 | teaspoon grated fresh orange peel |
| 1 | teaspoon vanilla extract |
| 1/2 | teaspoon orange extract |
| 3 | egg whites (Egg substitute will not work here.) |

Preheat oven to 350°.

Combine margarine and honey in a 9-inch pie pan. Add graham cracker crumbs and cinnamon; mix until crumbs are moistened. Press crumbs into bottom and sides of pan to form a crust. Bake 5 minutes. Let crust cool.

In a large bowl, combine *half* of the sugar with remaining ingredients *except* egg whites. Beat on low speed of an electric mixer until combined. Then beat on medium speed 1 minute.

In another bowl, using clean, dry beaters, beat egg whites until stiff. Gradually add remaining sugar, beating well after each addition.

Fold into orange mixture gently but thoroughly. Pour mixture into prepared crust.

Bake 25 minutes, until set and lightly browned.

Cool on a wire rack for 10 minutes, then chill.

---

Each serving provides:

**198 Calories**

| | | | |
|---|---|---|---|
| 1/4 | Protein Serving | 6 g | Protein |
| 1/2 | Bread Serving | 3 g | Fat (14% of calories) |
| 1/2 | Fat Serving | 36 g | Carbohydrate |
| 1/2 | Fruit Serving | 170 mg | Sodium |
| 1/4 | Milk Serving | 1 mg | Cholesterol |
| 77 | Additional Calories | 1 g | Fiber |

# Marbled Cheese Pie

*This easy pie is lovely to look at and delightful to eat.*

*Makes 8 servings*

## Crust
1       tablespoon plus 1 1/2 teaspoons margarine, melted
1       tablespoon plus 1 1/2 teaspoons honey
3/4     cup graham cracker crumbs

## Filling
2       envelopes unflavored gelatin
1/2     cup water
2       cups part-skim ricotta cheese
1       cup evaporated skim milk
1 1/2   teaspoons vanilla extract
1/2     cup sugar
1/4     teaspoon rum extract
2       tablespoons cocoa (unsweetened)
1/4     teaspoon almond extract

Preheat oven to 350°.

Combine margarine and honey in a 9-inch pie pan. Add graham cracker crumbs; mix until crumbs are moistened. Press crumbs into bottom and sides of pan to form a crust. Bake 5 minutes. Let crust cool completely.

Sprinkle gelatin over water in a small saucepan. Let soften a few minutes. Heat over low heat, stirring frequently, until gelatin is completely dissolved.

In a blender container, combine gelatin mixture, ricotta cheese, milk, vanilla, and *half* of the sugar. Blend until smooth. Pour *half* of the mixture into a bowl and stir in rum extract.

To remaining mixture, add remaining sugar, cocoa, and almond extract. Blend until combined. Pour into a second bowl.

Chill both mixtures 5 to 10 minutes, until slightly thickened.

Using 2 large serving spoons, drop mixture alternately into cooled crust. Marble the top with a knife in a crisscross pattern.

Chill until firm.

---

Each serving provides:

**247 Calories**

| | | | |
|---|---|---|---|
| 1 | Protein Serving | 12 g | Protein |
| 1/2 | Bread Serving | 8 g | Fat (29% of calories) |
| 1/2 | Fat Serving | 32 g | Carbohydrate |
| 1/4 | Milk Serving | 210 mg | Sodium |
| 66 | Additional Calories | 20 mg | Cholesterol |
| | | 1 g | Fiber |

# Pineapple Cheese Pie

*Light and delicate, this easy pie makes a refreshing, light-tasting dessert.*

*Makes 8 servings*

### Crust
| | |
|---|---|
| 1 | tablespoon plus 1 1/2 teaspoons margarine, melted |
| 1 | tablespoon plus 1 1/2 teaspoons honey |
| 3/4 | cup graham cracker crumbs |

### Filling
| | |
|---|---|
| 1 1/2 | envelopes unflavored gelatin |
| 1/2 | cup water |
| 1 1/3 | cups lowfat (1%) cottage cheese |
| 1 | cup cold orange juice |
| 2/3 | cup nonfat dry milk |
| 1/4 | cup sugar |
| 2 | teaspoons vanilla extract |
| 1/4 | teaspoon lemon extract |

### Topping
| | |
|---|---|
| 1 | cup canned crushed pineapple (packed in juice), drained (Reserve 1/4 cup of the juice.) |
| 1 | tablespoon sugar |
| 2 | teaspoons cornstarch |
| 2 | tablespoons water |

Preheat oven to 350°.

Combine margarine and honey in a 9-inch pie pan. Add graham cracker crumbs; mix until crumbs are moistened. Press crumbs into bottom and sides of pan to form a crust.

Bake 5 minutes. Let crust cool completely.

Sprinkle gelatin over water in a small saucepan. Let soften a few minutes. Heat over low heat until gelatin is completely dissolved, stirring frequently. In a blender container, combine gelatin mixture with remaining filling ingredients. Blend until smooth. Pour into cooled crust. Chill until firm.

In a small saucepan, combine pineapple, reserved juice, and sugar.

Stir cornstarch into water in a small bowl and add to pineapple mixture. Cook over medium heat, stirring constantly, until mixture comes to a boil. Boil 1 minute, stirring. Spread evenly over cold pie. Chill.

| Each serving provides: | | |
|---|---|---|
| **198 Calories** | | |
| 1/2 Protein Serving | 9 g | Protein |
| 1/2 Bread Serving | 3 g | Fat (15% of calories) |
| 1/2 Fat Serving | 33 g | Carbohydrate |
| 1/2 Fruit Serving | 280 mg | Sodium |
| 1/4 Milk Serving | 3 mg | Cholesterol |
| 46 Additional Calories | 1 g | Fiber |

# Almond Buttermilk Pie

*Buttermilk gives the flavor of this quick, no-crust pie a tangy surprise.*

*Makes 8 servings*

| | |
|---|---|
| 1 1/2 | cups buttermilk |
| 1 | cup liquid egg substitute |
| 1/2 | cup sugar |
| 1/4 | cup plus 2 tablespoons all-purpose flour |
| 1/4 | cup tub-style diet margarine |
| 2 | tablespoons plus 2 teaspoons nonfat dry milk |
| 2 | teaspoons baking powder |
| 2 | teaspoons vanilla extract |
| 1 | teaspoon almond extract |

Preheat oven to 350°.

Spray a 9-inch pie pan with nonstick cooking spray.

In a blender container, combine all ingredients. Blend on low speed until all ingredients are moistened. Blend on high speed for 1 minute.

Pour mixture into prepared pan. Let stand for 5 minutes.

Bake 35 minutes, or until pie is set and lightly browned.

Cool 10 minutes, then chill.

---

Each serving provides:

**138 Calories**

| | | | |
|---|---|---|---|
| 1/2 | Protein Serving | 5 g | Protein |
| 1/4 | Bread Serving | 4 g | Fat (23% of calories) |
| 3/4 | Fat Serving | 21 g | Carbohydrate |
| 71 | Additional Calories | 275 mg | Sodium |
| | | 2 mg | Cholesterol |
| | | 0 g | Fiber |

# Fresh Orange Pie

*Fresh oranges make a cool, refreshing filling for this scrumptious pie. Any variety of orange can be used, but navel oranges definitely get our vote!*

*Makes 8 servings*

## Crust

| | |
|---|---|
| 1 | tablespoon plus 1 1/2 teaspoons margarine, melted |
| 1 | tablespoon plus 1 1/2 teaspoons honey |
| 3/4 | cup graham cracker crumbs |
| 1/4 | teaspoon ground cinnamon |
| 1/4 | teaspoon grated fresh orange peel |

## Filling

| | |
|---|---|
| 2 | tablespoons plus 2 teaspoons cornstarch |
| 1 1/2 | cups orange juice |
| 1/4 | cup sugar |
| 1 | tablespoon lemon juice |
| 1/4 | teaspoon orange extract |
| 2 1/2 | cups fresh orange sections, drained, white membranes discarded |

Preheat oven to 350°.

Combine margarine and honey in a 9-inch pie pan. Add graham cracker crumbs, cinnamon, and orange peel; mix until crumbs are moistened. Press crumbs into bottom and sides of pan to form a crust. Bake 5 minutes. Let crust cool completely.

Dissolve cornstarch in a small amount of the orange juice in a small saucepan. Add remaining orange juice, sugar, lemon juice, and orange extract. Bring mixture to a boil over medium heat, stirring constantly. Boil 1 minute, stirring. Remove from heat and stir in orange sections. Pour into crust.

Chill.

---

Each serving provides:

**159 Calories**

| | | | |
|---|---|---|---|
| 1/2 | Bread Serving | 2 g | Protein |
| 1/2 | Fat Serving | 3 g | Fat (16% of calories) |
| 1 | Fruit Serving | 32 g | Carbohydrate |
| 48 | Additional Calories | 94 mg | Sodium |
| | | 0 mg | Cholesterol |
| | | 2 g | Fiber |

# Chocolate Cheese Dream Pie

*Two kinds of cheese blend in a delicious pie!*

*Makes 8 servings*

## Crust
1      tablespoon plus 1 1/2 teaspoons margarine, melted
1      tablespoon plus 1 1/2 teaspoons honey
3/4    cup graham cracker crumbs

## Filling
2      envelopes unflavored gelatin
1 1/2  cups water
2/3    cup nonfat dry milk
2/3    cup lowfat (1%) cottage cheese
1/2    cup part skim ricotta cheese
1/3    cup sugar
2      tablespoons plus 2 teaspoons cocoa (unsweetened)
2      teaspoons vanilla extract
1      teaspoon rum *or* almond extract
1      teaspoon chocolate extract
12     medium ice cubes

Preheat oven to 350°.

Combine margarine and honey in a 9-inch pie pan. Add graham cracker crumbs; mix until crumbs are moistened. Press crumbs into bottom and sides of pan to form a crust. Bake 5 minutes. Let crust cool completely.

Sprinkle gelatin over water in a small saucepan. Let soften a few minutes. Heat over low heat, stirring frequently, until gelatin is completely dissolved.

In a blender container, combine gelatin mixture with remaining ingredients *except* ice cubes. Blend until smooth. While continuing to blend, carefully add ice cubes, two at a time. Blend until mixture thickens. (You may need more or less ice cubes, depending on their size.) Spoon into cooled crust, discarding any remaining bits of ice. Chill.

Each serving provides:

**181 Calories**

| | | | |
|---|---|---|---|
| 1/4 | Protein Serving | 9 g | Protein |
| 1/2 | Bread Serving | 5 g | Fat (23% of calories) |
| 3/4 | Fat Serving | 26 g | Carbohydrate |
| 1/4 | Milk Serving | 224 mg | Sodium |
| 51 | Additional Calories | 7 mg | Cholesterol |
| | | 1 g | Fiber |

# Strawberry Cream Pie

*This luscious pie chills quickly thanks to the frozen strawberries, making it a great last-minute dessert.*

*Makes 8 servings*

### Crust
1       tablespoon plus 1 1/2 teaspoons margarine, melted
1       tablespoon plus 1 1/2 teaspoons honey
3/4    cup graham cracker crumbs

### Filling
1 1/2    envelopes unflavored gelatin
3/4    cup water
1 1/2    cups part-skim ricotta cheese
1/4    cup sugar
1 1/2    teaspoons vanilla extract
3/4    teaspoon strawberry extract
3       cups frozen strawberries, unsweetened (Do not thaw.)

Preheat oven to 350°.

Combine margarine and honey in a 9-inch pie pan. Add graham cracker crumbs; mix until crumbs are moistened. Press crumbs into bottom and sides of pan to form a crust. Bake 5 minutes. Let crust cool completely.

Sprinkle gelatin over water in a small saucepan. Let soften a few minutes. Heat over low heat, stirring frequently, until gelatin is completely dissolved.

In a blender container, combine gelatin mixture with remaining filling ingredients *except* strawberries. Blend until smooth. Add strawberries. Blend, stopping blender to stir frequently, until berries are pureed and mixture is smooth. Spoon into crust.

Chill.

Each serving provides:

**192 Calories**

| | | | |
|---|---|---|---|
| 3/4 | Protein Serving | 7 g | Protein |
| 1/2 | Bread Serving | 7 g | Fat (31% of calories) |
| 1/2 | Fat Serving | 26 g | Carbohydrate |
| 1/4 | Fruit Serving | 154 mg | Sodium |
| 45 | Additional Calories | 14 mg | Cholesterol |
| | | 0 g | Fiber |

# Strawberry-Topped Cheese Pie

*This luscious, creamy pie is so pretty when fresh strawberries are in season. For another variation, you can also use blueberries, raspberries, or a combination of all three.*

*Makes 8 servings*

### Crust

| | |
|---|---|
| 1 | tablespoon plus 1 1/2 teaspoons margarine, melted |
| 1 | tablespoon plus 1 1/2 teaspoons honey |
| 3/4 | cup graham cracker crumbs |
| 1/4 | teaspoon ground cinnamon |

### Filling

| | |
|---|---|
| 2 | cups part-skim ricotta cheese |
| 1 | cup liquid egg substitute |
| 1/2 | cup sugar |
| 1 | tablespoon all-purpose flour |
| 2 | teaspoons vanilla extract |

### Topping

| | |
|---|---|
| 1 | cup orange juice |
| 1 | tablespoon plus 1 teaspoon cornstarch |
| 1 | tablespoon sugar |
| 1 | teaspoon strawberry extract |
| | Few drops red food color (optional) |
| 2 | cups fresh strawberries, cut in half lengthwise |

Preheat oven to 350°.

Combine margarine and honey in a 9-inch pie pan. Add graham cracker crumbs and cinnamon; mix until crumbs are moistened. Press crumbs into bottom and sides of pan to form a crust. Bake 5 minutes.

Increase oven temperature to 375°.

In a blender container, combine all filling ingredients. Blend until smooth. Pour filling into crust. Bake 25 to 30 minutes, until filling is set.

In a small saucepan, combine orange juice, cornstarch, and sugar, stirring to dissolve cornstarch. Cook over medium heat, stirring constantly, until mixture comes to a boil. Continue to cook, stirring, for 1 minute. Remove from heat and stir in extract. Add food color if desired. Arrange strawberries over top of pie. Spoon glaze evenly over berries.

Chill.

Each serving provides:

**269 Calories**

| | | | |
|---|---|---|---|
| 1 1/2 | Protein Servings | 11 g | Protein |
| 1/2 | Bread Serving | 8 g | Fat (27% of calories) |
| 1/2 | Fat Serving | 38 g | Carbohydrate |
| 1/2 | Fruit Serving | 220 mg | Sodium |
| 77 | Additional Calories | 19 mg | Cholesterol |
| | | 1 g | Fiber |

# Coconut Custard Cheese Pie

*"Rich and delicious" is the only way to describe this heavenly pie!*

*Makes 8 servings*

## Crust

| | |
|---|---|
| 1 | tablespoon plus 1 1/2 teaspoons margarine, melted |
| 1 | tablespoon plus 1 1/2 teaspoons honey |
| 3/4 | cup graham cracker crumbs |

## Filling

| | |
|---|---|
| 2 | cups part-skim ricotta cheese |
| 1 | cup liquid egg substitute |
| 1/2 | cup sugar |
| 1 | tablespoon all-purpose flour |
| 2 | teaspoons vanilla extract |
| 1 | teaspoon coconut extract |
| 1 | tablespoon shredded coconut (unsweetened) |

Preheat oven to 350°.

Combine margarine and honey in a 9-inch pie pan. Add graham cracker crumbs; mix until crumbs are moistened. Press crumbs into bottom and sides of pan to form a crust. Bake 5 minutes.

Increase oven temperature to 375°.

In a blender container, combine all filling ingredients *except* coconut. Blend until smooth. Stir in coconut. Pour filling into crust.

Bake 25 to 30 minutes, until filling is set.

Cool slightly, then chill.

---

Each serving provides:

**236 Calories**

| | | | |
|---|---|---|---|
| 1 1/2 | Protein Servings | 11 g | Protein |
| 1/2 | Bread Serving | 8 g | Fat (31% of calories) |
| 1/2 | Fat Serving | 29 g | Carbohydrate |
| 67 | Additional Calories | 220 mg | Sodium |
| | | 19 mg | Cholesterol |
| | | 0 g | Fiber |

# Apple Custard Squares

*Served warm or cold, this is one of the tastiest fruit puddings. Using unpeeled apples adds more fiber to the dish, so unless the apple skins are especially tough, there's no need to peel them.*

*Makes 8 servings*

| | |
|---|---|
| 1/3 | cup Grape Nuts cereal, crushed (1 1/2 ounces) |
| 1 | tablespoon plus 1 teaspoon margarine, melted |
| 1 | cup liquid egg substitute |
| 1 1/3 | cups nonfat dry milk |
| 3 | tablespoons sugar |
| 2 | teaspoons vanilla extract |
| 1/2 | teaspoon ground cinnamon |
| 1/8 | teaspoon ground nutmeg |
| 4 | small, sweet apples (such as Golden Delicious), unpeeled, coarsely shredded |

Preheat oven to 350°.

Combine cereal and margarine in an 8-inch square baking pan. Mix until cereal is moistened. Press crumbs lightly in bottom of pan, forming a thin crust.

Bake 8 minutes.

In a large bowl, combine egg substitute, dry milk, sugar, vanilla, cinnamon, and nutmeg. Mix with a fork or wire whisk until blended. Stir in apples. Spoon mixture over baked crust. Gently press apples down into custard. Sprinkle with additional cinnamon.

Bake 25 minutes, or until custard is set.

Serve warm or cold.

---

Each serving provides:

**144 Calories**

| | | | |
|---|---|---|---|
| 1/2 | Protein Serving | 8 g | Protein |
| 1/4 | Bread Serving | 2 g | Fat (14% of calories) |
| 1/2 | Fat Serving | 24 g | Carbohydrate |
| 1/2 | Fruit Serving | 166 mg | Sodium |
| 1/2 | Milk Serving | 2 mg | Cholesterol |
| 18 | Additional Calories | 2 g | Fiber |

# Cinnamon Raisin Cheese Squares

*Guaranteed to be a hit, this rich dessert gets its flavor and moistness from
two sweet, fruity ingredients—applesauce and orange juice concentrate.
That's why it tastes so luscious yet is so low in fat.*

*Makes 8 servings*

### Crust

| | |
|---|---|
| 2 | tablespoons honey |
| 2 | teaspoons margarine, melted |
| 2/3 | cup Grape Nuts cereal (3 ounces) |
| 1/4 | teaspoon ground cinnamon |

### Filling

| | |
|---|---|
| 1 2/3 | cups lowfat (1%) cottage cheese |
| 3/4 | cup liquid egg substitute |
| 1 | cup applesauce (unsweetened) |
| 1/4 | cup sugar |
| 2 | tablespoons frozen orange juice concentrate, thawed |
| 3 | tablespoons all-purpose flour |
| 1/2 | teaspoon ground cinnamon |
| 1/4 | teaspoon ground nutmeg |
| 1 1/2 | teaspoons vanilla extract |
| 1/4 | cup plus 2 tablespoons raisins |

Preheat oven to 325°.

In an 8-inch square baking pan, combine honey, margarine, Grape
Nuts, and cinnamon. Mix until cereal is moistened. Press firmly in
bottom of pan.

Bake 10 minutes.

In a blender container, combine all filling ingredients *except* raisins. Blend until smooth. Stir in raisins. Pour over crust.

Bake, uncovered, 40 minutes, or until set.

Cool slightly, then chill.

Each serving provides:

**186 Calories**

| | | | |
|---:|---|---:|---|
| 1 | Protein Serving | 10 g | Protein |
| 1/2 | Bread Serving | 2 g | Fat (8% of calories) |
| 1/4 | Fat Serving | 34 g | Carbohydrate |
| 3/4 | Fruit Serving | 306 mg | Sodium |
| 50 | Additional Calories | 2 mg | Cholesterol |
| | | 2 g | Fiber |

# Apple Crisp

*Few can resist our apple crisp. The milk baked right into the topping adds a delectable flavor. This is a comfort food they'll love.*

*Makes 6 servings*

### Apples

| | |
|---|---|
| 6 | small, sweet apples, peeled, cored, and very thinly sliced |
| 1 | cup water |
| 3 | tablespoons sugar |
| 2 | teaspoons lemon juice |
| 1 | teaspoon vanilla extract |
| 1 | teaspoon ground cinnamon |
| 1/8 | teaspoon ground nutmeg |
| 2 | teaspoons cornstarch dissolved in 1 tablespoon water |

### Topping

| | |
|---|---|
| 1 | cup nonfat dry milk |
| 1 | cup Grape Nuts cereal (4 1/2 ounces) |
| 3 | tablespoons sugar |
| 1 | teaspoon ground cinnamon |
| | Dash ground nutmeg |
| 3 | tablespoons reduced-calorie margarine |
| 2 | tablespoons water |

Preheat oven to 375°.

Spray a 9-inch pie pan with nonstick cooking spray.

Place apples in a large saucepan. Add water, sugar, lemon juice, vanilla, cinnamon, and nutmeg. Toss to combine. Bring to a boil over medium heat, stirring occasionally. Add cornstarch mixture. Cook, stirring constantly, until mixture has thickened and apples are slightly tender, about 5 minutes. Spoon apples into prepared pan.

In a medium bowl, combine all topping ingredients *except* water. Mix with a fork until milk and margarine are evenly distributed. Add water and mix well. Sprinkle topping evenly over apples.

Bake, uncovered, 20 minutes, or until lightly browned.

For best flavor, serve warm.

---

Each serving provides:

### 251 Calories

| | | | |
|---|---|---|---|
| 1 | Bread Serving | 6 g | Protein |
| 3/4 | Fat Serving | 4 g | Fat (12% of calories) |
| 1 | Fruit Serving | 52 g | Carbohydrate |
| 1/2 | Milk Serving | 259 mg | Sodium |
| 51 | Additional Calories | 2 mg | Cholesterol |
| | | 4 g | Fiber |

# Pineapple-Cranberry Crisp

*This easy, colorful crisp is sweet yet tart with a deep, fruity flavor that's accented and brought to life by the almond extract.*

*Makes 8 servings*

### Fruit
| | |
|---|---|
| 1 | 1-pound can whole-berry cranberry sauce |
| 1 | 1-pound can pineapple tidbits (packed in juice), drained (Reserve 2 tablespoons of the juice.) |
| 1 | tablespoon sugar |
| 1/2 | teaspoon almond extract |

### Topping:
| | |
|---|---|
| 3/4 | cup rolled oats, uncooked (2 1/4 ounces) |
| 3 | tablespoons all-purpose flour |
| 2 | tablespoons sugar |
| 1/2 | teaspoon ground cinnamon |
| 2 | tablespoons vegetable oil |

Preheat oven to 350 °.

Spray a 9-inch pie pan with nonstick cooking spray.

In a large bowl, combine cranberry sauce, pineapple, sugar, and almond extract. Mix well. Place in prepared pan.

In another bowl, combine oats, flour, sugar, and cinnamon. Mix well. Add oil and reserved pineapple juice, mixing until all ingredients are moistened. Sprinkle evenly over cranberry mixture.

Bake 30 minutes, or until lightly browned.

Serve warm or cold.

---

Each serving provides:

**211 Calories**

| | | | |
|---|---|---|---|
| 1/2 | Bread Serving | 2 g | Protein |
| 3/4 | Fat Serving | 4 g | Fat (17% of calories) |
| 1 | Fruit Serving | 43 g | Carbohydrate |
| 100 | Additional Calories | 17 mg | Sodium |
| | | 0 mg | Cholesterol |
| | | 1 g | Fiber |

# Blueberry Cobbler

*You can use fresh or frozen berries for this popular favorite. If using frozen, be sure to buy the unsweetened ones and thaw them before using.*

*Makes 4 servings*

| | |
|---|---|
| 2 | cups blueberries |
| 3 | tablespoons sugar |
| 2 | teaspoons cornstarch |
| 1/2 | cup all-purpose flour |
| 1/4 | cup whole wheat flour |
| 1 | teaspoon baking powder |
| 1 | tablespoon plus 1 teaspoon margarine |
| 1/3 | cup skim milk |

Preheat oven to 375°.

Spray a 1-quart baking dish with nonstick cooking spray.

Place blueberries in a bowl. Add sugar and cornstarch and toss to coat berries. Place berries in prepared baking pan.

In a medium bowl, combine both types of flour and baking powder. Mix well. Add margarine. Mix with a fork or pastry blender until mixture resembles coarse crumbs. Stir in milk.

Drop batter in 4 equal mounds onto blueberries.

Bake 25 to 30 minutes, until lightly browned.

Serve warm for best flavor.

---

Each serving provides:

**208 Calories**

| | | | |
|---|---|---|---|
| 1 | Bread Serving | 4 g | Protein |
| 1 | Fat Serving | 5 g | Fat (19% of calories) |
| 1/2 | Fruit Serving | 40 g | Carbohydrate |
| 59 | Additional Calories | 182 mg | Sodium |
| | | 0 mg | Cholesterol |
| | | 3 g | Fiber |

## COOKIES AND CANDIES

# Cinnamon Roll-Ups

*These rolled-up, cinnamon-filled pastries are finger-licking good!*

*Makes 8 servings*
*(3 pastries each serving)*

### Pastry
3/4     cup all-purpose flour
1/3     cup lowfat (1%) cottage cheese
2       tablespoons sugar
2       tablespoons plus 2 teaspoons reduced-calorie margarine
1       teaspoon vanilla extract

### Topping
1       tablespoon plus 1 teaspoon sugar
1/2     teaspoon ground cinnamon

Preheat oven to 375°.

Have a nonstick baking sheet ready.

In a medium bowl, combine flour, cottage cheese, sugar, margarine, and vanilla. Mix with a fork until all ingredients are moistened. With your hands, work dough into a ball.

Place dough on a lightly floured surface and roll into an 8 × 12-inch rectangle.

Combine sugar and cinnamon for topping and sprinkle 1 tablespoon of the mixture evenly over the dough.

Starting with one long side, roll dough up tightly like a jelly roll. Using a sharp knife, cut dough crosswise into 24 slices, each ¹/₂-inch wide. Place rolls on baking sheet, cut-side down. Sprinkle rolls with remaining topping mixture.

Bake 15 minutes, or until bottoms of rolls are lightly browned. Remove to a wire rack to cool.

Serve warm or at room temperature.

Each serving provides:

**92 Calories**

| | | | |
|---|---|---|---|
| ¹/₂ | Bread Serving | 2 g | Protein |
| ¹/₂ | Fat Serving | 2 g | Fat (20% of calories) |
| 28 | Additional Calories | 15 g | Carbohydrate |
| | | 83 mg | Sodium |
| | | 0 mg | Cholesterol |
| | | 0 g | Fiber |

# Pastry Crisps

*Nice and crispy-crunchy, these cookies make a wonderful snack or accompaniment to any fruit dessert.*

*Makes 8 servings*
*(about 5 crisps each serving)*

## Pastry

| | |
|---|---|
| 1 | cup plus 2 tablespoons all-purpose flour |
| | Pinch salt |
| 1/4 | teaspoon baking powder |
| 1/4 | teaspoon baking soda |
| 1/2 | cup quick cooking oats, uncooked (1 1/2 ounces) |
| 3 | tablespoons sugar |
| 1/4 | cup margarine, melted |
| 1/4 | cup plain nonfat yogurt |

## Topping

| | |
|---|---|
| 1 | tablespoon plus 1 teaspoon sugar |
| 1 | teaspoon ground cinnamon |

Preheat oven to 400°.

Have a nonstick baking sheet ready.

Into a medium bowl, sift flour, salt, baking powder, and baking soda. Stir in oats and sugar.

Add margarine and yogurt. Stir until well blended. Knead dough a few times until it holds together.

Roll dough between 2 sheets of wax paper into a rectangle 1/8-inch thick. Carefully remove top sheet of wax paper. Combine topping ingredients and sprinkle evenly over dough.

Cut dough into 1 × 3-inch strips and place on baking sheet.

Bake 8 minutes, until golden.

Remove crisps to a wire rack to cool.

---

Each serving provides:

**165 Calories**

| | | | |
|---|---|---|---|
| 1 | Bread Serving | 3 g | Protein |
| 1 1/2 | Fat Servings | 6 g | Fat (34% of calories) |
| 30 | Additional Calories | 24 g | Carbohydrate |
| | | 143 mg | Sodium |
| | | 0 mg | Cholesterol |
| | | 1 g | Fiber |

# Shortbread Cookies

*This is our delicious version of a traditional butter cookie. The butter flavor extract adds the butter flavor without all of the fat.*

*Makes 8 servings*
*(3 cookies each serving)*

3/4     cup all-purpose flour
1/2     teaspoon baking powder
1/4     cup reduced-calorie margarine
2       tablespoons sugar
2       teaspoons butter flavor extract

Preheat oven to 375°.

Have a nonstick baking sheet ready.

In a small bowl, combine flour and baking powder. Mix well. Add remaining ingredients and blend well with a fork to form a dough.

Work dough into a ball with your hands. Divide dough into 24 pieces and roll each into a ball. Place on baking sheet. Flatten each cookie to 1/4-inch, using the bottom of a glass.

Bake 10 minutes, until bottoms of cookies are lightly browned. Remove cookies to a wire rack to cool.

---

Each serving provides:

**81 Calories**

| | | | |
|---|---|---|---|
| 1/2 | Bread Serving | 1 g | Protein |
| 3/4 | Fat Serving | 3 g | Fat (32% of calories) |
| 12 | Additional Calories | 12 g | Carbohydrate |
| | | 99 mg | Sodium |
| | | 0 mg | Cholesterol |
| | | 0 g | Fiber |

# Orange Cookies

*For another delicious variation, these cookies can be made with lemon extract and grated lemon peel.*

*Makes 8 servings*
*(3 cookies each serving)*

| | |
|---|---|
| 3/4 | cup all-purpose flour |
| 1/2 | teaspoon baking powder |
| 1/4 | cup reduced-calorie margarine |
| 2 | tablespoons sugar |
| 1 | teaspoon orange extract |
| 1/2 | teaspoon grated fresh orange peel |

Preheat oven to 375°.

Have a nonstick baking sheet ready.

In a small bowl, combine flour and baking powder. Mix well. Add remaining ingredients and blend well with a fork to form a dough.

Work dough into a ball with your hands. Divide dough into 24 pieces and roll each into a ball. Place on baking sheet. Flatten each cookie to 1/4-inch using a fork, and make a crisscross pattern.

Bake 10 minutes, until bottoms of cookies are lightly browned.

Remove cookies to a wire rack to cool.

---

Each serving provides:

**82 Calories**

| | | | |
|---|---|---|---|
| 1/2 | Bread Serving | 1 g | Protein |
| 3/4 | Fat Serving | 3 g | Fat (32% of calories) |
| 12 | Additional Calories | 12 g | Carbohydrate |
| | | 99 mg | Sodium |
| | | 0 mg | Cholesterol |
| | | 0 g | Fiber |

# Oatmeal Raisin Drops

*An easy favorite without the fat of most oatmeal cookies, these chewy cookies are delicious warm. If you prefer crunchy cookies, freeze them and enjoy them right from the freezer.*

*Makes 6 servings*
*(4 cookies each serving)*

| | |
|---|---|
| 1/2 | cup plus 1 tablespoon all-purpose flour |
| 3/4 | cup rolled oats, uncooked (2 1/4 ounces) |
| 1/2 | teaspoon baking powder |
| 1/2 | teaspoon baking soda |
| 1/4 | teaspoon ground cinnamon |
| 1/3 | cup firmly packed brown sugar |
| 1 | tablespoon margarine |
| 1/4 | cup plus 2 tablespoons raisins |
| 1 | egg white |
| 2 | tablespoons apple juice |
| 1/2 | teaspoon vanilla extract |

Preheat oven to 375°.

Have a nonstick baking sheet ready.

In a medium bowl, combine flour, oats, baking powder, baking soda, cinnamon, and brown sugar. Add margarine. Mix well with a fork until mixture is crumbly and margarine is completely incorporated into the crumbs. Stir in raisins.

Add remaining ingredients, stirring until all ingredients are moistened.

Drop mixture by rounded teaspoonfuls onto baking sheet.

Bake 10 to 12 minutes, until bottoms of cookies are lightly browned.

Remove cookies to a wire rack to cool.

---

Each serving provides:

**180 Calories**

| | | | |
|---|---|---|---|
| 1 | Bread Serving | 4 g | Protein |
| 1/2 | Fat Serving | 3 g | Fat (13% of calories) |
| 1/2 | Fruit Serving | 36 g | Carbohydrate |
| 49 | Additional Calories | 183 mg | Sodium |
| | | 0 mg | Cholesterol |
| | | 2 g | Fiber |

# Banana Drop Cookies

*These soft, moist cookies are almost like little bites of banana cake.*

*Makes 4 servings*
*(3 cookies each serving)*

| | |
|---|---|
| 1/4 | cup rolled oats, uncooked (3/4 ounce) |
| 3 | tablespoons all-purpose flour |
| 1/4 | teaspoon baking powder |
| 1/4 | teaspoon baking soda |
| 1/2 | medium, very ripe banana, mashed |
| 1 | tablespoon sugar |
| 1/2 | teaspoon vanilla extract |
| 1/4 | teaspoon banana extract |

Preheat oven to 375°.

Have a nonstick baking sheet ready.

In a small bowl, combine oats, flour, baking powder, and baking soda. Mix well. Add remaining ingredients and stir until blended.

Drop mixture by rounded teaspoonfuls onto baking sheet.

Bake 8 to 10 minutes, until bottoms of cookies are lightly browned.

Remove cookies to a wire rack to cool.

---

Each serving provides:

**69 Calories**

| | | | |
|---|---|---|---|
| 1/2 | Bread Serving | 2 g | Protein |
| 1/4 | Fruit Serving | trace | Fat (6% of calories) |
| 12 | Additional Calories | 15 g | Carbohydrate |
| | | 108 mg | Sodium |
| | | 0 mg | Cholesterol |
| | | 1 g | Fiber |

# Apple Chews

*These soft, chewy cookies can be made so quickly. They're perfect for a snack and go so well with a cup of hot coffee or tea.*

*Makes 4 servings*
*(5 cookies each serving)*

| | |
|---|---|
| 1/4 | cup plus 2 tablespoons graham cracker crumbs |
| 2/3 | cup nonfat dry milk |
| 1 | tablespoon plus 1 teaspoon sugar |
| 1/2 | teaspoon baking powder |
| 1/4 | teaspoon ground cinnamon |
| 1 | small, sweet apple, unpeeled, coarsely shredded |
| 1 | egg white |
| 1 | teaspoon vanilla extract |

Preheat oven to 350°.

Have a nonstick baking sheet ready.

In a small bowl, combine graham cracker crumbs, dry milk, sugar, baking powder, and cinnamon. Mix well. Add remaining ingredients, mixing with a fork until well blended.

Drop mixture by rounded teaspoonfuls onto baking sheet.

Bake 15 minutes, until bottoms of cookies are lightly browned.

Remove cookies to a wire rack to cool.

---

Each serving provides:

**126 Calories**

| | | | |
|---|---|---|---|
| 1/2 | Bread Serving | 6 g | Protein |
| 1/4 | Fruit Serving | 1 g | Fat (7% of calories) |
| 1/2 | Milk Serving | 23 g | Carbohydrate |
| 21 | Additional Calories | 204 mg | Sodium |
| | | 2 mg | Cholesterol |
| | | 1 g | Fiber |

# Chocolate-Raisin Peanut Butter Bars

*These scrumptious candy bars are easy enough for children to make.*

*Makes 8 servings*

| | |
|---|---|
| 2/3 | cup nonfat dry milk |
| 1/4 | cup water |
| 2 | tablespoons peanut butter (Choose one without added sugar or fat.) |
| 1 | tablespoon plus 2 teaspoons sugar |
| 2 | teaspoons cocoa (unsweetened) |
| 1 1/2 | ounces non-sugarcoated breakfast cereal, such as corn or oat flakes, crushed slightly (1 cup) |
| 2 | tablespoons raisins |

Have an ungreased 4 × 8-inch loaf pan ready.

In a small bowl, combine dry milk, water, peanut butter, sugar, and cocoa. Mix well. Add cereal and raisins. Mix until cereal is coated with peanut butter mixture.

Press mixture into bottom of pan.

Place in freezer for at least 1 hour.

Cut into 8 bars.

Refrigerate leftovers.

---

Each serving provides:

**84 Calories**

| | | | |
|---|---|---|---|
| 1/4 | Protein Serving | 4 g | Protein |
| 1/4 | Bread Serving | 2 g | Fat (22% of calories) |
| 1/4 | Fat Serving | 13 g | Carbohydrate |
| 1/4 | Milk Serving | 113 mg | Sodium |
| 19 | Additional Calories | 1 mg | Cholesterol |
| | | 1 g | Fiber |

# Marzipan

*The almond extract makes this fat-free candy taste a lot like the real stuff.*

*Makes 4 candies*

1/3     cup nonfat dry milk
1        tablespoon plus 1 teaspoon sugar
1 1/2    teaspoons water
1/4     teaspoon almond extract
1/4     teaspoon vanilla extract
2        drops food color, any color (optional)

In a small bowl, combine all ingredients. Mix until all ingredients are moistened. Divide mixture evenly and shape into 4 balls. Place on a wax paper-lined plate.

Cover and chill.

Serve cold.

---

Each candy provides:

**38 Calories**

| | | | |
|---|---|---|---|
| 1/4 | Milk Serving | 2 g | Protein |
| 16 | Additional Calories | trace | Fat (1% of calories) |
| | | 7 g | Carbohydrate |
| | | 31 mg | Sodium |
| | | 1 mg | Cholesterol |
| | | 0 g | Fiber |

# Rum Balls

*These delightful morsels are a wonderful holiday treat. No one will believe they're so low in fat!*

*Makes 6 candies*

| | |
|---|---|
| 1/3 | cup nonfat dry milk |
| 3 | tablespoons graham cracker crumbs |
| 2 | tablespoons sugar |
| 2 | teaspoons cocoa (unsweetened) |
| 1/2 | teaspoon vanilla extract |
| 1/4 | teaspoon rum extract |
| 2 3/4 | teaspoons water |

In a small bowl, combine dry milk, graham cracker crumbs, sugar, and cocoa. Mix well. Add remaining ingredients. Mix until all ingredients are moistened.

Divide mixture evenly and shape into 6 balls. Place on a plate.

Cover and chill.

Serve cold.

For different taste treats, in place of the rum extract try 1/4 teaspoon almond extract or 1/8 teaspoon peppermint extract.

---

Each candy provides:

**48 Calories**

| 46 | Additional Calories | | |
|---|---|---|---|
| | | 2 g | Protein |
| | | trace | Fat (7% of calories) |
| | | 9 g | Carbohydrate |
| | | 43 mg | Sodium |
| | | 1 mg | Cholesterol |
| | | 0 g | Fiber |

# Coconut Bon Bons

*Normally, foods made with coconut are extremely high in fat. These candies, made with nonfat milk, are a delicious exception.*

*Makes 4 candies*

| | |
|---|---|
| 1/3 | cup nonfat dry milk |
| 1 | tablespoon plus 1 teaspoon sugar |
| 2 | teaspoons shredded coconut (unsweetened) |
| 1/2 | teaspoon coconut extract |
| 1/4 | teaspoon vanilla extract |
| 1 1/2 | teaspoons water |

In a small bowl, combine all ingredients. Mix until all ingredients are moistened. Divide mixture evenly and shape into 4 balls. Place on a wax paper-lined plate.

Cover and chill.

Serve cold.

---

Each candy provides:

**42 Calories**

| | | | |
|---|---|---|---|
| 1/4 | Milk Serving | 2 g | Protein |
| 19 | Additional Calories | trace | Fat (10% of calories) |
| | | 7 g | Carbohydrate |
| | | 31 mg | Sodium |
| | | 1 mg | Cholesterol |
| | | 0 g | Fiber |

# Sauces and Toppings

Sauces can enhance even the simplest of foods. But all too often, these tasty additions add lots of unwanted calories and fat. Not so if you follow a few easy rules:

- Use low-sodium broth or reduced-sodium soy sauce as a base for sauces and marinades.
- Add spices to salt-free tomato sauce to create fat-free sauces for chicken and fish.
- Combine nonfat yogurt with herbs and spoon over cooked vegetables.
- Replace butter with reduced-calorie margarine to top pancakes and waffles.
- Use nonfat yogurt in place of sour cream to top baked potatoes.
- Top angel food cake and pancakes with fruit toppings.
- Combine nonfat yogurt with fruit to make creamy sauces to top desserts.
- Use evaporated skim milk to replace cream in cream sauces.

# Honey Mustard Sauce

*Use this delicious sauce to top sliced chicken or turkey, served either hot or cold, and either plain or on a sandwich.*

*Makes ³/₄ cup*

¹/₂      cup prepared yellow mustard
¹/₄      cup honey
2       teaspoons reduced-sodium soy sauce

Combine all ingredients in a small bowl, mixing well.
Serve right away or chill for later servings.

---

Each tablespoon provides:

**30 Calories**

| 20 | Additional Calories | 1 g | Protein |
|----|---------------------|--------|---------|
| | | trace | Fat (12% of calories) |
| | | 7 g | Carbohydrate |
| | | 164 mg | Sodium |
| | | 0 mg | Cholesterol |
| | | 0 g | Fiber |

# Chili Orange Barbecue Sauce

*This is a perfect sauce to brush on chicken or meat while broiling or grilling.*

*Makes 1/2 cup*

| | |
|---|---|
| 1/4 | cup plus 2 tablespoons bottled chili sauce |
| 2 | tablespoons frozen orange juice concentrate, thawed |
| 2 | teaspoons vegetable oil |

Combine all ingredients in a small bowl. Mix well.

---

Each tablespoon provides:

**30 Calories**

| | | | |
|---|---|---|---|
| 1/4 | Fat Serving | 0 g | Protein |
| 23 | Additional Calories | 1 g | Fat (33% of calories) |
| | | 5 g | Carbohydrate |
| | | 171 mg | Sodium |
| | | 0 mg | Cholesterol |
| | | 0 g | Fiber |

# Apricot Brandy Sauce

*Delicious on sliced chicken or turkey, this sauce can turn leftovers into an elegant meal.*

*Makes 3/4 cup*

| | |
|---|---|
| 1/2 | cup water |
| 2 | teaspoons cornstarch |
| 1/4 | cup fruit-only apricot spread |
| 1 | packet low-sodium instant chicken-flavored broth mix |
| 1 1/2 | teaspoons brandy extract |

Place water in a small saucepan. Add cornstarch, stirring until dissolved. Add remaining ingredients. Bring mixture to a boil over medium-low heat, stirring frequently. Continue to cook, stirring constantly, 2 minutes more.

Serve hot.

Each tablespoon provides:
**19 Calories**

| | | | |
|---|---|---|---|
| 1/4 | Fruit Serving | 0 g | Protein |
| 8 | Additional Calories | trace | Fat (1% of calories) |
| | | 4 g | Carbohydrate |
| | | 0 mg | Sodium |
| | | 0 mg | Cholesterol |
| | | 0 g | Fiber |

# Orange "Butter"

*Spread a little on baked sweet potatoes or on French toast or regular toast. It adds a wonderful flavor boost.*

*Makes 1/4 cup*

1/4     cup reduced-calorie margarine
1 1/2   teaspoons grated fresh orange peel
3/4     teaspoon orange extract

   Combine all ingredients in a small bowl or custard cup. Mix well. Serve right away or chill and use for later servings.

---

Each teaspoon provides:

**18 Calories**

| | | |
|---|---|---|
| 1/2   Fat Serving | 0 g | Protein |
| | 2 g | Fat (98% of calories) |
| | 0 g | Carbohydrate |
| | 45 mg | Sodium |
| | 0 mg | Cholesterol |
| | 0 g | Fiber |

# Baked Potato Topper

*Turn a baked potato into an elegant dish without adding fat. This simple mixture also doubles as a salad dressing, and the herbs can be varied to accommodate everyone's taste.*

*Makes 4 servings*
*(1/4 cup each serving)*

| | |
|---|---|
| 1 | cup plain nonfat yogurt |
| 1/2 | teaspoon dill weed |
| 1/4 | teaspoon salt |
| 1/8 | teaspoon pepper |
| 2 | teaspoons imitation bacon bits |
| 2 | teaspoons dried chives |

In a small bowl, combine yogurt, dill, salt, and pepper. Mix well. Chill.

To serve, spoon 1/4 cup of the yogurt on a baked potato. Sprinkle each potato with 1/2 teaspoon of the bacon bits and 1/2 teaspoon of the chives.

---

Each serving provides:

**37 Calories**

| | | | |
|---|---|---|---|
| 1/4 | Milk Serving | 4 g | Protein |
| 13 | Additional Calories | trace | Fat (6% of calories) |
| | | 5 g | Carbohydrate |
| | | 209 mg | Sodium |
| | | 1 mg | Cholesterol |
| | | 0 g | Fiber |

# Whipped Topping

*Creamy, smooth, and glossy, here's an almost fat-free topping that you can make yourself. And you can flavor it any way you like by adding a few drops of your favorite extract. Try coconut, lemon, almond . . . .*

*Makes 4 servings*
*(1/4 cup each serving)*

| | |
|---|---|
| 1/2 | teaspoon unflavored gelatin |
| 1/4 | cup water |
| 2/3 | cup nonfat dry milk |
| 2 | tablespoons sugar |
| 3/4 | teaspoon vanilla extract |
| | Few drops any other extract (optional) |
| 1/4 | cup ice water |

Chill a medium bowl and the beaters from an electric mixer in the freezer for at least 30 minutes.

Sprinkle gelatin over 1/4 cup of water in a small saucepan. Heat over low heat until gelatin is completely dissolved.

Remove bowl from freezer and place it in a large bowl of ice cubes. In the chilled bowl, place dry milk, sugar, vanilla, optional extract, and ice water. Beat on low speed of electric mixer, gradually adding gelatin mixture.

Increase speed to high and beat until soft peaks form.

Chill in a covered container 10 to 15 minutes before serving.

*Note:* Topping will keep well in the refrigerator for 1 to 2 days.

---

Each serving provides:

**69 Calories**

| | | | |
|---|---|---|---|
| 1/2 | Milk Serving | 4 g | Protein |
| 24 | Additional Calories | trace | Fat (1% of calories) |
| | | 12 g | Carbohydrate |
| | | 63 mg | Sodium |
| | | 2 mg | Cholesterol |
| | | 0 g | Fiber |

# Raspberry Melba Sauce

*A gourmet's delight, this versatile sauce can be serve hot or cold over fruit, angel food cake, or vanilla lowfat frozen yogurt.*

*Makes 8 servings*
*(2 tablespoons each serving)*

1     10-ounce package frozen raspberries, in light syrup
3     tablespoons sugar
3     tablespoons water
1     tablespoon plus 1 teaspoon cornstarch*

In a small saucepan, combine raspberries, sugar, and 2 tablespoons of the water. Bring to a boil over medium heat.

In a small bowl or custard cup, combine remaining water with cornstarch, stirring to dissolve cornstarch. Add to berries. Continue to cook, stirring constantly, 1 minute.

Pour mixture through a strainer into a small bowl. Discard seeds. Serve sauce hot or cold.

*If you are going to serve this sauce cold, use only 1 tablespoon of cornstarch.

---

Each serving provides:
**60 Calories**

| | | | |
|---|---|---|---|
| 1/4 | Fruit Serving | 0 g | Protein |
| 23 | Additional Calories | trace | Fat (1% of calories) |
| | | 15 g | Carbohydrate |
| | | 1 mg | Sodium |
| | | 0 mg | Cholesterol |
| | | 0 g | Fiber |

# Strawberry Yogurt Sauce

*Great over fresh berries or fruit salad, this sauce can turn a simple fruit dish into a fancy dessert.*

*Makes 8 servings*
*(1/4 cup each serving)*

1    cup vanilla nonfat yogurt
1    cup fresh or frozen (unsweetened) strawberries (If using frozen
        strawberries, thaw and drain them well.)
1    tablespoon sugar
1    teaspoon vanilla extract

In a blender container, combine *half* of the yogurt with remaining ingredients. Blend until smooth. Stir in remaining yogurt.
    Chill thoroughly.

| Each serving provides: | | |
|---|---|---|
| | **39 Calories** | |
| 37    Additional Calories | 2 g | Protein |
| | trace | Fat (2% of calories) |
| | 8 g | Carbohydrate |
| | 20 mg | Sodium |
| | 1 mg | Cholesterol |
| | 1 g | Fiber |

# Double Strawberry Sauce

*You get a double dose of berries in this delectable, sweet sauce. Use it to top French toast, pancakes, fruit salad, lowfat ice cream, or angel food cake. It's so versatile.*

*Makes 4 servings*
*(1/4 cup each serving)*

1     cup frozen strawberries (unsweetened), thawed and drained
          (Measure while still frozen.)
1     tablespoon fruit-only strawberry spread

Combine berries and fruit spread in a small bowl and mix well. Use right away or chill for later servings.

Each serving provides:

**24 Calories**

| | | |
|---|---|---|
| 1/2 Fruit Serving | 0 g | Protein |
| | trace | Fat (2% of calories) |
| | 6 g | Carbohydrate |
| | 1 mg | Sodium |
| | 0 mg | Cholesterol |
| | 0 g | Fiber |

# Cinnamon Yogurt Sauce

*Here's an easy mix to spoon over baked apples or cooked winter squash.*

*Makes 4 servings*
*(1/4 cup each serving)*

| 1 | cup vanilla nonfat yogurt |
|---|---|
| 1 | tablespoon firmly packed brown sugar |
| 1 | teaspoon ground cinnamon |
| 1 | teaspoon vanilla extract |

In a small bowl, combine all ingredients, mixing well.
Chill thoroughly.

Each serving provides:

**68 Calories**

| 1/4 | Milk Serving | 3 g | Protein |
|---|---|---|---|
| 37 | Additional Calories | 0 g | Fat (0% of calories) |
| | | 13 g | Carbohydrate |
| | | 42 mg | Sodium |
| | | 2 mg | Cholesterol |
| | | 0 g | Fiber |

# Hot Fudge Sauce

*A practically fat-free hot fudge sauce? Fantastic! Spoon over lowfat ice cream or use as a luscious fondue for dipping fresh fruit.*

*Makes 8 servings*
*(2 tablespoons each serving)*

| | |
|---|---|
| 2 | tablespoons cocoa (unsweetened) |
| 1 | tablespoon plus 1 teaspoon cornstarch |
| 3 | tablespoons sugar |
| 1 | cup evaporated skim milk |
| 1 | teaspoon vanilla extract |

In a small saucepan, combine cocoa, cornstarch, and sugar. Mix well, pressing out all lumps with the back of a spoon.

Gradually stir in evaporated milk, mixing until cornstarch and cocoa are dissolved.

Bring to a boil over medium-low heat, stirring constantly. Continue to cook, stirring, 1 minute.

Remove from heat and stir in vanilla.

Serve hot.

---

Each serving provides:

**53 Calories**

| | | | |
|---|---|---|---|
| ¹/₄ | Milk Serving | 3 g | Protein |
| 27 | Additional Calories | trace | Fat (4% of calories) |
| | | 10 g | Carbohydrate |
| | | 37 mg | Sodium |
| | | 1 mg | Cholesterol |
| | | 0 g | Fiber |

# Chocolate Pineapple Sauce

*Delicious, delicious, delicious! Serve over lowfat ice cream or on angel food cake and you've created an elegant dessert.*

*Makes 8 servings*
*(2 tablespoons each serving)*

2/3     cup nonfat dry milk
1       tablespoon plus 1 teaspoon cocoa (unsweetened)
1       tablespoon plus 1 teaspoon sugar
1/2     cup canned crushed pineapple (packed in juice), drained
            (Reserve 2 tablespoons of the juice.)
1       teaspoon vanilla extract

In a small bowl, combine dry milk and cocoa. Mix well, pressing out any lumps with the back of a spoon. Add remaining ingredients and mix well.

Chill several hours.

| Each serving provides: | | | |
|---|---|---|---|
| | | **42 Calories** | |
| 1/4 | Milk Serving | 2 g | Protein |
| 18 | Additional Calories | trace | Fat (4% of calories) |
| | | 8 g | Carbohydrate |
| | | 32 mg | Sodium |
| | | 1 mg | Cholesterol |
| | | 0 g | Fiber |

# Lemon Sauce

*This delicate sauce is great to spoon over bread pudding, rice pudding, or noodle pudding.*

*Makes 1 cup*

1    cup water
2    tablespoons plus 2 teaspoons sugar
1    tablespoon plus 1 1/2 teaspoons lemon juice
1    tablespoon plus 1 teaspoon cornstarch
2    drops yellow food color

Combine all ingredients in a small saucepan. Stir until cornstarch is dissolved. Cook over medium heat, stirring constantly, until mixture comes to a boil. Continue to cook, stirring, 1 to 2 minutes.

Serve hot.

Each tablespoon provides:

**11 Calories**

| | | |
|---|---|---|
| 11 | Additional Calories | 0 g | Protein |
| | | 0 g | Fat (0% of calories) |
| | | 3 g | Carbohydrate |
| | | 0 mg | Sodium |
| | | 0 mg | Cholesterol |
| | | 0 g | Fiber |

# Index